A Soldier First

GENERAL RICK
HILLIER

A SOLDIER FIRST

BULLETS, BUREAUCRATS
AND THE POLITICS OF WAR

HarperCollinsPublishersLtd

A Soldier First
Copyright © 2009, 2010 by Rick Hillier.
All rights reserved.

Published by HarperCollins Publishers Ltd.

Originally published in a hardcover edition by HarperCollins Publishers Ltd: 2009
This trade paperback edition: 2010

All photos reprinted courtesy of General Rick Hillier.

HarperCollins books may be purchased for educational, business,
or sales promotional use through our Special Markets Department.

HarperCollins Publishers Ltd
2 Bloor Street East, 20th Floor
Toronto, Ontario, Canada
M4W 1A8

www.harpercollins.ca

Library and Archives Canada Cataloguing in Publication

Hillier, Rick, 1955–
A soldier first : bullets, bureaucrats and the politics of war /
Rick Hillier.

Includes index.

ISBN 978-1-55468-492-2

1. Hillier, Rick, 1955–. 2. Canada. Chief of the Defence Staff.
3. Generals—Canada—Biography. 4. Canada. Canadian Armed
Forces—Biography. 5. Canada—Military policy. 6. Canada—Biography.
I. Title.

U55.H54A3 2010   355.0092   C2010-903570-4

Printed in the United States
RRD 10 9 8 7 6 5 4 3 2 1

CONTENTS

ACKNOWLEDGMENTS

This book is dedicated to Canada's sons and daughters who serve our nation in the Canadian Forces and to their families who, despite not being volunteers, also serve, albeit differently. For more than thirty-five years, I enjoyed being a part of this group—I marvelled at their resilience, laughed at their jokes, grieved at their losses, celebrated their successes and treasured each day. I was privileged, for three and a half years, to command these heroes, represent them, support them in their missions and fight their battles publicly. In my post-military life, I continue to support, defend and appreciate them.

No family could be more supportive than mine. I could never have completed my career as a soldier without my bride, Joyce, and have often said that if I had my life to live all over again, I would do two things: join the army and marry that girl. Our sons, Chris and Steven, have lived, and tolerated, different lives because of my service, and now Chris' family does the same because of his. God bless them, and my love and thanks to them.

I could write another book in thanks to the people who've been there along the way (many are named in the pages that follow), but I'd like to especially acknowledge a few people who were key in putting this book together: John Pearce, my literary agent, for finding the right home for it; Chris Wattie, for many hours of discussion and for his keen insights into my career; and the people at HarperCollins—David Kent, Iris Tupholme, Jennifer Lambert, and my editor, Jim Gifford, for walking me through an often challenging process.

Lastly, life in this great country is good. Much of that is thanks to the stability we enjoy because of the sacrifice of soldiers, sailors, airmen and airwomen. To those Canadians who support them, thank you—your support is needed now, as never before. God, it's great to be Canadian!

A Soldier First

BREAKFAST WITH THE PM

It was a Saturday morning in early December in Ottawa and I was late. Again. Not a good start to a job interview with the Prime Minister of Canada.

The interview was to determine if I was to become the next Chief of the Defence Staff. The process had commenced in the fall of 2004, when Eugene Lang, Chief of Staff to Minister of Defence Bill Graham, approached me in the last week of November and asked, on the Minister's behalf, whether I wanted to be considered for the Chief's appointment.

I had met the Minister several times, had briefed him extensively on the situation in Afghanistan immediately after I relinquished command of the NATO mission in Kabul (the International Security Assistance Force, or ISAF) and had travelled with him to Quito, Ecuador, to participate in a Defence Ministers of the Americas conference. During that trip we had discussed, in some detail, the state of the Canadian military, the kind of forces needed for the threats we faced and the changes we would have to begin to launch us on the road to building those forces. I had drawn a series of diagrams to illustrate my ideas during the six-hour flight to Quito, and we chewed over many of the problems those necessary changes would both cure and cause.

I had come to appreciate the tremendous character that Graham brought to his appointment, and we had certainly established a rapport early during his tenure as Minister. We were comfortable with each other, we spoke frankly and both of us enjoyed the funnier side of events and focused on the serious issues as well. I was confident that if I did become Chief, he and I would work well together.

My response to Gene's approach was pretty quick and, I thought, clear. Yes, I was willing to throw my hat into the ring, but even if the government offered me the job and the promotion to full general that followed, I would not necessarily accept it. In short, I told him that if I was to take the job, it had to be a two-way contract, with direct support from the Prime Minister, the Minister of Defence and the entire Cabinet. They also had to commit to financial support in future federal budgets for the changes I wanted to introduce. I was not about to take on responsibility for the enormous changes that the Canadian Forces required on my own. I truly believed that all Canadians had to be a part of this rebuilding of their armed forces if it was going to be successful. Our business involved putting men and women in areas of high risk, from the high seas to search-and-rescue missions to combat operations in faraway lands, so once we started down that road of change we could not afford to fail.

The first step in the process of selecting the new Chief was an interview with the Minister, with Gene present as well. I knew that at least five other officers, including one recently retired general, were also being considered and that there was considerable support for some of them within military and government circles—and little for me. Part of the reason was a memorandum that I had written to the current Chief of the Defence Staff, General Ray Henault, a few months previous, that had not made me popular. I had suggested that the Canadian Forces focus on coherently and cohesively delivering a strong punch in limited geographical areas while concentrating on major centres of population both in Canada and overseas. The memo had been widely distributed (one of my first lessons on how leaky National Defence Headquarters was) and had found its way to the media. That memo had engendered much backlash and emotion, not so much because of what it said as because of what many people, in our survival mentality, read into it.

In the backwards-looking, bureaucratic, cumbersome and risk-averse Canadian Forces that we had become, no one encouraged the ability to work as one organization, and any suggestion of strategic change was fought tooth and nail by almost all concerned. I wrote the memo out of frustration that the Canadian Forces did not appear to know where it was going, and with fear that catastrophic failure was looming for all of us. My words, however, were used to paint me as a narrow-minded, land-oriented army officer who would use any increases in the defence budget to rebuild the army at the expense of the navy and air force. There was, therefore, much nervousness in military circles at the prospect that I would be chosen as the new Chief, a position that some presumed I would use to promote only the land component of the Canadian Forces. There was also some nervousness elsewhere that I would be impossible to control if appointed as the senior military officer in Canada.

The interview was scheduled for 4 p.m. on November 23, 2004, immediately following that day's parliamentary session, in Bill Graham's office. Since the selection committee was working in confidence to keep speculation to a minimum, essentially all I was told was the date and time of the interview. My office as army commander was on the nineteenth floor of National Defence Headquarters, in the centre of Ottawa, and the Minister's was directly beneath me on the Executive Floor (which happened to be the thirteenth floor but was never referred to as such, whether out of tradition or superstition I was never sure). I planned to be there right on time and came off the elevator at the Minister's floor about one minute before the scheduled interview. It was only then that I was told that the meeting was scheduled for the Minister's parliamentary office, in the Centre Block on Parliament Hill. Fortunately, the corporal who was Graham's driver was on hand and immediately offered to drive me over to the Centre Block and escort me through the time-consuming rings of security, a necessary evil in government buildings. Still, I was thirty minutes late for my first interview as a potential CEO. In an organization in which punctuality and timeliness are virtues, this was clearly not a good start.

The interview, however, went fine; it wasn't a great job interview, but it wasn't a bad one either. In Graham's badly lit office, equipped with the most uncomfortable chairs imaginable and in the depressing darkness of an early Ottawa winter, we discussed the potential missions for the CF, international and

domestic, the changes needed to execute those missions successfully, the importance of international relationships, particularly
those within the North Atlantic Treaty Organization (NATO),
and our relations with the United States and other allies. I think
Graham had already perceived my enormous disdain for the
inept and inflexible institution that I believed that NATO, the
Western military alliance, had become since the end of the Cold
War. I didn't hold back, and told him as clearly as I could what
I believed had to be done and why, what the priorities had to be
and what it would all cost. Gene Lang took some notes and did
not say a word.

The last item we discussed was my idea of a two-way contract.
Clearly, Gene had passed this on to Graham, and the Minister
seemed intrigued. What did I mean by that? he asked. I explained,
again, that it was pointless to ask any one person to take on the
task of making changes of such magnitude and importance, and
that if we tried to put it on one person's shoulders, we could
expect failure. A Chief of the Defence Staff without clear government support in the form of actions, not just speeches and policy
statements, was doomed to preside over an organization on its
way to irrelevance, just as the country needed us most. As Walt
Natynczyk, my eventual successor as Chief, used to say, the Canadian Forces had become a "self-licking ice cream cone," too big to
be cheap and too small to do much more than administer itself.
I had no intention of presiding over that kind of army, navy and
air force and told Graham so. I said that if the Government of
Canada wanted to do something for its armed forces—hopefully,
changes along the lines of what I had proposed—they might want
to consider me as one of the candidates for Chief of the Defence

Staff. If not, I told him, I was clearly not their man and had no interest in the job.

After about an hour, we ended on a positive note and I walked out of his office, fully expecting that would be the end of the application process for me. No one in the army staff, except for my executive assistant, Lieutenant-Colonel Grant Dame, or anyone anywhere else in National Defence Headquarters was aware of our meeting. My expectations were not high: I knew I was not considered one of the front-runners to become Chief.

After a couple of weeks with no word about the selection process, Graham, who was in his home riding in Toronto at the time, called me. The Minister asked if I was available to meet the Prime Minister for another job interview. Paul Martin wanted to have me over to breakfast at 24 Sussex on the following Saturday morning, where I would meet with him, Graham and Tim Murphy (Martin's Chief of Staff), in what amounted to a second interview for the job of Chief of the Defence Staff. Clearly, Graham had recommended that the Prime Minister interview me in person, but I had no idea if any others had been recommended or, if so, how many were on the short list for a meeting with the PM himself. After careful consideration (all of two seconds), I said that yes, I was available for breakfast at our prime minister's home. We confirmed the appointment for 8:30 a.m. and agreed that Graham and I would meet in a coffee shop in the Byward Market, near his Ottawa apartment, and go to 24 Sussex together to avoid unwanted speculation.

Now I was late for that meeting too. It had snowed heavily the night before, and I found myself stuck behind several snowplows on the way into downtown Ottawa, trying desperately to figure out how I could get away with being late not just once, but twice. Even though I had never aspired to be Chief of the Defence Staff, by now I was excited at the chance to really help change the organization that had been such a huge part of my life for more than three decades. All of us who had operational experience believed we needed to make dramatic changes, and I had decided that if offered the job, within the right context, I'd take it.

My worries about blowing the biggest interview of my life turned out to be for naught. The snowplows that had been blocking my way took an off-ramp; I picked up speed, found my way to the Market and into a parking spot, and quickly met up with Graham. Gene and Graham's public relations aides were there as well. They remained in the café while we jumped in the staff car and headed to 24 Sussex.

It was surreal to be welcomed to the Prime Minister's official residence. Like most Canadians, I had never been in the house before and had wondered numerous times, whenever I passed the front of the grounds on Sussex Drive, what it was like inside. Three things about 24 Sussex struck me immediately. First, about twenty suitcases, packed and labelled, were lined up in the foyer when we arrived, and I nearly tripped and fell flat on my face trying to get around them. I later learned that as soon as our breakfast was over, the Prime Minister, his family and key staff were off on a combination Christmas holiday and official visit to Europe and North Africa. I was the only thing that stood between them and warmer climates. The second thing that attracted my attention was the enormous natural Christmas tree that took up much of the living room. My wife,

Joyce, and I had always gone overboard on Christmas decorations, including putting up our own enormous tree just the previous week, and I wished that she could be there to see—and smell—this tree. Lastly, I was astonished at how cold the house was. The windows of the sunroom, just off the living room, overlooked the Ottawa River, but you wouldn't have known it that morning—they were covered in frost that seemed inches thick. Obviously, the renovations recently publicized by the National Capital Commission as necessary for 24 Sussex were desperately needed.

Within minutes Tim Murphy arrived and Prime Minister Martin joined us in the living room, next to that enormous, beautiful tree. I was in my dress uniform and the other three men were dressed casually in shirts, sweaters and slacks. After the residence staff brought in a large pot of coffee, we sat down and started talking. I sat next to Graham on one sofa, facing the Prime Minister and Tim on another. I listened for a while as Martin talked about his belief in the Canadian Forces, his admiration for the men and women who served and his desire to rebuild our military. We sat for about forty-five minutes, with the Prime Minister and me doing most of the talking, covering much of the same ground I had in my first interview with Graham. What kind of forces did we need and why? How would we focus them at home? What equipment did we need, and in what order should we buy it? What were our most important international relationships, and in what condition were the military component of those relations? There was also a lot of discussion about the international scene, particularly NATO, the crisis in Sudan's troubled Darfur region, and Afghanistan.

It was immediately clear that the Prime Minister thought that NATO was in difficult straits, searching for a new raison d'être now that the Cold War was over. It was equally obvious that although both Foreign Affairs and Defence had recommended Afghanistan as the focal point for Canada's international policy in the immediate future, he remained unconvinced. Darfur and particularly the plight of women and children in that desperate land dominated his thought process. He showed obvious frustration at the lack of clear choices for action abroad.

Graham interjected at one point to tell the Prime Minister that I was most comfortable drawing out my ideas on paper, and that might help our discussion. Martin immediately got up and went in search of something to write on, and returned with a small book of lined paper. I had started sketching out some of my thoughts when we were interrupted by Sheila Martin, who came in to say hello. I introduced myself, and we talked a little bit about family and, specifically, about our new grandson, Jack, who had been born two months earlier, on October 8. Although I did not know it at the time, this was the start of a friendship that would develop over the next year between Martin, Sheila, my wife, Joyce, and me, and that would become one of the more enjoyable memories of my time as Chief.

We were then interrupted by the Prime Minister's chef, who announced that he had prepared breakfast. We adjourned to the dining room, where I sat at the end of a small table, with Graham on my right, Tim Murphy on my left and the Prime Minister across from me. We dined on eggs Benedict and pastries while continuing the discussion, and I sketched my thoughts furiously all the while. I drew diagrams outlining the status quo of the

Canadian Forces as I saw it: three very separate arrows focused below the sea, on the ground and high overhead, arrows that were completely unconnected. I then scribbled out a second diagram showing how that should change, focusing all of them into one big arrow representing the Forces united to achieve one effect for Canada, no matter where they were sent. To do that, I drew a bubble that showed how we would focus our operations. The bubble surrounded areas where people lived, since that is where we were most often needed, along the coasts and shores where over 70 per cent of the world's population resides. My simple drawing demonstrated a new and refocused CF, including a much enlarged and empowered special forces command, which would allow us to be successful in any mission.

A picture or sketch may be worth the proverbial thousand words, but as a Newfoundlander I liked to use both the sketch *and* the thousand words to describe the Canadian Forces I wanted to build, a Canadian Forces that would be ready for the threats that faced us. I foresaw a learning organization that could adapt quickly and that reflected Canada's needs. I took pains to point out that a foreign policy that focused on failed states and concentrated our efforts on one mission at a time could allow us to punch at our proper weight: that of a G8 nation, a founding member of both NATO and the UN and the originator of the responsibility-to-protect resolution in the UN. Many of us in uniform felt that our lack of preparedness—in people, equipment and culture—had not permitted us to be as effective an organization as our nation deserved.

Although much of our conversation during the breakfast and afterwards, when we adjourned to the living room again, focused on the international responsibilities and demands, we also spoke at length about the arctic, search and rescue, basing issues and the size of the Canadian Forces. I was not up to speed on all these issues, and indeed felt that much of what needed to be done would become clear later on. If I was offered the job of Chief of the Defence Staff, I would commission studies to seek solutions to those challenges.

By now we were on our third or fourth pot of coffee. Martin matched my consumption cup for cup, and after about two and a half hours, the Prime Minister asked me to give them a few moments to confer among themselves. I went out into the icy sunroom and they disappeared into the study. The only way to stay warm in that frigid room was by drinking more coffee, and after several cups I was now experiencing some discomfort and there was no bathroom in sight. About twenty minutes later Martin invited me back into the living room and, in the presence of Graham and Murphy, asked if I would become the next Chief of the Defence Staff. Before I could answer, the Prime Minister said that he understood I had some conditions or concerns and asked what they were. I articulated my belief that without commitments of support from both him and his Cabinet, including a significant financial commitment, and without the determination by his government to withstand the screams from partisan groups when we started the necessary changes, taking the job would be pointless.

Like every politician I have ever met, Martin started his response by saying that he wanted to rejuvenate the Canadian Forces and would commit more money but didn't see much coming available in the next couple of years. He said that he

expected that more funding would be available later, at the three-
to five-year mark. Clearly that would not do, because the immediate and radical changes I had in mind could be started only
by immediate and substantial funding for the Canadian Forces.
Our top spending priorities—including tactical transport aircraft, search and rescue planes, heavy lift helicopters, new trucks
and supply ships—could be put off no longer. In addition, we
had to start dramatically improving the basics (such as training),
increase our supply of parts, ammunition and vehicles, rebuild
the medical support system and much more, right away. After
much discussion of the practical implications of this, including
how much it would cost in general, we reached an agreement. We
were going to change the Canadian Forces!

I left 24 Sussex with Bill Graham, clutching my sheets of
drawings (which I would find crumpled up in the spare-wheel
well of my car some three years later), wishing Paul and Sheila
Martin a Merry Christmas and safe travels as I was going out the
door. We returned to the coffee shop, where I immediately found
the bathroom and then had a brief discussion with Graham and
Lang on where to go from here. Surprisingly, despite the fact
that Ray Henault, the incumbent CDS, was not due to begin his
next job, with NATO, until June 2005, both Martin and Graham
were determined to have me assume command much sooner
than that. Graham initially wanted me to take over on January
2, 2005, in just over three weeks' time. They were eager to get on
with drafting a new defence policy for the government along the
lines of my vision. Both men wanted the policy work finalized
to drive the budgetary allocations in late winter, and thus speed
was important.

I left the coffee shop, headed home and broke the news to Joyce. She gave me her support (it would have been impossible to accept the job without that), and I started cleaning out my basement and garage in preparation for the intense and demanding times ahead. I knew that this would likely be my last chance to get some chores done for Joyce for some time, because the years ahead would leave precious little room for anything but the job. Little did we know just how intense, demanding, satisfying and exhilarating it would be.

13

CHAPTER 1

NEWFOUNDLAND DAYS

Becoming a general and Chief of the Defence Staff was the furthest thing from my mind growing up in outport Newfoundland. I was no different from any other boy in my community, or anywhere else in Canada: I wanted to be a policeman or a fireman. Which one I wanted to be depended on which day you caught me—one day I wanted to be a fireman, the next it was a policeman. But that started to change when I was eight and started reading military history. I had already become an avid reader, but Campbellton, about an hour north of Gander along the northern coast of Newfoundland, was a pretty small community—we didn't have a library or access to many books.

There was an older fellow that was living just up the road from our house named Smokey Elliott. I'm not sure why he was called Smokey, unless it was because of the pipe he was always smoking, but the story about him was that he had been in military intelligence during the Second World War and did some stuff that nobody knew or talked about. He was certainly a well-educated man and he had an enormous collection of military history books, especially about the First and Second World Wars.

I went to visit him with my dad one day and while they were chatting I looked up at all the shelves of books for the first time. In hindsight, I'm not sure how big his library was, but through the eyes of this very young kid, it appeared vast. Certainly, it was a far bigger collection than anyone else in Campbellton could claim. We had to mail-order the few books we had. Remembering the rumour that Smokey had been in military intelligence in the war, when he asked me what I wanted to do when I grew up I took a bit of a risk and shot back, "I want to go and join MI6 or MI5."

I had no idea what I was talking about. I wasn't quite sure what MI5 was, whether it was the British foreign intelligence service or the domestic one. I just knew it was something related to intelligence, and wanted to see what kind of response I would get. All of a sudden, Smokey's eyes brightened and he started looking at me as though he recognized something. I was no more than eight or nine years old, and he was probably thinking, What kind of eight-year-old already knows about MI5?

"So, you want to go into military intelligence, eh?" he asked.

I mumbled something clever, like "Mmm hmm." He just nodded and handed me one of his books, the first of many that he loaned me over the next few years.

In those days in rural Newfoundland, you would just invite yourself over; you'd never wait for an invitation. Nobody bothered to knock on the door. People just came up the walk, opened the door and walked on in. So that's what I would do: go over to Smokey's house every week or so, bring back the three or four books that I'd borrowed before and leave with an armful that he'd recommended. I read them and looked at the pictures in great detail.

I don't know if it was the first book Smokey loaned me, but I do remember reading Barbara Tuchman's *The Guns of August*, a detailed and very complex book about the start of the First World War. I had a tough time wading through parts of it, but I recall that book vividly. I've reread it several times since, and Tuchman's description of the troop trains that began to roll in the days leading up to the start of the First World War in the summer of 1914, full of recently mobilized soldiers headed for the front, and of the irreversible momentum thus created that inevitably led to war captivated me. Once the trains rolled, that was it—there was going to be a war no matter what anybody said or did. All those troops were going to go somewhere and do something.

That book, and its lesson about momentum, came back to me during the Winnipeg floods of 1997, when I was the brigade commander in Petawawa, Ontario. One brigade of soldiers had already come into southern Manitoba from Edmonton and was working south of Winnipeg, but the political and military chains of command were waffling over whether or not to send my brigade as well. They weren't sure how big the flood was, when the Red River would crest or how much help they would need, so there was a great deal of ambiguity: Should we send two brigades or not? My brigade, of just over 4,000 soldiers, was in the midst of deploying to Gagetown, New Brunswick, for a major exercise, and we already had our advance parties moving out in exactly the opposite direction from Winnipeg. The train carrying all of our tracked vehicles was heading toward Montreal.

I was in Ottawa on the phone to Major Mike Jorgensen, my head of operations, and he was asking me, "Okay, should we send the brigade to Gagetown, or should we hold here in case we get ordered to turn around and head for Manitoba?"

Our headquarters in Toronto couldn't really tell us anything, and nothing was coming out of National Defence Headquarters in Ottawa. So I told him, "Okay, let's go ahead and deploy the brigade to Gagetown."

That was at 4:00 p.m.; the first packet of troops was departing, by road convoy, at 4:30. I sat there and thought for about ten minutes, phoned Mike back and said, "Stop that packet. Let's give it another twenty-four hours and see what develops."

As it turned out, the flood was much more serious than anyone had thought, and twenty-four hours later, most of the brigade was moving toward Winnipeg. Then somebody came up with the idea that we were going to hold up at Thunder Bay and wait for further orders; but I knew that once we started heading out from Petawawa, we were going to have media and press all over us. With 4,000 troops and a thousand vehicles on the move, there was no way we were going to stop.

"Don't be stupid," I said. "Once we start moving, once we leave Petawawa, we're going to Winnipeg and we ain't stopping until we get there." It was just like *The Guns of August:* once the trains started moving, the war was going to start. When we rolled our first convoy toward Winnipeg, there was no way we were going to be able to stop until we got there.

So that was my first introduction to the military: through reading history. I became so engrossed in it that for one of my birthdays my mom ordered me an eighteen-book set on the Second World War from Time-Life Books, a set I still have in my library.

It shouldn't have come as much of a surprise, therefore, to Mom and Dad when one day I told them that I wanted to be a soldier. I didn't quite know what that was, or what it meant, but I knew that that was what I wanted to be. All that military history had filled me with the idea of soldiers and what they did, even without understanding all of it. I was determined to find out all I could, though, and wrote to the recruiting station in Gander just after I turned nine, looking for information on joining the Canadian Forces. They mailed me an entire package in reply, including a letter inviting me to come to a recruiting centre to apply. Obviously I hadn't told them how old I was, and I would later joke that maybe that was indicative of the educational standards that they were accepting at the time. I pored over all the brochures, particularly the ones about the Combat Engineer and Demolition Diver classifications, reading and rereading the descriptions of each of those specialties for hours and hours.

Beyond the fixation on military history and reading, I experienced a pretty typical boyhood, growing up in rural Newfoundland. Campbellton was a great community to grow up in, and as it turned out it was actually a great training ground for being a soldier. It's a small community in Notre Dame Bay, built around an inlet from the ocean that's about thirty kilometres in from the wide-open North Atlantic. People all built their homes around that little horseshoe-shaped inlet, the vast majority of them right on the edge of the water. The Indian Arm River emptied into the ocean nearby, with a long-abandoned pulp mill close to it. Campbellton was, and still is, a beautiful community. When you come over the hills from either direction it suddenly appears in front of you, an absolutely gorgeous spot with several small islands out in the middle of the bay.

It's still, now, like it was when I was a boy.

The lifestyle in Newfoundland and Labrador produces characteristics in men and women that make them great soldiers, sailors, airmen and airwomen. Determination to carry on even when conditions are tough is part of the Newfoundlander character, because on that windswept rock where the population clings to the edge of the stormy North Atlantic, if you were to let bad weather or adversity bother you, you'd never enjoy life. We would go fishing a lot, and even though it was wet and cold most of the time, when we were out in a boat that didn't bother us—we just carried on with whatever we were doing. As boys we got used to handling equipment and vehicles, whether it was snowmobiles or chainsaws or firearms. We were always doing all those things that can come in handy later in life if you join the army or the navy or the air force. Most importantly, we learned to do those things and live our lives with a sense of humour.

Newfoundlanders also have an independence of mind (sometimes referred to as stubbornness), and a get-the-job-done attitude. That, combined with their sense of humour, gives most of the island's sons and daughters the innate ability to get along with people. We're always out doing things with friends and neighbours, the kinds of activities that really help to prepare young men and women for life, as part of a team, in the Canadian Forces.

One of the things we used to do in Newfoundland every spring—I'm sure it still goes on and is just as dangerous now as it was then—is what we used to call "copying." We'd go out on the edge of the bay, right along the shore, when the ice was starting to break up and turning into little floating pans and play something like follow the leader—in other words, try to "copy" each other's moves. We would jump from one small ice pan to the next and immediately to the one after that, trying to be more daring than our friends so they would chicken out rather than follow us. The braver or more audacious you were, the more likely you'd hop onto a piece of ice that couldn't really bear your weight, so that if you didn't keep going, you fell into the water. Invariably, every year, one or two kids across the province would drown, and every parent in Campbellton—indeed, every parent in Newfoundland—would threaten their kids every spring: Don't go copying! One spring I snuck out anyway to go copying, fell into the water and went home soaking wet and icy cold. My big heavy wool sweater and heavy wool pants dripped with sea water, and if it had not been for a friend who pulled me from the freezing water, my life would have been short. My mom certainly gave me my comeuppance for that.

Myrtle Hillier, my mom, was a strong lady. She believed in education and made sure I knew that I was going to university after high school. She was crystal clear on that: I was going to university. Like most Newfoundland women, she was the one who held the family together because Dad was always away working—she ran the family. My dad, Jack Hillier, was a typical

Newfoundlander. He believed in family, hard work and family, in that order. He was a mechanic, but like everyone else on The Rock, he was also a Jack-of-all-trades (a great pun on his name), and at various times in his life he was a trapper and a fisherman. He farmed a little bit as well, and he was a truck driver. A typical Newfoundlander, he did whatever was necessary to feed his family and put a roof over their heads.

22

I had five sisters, four of them older than me, so I was surrounded by females all my life. I ended up wearing so many of my big sisters' hand-me-downs, I would later joke that I joined the army just so I could finally wear men's clothing. In fact, having worn hand-me-down slacks for years, it was only when I was nine, getting bigger and with new pants, that I realized that men's pants had the zipper in the front. It certainly was a different life with five girls in the house. My sisters used to call me King Richard because I was the only boy and tended to get my way, especially when I was small.

When we got a little older, Mom and Dad let us know they expected us to do certain things around the house. When Dad was away, I was responsible for getting the wood for the stove. So whenever Dad was off to work, I would go out with the chainsaw to cut up wood. Not too many parents these days would be comfortable letting their eleven-year-old child use a chainsaw, but in those days you just did the business. I would go hunting or take the boat out fishing, and I would have to row that boat all by myself—there was no motor, of course, and there were certainly no life jackets, which would be unthinkable today. We didn't have running water in the house, which was very common in Newfoundland in the 1950s and '60s, so my sisters and I had to haul it in from the well. If it snowed, we shovelled the snow. But in spite of the hard work, it was a pretty enjoyable life.

What was important when I was growing up was school and church. Communities revolved around their small denominational churches. In Campbellton there was a Pentecostal church, a United Church and the Salvation Army, to which we belonged. The church really became the hub of our social life. I used to play piano in church and a horn in the brass band, and that essentially was the extent of my social life as a young teenager.

Our local school was very tiny until I was in grade 8, when we finally had a new high school built just on the edge of town, for students from all the surrounding communities. We had one high school for the whole region. I attended Greenwood High School until graduation in grade 11 in June of 1972 (at that time Newfoundland high schools only went up to grade 11).

I found school boring, probably because I was reading so much on my own, continuing to borrow books from Smokey Elliott. Geography, history and literature were easy subjects for me, math a little harder, but I was never challenged in school like students are today, and I wish that I had been. I really enjoyed math though, particularly geometry, and although I was not a great artist, I always managed to get at least a passing grade in art class. Our sons find this amusing now, because as my career in the military progressed I often found myself trying to communicate by sketching and drawing. Those sketches were usually atrocious because I have no artistic talent whatsoever. I persist, though— did I mention that Newfoundlanders sometimes are stubborn?

One of my most memorable teachers, Art Sparks, is now my brother-in-law. Joyce was staying at his house and teaching in Comfort Cove, the community next door. She was originally from a town over 300 kilometres away from my home, but after a year of university she was already teaching in this community next to ours and staying with her brother. I've always thought the best thing about Campbellton is that's where I met Joyce.

In a small community, everybody knew everybody else. I'd first seen Joyce when she came to Campbellton for Art and Eileen's wedding when she was nine. She had been down before, visiting folks and staying with her brother, and I had seen her, but I didn't know her. I did remember her as the flower girl coming out of church at her brother's wedding. I'm not a particularly spiritual guy, but I remember seeing her coming down the steps of this tiny United Church, a pretty little church built up against a rocky hill. I don't remember anybody else from that wedding, but I do remember her.

I didn't really get to meet her until her eighteenth birthday party. About a month after that party, I saw her at a school dance. We had one dance and never looked back. We've been married now for thirty-five years.

———————

When I was sixteen, university was looming and I was determined to join the military. My dad hadn't been overly fond of me joining the Canadian Forces from the time I first mentioned it and still needed some convincing by the time I was ready to apply. He was worried that we were going to end up in a war somewhere and that his only son would be lost.

There was no military role model in the family, an uncle or

a cousin in uniform that I could look up to or ask for advice. But I did hear a lot about my dad's uncle, John Clark. Uncle John joined the Royal Newfoundland Regiment as a nineteen-year-old private in 1916. He went to France and Flanders and was killed in August 1917 in the trenches. All my life I heard stories about Uncle John, almost as if he was still alive; I have a picture of him on the wall in our entranceway at home. He had just turned twenty when he was killed, and my dad's great fear was that his son was going off to join the army and be lost, just like Uncle John.

Even at this late date, many decades after the war, the losses of the Royal Newfoundland Regiment remain deeply felt in the province. On July 1, 1916, during the Battle of the Somme, the regiment had been virtually wiped out at a place called Beaumont Hamel; hundreds of young men were killed or horribly wounded in less than an hour early that day, and the impact on what was then a very small island population was devastating. Almost every family in every community across Newfoundland lost someone. To this day, July 1—Canada Day, but also the anniversary of the day Newfoundland lost so many of its sons—is a day of remembrance and great sadness in Newfoundland.

In the summer of 2006, Joyce and I had the privilege and pleasure of visiting Beaumont Hamel on the ninetieth anniversary of that battle. We toured the battlefield and the Caribou memorial, which is now a Canadian national historic site, despite its being in central France, along with a delegation of other Newfoundlanders and Canadians, including Premier Danny Williams, who I'd gotten to know fairly well. That night we held a regimental mess dinner in a big tent on the site, with about

250 dignitaries from the military and the French and Canadian governments. The band of the Royal Newfoundland Regiment played for us all through that dinner, and I was sitting at the head table, facing the monument commemorating the battle: a massive bronze caribou set on a mound of earth overlooking the site, lit by floodlights. You could look out over the trench lines to where the regiment had formed up, no man's land, the German trenches beyond and the Danger Tree, the small tree that marked the spot where many men instinctively gathered to seek comfort from their friends or to shelter under the withering fire of German machine guns. It was a very emotional event. We were all dressed in our best, formal regimental mess kit and the band was playing Newfoundland songs, all the ditties that get you singing along. As I looked out over that battlefield, listening to the music, I couldn't help but think of the bodies that are still buried there and the boys who were buried in the cemeteries close by, all those young Newfoundland boys who went over the top that morning in 1916. Did they know we were here? Could they hear that music and know that the province and, indeed, the country was there to pay tribute to them ninety years later? Did they know that we still remember them? I believe yes, they do, and it made it all the more moving and emotional for me.

Beaumont Hamel was at least part of the reason that my dad wasn't particularly enthused about my joining the military. But I needed his signature on the application form, witnessed by a Justice of the Peace, to join up, as I was not yet eighteen years old. My dad and my mom had some discussions about it and Mom finally said to Dad, "Well, if you don't sign for him now, he's going to join as soon as he's old enough, and then maybe he'll be resentful about that. So maybe you should reconsider."

Dad got through his concerns and we both went to the Justice of the Peace and signed the application in his presence, with him as witness. I sent the application off (at least I was old enough to join now), the recruiters came to the school to interview me and soon afterwards I went into St. John's to the recruiting centre to complete the detailed application process to become an officer.

Like many who walk into a recruiting centre, I wanted to be a fighter pilot. There were eleven of us from across the province who wanted to enlist during the Easter break of 1972, and the first thing we had to do was get our medical examinations. As we were all sitting, waiting to have our eyes tested, I came to the realization that I had to be able to see pretty well to be a pilot. We were getting tested one at a time and I was almost the last guy in line. My eyes were already going downhill a little bit by then, and I was afraid that I might not be able to pass the test. I knew that I would need to prove that I could see well to fly fighter jets—that's all I was thinking about at this stage. I was sixteen years old, after all. I listened to the guys ahead of me read the bottom two lines on the eye chart so many times that I was able to memorize them. I thought to myself that if I can pass this test, that's it, I'm going to be a pilot. My turn finally came and those bottom lines of the eye chart were nothing but a blur, but I repeated them from memory and got the thumbs-up from the medic.

I was ecstatic. That's it: my eyes have been tested and I'm off to flight school to be a pilot. Of course, the next step was to send us to an optometrist for a more thorough eye test. The doctor walked into the room, looked me over from six metres away and

27

said, "You're never going to be a pilot. I can tell that your eyes are bad from here."

So of course I was rejected as pilot material. I went back to the recruiting centre and the officer looked over the results, scratched his head and said, "Jeez, I can't believe there's such a difference in the tests." I confessed that I had a bit of familiarity with the eye chart, having sat there for an hour listening to the other guys repeat the letters. They flipped the chart over, tested me again and of course I couldn't read the bottom two lines at all. My expectations and desire to become a pilot were dashed then and there.

I applied to join as an officer cadet and to follow my studies at the Royal Military College in Kingston, Ontario. Unfortunately, a few weeks after my application was processed, the recruiting centre called me back and told me that I hadn't been accepted. I never did find out why. The folks at the recruiting centre in St. John's were disappointed too: of the eleven of us who had applied together, none was accepted. The recruiters felt that out of our group, at least *some* of us would have made absolutely the right kind of officer cadets, and future leaders, that the Forces needed. They encouraged me to reapply, but I had already been accepted into Memorial University and I was a little pissed about not getting accepted into the CF, so while I immediately reapplied to become a soldier, I also applied to the Royal Canadian Mounted Police. I wanted to be in uniform one way or the other. My second application went through in several months; I was accepted as an officer cadet, and since I was already studying at Memorial University, I stayed there as a member in the Regular Officer Training Plan. ROTP let me go to classes at Memorial during the school year (with tuition and a small monthly stipend paid by the Canadian Forces) and spend my summers training with the army.

At Memorial, I was studying biology, which wasn't a very good fit with either my interests or my career aspirations. We really lacked guidance or a mentoring system in the schools in those days. In hindsight, with some guidance, I might have been able to focus more and maybe have gotten into a program more applicable to what I wanted to do in life, whether it was business or political affairs (even though I'm not and never have been a politician). Nobody sat you down and asked, "Okay, what is it you want to do in life? How are you going to prepare yourself for that; what kind of programs would fit within that preparation best and what would fit least?" If someone had done that for me, biology probably would have been the last subject on my list. It was a good general education, but not much preparation for what I was heading into in life.

My fondest memory of my time at Memorial was proposing to Joyce. She had taught school for one year in Comfort Cove. We started dating in the fall of that year and both went to Memorial University the following summer. I proposed to her on Christmas Eve. I had bought a relatively inexpensive ring for her, and we were married the following Victoria Day weekend, on May 24. We used to joke that I'd always be around for our anniversary because it was the holiday weekend. Looking back, I think I've been home for exactly three of our anniversaries, because the army had me out training or deployed overseas almost every year at about that time.

We got married on a windy, cold and wet day at Joyce's home in Lower Island, Conception Bay, in a small community wedding with maybe fifty guests. We've been together ever since, and Joyce has been the high point of my life, without question. I tell stories about her to the troops all the time, about what a great lady she is, and I always add in a little humour, although Joyce beats up on me all the time about it.

One story, especially, always made a big impression. Whenever I spoke to a group of troops who were deploying overseas, I would gather them together and say, "Okay, just remember: you're well trained, you're well prepared, you've got great leaders, you've got good equipment and you have the support of a country. If there's anything else you need, we're going to get it for you. You're ready to go and do this mission. Now, you guys all understand your job when you're over there?"

"Yes, sir," they would all tell me.

I would ask them, "What's your job?"

They would say, "We're going to go and help make an area more secure" or "take on the Taliban . . ."

That's when I would interrupt and say, "Stop that bullshit! Your job, when you're in Afghanistan and on the phone back to your wife or husband or your partner, is to support whatever they're doing. Because you're going off there to do this mission; you're all fired up, you're with your team and all that. But your families are left back here. So they're going to say things to you about what they have done. They're not actually looking for your approval. All they want is for you to acknowledge what they're doing, that they're handling things and they've got them squared away despite the stress of you being away and at risk. They are being successful on their mission also, and they just want you to know that."

I would tell them the story about my fridge. I phoned Joyce when I had been deployed to Afghanistan for about five months. I could tell immediately that she was stressed, and she does not stress easily. She told me the fridge had broken down. I said, "You know, that fridge is probably not even three years old, it's probably still under warranty. Why don't you call the technician in and just get it repaired?"

"No," she said, "I've already bought a new fridge."

I said, "That's good, that's excellent, because that fridge was almost three years old, and obviously needed to be replaced. I'll tell you what—when the guys come and bring in the new fridge, have them put that old one out in the garage, and when I come home I'll get it repaired and then I'll have a beer fridge in the garage."

"Nope, too late," she said, "I've already thrown it out. I didn't want it around the house."

I said, "That's perfect, Joyce, because the garage is already full of garbage and the last thing we need is more, so well done—I didn't need that fridge anyway."

I told those soldiers, "You guys remember, your job is to support your families back home by saying, 'Yes, honey, you're absolutely right. If it had been me, I would have made that exact same decision.'"

I still get e-mails about that story. One young captain who was just moving to Kingston recently sent me a note that said, "I've got to tell you, General, about this story you told me about the fridge. My husband and I just had a stressful conversation and I didn't handle it like you did. He'd gone off and bought a 'Cadillac of a kitchen set,' and I thought he'd spent too much money. Here he was trying to set up the house so that I'd be happy and all I had to do was say what you suggested since he'd already done it. All I had to do was say, 'My love, absolutely right, that's exactly what I would have done if I had been there.' I didn't do that, we hung up the phone angry at each other and now we are not going to see each other for six weeks. I wish that I had listened more closely to you and done what you did."

The troops I have spoken to since say the same thing. When I saw them in Afghanistan, they would say, "Sir, you're absolutely right. When I'm talking to my wife or when I'm talking to my partner, that's what I do." So Joyce became the central character in one of my favourite stories, and great soldier that she is, she puts up with it all.

CHAPTER 2

BASIC TRAINING

After completing my first year at Memorial, I went to basic officer training in Chilliwack, British Columbia. We had to take a Canadian Forces Boeing 707 flight across the country, the longest trip I'd ever taken in my young life. I flew from St. John's, Newfoundland, into Canadian Forces Base Shearwater, in Halifax, then got into the Boeing and went to Quebec City; then to Trenton; on to Winnipeg and Calgary; and finally, many hours later, I landed in Vancouver. All of us spent the entire day sitting on that plane going across the country in our dress uniforms, as uncomfortable as we could be, especially since none of us had worn the uniform before.

After finally getting to Vancouver, we got on a bus for the two-hour trip up the Fraser Valley to CFB Chilliwack. On arrival, getting off the bus, we all put on our berets, which nobody had yet told us how to wear properly. The berets had two little ventilation holes in the side. One of the guys thought that, logically, if you pull the beret flat down on the side with the ventilation holes, you cover them up, and since they then cannot breathe, they're useless, so obviously the beret must be pulled down the left side. He got off the bus, wearing his flap on his beret down over his left ear.

That was my, and our, first introduction to Sergeant Cy Clayton, who proceeded to tell that poor guy in a very loud voice, with his face really up close and personal, in great detail, how to properly wear a beret. It was quite funny. The guy's thought process was right on the money, completely logical and completely wrong.

Sergeant Clayton was the first individual in the Canadian Forces who really, really made a lasting impression on me. It's been thirty-five years since that first day of basic training in Chilliwack and I still recall him clearly. A non-commissioned officer, he was an incredible leader and made his mark on everybody on that course in the most positive sense. We were scared to death of him—after all, most of us were only seventeen years old—but at the same time we lived for a word of praise, any sign that we pleased him. One day, after he had raked us over the coals for some infraction, we were forming up as a platoon, getting ready to march to our training, and he was heading off to the training building. He got into his car and, as he drove by the platoon, put his hand up to block us from his view, pretending that he didn't want to see us because we were such a group of sad sacks. We were convinced that this guy was watching everything we did, forcing us shape up to his standards. When we didn't put 100 per cent into what we were doing, watch out.

We didn't have combat uniforms yet. The first morning, in formation on parade, all of us were wearing sport jackets and ties.

Sergeant Clayton went along inspecting each of us. He walked past me, stopped and backed up. "Mr. Hillier, did you shave this morning?" he asked me.

Shave—why would I shave? I thought. I didn't grow a beard overnight. And my practice until now had been to shave about once a week.

Well, guess what: after Sergeant Clayton was done chewing me out, I made sure I shaved the next day. Clayton was a leader. He didn't suffer fools gladly, he had no time for incompetence or laziness and he drove each of us to excel as individuals and perform superbly as a team. He was one of only a handful of black non-commissioned officers in the Canadian Forces at the time and went on to become a regimental sergeant major of the army's Combat Training Centre in Gagetown, New Brunswick, from where he retired in the early 1990s.

Another instructor who made a big impression on me was Regimental Sergeant Major Slaney. He was a legend throughout the CF, particularly for his incredible eyesight and uncanny ability to remember people. He had met me only once, in a crowd of 500 other officer cadets. One day as I was sauntering down the road toward the Officer Cadets' Mess with my hands in my pockets, he spotted me from where he was standing out by the main gate, a long distance away. Suddenly I heard him shouting, "Mr. Hillier, what are you doing? Get your hands out of your pockets." I got my hands out of my pockets pretty quickly, because RSM Slaney was like God to us and we feared his retribution.

I loved the army from the start. We were the first out of the four platoons on the basic course that summer to get our combat uniforms, and when we finally put them on we felt like commandos. Despite the incredibly long hours, demanding fitness training, barracks life and working all summer, I don't think we went to Chilliwack or Vancouver or anywhere else even for a weekend. I really enjoyed basic training, despite not being taught enough soldiering skills. I wanted to shoot more and do that kind of stuff, even though the physical fitness training was a bit challenging for me, especially the running. I wasn't a runner then—it just wasn't something we did back in Newfoundland, so it took me a while to get into it. We did a lot of walking up a mountain in Chilliwack, with rucksacks on our backs, in the pouring rain, then walking back down that mountain at night while it was still pouring rain. It was fun, and all of us, in this team-building environment, made friends for life—guys like my roommate, Dennis Hartnett, an artillery officer who later became lieutenant-colonel and now lives in Kingston; Brad Harper, who was in the same platoon with us; and Eric Reid. (Both Brad and Eric became dentists and also good friends. Brad, tragically, committed suicide in 1992.)

A lot of people will tell you that training was much tougher back then (the "back in my day" syndrome), but I actually think it's tougher now. We did lots of rucksack marches, and until my body got used to running, the physical training (or "PT" for short) was just a little tough. Halfway through the course, however, we stopped doing our morning exercise because we were going into the field. Sergeant Clayton said, "Okay, you've stopped doing morning PT. So let me just tell you, platoon, you need to be out there every morning doing PT, despite its not being compulsory, to keep yourself fit, to keep yourself in shape and keep yourself flexible, so when you're in the field, you don't get hurt."

We didn't face a concerted build-up to a higher level of physical fitness that would make us ready to go off and tackle the next level of training or eventually go off to fight a war. It's quite different now: the Canadian Forces runs a thirteen-week basic course that builds our women and men to a fitness level that most soldiers have not reached in a long, long time. The physical fitness and knowledge that we're building our soldiers up to is superb—better, in my view, than anything we have done before.

Training is now focused much more on operations than ever. We train, and train, and train some more until the soldiers are ready to go overseas. That was never really the case during training in the '70s. We would show up for our summer of training, the guys would be at various levels of fitness, the correlation between what we were doing and operations was limited and a great deal of time was wasted. When I finished basic training, I went right back to university and the next spring started the next phase of my introduction to the army.

CHAPTER 3

BETWEEN A ROCK
AND A HARD PLACE

Gagetown, New Brunswick, Home of the Army, was where I truly began the process of becoming a fully trained Armoured officer. I had picked the Armoured Corps largely because my roommate in basic, Dennis Hartnett, had decided he wanted to go into the Artillery. I had also been thinking about joining the Infantry; but I just wasn't sure what I wanted do, and between the two of us we had discussed the three combat arms specialties in detail. Dennis and I would talk in the barracks while we were cleaning our kit, polishing our boots and waxing the floor, which we did a lot. We had been given very little information on the various career options open to us.

The only real information I had about the different branches were those pamphlets the recruiter had sent me when I was eight. I really wasn't even sure what becoming an Armoured officer actually meant. Later, when I became the training officer at the Armour School, in the early 1980s, we started bringing potential officer recruits through the different combat arms schools—the Artillery, Infantry and Armour—to show them what each branch did. I decided we were going to market the Armoured Corps to these young kids who were applying to become officers. We took them into the school, sat them down and said, "We're the Armoured Corps. We've got big phallic symbols that we ride around on, and this is what we do." We tried to excite them, fire them up and get them to want to join us. Sometimes we'd succeed and sometimes we didn't, but we helped people make logical decisions about their career in the army. In our day, we didn't have that exposure, just those talks in the barracks with the other recruits. At some point during those discussions with Dennis, I came to realize that the idea of riding into battle on a tank was an appealing one, and chose the Armoured Corps. What I didn't realize at the time was that the front-line battle tank then in service with the Canadian army was the Centurion Mark V, a vehicle first designed and built at the end of the Second World War that by then was older than me—Canada had bought the tanks nearly a quarter century before. If I had known that at the time, I might have made a different choice. I learned about the Centurions the hard way—the first time I went into the field to train on them. I was told, "Right, you're the troop leader today, Mr. Hillier. Here are your orders and off you go."

My first mission was to take up a defensive position. I had to set up my troop of four tanks, with three officer cadets commanding the other tanks and me as their leader, to defend part of the training area in Gagetown. I went forward on foot, leaving the tanks in a wooded area under cover, did my reconnaissance, prepared my plan, gave my orders, planned a rehearsal and got ready to move the troop into the position first thing in the morning. During the rehearsal, we brought the tanks forward and marked the positions they would roll into at first light (this was before we had any real night-vision equipment, so we drove stakes into the ground to mark our positions so that we could approach them accurately in the dark of night). When the time came to move back to the woods, not one of those four tanks would start. That was my introduction to the venerable Centurion. For most of that summer, we trained as tank commanders on armoured personnel carriers, pretending they were tanks, while the Centurions were in the shop.

In the summer of 1976 I entered Phase 4, the culmination of my training as an Armoured officer, which would qualify me to command a troop of four tanks and the sixteen soldiers who crewed them. Phase 4 was the culmination of months of courses over several years, putting the finishing touches on all the young men who had gone through university or other educational institutions, passed basic and advanced training and were almost ready to become officers in command of Canadian soldiers. What was supposed to be a great learning and developmental experience instead turned out to be a low point, for the Armoured Corps and for the army, as far as I was concerned.

Someone had screwed up. We started off in June 1976, with sixty-five officer candidates on the parade square, ready to train. Unfortunately, the Armoured Corps just couldn't handle sixty-five new officers in the four regular-force regiments it had at the time; that many new officers would have overwhelmed the units.

At most, the corps could have handled ten new junior officers per unit, and even that, as it turned out, was almost too many.

So that summer became an exercise in survival. In fact, it was a slaughterhouse: out of the sixty-five who started the course, only twenty-eight graduated at the end of the summer. The rest failed. Some of those who didn't make the cut went off to other specialties in the army, becoming Artillery or Infantry officers. A few jumped before they saw the axe coming, but most ended up getting released from the Canadian Forces. These were young men (there were no women on that course) the army had already made a huge investment in. Some pretty good people went out the door that summer, and the experience left an overwhelming impression in the minds of everybody who was on that course that this was just not the way to do business. It says something about the state of the leadership of the military and the incredibly poor training process at the time that we lost so many good young men. It was appalling.

We spent the first week of the course in garrison, taking classes, refreshing skills from previous courses, and then deployed to the training area, or "into the field," for the practical-training part of the course. The instructors began weeding people out right away. By the time that first week was over, some of the men were already on formal warning of shortcomings because their inspections weren't good enough or they had not received a high enough mark on one of their tests. If you got three warnings from the course staff, you were out. By the time we got out into the field to actually start learning how to command our vehicles and later a troop of tanks, some guys were already more than halfway out the door.

By the end of that week, we knew what was happening and became very cynical about it. We'd go out to the training area every Monday morning in the old deuce-and-a-halfs (the '50s-era 2.5-tonne trucks that were the army's main transport at the time), and we could barely cram all of us into the cargo or passenger compartments. By the time we came back on Friday afternoon after a week of practical tests, there'd be just six or seven of us left. We'd get on the truck the next Monday morning and our "gallows" humour would kick in. We'd say things to each other such as "Hey, what size are your combat boots?" or "That's a nice scarf you've got there buddy, I'd like that when you go home."

The experience shaped, in a dramatic way, my approach to leadership. I believe in doing things almost the exact opposite of what we encountered that summer—respecting individuals, bringing them along, training and developing them, occasionally jacking them up but always on a path to make as many as possible the leaders we needed. Instead, the CF, and specifically the army, treated great young men deplorably, created a culture of survival, and as a consequence, lost many of the very good ones. Every day that summer we all worried that we would be the next to go.

During that awful Phase 4 training, I met guys like Mike Maissonneuve, who went on to become a lieutenant-general. We became great friends during training and have remained so ever since. Mike and I chased each other around the Gagetown training area armed only with our pistols, doing fire and movement drills, which, if you know anything about fire and movement, is pretty stupid to do. We'd been out for a week, though, were exhausted and thought that pretending to conduct fire and movement drills with pistols was hilarious.

When we went out into the brush and scrub of the sprawl-ing training area around Gagetown on either the Centurions or the pretend-a-tank, we knew that we had only one chance to impress our instructors. The course staff even started a bit of a competition among themselves to see who could fail the most students. I failed my share of tests but was never on warn-ing and so wasn't concerned that I was going to be kicked out, but we were so gun-shy about the way things were being run and had so little faith in our instructors that we didn't believe a thing they said. On one of my tests, I had received orders from the instructor, completed my plan and issued my orders to the other students. We were moving through the area to our start-ing point for this particular operation when the instructor, a captain, who was in the back of my armoured personnel car-rier, leaned forward and said, "Mr. Hillier, I just got a call on the other radio saying that your wife had to go into the hospital for an emergency operation. So you have a choice: do you want to go back right now and be with her, or do you want to finish your task and then we'll have transportation waiting for you to go back immediately? Your choice."

I was immediately suspicious, because I hadn't heard any-thing on the other radio, and thought that he was throwing this at me to see if he could shake my confidence and assess my resolve. I was going to show him! I replied, "Well, I'll carry on, and if you can have transportation waiting for me after, I'll go back to join her then."

I completed the test successfully. To my surprise, the captain said, "The transport will take you back to see your wife now—she's in Oromocto Hospital."

I looked at him in astonishment. "What? My wife's really in the hospital?" I couldn't believe it. I actually thought he had made it up as an additional test to stress, and possibly fail, me. That's how little we trusted the instructors.

When I became Chief of the Defence Staff, I remembered the lessons I'd learned on that course: not how to be a tank troop leader, but how *not* to lead soldiers. As Chief, I constantly harped about making our officers leaders, not managers, and that one of the most important differences was treating your people right, with respect for them a large part of that "right." A big part of leadership is taking care of people; Phase 4 was the antithesis of that.

Toward the end of that summer there was an inquiry into how the course was handled. Colonel Nicholson, the Combat Training Centre commandant, stood up at the mess dinner at the end of our course and said, "The inquiry's done and we've proven that the leadership is great, and everything is exactly as it should be." Everybody in the room thought this was great and applauded, except for the handful of us who had survived. We sat there shaking our heads. That course had almost nothing to do with learning how to lead a troop of tanks: it was about hanging on desperately until it was over.

The top four or five students who survived Phase 4 were immediately posted to our base in southern Germany to become tank troop leaders. The rest of us stayed in Gagetown and completed the Armoured reconnaissance course (we called it Phase 5) in the fall. We again had one week in garrison, learning reconnaissance doctrine, then a full month in the field, doing reconnaissance jobs as part of a patrol or a troop. That course, conversely, was immensely enjoyable. The culling had been completed the previous phase, the army had decided all of us were needed at the regiments and so we really did learn how to be both leaders and reconnaissance (recce) specialists. On completion of this formal training, six of us went to join each of the regiments. Because, even with this reduced output, there was still a surplus of junior officers, most ended up not getting to be troop leaders—the appropriate first job as a young officer—right away. I went to the 8th Canadian Hussars in Petawawa, Ontario, a short drive up the highway northwest of Ottawa, arriving there at the end of October 1976 with my family, and I became the intelligence officer for the regiment, my first job in the army. Eventually, I became a reconnaissance troop leader, the first of many command appointments, then later got a tank troop of my own.

When I arrived in Petawawa and joined the regiment, I saw that what had occurred in that Phase 4 was not the exception, but the rule. The same attitudes and approaches that we had experienced were reflected throughout the army. The regiment had no direction. There was no focus on operations; there was no focus on physical fitness; there was no focus on cohesion or morale in any way, shape or form.

The biggest problem was a distinct lack of leadership, so much so that it was invisible—the commanding officer and his senior officers, with a few, rare exceptions, seldom, if ever, went out to see their soldiers at work, and it was even rarer for them to actually talk to them. There was little communication and most in the unit had no idea what was going on around them. Many of those in leadership positions were distinctly uncomfortable around their subordinates and couldn't seem to relate to them. That discomfort often led to their acting very harshly on disciplinary matters, or to their coming across as bureaucratic and pedantic. They just didn't seem to understand their soldiers and certainly could not relate to them.

The actions of many of the regiment's leaders articulated what I thought were questionable values. Some of them were more concerned with looking after themselves or their careers than looking after their men. There is an old army adage that an officer's priorities are supposed to be his mission, his soldiers and then himself, but that certainly wasn't the rule in the 8th Hussars. Many of us really did believe in those priorities, but the actions of others made me question whether they did. It was a tough baptism.

When the commanding officer handed over the regiment to his replacement a few months after I arrived, he stood up at his change of command ceremony and actually apologized to the soldiers drawn up in the ranks in front of him for spending too much time in his office. I thought, "Never, ever lead in such a way as to have to make a statement like that."

The army and the rest of the Canadian Forces—after decades of training, few operations, a Cold War, government inattention and being on the back burner in Canada—were becoming a bureaucratic organization, just another department of the Government of Canada, administered by managers, not leaders. We had moved away from many of the best characteristics of leadership—focusing on getting the job done and giving the soldiers a vision of how to get it done—and had replaced it with bureaucratic process, turning the military into a risk-averse organization that didn't give us the results needed.

The same problems were evident throughout the entire brigade command structure, not just the 8th Hussars, and caused me to ask, numerous times, what the hell we were doing. I saw little in that first year that inspired me to want to continue to be a leader, an officer, or to continue to serve in the Canadian Forces.

Adding to the difficulties, the 8th Hussars, like the other regiments in the Armoured Corps, had real problems with its equipment. In what was a continuation of the situation with the elderly Centurions in Gagetown, the Lynx armoured reconnaissance vehicles were extremely worn (in fact, they would later be grounded—that is, prohibited from being used—because of a problem with their tracks that caused them to be hazardous to operate), and the Ferret armoured scout cars were completely unreliable because of their tendency to break down frequently. These were all vehicles from the 1950s, immediately post–World War II, and the same age as the Centurions.

There were a couple of bright spots. When things are going badly, some individuals always seem to step up and meet the challenge. Almost a year after arriving in Petawawa, I became a recce troop leader, and two of the soldiers in that troop turned out to be standouts—examples for me, their boss, to emulate. One of them was a young master corporal (the first military rank with formal leadership responsibilities), Rick Round, who later went on to become a major, retiring from the Canadian Forces after eight UN missions around the world. He was a consummate professional, a values-based individual who became a good friend. Rick was always impeccable in his dress and deportment and was always thinking ahead. To me, he was the epitome of a soldier and a leader.

The second was my troop's senior non-commissioned officer, Warrant Officer Paddy Lawrence. Paddy was the second black Canadian who really had a major impact on me. He mentored and guided me, often saving me from myself, during my time as a troop leader. He had been a Golden Gloves boxer, was still superbly fit and had great instincts about how to be a leader. Paddy looked after his soldiers as well as looking out for me and became the Rock of Gibraltar for young Lieutenant Rick Hillier.

By this time Joyce, our baby son, Chris, and I were a small, happy family settled in Petawawa. In that first year in the army, however, I saw precious little in the Canadian Forces to inspire me to continue to want this as my lifelong profession. Joyce and I had many conversations about whether we were going to do this for the rest of our lives, and at points during that first year, I would turn to her and ask, "Do we really want to belong to this organization? Do we really want to be a part of this for any more time than we have to?"

Joyce said, "No, probably not."

CHAPTER 4

TANKS, BUT NO TANKS

That first year in the regiment in Petawawa, so depressing, almost caused my career in the military to end soon after it began. About a year after I joined the regiment, however, one man, demonstrating the impact that a single person can have, changed my mind about staying in the army.

Lieutenant-Colonel Bob Billings, who took over as commanding officer of the 8th Hussars in the summer of 1977, was a man who inspired. He made communications a priority and talked to everybody in the regiment, from senior officers to the most junior soldiers—a real and positive change from previous commanders. He wasn't the sort of commander to sit in his office all day; that much was also clear as I bumped into him in my troop parking area on the second day of his appointment. The shock of seeing the CO in his work area was significant for our soldiers, and for us; and to have him talk to us, seeking our opinion, was almost unbelievable. Word about this new guy spread quickly.

Soon after he took over, Bob got the regiment together on the parade square to talk with all of us, again—a new experience for a lot of us young soldiers. He told us what we were going to be doing, why and how: "You might love it, you might hate it, you might be tested by it. But we're all going to do it together, and we're all going to look after each other while we do it. We're going to look after our families, and we're going to make sure we all know what's going on. Yes, there are going to be tough times, and no, we don't have enough equipment. But we're going to do it anyway."

We lined up behind Bob Billings, his approach and his ideas. He brought the unit together in a variety of fun ways—regimental games, sports events—and he attended all of them. He was always visible, and he also did exactly what he asked every soldier to do. Bob led the hockey team in brigade competitions against the other combat units, and while his scoring ability didn't have an impact, the one fight he got into inspired the rest of us unbelievably. He made physical fitness a priority, and when he organized regimental physical training days, he was out there with his staff and senior NCOs, like everyone else.

Bob insisted on ethical behaviour, set the example himself and held people accountable for their actions. He told us, "My principles of behaviour are honesty, integrity, loyalty," and he walked through what that would mean to all of us, from the most junior, newly enlisted soldier to the most senior officers in the regiment. He built little teams, then merged those teams into one bigger team, and did so with a number of activities, most of which were common sense but which no one had ever tried before. Billings made sure that every event was just that—an event, with flair, drama and excitement. If it was a family day, he made sure the organizers made it as exciting as possible, the best family day ever, with lots of different things for children to do and with special attention paid to our wives. He initiated the first family day early after his arrival, brought all the soldiers' families into the base, put on rides for them, put the kiddies on the few Lynxes that were running, let them ride heavy trucks and every other kind of wheeled or tracked vehicle that would work. He paid attention to "his" families and made it so much fun that even the soldiers' spouses and children started to feel like they were part of something special.

53

Bob turned training exercises from mundane, routine affairs into free-play challenges that were fun, valuable and demanding, all at the same time. He talked to everybody. He talked to each troop and squadron of soldiers, spoke to the NCOs, got all the officers together and worked on building camaraderie within the entire unit. Bob invited the junior officers, or subalterns—young lieutenants like me—and their wives to his house for dinner, rotating evenings so he could fit everybody in. When our turn for dinner with the commanding officer came, and Joyce and I walked into his house, I was frightened to death. To a subaltern like me the commanding officer was God, and I almost dreaded that dinner. Bob and his wife, Sheila, went out of their way to make us feel at home, however, and it turned out to be an incredible evening for all of us.

Up until then, I had not experienced leadership like that— not from any officer, let alone from a commanding officer; none of us had. Bob made it fun to be in the unit, despite the fact that we had almost no working equipment. The little equipment we did have was older than most of the soldiers who were using it, and even the few newer vehicles were falling apart for lack of spare parts. That somehow didn't seem to matter. Bob was later promoted to colonel and became the Director of Studies at the Army College in Kingston, from where he retired. He and Sheila still live in Kingston.

One of the best lessons I learned, or perhaps had reinforced, from Bob was the importance of having a sense of humour. When I was building up my headquarters to go to command the mission in Afghanistan in 2004, I brought my entire staff of 200 together at the start and end of every day in Kaiserslautern, Germany, during two and a half weeks of preparation, when I would talk to them—what we were doing, why and how. After training together for ten days, getting to know most of the staff team and observing and participating in many activities, we were going to culminate the training with an intensive five-day package replicating, as closely as possible, Afghanistan and what we would be doing there. Wanting to focus my team on key priorities, I walked through nine rules on how we would approach the test. Rule 9 was to have—and use—a sense of humour to relieve stress, lighten the mood and help keep people healthy. That started a ball rolling, and at every meeting or event thereafter, someone had a joke, an anecdote to relate where they had screwed up or a slide to show relating to something close to our mission that was funny. Rule 9 became almost a compulsory part of our life and, years later, I still receive e-mails from members of that team with the subject line "Rule 9."

At the same time, Bob also taught me the importance of optimism and how it can become a force multiplier more powerful than a battery of artillery or a squadron of tanks. When I became Chief of the Defence Staff, I met a lady named Jackie Girouard, who reminded me yet again about the importance of optimism. Jackie had lost her husband, Regimental Sergeant Major Bobby Girouard, in a November 2006 attack by a vehicle-borne suicide bomber in Kandahar province. After much soul-searching, Jackie decided, about a year after her husband's death, that she wanted to realize her dream and join the Canadian Forces and, at age forty-six, did so. She was due to commence basic training in February 2008, and just a day or so before that I ran into her at the Garrison Ball, a military gala dinner for about a thousand people, in Toronto. I put my arm around her and said, "How is it going, Jackie?"

She told me that it was still hard to think about her loss but that she was bolstered by her two sons and her daughter. "But I notice that when I smile more, they smile more!" she said.

I thought, what an incredible lady and what a great lesson: optimism is not only contagious, it's a necessary part of being a leader. Jackie's optimism enabled her to get through life after losing Bobby, helped her family cope each day, and certainly got her through basic training, including the hard physical fitness training and running of stairs. (At the training centre in Saint-Jean, Quebec, the recruits live on the top floors—10 to 12—and are not permitted to use elevators. Jackie swears she will never walk another stair after the weeks of doing so in Saint-Jean!)

When I became Chief, I made it my personal goal to be optimistic, always, but particularly around National Defence Headquarters in Ottawa. On stressful days, if you walk around with a long face and a frown all the time, you can create a negative atmosphere in a heartbeat. Your actions and physical expressions communicate to those around you how you feel and dramatically affect how *they* feel. In short, if you are perceived as downcast or pessimistic, your organization will become that way overnight.

There were some tough days when we really needed to remember that lesson. On July 4, 2007, in a tragic attack, we lost six soldiers, all in one vehicle in Kandahar. The next morning, at our weekly leaders' meeting of about twenty-five men and women, civilian and military, we were briefed on the attack. It was clear that much of the team was in shock, and there were tears running down the cheeks of more than one person around that table. When the briefer finished, I spoke. "You know," I told them, "yesterday was a tough day. We lost six awesome, great, young Canadians who died because of their service to Canada. We're going to mourn each one of those individuals as the fine young men that they were; we're going to bring them home, and we're going to show them all the respect and honour that they have earned and deserve. We are going to ensure that they are returned to Canada for the final time with full military honours and with dignity. We are going to look after their buddies, who are stressed; we're going to support their families in this, the worst time of their lives, making sure they are looked after every step of the way, and there are not going to be any limitations on that help. We are going to do all of that as senior leaders, while we are in this room, in the next few minutes, and then we are going to refocus immediately on our responsibilities. If we step out of this room looking like we're finished, the men and women who work for us—all those other servicemen and servicewomen who are serving Canada—will be devastated. We can't do that to them. We must do our job if they are going to do theirs and if we are to meet our moral obligation to them."

So that's what we did. That story shows how you can go through a tragedy and just keep going. If, as a leader, you can't shake that reversal, you can't do your job. In our case, that would have put the lives of Canada's sons and daughters in Afghanistan even more at risk.

Optimism and humour go together. I started to realize how important both were as early as basic training. A few times when things were tough or we had made some kind of major mistake—or what at the time *seemed* like a major mistake—Sergeant Cy Clayton would make a bit of a joke and get us all laughing. The insecurity and fear we felt would dissipate and we'd understand that we'd screwed up, would laugh about it and would never doubt that we were going to be successful at what we had set ourselves to do.

———————

In 1979, I was looking forward to, with the 8th Hussars and Lieutenant-Colonel Billings, a tour of duty in Cyprus, where Canada was contributing a battalion to the United Nations peace-keeping mission. One day during the regiment's preparations for that deployment, Bob called me to his office and said, "Rick, we're going to Cyprus, but you're not. I want you to become one of the tank troop leaders in Germany from January to July 1979."

I had mixed emotions. I wanted to go with the unit to Cyprus, but at the same time I wanted the chance to lead a troop of tanks. I had already led a reconnaissance troop by that time and had had a little taste of tank troop leading when we completed a small unit exchange in 1978 with the U.S. Army down in Fort Hood, Texas. The plan was that I would stay back for a couple of months as part of the rear party, supporting the families of the troops that were in Cyprus. Then, just after Christmas, I would go to Germany to be a troop leader with the Royal Canadian Dragoons, the Armoured regiment based in Germany. My family would stay in Petawawa for that time.

Bob had asked me to do it, so I did it, departing on the first of January 1979. I had tried to set up Joyce for success before I left by buying a new car for her. She was working that winter and our son Chris was just three years old, so I wanted her to have reliable transportation. I researched all the different models and picked a car that had been named Car of the Year in 1978—a Plymouth Volare. I thought, "Awesome, I have to buy this one— that way Joyce won't have any problems."

From the time we got it until we finally got rid of it ten years later, that car was a lemon. Joyce would be going to work and the brakes, which had somehow corroded, wouldn't fully release and stuck halfway all the time. If there was even a little bit of ice and snow, on level ground, the wheels would spin. The car would break down constantly, and we would have to get it towed to the shop and fixed. Meanwhile, she was going to work and dealing with everyday life. While I tried to do everything I could before I left for the six months, it just did not work out at all. I have never forgiven Chrysler for that car.

I arrived in Germany on the second of January and went to work the very next day. I took command of my tank troop of sixteen soldiers in B Squadron and immediately went down to accept four brand-new Leopard C-1 tanks, right from the factory. They even had that new-car smell, which was pretty refreshing to me after having spent so much time training in old vehicles like the Centurion.

Three weeks later, at the end of January 1979, we were to deploy on a big NATO winter exercise involving troops from North America and all across Europe, a total of about 200,000 soldiers. In order to be ready, we had to learn how to operate these brand-new tanks and, more importantly, use them effectively. We also had to put enough kilometres on them to make sure all their tracks could be torqued properly, so we spent hours upon hours driving them around the airfield at the big Canadian air force base in Germany, having a lot of fun in the process. We were like kids with new cars, and looked forward to using these superbly designed fighting vehicles for years. Little did we know how many that would be.

In late 2006, on a visit to Afghanistan, I went to take a close look at the Leopards that we had just sent to Kandahar to give the battle group more firepower. Sure enough, one of those tanks in Afghanistan was one of those four brand-new ones that my troop had driven out of the factory in 1979. It certainly didn't have the new-car smell anymore. Its belly armour was worn thin and the vehicle didn't function well at all in the heat of the Afghan summer. It was the best, and the only, tank that we had, however, and we needed it in the fight, so there it was, still serving after all those years.

We had gone through the whole process of trying to replace those Leopards with something lighter and easier to lift by aircraft but that still had the same firepower, protection and mobility. We thought the answer would be something like the U.S.-built Mobile Gun System, or MGS, but we found as we went down that road that the MGS just could not deliver. What we had was the Leopard C-1, so that's what we sent to Afghanistan.

During this first tour of Germany I met the commanding officer of the Royal Canadian Dragoons, Lieutenant-Colonel Gordon O'Connor, who would later become Minister of National Defence while I was CDS. Although he had been my commanding officer during the latter part of Phase 4 training in the Armour School in 1976, I had never met him. I talked to him briefly when I first arrived, but I was just a young officer at the time, doing things typical for many young officers, such as pushing on doors marked "pull" and so forth. He was very senior to me, of course, so I never really saw that much of him during the first few weeks of breaking in the Leopards. During the winter exercises we were detached from the regiment and operating with a combat team from the Infantry, so, again, I was never really directly under his command and saw him not at all.

———————

When I arrived in Germany, the Dragoons were somewhat in shock. Just prior to Christmas, one of the soldiers had been arrested by the German police for drunk driving. The Canadian Forces in Europe had its own military justice system that handled such offences for soldiers and their families, so the offender was handed over to the regiment. The guy who'd been arrested was married with several kids, and the feeling in the regiment had been that the right thing to do would have been to delay sentencing him until after Christmas, to minimize the impact on his family. Instead, Gord, who had the reputation of being a disciplinarian, threw the book at him. He gave him a term of detention that started just before Christmas Day. Right or wrong, there was a great deal of hard feeling in the regiment that this corporal, the father of two children, was behind bars over Christmas. The consternation in the ranks was significant, and Gord O'Connor's legacy in the regiment was that he was a harsh disciplinarian who did not relate well to the soldiers and their families.

Obviously, all leaders have to be ruthless on occasion and have to have a core of steel somewhere in their makeup. Being a leader means that sometimes you're going to piss people off, because you have to do the tough things. It doesn't mean that you have to be like that all the time, though, and most good leaders find the right balance, because being a leader means finding that balance between hard and soft. If you handle everybody in a hard manner all the time, then the amount of respect and loyalty they have for you will dissipate quickly. The biggest part of a leader's job, I found, was going around thanking people and trying to motivate them by showing them that what they're doing is appreciated. I didn't see that in the Royal Canadian Dragoons when Gord O'Connor was commanding. Although he was extremely capable, communicating with and motivating the soldiers was just not his forte. Those soldiers were all completely surprised when Gord decided to run for Parliament many years later, and equally surprised when he was elected! The media would make much out of my relationship with Gord, but I can say that I enjoyed my time in Germany under his command, undergoing simple, great training on brand-new, state-of-the-art equipment.

When we were satisfied that the Leopards were ready and we were prepared to use them effectively, we loaded them onto a train and deployed to Bavaria for a big exercise called Winter Reforger, along with 200,000 American, British, German, French and other Canadian soldiers. It quickly became clear that our new tanks gave us a significant advantage. This was the first time I'd seen how technology could really change the battlefield, particularly when complementing a superbly trained network of motivated soldiers.

We moved our tanks with a combat team of infantry from the Royal Canadian Regiment, running at night, really fast, trying to get to the rear of the enemy (some U.S. Army units), come at them from behind or from a flank and catch them unawares. A surprised enemy was an incoherent and therefore vulnerable enemy. The Leopards had the new night-vision camera mounted on the turret that would magnify any kind of ambient starlight or moonlight and really light things up. We could move very quickly at night without lights, see for quite a distance and fire on anyone we saw. Again and again, we would come upon enemy units—mostly American, because they were the largest body of troops involved in the exercise—hiding in the woods and usually fast asleep. We could see them from up to a kilometre away, make out every single vehicle and count individual soldiers. We'd start firing on them with blank ammunition and catch them completely by surprise.

I watched one American tank lieutenant asleep in a line of trees along with all of his men and could actually see him coming up through the hatch of the tank, stretching his arms and yawning. We got all of our tanks and the infantry in position and opened fire. All of a sudden there were people popping up and running around everywhere. It was mayhem at the other end, but it was perfect for us; we just sat back and blazed away. The only problem was that none of the other Canadian units had anything like the Leopard's night camera, so we were banging away at the Americans in the woods a kilometre away and the infantry right beside us in their armoured personnel carriers had no idea what we were shooting at—they couldn't see a single thing.

The American units didn't have the night capability on their old M60 tanks. I found it quite incredible to see what we could accomplish with only a small technological edge, particularly when it augmented that well-trained team of people. Now, of course, the night-vision technology is much improved, with scopes and sights that can see through all light and weather conditions and make the low light level television that we had on the Leopards look an antique. For that one shining moment in 1979, however, the Canadians had the advantage.

We also had some disadvantages. After that exercise, we transported the Leopards by tank train to an enormous tank range in northern Germany, next to the site of the infamous Bergen-Belsen concentration camp, to participate in a live-fire gunnery exercise. We picked the team during that exercise to take part in the Canadian Army Trophy competition, a prestigious competition with a prize for the most accurate shooting from tanks representing the Central European and North American nations in NATO. The original trophy, donated by Canada (hence the name), had been the trigger for a competition between the tanks of the various countries in the alliance to improve NATO's standard of tank gunnery. So we had Germans, Brits, Belgians, Dutch, Danes, Americans and Canadians all competing for our tankers version of "top gun." I was selected as one of the troop leaders on that team. We trained for the next two months, and then set off to take part in the competition, again in Bergen, in northern Germany. That's when we first discovered that we had a problem with the tanks' fire control system, the device that automatically calculates the angle of the gun, the temperature, the kind of ammunition being used and the range to the target so that the gunners only had to lay the crosshairs on the target in order to hit it.

All of our training was in vain. We'd go out on a cool day and shoot accurately, never missing a target. Then we'd go shoot on a hot, sunny day and we would miss almost every single target, requiring multiple shots to hit the ones we did kill. Our procedures were right; our troops were working together well; we were acquiring targets, allocating them and then shooting quickly. We were probably the best team out of all the nations involved in the competition in those categories, but it seemed that the hot weather was causing a technical problem with the tank.

When we bought the Leopards from the Germans, someone in Ottawa had decided that the German fire control system wasn't good enough for Canadians, so we had to put in our own. We bought a unique-to-Canada computerized fire control system. Once the gunner fed the range and all the other factors into the system, the gun did the rest; we were supposed to get a kill every time. In cold weather, the system worked like magic. What nobody realized was that the system was connected to the interior roof of the tank's turret—in reality a thin piece of metal. In hot weather, the turret roof would buckle slightly—just a few millimetres, but more than enough to shift the sight completely out of alignment. We would set our sights early in the morning, when it was cool, then go out and wait in a concentration area for our turn to shoot. It wasn't uncommon to wait for five or six hours, and in that time the sun would warm the top part of the turret, warping it just enough to pull the sight off target. To our great disappointment, our scores in the competition were absolutely abysmal. We didn't hit a thing.

It took more than seven years for the Canadian Forces to solve that problem. It took the army more than three years just to admit that there even *was* a problem. Everyone who looked into the issue said, "No, it's the gunners' fault," or "Put a few wet sandbags on the roof of that turret and we'll be good to go." In 1987, when we finally rectified that problem with the sights, we were part of the by now combined multinational team that won the trophy even though by that point we were up against a whole new generation of tanks that were much more advanced—M1 Abrams tanks (American) and Leopard 2s (German). It was much tougher to go out and win, but we did it.

Our problems with the tank sights were caused by our tendency to Canadianize everything that the Canadian Forces purchased, taking something that worked perfectly well for others and deciding that it wasn't good enough for us. The Canadian Forces have thought that way for decades, and we worked really hard over the past few years to change that thinking. If an American-built weapon is working fine or a British vehicle drives beautifully, then let's buy it as is. Otherwise we end up with a unique,

Canadian-modified beast that causes us technical headaches and costs us money. Canadianized pieces of kit are hugely expensive to maintain because there are usually fewer of them. Secondly, if there are problems, they end up being uniquely Canadian problems, and the CF has to go through long and expensive procedures to identify and resolve them. I learned in Germany to put an appetite suppressant on Canadianization. Despite our efforts, this is still a major challenge.

We had also highlighted something even more important, but it took a while for it to resonate with me. The Canadian Forces was not a learning organization; we didn't conduct analyses and come to logical conclusions following complaints from the field or clearly identified problems. We just had not gotten to the point where we could really self-critique our problems; we didn't look to improve or at how to learn. Whether it was the Leopard fire control system problem, raincoats that were not waterproof or anything else, we appeared to be incapable of accepting there was a problem, identifying it, finding solutions and then implementing those solutions quickly. That was probably the most important change in the last five years: taking a lesson learned in Afghanistan and, in a matter of days, starting to teach that lesson back here in Canada.

CHAPTER 5

STRIKING IT RICH IN FORT KNOX

When I came home from Germany in July 1979, Bob Billings called me into his office and told me he had a new job for me: "I want you to become part of our support team for the militia." So I moved into an office in a different building in Petawawa and began work-ing from there for the Central Militia Area, which comprised the land reserve in Ontario, as a liaison, essentially, between the reserve army (citizen-soldiers rather than soldier-citizens) and the regular-force brigade in Petawawa. My family and I continued to live in Petawawa and I supported reservists who came there to train.

Until then my only exposure to the reserves had been when we brought groups of reservists from the various Armoured mili-tia units across Ontario to Petawawa for a weekend on the gun-nery range. That had been Billings' idea: he wanted to strengthen the relationship between the regular force and the militia. I spent a weekend with my non-commissioned officers running the militia soldiers through their gunnery drills and ensuring that they were ready to fire live, but that had been my only exposure to the reserves up until then. The regular army and the reserves were different worlds. It took me a while to get used to the idea of troops under my command being plumbers, doctors or police officers during the week and then putting on their uniforms to become soldiers on weekends and evenings. There was certainly a huge disparity and a large gap in the understanding between the regulars and the reserves. Although we all wore the same uniforms, neither side really trusted the other. At times we barely spoke to each other. The regulars could be quite arrogant, looking down our noses at part-time soldiers, and the reservists could be touchy and often had an inferiority complex. The regular army—in fact, the entire Canadian Forces—had lost touch with its reservists, and that loss was but one indication that we had lost touch with the Canadian public.

I'm not sure that the CF ever had a significant relationship with the people of Canada. Since the Second World War, our military was never really regarded as the armed forces of Canada by Canadians themselves; Canadians never took ownership of the military. That gap was exacerbated during the Cold War, when the army, navy and air force spent most of their time training constantly for a war with the big bad Russian bear that never came. Much of that training took place on the ground or in the skies of Europe or on the North Atlantic and hence was never seen by ordinary Canadian men and women. We were becoming, outside of the NATO mission, a large bureaucracy, with a tendency to avoid making waves and taking risks. The events that occurred during the Somalia mission with the Airborne Regiment in the early 1990s made people in uniform duck even farther below the waterline until they effectively disappeared.

That was also true of the relationship between the regulars and the reserves—it had also disappeared. I don't know what it was like before I joined, but by that time each component was a separate entity that largely ignored the other. They would occasionally snipe at each other across the divide, a gap that very few people managed to bridge. It's only during the last ten years that that chasm has really been bridged, driven by the fact that during the mid-1990s and the early 2000s both regular and reserve forces were needed to carry out the many missions that the Canadian Forces were asked to do, and the relationship had to improve. With the cuts to personnel and funding, the regular force needed the reserve force to accomplish all those missions, and the reservists needed the regulars to really hone their skills so that they could be successful.

The navy and air force led the way in integrating their regular and reserve forces in order to accomplish their mission, but the army had been slow to follow. The Canadian Forces came out with a plan in 1998 to significantly change the land reserves, amalgamating some of the smaller reserve regiments, and redefining the roles and focus of most of them. In the view of the reserves, that shake-up was mostly a bad idea; and even where it was a good idea, the changes were made totally without consulting them. The regular force imposed the changes on them and, essentially, the reserve community rebelled. The few tentative ropes that had been strung across the divide were cut or burned, and the relationship collapsed. Everything to do with the changes came to a crashing halt.

Lieutenant-General Mike Jeffery, my predecessor as head of the army, was faced with the challenge of resolving the crisis. Mike was brought in to start to put things back on track. He went out of his way to consult the reservists and move forward with ideas from both them and the regulars. He brought people together until there was no fence and everyone, almost without exception, was working toward one vision. Mike's work was instrumental in bringing us together, and now the army works together as one unit.

My continuation of that approach was to tell people to be proud. I told those in uniform to be proud of who they were and what they did. Everywhere I went I said, "Look, be proud that you're a soldier; be proud you're a sailor; be proud that you're an airman or airwoman, but don't be so proud that you're freaking stupid and can't work well with the other sailors or soldiers or airmen and airwomen, who are all—guess what?—Canadians. We're all trying to achieve one thing and in order to be successful, we need to do it together."

I always told the reservists to be proud, whether they were students or teachers or medics or business people. I used to say, "My God, you spend time doing things for Canada in uniform and I cannot even imagine trying to do something like that, holding down a civilian job, a profession, and also being a soldier."

My first contact with the reserves was a great experience. It was a very short posting, but I got to meet and work with a lot of very good people, under a different timeline and set of conditions than I had experienced in Germany and in the 8th Hussars. Then, in late 1979, my career manager (the personnel officer assigned to every Canadian Forces officer to help guide his or her military career) showed up in Petawawa and said, "We're going to polish you."

"Okay, great, sir," I said. "Where am I going—to Gagetown?" If I could not be with a combat unit, I wanted to work at the Armour School as an instructor.

"No, no, you're going to Fort Knox, Kentucky, to take the U.S. Army's Armor Officer Advanced Course."

He went on to say something else, but I couldn't hear anything—the blood was roaring in my ears. I thought to myself, "I'm going to Kentucky. I've never been there before." I ran over to where Joyce was working, in the Bank of Montreal on the base in Petawawa, and said, "Joyce, we're posted."

She said, "Where?"

"To Fort Knox, Kentucky."

"What are you going to do there?"

"I have no idea," I said, and I was laughing because I was so excited. "But we're going to Fort Knox, Kentucky."

Her response was slightly different. She started crying at the thought of leaving friends, uprooting our son, giving up her job, moving houses, and re-establishing ourselves in another country. She soon came around though, great wife that she is, and reconciled herself to what we were going to be doing.

At the end of February 1980, we drove to Fort Knox, which is not just the U.S. Treasury's gold bullion depository, but also their army's biggest training centre for Armored officers. The Armor Officer Advanced Course is the equivalent of our Army Operations Course, run for junior captains at the Staff College in Kingston, Ontario, and would act as the equivalent qualification for me.

We arrived in Kentucky on a Sunday night and found the guest house on post. I phoned the liaison officer, Major Randy Hoodspith. He and his wife, Shirley, came over and visited with us. By 9:30 the next morning we had been assigned a permanent house on the base. The house was just a few blocks from the gold depository, where they filmed parts of the James Bond movie *Goldfinger*. In the scenes where Pussy Galore and her Flying Circus are flying over the depository building, you can actually see where we lived, which we have pointed out endless times to our friends. We always take pleasure in watching that movie.

By noon on Monday, everything was unpacked, an indicator of how little furniture we had, and I went into the student liaison office to report formally. I said, "I'm Captain Hillier, here to start the Armor Officer Advanced Course."

"Okay, great, sir. As long as you're back here by 10 April, that's good." It was only March 1.

I had no idea that we were so early, but I wasn't complaining: it gave me more than a month to spend with Joyce and our son, Chris, and we all got the opportunity to really learn about Fort Knox and visit many parts of Kentucky. The fort itself was huge, especially in comparison to Canadian army bases. The actor Bill Murray had just finished filming *Stripes* at Fort Knox, and when watching that movie a little while ago I recognized all the old World War II–era barracks, and a part of my daily running route.

The course, once it started, was incredible. There were 120 officers taking part, with the program broken into five major components, the first of which was Offence. We spent two months learning about how to handle offensive operations, manoeuvre a battalion or brigade and attack an enemy. At the end of the phases, the students received orders as battalion commanding officers and had to prepare a plan and the corresponding orders for their battalion, and hand them in to be marked. It was a day-long test: at 8 a.m. we got our orders and had until 6 p.m. to complete the work. Every part was marked with a "Go" or a "No Go," and if you got a "No Go" you had to go back and redo the test until you got it right. There were almost 120 separate items to be checked, and I was the only guy in the class who got all "Go's" on the first try. In celebration, I went out and treated myself to a pair of Dingo cowboy boots, which I had wanted for a long time. I still wear them.

We had a great time on that course. All the foreign students (there were officers from many other nations) were taken to Washington, D.C., for a week. That was the first time I'd ever been to Washington. I loved visiting monuments such as the Lincoln Memorial, and the Smithsonian Institution's National Air and Space Museum, with the capsule from *Apollo 11* (the part that they had brought back from the moon landing) and the Wright brothers' first airplane. I also enjoyed the Jefferson Memorial, the Washington Monument, the White House and the Reflecting Pool, and managed to get in several distance runs around the Mall.

This wasn't my first exposure to the American way of doing things. About a year earlier I had gone with the 8th Hussars for a small unit exchange to Fort Hood, Texas, a place I later got to know quite well. That exchange lasted only for six weeks, with three troops of tanks plus a small headquarters and a very small support unit participating. I knew the two other troop leaders well: Lieutenant Brad White, a good friend of mine, and Lieutenant Bill Brough, who became one of my better friends through life. We flew down in a Hercules, which then turned around and loaded an equal number of American soldiers and took them back to Petawawa. We left Ottawa early on a cold May morning, bundled up in our combat jackets with scarves and gloves, so we kind of pitied the GIs heading north. When we landed in Fort Hood that afternoon, however, it was at the hottest part of the day, 36 degrees Celsius on the tarmac when we disembarked the aircraft, and we would have gladly traded Canadian weather for the stifling and dry heat. We formed up in parade format to be welcomed by the Americans. None of us were acclimatized to the heat, least of all this boy from Newfoundland: I got a terrible sunburn on my face the first day in Texas, and it just got worse over the next days.

We spent the next few weeks training on the American M60 tanks, firing the tanks' guns on the range, doing tactical training in the field and following it up with some sightseeing in what was, for almost all of us, an entirely new and exciting region. We went to Houston to watch a baseball game, and to San Antonio to sightsee on the River Walk. We were a pretty closely knit group and had a great time.

On our third week of the exchange we got a call from Canada asking for Warrant Officer George Halfkenny. George was a great non-commissioned officer and a really good guy. He had gone off with other NCOs that day (it was a Sunday) and we had to go track him down because he had to phone home. Two of his sons and another boy, aged about twelve to thirteen, had gone to Algonquin Park, near Petawawa, to go fishing, which they'd done frequently in the past, and had not come back. George was obviously in shock that his sons were missing, and we got him home as quickly as possible. He flew to Montreal, and Bob Billings arranged for a helicopter to pick him up and take him to Petawawa immediately. Bob had sent almost the entire regiment to Algonquin Park to look for these boys.

Unfortunately, the day George got back the boys' remains were found. A black bear had hunted down and killed all three. It was devastating for all of us and a pretty tough time for the whole regiment. It demonstrated to me that while it can be difficult to lead during times like those, if you are adamant about doing what is right, as opposed to worrying about how your actions will look to superiors or others, you can get through it. Bob Billings, again, had done what was right.

The Texas exchange was my first exposure to the U.S. Army, and it was not pretty. What struck me immediately was that it was a huge organization: Fort Knox and Fort Hood each had more soldiers than the entire Canadian army, but even to my relatively uneducated, inexperienced and naive eye, I could see that the U.S. Army was in crisis. There were major disciplinary challenges and enormous problems with crime, including major, violent crime. There were places on Fort Hood that you simply did not go, certainly not at night—it was just too dangerous. A year later, I found that Fort Knox was no different. They had big problems with drugs, violence, absenteeism and desertion. Their leadership was almost autocratic, and their equipment, despite the enormous quantities, left much to be desired. The U.S. Army was still in the grip of the crisis of confidence following Vietnam, and that really didn't resolve until the first Gulf War.

It was obvious as well that the Americans had big muscle. They're a huge military force—army, navy, air force, the Marine Corps, the reserves and the active-duty and National Guard components. They can conduct brigade operations effectively and division and higher-level operations really well—that is, when all the pieces come together. In the Canadian Forces, our strong point was the professionalism of our men and women in uniform, who, when they were well equipped, well led and well motivated, could have an enormous impact. The Americans had that big stuff squared away, but although we Canadians didn't have that massive army, navy or air force, we did have great young men and women, superbly and extensively trained and, at the smaller-unit level (the battle group up to brigade group level), we were as good as any force in the world and better by far than most.

Canada put lots of effort into the individual training, teaching our soldiers the shooting, movement and other skills they needed to do their jobs, but far too little into the collective training—bringing all the soldiers, in their units, together to train as one large team. Not only did we not have those big units like the U.S. Army, we didn't have the financial resources to do the higher-level training with the units we did have. Unfortunately, it got worse, not better, over the next decade or so.

In fact, during the 1990s, when what seemed like annual financial cuts hit hardest, we were actually prohibited from doing collective training. Walt Natynczyk and I, serving together in Petawawa, coined a phrase to describe the situation: "We need to train to fight as opposed to having to fight to train." That was a real issue: we weren't doing the collective training because we couldn't afford it. We weren't doing things at the combat team level, and we certainly weren't doing them at the battle group level, and we never did them at the brigade level after the early 1990s. As a result, we lost most of those skill sets, and we're still struggling to get them back. In an organization that must develop its own leaders, stopping that training for only a few years means an entire generation of leaders are ill-prepared for their primary jobs.

I learned a lot about how to do things well in Fort Knox, and, equally important, learned a lot of what not to do, by watching the mistakes the Americans were making. A lot of their problems came down to posture: they were posing as an army. It was really, when you got down to it, a group of poorly equipped, poorly trained and undisciplined soldiers who weren't motivated. They felt, perhaps correctly, that nobody in American society really wanted too much to do with the United States Army in those days. These were lessons there that resonated with us in the CF in the mid-'90s.

Our experience in Fort Knox was overwhelmingly positive, however. One person I remember most fondly was the lady who was the assistant to the officer in charge of the student liaison office. Diane Hatcher was an incredible woman. Fort Knox was home to an enormous number of foreign students for training, and it was her job to look after them. Even though she was just the assistant in the liaison cell, in reality there was a constant rotation of officers coming and going through that job, so it was Diane who really ran the place.

All the foreign students learned very quickly that if you wanted something done, you went to see Diane. We got to know her well; she loved the Canadians because we were "zero maintenance." When students from Third World countries arrived, including some families who showed up to start the course with their own servants in tow, she often had numerous, complex and sometimes impossible issues to handle. We have stayed in contact all these years since. Diane became a strong supporter of every Canadian student who ever went to Fort Knox.

In the autumn of 2005, I finally got the opportunity to repay this incredible lady for twenty-five years of looking after Canadians. Diane has multiple sclerosis and is confined to a wheelchair most of the time. We heard that she was retiring from the student liaison office in Fort Knox and so we gathered together five of her former students and flew to Kentucky to present her with the Canadian Forces Medallion for Distinguished Service to Canada and the Canadian Forces. All five of us spoke at her retirement ceremony as our way of thanking her publicly for her excellent work. It was one of those great moments in life and a good lesson: remember, and recognize, good people.

When I finished the Armor Officer Advanced Course, in December 1980, Joyce and I drove north, a little reluctant to return to the Canadian winter. We stopped in Boston and visited long-lost relatives, second-generation Americans whose families had left Newfoundland before the Second World War, during the Great Depression. They, and many others, travelled down the eastern seaboard in search of work, and so we discovered people from both sides of our family in the Boston area. Then we went on to Newfoundland for Christmas with family and back to my next job, at the Armour School in Gagetown, New Brunswick. I had finally got to Gagetown, if a bit indirectly.

Gagetown was the epitome of winter. We moved into our military quarters on January 4, 1981, and over the next days had a snowfall of more than 100 centimetres. It was quick to work for me, as I spent the first eight months as a training officer for students, teaching and leading on various courses. One of those was a two-week course in which we conducted tactical training for all the helicopter pilots, so they could work effectively with the ground troops, but the course I remember most was training sergeants to become warrant officers. This gave me the opportunity to test a few new concepts I had picked up in Fort Knox, to try them in the Canadian system and see how they worked in the field. There were twenty-five sergeants on that course, some of the best non-commissioned officers in the Armoured Corps—indeed, in the army—so we were like our own little squadron, which gave me the chance to operate at another level up from what I had been doing until then.

Of those twenty-five students, only one guy didn't pass the course, and within a couple of weeks it was obvious to everybody involved—the instructors, the students and even the individual himself—that he just wasn't ready for this next level. What was interesting was that out of the twenty-four sergeants who did succeed, eighteen went on to become chief warrant officers, our highest non-commissioned rank. It was an incredibly talented group, including guys who later became regimental sergeants major and with whom I had the great privilege of soldiering while I was brigade commander in Petawawa and later a division commander in Bosnia, men like Bruce Prendergast and Roger Munger. They were such a great group of students. As their instructor, I learned about ten times more than they did.

I also had the chance to be part of the instructor cadre for a Phase 4 course, which I was determined to help make a much better experience for the young Armoured officers than my Phase 4, in 1976, had been. Because there was a large-scale division exercise under way in Gagetown in 1981, we moved the Phase 4 course to Wainwright, Alberta, a huge training area that we had virtually to ourselves. We had sixteen students training to become Armoured officers, and fifteen passed, including several who are now generals. Almost everyone who was on that course made their mark in the army, regardless of what rank they later achieved.

After the first week or so it was obvious that we had truly talented young student officers. Instead of giving each of them two or three hours in the "hot seat," we put them in as troop leaders and left them there for two to three days. I remembered my Phase 4 in 1976 and how we'd had only two or three hours to prove we could do the job, and if we failed even once we were given formal warnings and were halfway to failing entirely. So I left those students in the command chair for a long time before we rotated the next guy in. The students used the time, with mentoring from the instructors, to learn what they needed to do to be successful. We mentored, talked, demonstrated, accepted failure and worked hard with all of them to achieve the maximum training value. At the end of their time as leaders for a specific operation, we would assess and debrief and discuss what went right and chuckle over what went wrong. Once in a while we got a little angry and kicked the tires on the vehicles too, as we talked about what had not gone right. That training course also became one of the best learning experiences in my career, and one of my most satisfying memories.

What it did was help me consolidate and cement those leadership attributes I'd learned from Cy Clayton and Bob Billings and from my time at Fort Knox. It even taught me a few things I hadn't learned. I always found it hugely satisfying being an instructor, not because it meant I got to lord it over people but because I learned thousands of things by teaching a course, more than any of the students. Helping those young officers or those more senior and experienced sergeants develop and grow was incredibly satisfying. If I couldn't be at the combat unit, I wanted to be at the school, teaching.

That Phase 4 was also a lot of fun. We trained hard and worked hard, but one weekend we took the students down to Calgary to visit the base of Lord Strathcona's Horse, the Armoured regiment there. It also happened to be the first weekend of the Calgary Stampede, and we spent a little time enjoying that great Canadian tradition. It was my first visit to the Stampede but not my last: I went back several decades later as Chief of the Defence Staff.

Those training courses were also a chance to get to know many people in my profession, the Armoured Corps specifically and, more generally, the army. People from every regiment came to the school, so we got to know them all. Most of those sergeants or young officers are still around, although no longer quite so young. More than half of them are still in uniform, most, if not all, in the senior ranks.

After I spent almost a year running courses, the commandant stuck me in the Armour School's standards section, where I made sure that all the training at the school was being done properly and at the right level, or standard. After five months of that, I had, again, to make the transition to student, joining the combat team leaders' course, a three-month course that qualified captains to become majors. That was a lot of fun, not least because it was one of the times when I was actually at home and could spend time with Joyce and Chris. When we happened to have an extra day off during Easter, I was home and could spend it with the family—all too rare during my career.

I have to admit that I did not enjoy my work as a standards officer, an entirely uneventful time in a forgettable position. In fact, I was bored, spending my days working through training manuals and course training reports and reading all the nitty-gritty details. I was terrible at it and admitted it. Alleviating the boredom became the main preoccupation for me and the two other standards officers I shared an office with, Johnny Stuckart and Bruce Finn. Our office was quite tiny, tucked away in the Armour School's headquarters building, which dated back to the Second World War. The doorway opened onto the main corridor of the building, and people on their way to the commandant's, deputy commandant's or administrative offices would walk past our office. The first thing we did was put a green divider screen in front of the door so that nobody could see in. Well, it was amusing how much that disturbed folks. Everyone was whispering, "What are they doing in there? What's going on? Who do they think they are?"

That only got worse when we began doing what we called "tactical troop training" with our desks. Every day we would arrange them into a different one of the dozen or so formations that a tank troop would use. One day we'd put them in an arrowhead formation, with one desk up front and the other two behind and to either side, all facing the same way just like a troop of tanks in arrowhead formation. The next day we'd be in Line Abreast, and the day after that we put them in Echelon Right, and so on. Despite the green divider in front of our door, people would drop into our office to chat or gossip, and word spread pretty quickly about what we doing. Lots of people were perturbed by it, silly as it sounds—they just didn't like it at all, which probably should have rung a bell about the challenges of change to people, no matter how small or insignificant it may be. Change makes people insecure.

I also created my own office space within the small office we all shared. *WKRP in Cincinnati* was a popular TV program then, and I was struck by how the character Les Nessman put tape around his desk to mark off his "office." I did that to my desk every morning, no matter what formation we were in. I'd take the roll of tape and mark out my office space and say, "This is my private office, and here's my door." This went on for about two months, and everybody would use the doorway to come into my office, including the cleaning lady who came in once a week to sweep up and empty the garbage cans.

Once the entertainment value of those immature actions started to fade, we began to use our blackboard to list predictions about where all the captains in the Armour School were going to be posted over the next year. We would sit in our chairs every day and say things like, "Okay, Smith's staying here in Gagetown to go to D&M squadron [where we taught soldiers driving and maintenance of armoured vehicles].” Nobody wanted to go to D&M squadron, because it was seen as a fate worse than death—career death, certainly. We had great fun skewering our buddies and would put ourselves down for the plum postings: “Hillier's going to Germany,” and so on.

One day Lieutenant-Colonel Dick Lawrence, the school commandant, walked into our office to take a look at our career planning. Dick sat down in the chair, looked at the blackboard and said, “So, I heard about this great career plot you've worked out. Tell me your reasoning and rationale behind some of these.”

Dick was a pretty easygoing guy and had a sense of humour, so we tried to answer by making a joke, because we certainly didn't want this thing taken seriously. “Well, sir,” I said. “Hillier is going to Germany because he's worked hard all year and done everything you've asked of him.”

He left chuckling to himself and we thought it was all in good fun. Unfortunately, word spread like wildfire around the school that the boss had been in our office, and the other officers thought there might just be something to these plans of ours. Within the next two days, every officer dropped into our office to quiz us about that plot. “So why have you got me down going to D&M squadron? Why can't I go to Germany?” My God, it was funny, but we soon realized that it had gotten far too serious—the joke had reached its best-before date—and so we quickly erased those blackboard scribblings.

A few months later I finished my tour at the school and, sure enough, got my posting to Germany. I was still a relatively junior captain; the fact that I had gone to Fort Knox had given me a tiny bit of a jump on some other captains in our quest for the next, best challenge, but I was still far down the seniority list. I don't know if our work on the blackboard had anything to do with it or not, but off the family went to Germany in June of 1983.

CHAPTER 6

GERMANY

On arrival in Germany I was appointed the administrative officer for A Squadron of the Royal Canadian Dragoons, responsible for administration, both personnel and logistics, in the
squadron of 120 soldiers. Captain Georges Rousseau, who was
the squadron's battle captain and responsible for operations, his
wife, Maureen, and their two daughters met us when we got off
the plane after that long trip from Canada. We have been close
friends ever since, as have our children. In fact, Georges's eldest
daughter, Tina, is now our grandson's teacher in Pembroke.

Georges and I worked together that first year in Germany,
a great time for both of us. We worked hard, preparing for the
Soviet Union and the Warsaw Pact nations to come across the
border, keeping up that great Cold War deterrent for a threat that
never materialized. We trained hard, away from home a lot on
exercises, but it was all predictable. That predictability made it

possible to have something resembling what the rest of the world (outside the CF) called a normal family life.

Germany was really the last time when we managed to find that balance between family and work. Because the work was predictable and we knew when we were going to be away, we could make plans with some certainty that they would go ahead. We spent a lot of time in the field throughout Germany, training, but we came back with the knowledge that we'd have a long weekend at home and, most importantly, a good idea of what we were going to be doing for months ahead of time. We'd be away throughout the summer and into early fall, but as winter approached our workload would lighten, and we would catch up on things: participating in a brigade sports day (Georges and I tended to bring up the rear in the forced march team), getting all the maintenance done on the tanks, doing individual training for crewmen and, in the Royal Canadian Dragoons, celebrating our regiment's past glories. In 1983, our first year at the base in Lahr, the regiment celebrated its 100th anniversary as Canada's senior regiment and marked the occasion on November 7, the day three Dragoons won the Victoria Cross during the Boer War. This became a gathering of the entire regimental family and a chance to renew acquaintances with old friends living in far-flung places.

For some reason, and clearly after not nearly enough discussion, we decided to have a small team celebrate the regiment's centennial by running from our training range in northern Germany back to our home base in Lahr, a distance of over 850 kilometres. Georges and I would anchor the team (in every sense of that word), and while our squadron was moving up to the area by tank train, I drove up the back roads in a truck to scout the route.

"What's it like?" the other nine members of the team asked when I arrived to join them.

"Flat as a pancake, boys," I said confidently, "flat as a pancake. Its going to be easy"—words for which I have been ridiculed ever since.

The difference between driving a route in a vehicle and running it on foot is vast, and from the time we left until we arrived, we seemed to be running steadily uphill. Georges and I still joke about selecting our running routes based on their being "as flat as a pancake."

Christmas invariably included a break with the family, and many of the single soldiers went home to Canada. In the winter months the family went skiing. By spring, the other officers and I focused on gunnery training to ensure that our effectiveness with the Leopard C-1 tank was high, and every May the regiment would do its helicopter-tank coordination exercise. Then the annual rotation of new troops coming in from Canada and old troops leaving to go home would occur, and we would start the cycle again. It was a well-planned life, and immensely enjoyable. Europe was at our feet, and Joyce and I couldn't pass up the chance to visit all the places we had only read about until now.

Everything you experience in life becomes a little part of who you are and what you do as a commander, a leader and a person. For me, the fondest memory I have of our time in Germany was when our second son, Steven, was born.

Our first son's birth had been eventful enough. When Chris was born, we were in St. John's, Newfoundland, and very much in transition to go to Gagetown, New Brunswick, so I could complete my training as an Armoured officer. Joyce was due just before New Year's, and our doctor clearly had plans for that festive time and didn't want them interrupted by having to deliver a baby, so he suggested bringing her into hospital early, to induce labour. On December 29, Joyce was admitted. I went with her and then left at ten o'clock to go back to my sister's, where I had been staying. I opened the fridge door to take out a bottle of beer, but didn't even have it open when the phone rang. It was Joyce.

"Come on down," she told me, using the popular line from *The Price Is Right*, "because I've started having contractions."

So I put the beer in my pocket—still unopened—and drove to the hospital. Within two hours, Chris was born and I went out to sit in the waiting room. At three o'clock that morning, I popped the cap and celebrated Chris's birth with a beer.

It was a similar scenario when our younger son, Steven, was born soon after we arrived in Germany. The regiment had deployed into one of the training areas for late July and early August, and of course I was with them in my new job. Joyce was due. Unfortunately, one of our tracked vehicles, an M113 armoured maintenance vehicle, rolled during the last day of training, and Corporal Mike Ward, one of our young mechanics, was killed. Since I was the administrative officer and thus responsible for the maintenance troop, I was designated to escort his body back across the Atlantic. Mike's dad was Captain Jack Ward, an air force ground support officer in Cold Lake, Alberta. I escorted the remains back from Germany to Grand Centre, next to Cold Lake, and participated in the final funeral arrangements with both the base command team and the family. Jack and his wife, Nancy, made an incredibly strong couple with two daughters who were equally special. In 2006, when at Cold Lake, I took the opportunity to visit Jack (unfortunately, Nancy had passed away) and reconnect with this fine man. Mike's death was my first experience in losing someone I had worked with, and it was tough.

By now it was late August, Joyce was about ready to give birth and I was in a hurry to get back from Alberta to the base in Lahr. Happily, she hadn't gone into labour yet. Brian and Rachel Forsyth, the couple who lived in the apartment underneath ours in the military building complex, were good friends; Brian was also with the regiment, which had already redeployed for the second stage of fall exercises in the Bavarian part of Germany.

When, several hours after I returned to Lahr, the baby started coming, we put Chris to sleep at Rachel's, got Joyce into the car and headed to the military hospital. I ran in and said, in a slight panic, "My wife's in the car, she's going to give birth."

The lady at the hospital entrance, familiar with overexcited fathers-to-be, said, "There's a wheelchair right there. Put her in it and bring her in."

I took the wheelchair, helped Joyce out of the car, got her into it and started pushing. In our state of excitement, when I start to push her up the ramp, I realized that I had not locked the wheelchair frame and so squeezed Joyce until she popped out and landed on the bridge. We were both laughing madly, and all the time she was having contractions.

When we finally got her into the hospital, she went into the delivery room right away, and two hours later Steven was born, like his big brother, Chris, in the early hours of the morning. I went to sit in a rocking chair in the waiting room, and a nurse brought Steven out and put him in my arms. I was rocking away when she said, "That's a picture of perfection."

"Yeah, the only thing that could make this better would be a cold beer," I said. "But I don't suppose you can handle that in a hospital."

"Just a minute," she answered. She opened the refrigerator door and I could see it was stacked full of the distinctive green cans of Heineken. "We keep this on hand for nursing mothers, because of the yeast they need to boost their milk production."

She popped open a can of beer for me and I sat there holding my second son in one hand and a cold beer in the other. I marked the births of both of my sons with beer, not champagne.

While it was good to have a predictable training and deployment cycle, so predictable that we coined a phrase for it—SALY (pronounced "Sally"), meaning "same as last year"—the implications were not good for the mindset of the Canadian Forces. Nobody really had to think, particularly at the strategic level, and consequently our leaders were not trained, selected or experienced enough to think beyond the stalemate in Europe. We paid a high price for that mindset later, because it led directly to some of the challenges that we faced in the 1990s and early 2000s. That "sameness" each year led inevitably to a focus on picayune detail or measurable process.

When the Soviet Union collapsed and the Cold War ended, we found ourselves amidst chaos, setting off on complex, difficult and sometimes ill-conceived missions in places like Somalia,

Rwanda, East Timor, the former Yugoslavia and, later, Afghanistan. We were not yet finished the peacekeeping mission in Cyprus and continuing significant deployments into the Middle East. At that same time, we found ourselves shelving plans to rebuild atrophied capabilities, saw our budgets cut by more than 25 per cent, our training slashed to an almost non-existent state, bases closed and the numbers of uniformed men and women reduced drastically. In a perfect storm, then, our confidence in who we were and our pride in being soldiers, in the most generic sense, was shattered. Several scandals, including those in Somalia and Bosnia, compounded our stress, while frozen, insufficient wages spoke eloquently as to our value in the eyes of our government and Canadians. Most of us in uniform, key to coping with humanitarian crises worldwide, were not making enough money to feed or house our own families.

The perception across the junior ranks was that we, the leaders, had broken faith with those we led, and if there is one thing I learned over the years, it is that perception is reality. Our soldiers did not trust us. We could do little to address the key issues that weighed so heavily on them and their families. The Canadian Forces moved into crisis and focused on survival, not excellence or shaping for the future or serving Canada. We were largely incapable of coping, and "SALY" had been responsible for a lot of that. After thirty to forty years in an organization where everything was the same, leaders could not handle the sudden, global changes or the enormous issues those changes created.

Unfortunately, many of the institutions around the world, including those in Canada, are in exactly the same boat; they still haven't gotten out of that Cold War frame of mind, either culturally or structurally. The Canadian Forces finally saw serious transformation in leadership, structure, training, education and equipment, but few other organizations have followed suit. The challenges that the United Nations faces on operations every day, and certainly the challenge that NATO is now facing in Afghanistan, reflect the fact that both organizations are still based on their Cold War model. Neither the UN nor NATO has changed fundamentally to face an enemy that is as different from the Red Army as night is from day.

I look back to that time in Germany and see the good and the bad of it. Getting the balance between family and work right was important to all of us and, recently, key to improving support for military families. It was obvious that we needed to significantly change the way we educate, train and season our leaders, to change the way we select them and, most importantly, to reassess what we ask them to do. We had to start looking for, and then reinforcing, intellectually agile people who could take their operational, command, staff, international, domestic, tactical and strategic experiences and, along with their training and higher education, within seconds be able to make key decisions, all while under a huge amount of stress, sometimes with men and women dying around them. I wanted leaders with the ability to put all of that into one pot and be able to shape the events around them, strategically, for Canada.

That was a key part of what drove me—and others—to change the Canadian Forces. We knew we needed to shake up the command structure, the people in that command structure and how we did business together as an army, navy and air force, versus each off in its own little world. This led to some significant changes in our succession planning, and to the departure of many leaders at various rank levels, most of whom had been extremely comfortable in the Cold War environment.

———————

After a year as administrative officer for A Squadron, I became the squadron's battle captain, working for the squadron commander, Lais Barsauskas, a big Lithuanian Canadian. He and his wife, Linda, were good friends of ours. I had met them back in my first brief tour of Germany in 1979, and we again served with them at Armour School.

In the spring of 1985 Brian Mulroney's Conservatives took power. One of their campaign promises was to rebuild the armed forces, which had languished under Pierre Trudeau and the Liberals. One of the first things to do was flesh out the under-manned units that were part of the army brigade in Germany, our land contribution to NATO at the time. We had two tank squadrons in Germany and a reconnaissance squadron, when the official order of battle called for three squadrons of tanks and a reconnaissance squadron. The infantry battalions only had three rifle companies on strength, but the structure called for four, so NDHQ created that third tank squadron and fourth rifle company in each battalion to bring our NATO contribution onto a sounder footing. The Dragoons stood up C Squadron in Germany in early summer of 1985 and, at the same time, I was promoted to major. To my delight I was given command of this new squadron.

The day I took command of the squadron, June 30, 1985, my mom and dad arrived in Germany for a family visit. That same day we had a military farewell to say goodbye to a retiring lieutenant-general, so Joyce brought Mom and Dad out to see the parade. It was the first time they'd ever seen a military parade or tanks or had even been in Europe, and so it was a big experience for them.

By then my dad was long over his resistance to my going into the army and proud of what I was doing, especially when he saw it all up close. He had been a little nervous that we were going to Germany in 1983, with Joyce over seven months pregnant, wasn't too sure about her having our baby in Europe and thought that maybe Joyce should stay home to have the baby in Canada. Joyce had a different opinion, so Steven spent his first four years in Lahr. The three weeks of their visit was one of the best family times we ever spent together.

I commanded C Squadron for the next two years and every day was memorable and satisfying. It was one of those rare opportunities where as a commander I had the chance to take a group of talented individuals and build them into a team that was recognizable as capable by everyone who watched them in action. It was an opportunity to show people what could be done by this team when each individual gave it his all. Matt Macdonald was my battle captain, a squadron commander's right-hand man, and he was, and is, an incredibly capable leader. I had met him and his wife, Anne, when I first arrived in Germany in 1979—we were troop leaders in the same squadron. We had then served in Gagetown together, both of us as training officers. Matt is now a major-general and the head of the defence intelligence branch.

Our sergeant major was Squadron Sergeant Major Jim "Tooner" Martin. His mark of distinction was that the top part of his right thumb had been cut off years before in a weapons accident. For some reason, the doctors had really not done a great job of cleaning up the stump and he had this massive club on his right hand. He was famous for waving that big misshapen thumb at anyone who'd earned his disapproval, saying, "You don't do this right, I'm going to stick my thumb up your nose and drag you around the barracks block until you get it." We all tried to avoid that!

We had great senior NCOs too, such as Warrant Officer Bob Braye, who was the squadron quartermaster. The SQ, as he was commonly called, was in charge of procuring things the troops needed (sometimes the difference between that and straightforward theft was hard to discern, but a good SQ was worth his weight in gold) and was part of a good mix of pretty experienced guys and a whole lot of fine young soldiers.

The first thing I did on forming the squadron was get all 120 soldiers together and suggest a few novel ideas. One was that when we deployed on exercises, which could last for six or seven weeks, we would pool some of the extra pay we got for being in the field (about $10 a day) and use it for some squadron luxuries that everyone could enjoy. I suggested that we get a TV and a VCR and build a special crate for them so we could take them with us into the field. That way, when there was downtime, when it was wet and cold and we had a few hours off, we could watch a movie. This was unheard of in those days. But I had more in store. I told them we needed a chip fryer. "When you're out in the field and you've been eating rations all week," I said, "wouldn't it be nice to get a little bag of french fries, to satisfy your taste buds?" This probably reflected my taste for the diet of Newfoundlanders!

The third thing I wanted to do was organize adventure training, which would give the squadron a common thread, something to look forward to and prepare for at the end of the year. My idea was to have the squadron learn to scuba dive and then dive somewhere for ten days. That meant anyone who was not a strong swimmer had to improve their skills. Everyone had to take first aid and CPR courses, and then learn how to scuba dive. On top of that, we had to raise enough money to pay for the equipment and training, which is expensive. Some of the young soldiers, particularly the married ones, couldn't afford it.

"Let's everybody put aside one day of field pay, just one day," I said. "You're not even going to miss it. What do you think about that?" Well, thanks to all my great NCOs, it snowballed. The most junior soldiers in the squadron contributed one day of field pay, corporals gave two, master corporals three, the sergeants four, and I—well, I just handed in all my field pay for the entire summer and fall training period. It was worth it. It helped mould 120 of us into a team that performed superbly. We completed our swim and dive training and spent some ten days in the Mediterranean diving near the island of Elba. It was fun and brought this disparate group of men, from many different organizations and provinces, together. We worked hard, but played equally hard, and morale in the squadron soared. Others came up with great ideas, for which I can take none of the credit, but they all helped build an incredible team that performed magnificently.

I had read in a military magazine about an American battalion commander who had tried to take annual refresher training, where you go over all the basics of soldiering so you are refreshed in your use of them—shooting individual weapons, first aid training, fitness testing, etcetera—and put a different face on it so it wouldn't just be the same old thing. He sent his company off on a biking expedition over two or three days and had them do their refresher training at stands set up along the way. I thought that was a great idea, and so we decided to do it. I had no compunction about using, and giving credit for, someone else's good idea.

When I was told I was going to command the regiment in 1990, my boss at the time, Brigadier-General Pierre Lalonde, called me in to congratulate me.

"Thank you, sir," I told him. "I'm pretty excited."

"Do you know what your job is as commanding officer of the regiment?"

I said, "It's obvious, sir. Provide leadership and make sure we've got a crackerjack fighting unit—all that good stuff."

"Yes, you're going to do all that. But do you know what your real job is?" he asked again—rhetorically, as it turned out, because he went on to answer his own question. "Your job is to protect your soldiers from good ideas. Do you know something?" he said. "There are twenty thousand good ideas a day out there, and if you try to implement even a small percentage of them, you will kill your soldiers. Your job is to protect your soldiers from good ideas."

As "Tooner" used to tell me, "Sir, you have about two good ideas a year; one of them won't work from the start and the other one, with a lot of help from us non-commissioned officers, well, we'll make something out of it." I've always kept that in mind: protect your soldiers from good ideas!

The American officer's ideas for refresher training stuck. I thought it was a good way to the enliven what was often a routine, sometimes boring, repetition of basic drills and skills. We turned that training into a contest, the Super Trooper competition. For two days on a thirty-six-kilometre course, we would reconfirm our basic training skills like navigating cross-country, handling prisoners of war, shooting, running an obstacle course and completing first aid on simulated casualties, all designed to build and refresh the individual soldier's skill set. We used money from the squadron fund and bought a shotgun as a prize for the winning soldier.

The troops had to navigate their way from one point to another and then complete an event at specific places. We put something in each of those events that went back to what we had been teaching for the previous months. We had all taken, for example, some Russian language training. At the prisoner-of-war handling stand, we then had to speak Russian to pass that test. The Russian training had been really popular. All the guys wanted to learn it. One of the soldiers in the regiment spoke Russian, and he came to our squadron for two or three days and taught the boys how to say things like "Stop!" and "Hands up, lay your weapon down!" This was back in Clint Eastwood's heyday as *Dirty Harry,* so everybody in the squadron wanted to know how to say "Go ahead, make my day" in Russian. The poor guy who was teaching had to tell them that there was no phrase like that in Russian. "Look," he said, "that's meaningless in Russian. There's no equivalent. The literal translation makes no sense."

I pulled him aside and said, "Look, you fail to understand the concept. Give them a phrase that is somewhat akin to 'Go ahead, make my day.' I don't care what it is. The boys want to know 'Go ahead, make my day' in Russian, and they are going to get it."

So he came up with a phrase, and for the next weeks, to the chagrin of everybody else in the regiment—probably everybody in Lahr—my whole squadron went around saying "Go ahead, make my day" in Russian, or what they assumed was the phrase. I never did find out what it actually meant.

We had a squadron party, or a "smoker," at the end of the refresher training, with a few pops, as Don Cherry likes to say. We talked about what had happened and told many war stories, some of which were even true. Everybody remembered jumping into a pond on the obstacle course and swimming across to the other side at night. It was cold, but it was a water obstacle and they had to cross it. How they got across was their business. Each person had his own little story from different parts of the competition, and that made it an overwhelming success. That refresher training approach later became a regimental activity, when I was CO of the Royal Canadian Dragoons, and eventually a brigade competition. It was one good idea that worked itself all the way through the system.

Being a squadron commander, particularly in Germany in the 1980s, was exciting, and I loved the job. I would have enjoyed doing that forever, really. Commanding a regiment, or a brigade or division—all jobs I held later in my career—brought a certain satisfaction, with many challenges and obviously a lot of stress. Certainly that was true as CDS. As the commander of 120 soldiers in a squadron, though, you have the chance to exercise direct leadership, with very obvious and real-time results and satisfaction. As the size of commands increased, it was easy to lose touch with people. It became harder to really know all of them the way I got to know the troops in C Squadron, RCD.

I knew every soldier in that squadron well, and spent a lot of time with them. One day we scheduled a vehicle inspection as we were getting ready for our annual technical inspection. The squadron was formed up, nineteen tanks, an armoured recovery vehicle (a battlefield tow truck for tanks) and the ten other armoured personnel carriers and trucks for our support. Everybody thought I would take an hour and a half, two hours tops, to inspect the vehicles. It took me fourteen hours to go through the squadron and I never even got to the support vehicles. I went through every tank, spoke to every crew member and asked them, "What's your job?" I had them walk me through and show me, comprehensively, what their part in a tank crew was, from driver to gunner, and how that tank had to be maintained and repaired.

A leader at that level gets to know all those in the command, their strengths and weaknesses and, with that knowledge, has the satisfaction of putting them all together to accomplish a mission—and can have fun doing it. Below that level, as a troop leader, I really never had the opportunity to control my own destiny. Once I moved to command beyond squadron level, although there were incredible and exciting challenges, the organizations were so big that much of that intimacy was lost.

It also helped that we had a very clear mission: defending Western Europe from the Soviets and keeping the Free World free. By and large we had the equipment that we needed at the tactical level to do that: we had Leopard tanks, the people to man them, good training, lots of ammunition and the opportunity to use it to hone our skills.

At the very end of our time in Germany, C Squadron had the great fortune to get picked to compete for the Canadian Army Trophy—still the most prestigious prize for tank gunnery in all of NATO, and my second exposure to it. The NATO commanders had started to realize that it was getting awfully expensive to compete as one nation against another. It became clear that the Americans were going to spend whatever it took to win, to showcase their tank for industry, while the Germans were going to do whatever it took to showcase the Leopard 2. The Brits, with their Challenger, were somewhat more challenged. The competition was starting to become unaffordable.

So the approach changed to allow a competition between the two army groups that were in Germany: Northern Army Group and Central Army Group. Each army would enter a team representing all nations in their group, thus reducing national competitiveness to a healthy level. The units competing weren't chosen until three months before the competition, and each country put in a list of all its operationally committed units from which that selection could be made. C Squadron ended up having its name drawn out of a hat ninety days before the competition to represent Canada in the Central Army Group, to which we belonged. For my last three months in Germany, April to June 1987, I was the team captain.

We had finally fixed the problem with the Canadianized gunsights and had great confidence in our training, our equipment and our soldiers. That all led to confidence in our shooting. We practised on an American computer simulator that was incredibly advanced for its time. This was long before computers were being routinely used as combat trainers, and we felt part of something special doing it. Our commanding officer, Lieutenant-Colonel Bob Meating, had literally tracked down the Central Army Group commander, an American four-star, and got him to turn his promise of access to the latest training gizmo into action. We ran shoot after shoot on that trainer, so that when we arrived for the competition we were ready and shot superbly. Our older Leopard tanks couldn't compete with the speed of the Americans' M1 Abrams or the new Leopard 2s, but we held our own and then some. The now advanced fire control systems in those tanks let them acquire and shoot targets much more quickly and accurately than we could. We didn't win, but out of the eighteen different tank troops that fired in that competition, our two troops place third and fourth, an enormous success.

When we—both our personal family and the entire regimental family (in a unit rotation)—returned to Canada in July 1987, I headed to French-language training in Ottawa. Joyce and I didn't know the city and spent a long time looking for a house until we finally obtained military quarters in Rockcliffe, near the Ottawa River. By Christmas I learned that the following summer, 1988, I would be posted again, going to Toronto for the year-long Canadian Forces staff course for majors. The family decided to stay in Ottawa because Joyce was working, the kids were both in school, Chris was playing hockey and we had friends all round. Stability was important. I went to Toronto.

Matt Macdonald had made a similar decision, leaving Anne and their son, Jason, in Petawawa, so he and I rented an apartment and, old friends that we were, settled in for the course, a year of figuratively putting our feet up and contemplating the world, including our country's place in it, while writing about and discussing specific strategic issues. Oh yes—and doing a lot of mindless, repetitive work to learn how to deploy large formations and work within them internationally. This was late 1988 and early 1989, so, needless to say, our entire focus was on the Cold War and the need to defend against the now disintegrating Warsaw Pact.

CHAPTER 7

DECADE OF DARKNESS

In December 1989, halfway through my Staff College course in Toronto, I was told that I was going to be promoted to lieutenant-colonel early in the new year and posted to army headquarters in Saint-Hubert, just outside Montreal. I immediately asked how long I was going to be there, as I needed to make some decisions, with my family still living in Ottawa. I was told I'd be in Montreal for three to five years for certain, and that I wouldn't be getting to command a regiment in the next cycle.

Joyce and I decided to uproot our family and move once more. We had already, in the time I had spent in Toronto, decided we were not going to be separated again, unless it was for operational deployments, where we would have no choice. She quit her job in Ottawa and we bought a house in Saint-Bruno on the south shore of Montreal and moved in that August, anticipating a long stay. Then, in January, just five months into my job as the senior staff officer for operations for the army, Lieutenant-

General Kent Foster, Commander of the Army, came down to my office early one afternoon, shook my hand and congratulated me, saying, "Well done—you're posted to Petawawa to command the Royal Canadian Dragoons."

I was more than a bit surprised, but I was ecstatic at the same time. I was back to soldiering, not doing staff work at headquarters. Most leaders will give their eye teeth to command a regiment.

The only problem was that Joyce didn't know the news yet, and I could not reach her at her work in downtown Montreal. I went home and, with the help of a senior non-commissioned officer at the headquarters who lived near me, Sergeant Briscoe, I quickly made up a large "For Sale" sign and she stuck it into the two metres of snow on our lawn on her way home.

It wasn't long before I received a panicky call from my son Chris. "Dad, somebody is selling our house!" And not long after that, a perturbed Joyce called, saying, "What's going on? Who put the sign there, and where are we going now?"

The great wife that she is, Joyce adjusted quickly, and we officially put our house up for sale in a depressed real estate market in early February 1990 and sold it just three weeks later. I was in Ottawa when I received a second panicky phone call from Joyce, saying that the deal had fallen through. She persevered and somehow managed to resell the house before midnight that same night. What a woman! We moved to Petawawa in June and I took command of the Royal Canadian Dragoons in early July, making Montreal one of my shortest postings.

Brief though it was, we enjoyed Montreal and Quebec. Joyce worked right downtown and both of my sons went to school there. Saint-Bruno is one of the prettiest places we've ever spent time in; indeed, it is one of the most beautiful spots in the country, with the Rivière Saint-Jean near the military college, a great park, ski hills and beautiful architecture.

In my ten short months at army headquarters I learned a lot, although it wasn't always positive. Again and again I found that we were not really the Canadian Forces: we were just an army, and not even a unified one at that. Here's but one example: 10 Tactical Air Group was part of the army headquarters complex, which was the command element for the air force's tactical helicopter squadrons that worked with us army types. But that air group headquarters worked for the air force, and at a time when budgets were being slashed by the federal Conservatives, there was great disagreement as to what value those helicopters could provide, what types we should have, who should command them and, most importantly, who should pay for them. The air force felt that since they carried or supported troops on the ground, they were army assets and the army should pay. The army felt that since they flew, they were air assets—lowest in their list of priorities—and that the air force should pay for them. That argument led, just a few years later, to one of the more idiotic decisions ever made in the Canadian Forces. With funding cuts reaching critical levels, the air force and the army couldn't agree on what to do with our helicopters. So we sold our big, heavy lift helicopters, the Chinooks, to the Netherlands, leaving us with only small civilian Griffon helos tarted up as utility helicopters. When we began serious operations in the Balkans, Africa and, particularly, Afghanistan in the following years, we all came to regret that decision.

Nothing irked me more than to arrive in Kandahar and have to wait for another nation's helicopter to take me and my team out to visit one of our forward operating bases. Most often, it ended up being the Dutch forces, and we could almost see the Canadian flag under the Royal Dutch Air Force roundel on the Chinooks. Other than hurting our pride, more importantly, those workhorse choppers with their huge carrying capacity are lifesavers, enabling operational flexibility and allowing us to jump our troops over Taliban ambushes and roadside bombs. In December 2008, after almost five years of work, we finally had our first operational flight by Canadian Chinooks in Afghanistan, and what a great moment that was. But in 1990 the squabbling over helicopters was almost the entire extent of the army–air force relationship. The relationship between the army and the navy was non-existent.

The Conservative budget of 1989 had closed bases, cut the size of the Canadian Forces by 2,500 personnel and cancelled many equipment purchases, the most high profile of which were the proposed nuclear-powered submarines. In all, the Department of National Defence was expected to cut $2.7 billion over five years. The budget also killed the Army 2000 plan, an enormous reorganization that everybody had been building toward during the 1980s, which would have given regular and reserve force units specific and detailed missions (which might have helped that regular-reserve relationship), created a corps structure and completely realigned equipment both new and old to those new missions. All of that was blown away by the spring budget. Instead, we wound up parking whole fleets of vehicles and mothballing aircraft. All the army's planning for the next two decades went out the window. Whatever vision there had been was gone, and there was nothing to replace it except further budget cuts and an ongoing struggle for survival. We were accelerating the long downhill spiral that spanned more than a decade.

I left Montreal at an interesting time. I was the senior staff officer in charge of operations, responsible for synchronizing and coordinating operations across the army at a time when the Berlin Wall was falling, the Warsaw Pact was starting to break up and Mikhail Gorbachev was having significant impact on the international order. Every single day we were trying to guess what would happen next. The old world order was crashing around us, nothing was replacing it and I don't think any of us had any idea of how dramatic the effect would be.

One of the things that perhaps might have taught us that the world was going to be a very different place happened during my last two months at army headquarters. We had a crisis on the Akwesasne reserve, on the border between Ontario and New York State. Suddenly the Province of Ontario requested that the army go in to relieve the Ontario Provincial Police because they felt the threat posed was greater than what police were designed to handle. I flew down to Cornwall to come to grips with that, and drove across to the reserve with the police and some of our soldiers to look at the place. We eventually conducted significant operations there, but mainly in direct support to police forces, not as the lead.

Then, during one of my last operational briefings to the army commander before I went off to command the Royal Canadian Dragoons, the subject of First Nations reserves as potential domestic hot spots came up. I told him, "Oh, by the way, there are some things happening up at the Oka reserve, and we're going to have to keep an eye on it."

One of the senior officers in the audience at that briefing said, "Oh, Rick, don't worry about that. Nothing is going to happen there."

I went off to command the Royal Canadian Dragoons, and within two months a third of the army was up at the town of Oka and the Kahnawake reserve, about an hour west of Montreal. The Mohawk Warriors had taken over a patch of disputed land, defied the Quebec provincial police and killed one officer in a shootout when the police tried to take down their barricades. The army was called in to restore order and, in my view, did a magnificent job defusing a potentially explosive situation.

But that briefing in which I had almost predicted the crisis was to me a telling incident. The mindset hadn't really changed, despite what was going on around us both abroad and here at home; it didn't change until about three or four years ago, and even then only because we forced it to change.

———

I was commanding officer of the Royal Canadian Dragoons for two years; with the support of an outstanding brigade commander and leader named Ray Crabbe, we managed to train for operations such as the intervention at Oka. We started to focus on training our soldiers for operations other than a conventional war, and really started to learn some lessons about the big challenges in front of us, whether those were in Canada, a country in central Africa or (little did we know at the time) in the middle of a country that was just starting to break up, the Republic of Yugoslavia. We were living in an entirely different world and facing an entirely different fight from the one we had been training for during the decades of the Cold War.

We also observed some incredible tactical lessons in other places throughout the 1990s, operating in Croatia, Bosnia, Macedonia, Somalia and all those other places we were sent. We saw what happened there and how best to react to those complex and dangerous situations, and should have learned some useful tactics that would have changed our entire training focus. Most of those hard-won lessons were, however, forgotten as soon as each mission was over. Even the individual rotations of soldiers we sent into those hot and dangerous locations—the new battle groups sent in every six months—had to relearn the lessons the previous group had learned on the ground. Every rotation we sent into places like the former Yugoslavia was almost like a first deployment: lessons weren't being captured, turned into training lessons or doctrine and therefore learned by the institution.

We went straight back to the same old, same old—that SALY, or "same as last year," mentality—and we continued to train in exactly the same way we had for decades. As one of my friends said, "We weren't in the former Republic of Yugoslavia for thirteen years. We were there for twenty-six individual unit rotations, most of them unrelated to each other."

To be absolutely fair, this leadership problem wasn't confined to the military: it was a Canada-wide problem. The focus in Canada during most of the 1990s was on reducing deficits, balancing the budget and paying off debt. Across all levels of government, nobody had a vision for either the world or Canada's place within it, much less the role of the Canadian Forces. The massive financial cuts that occurred in 1994, accompanied by a simultaneous and massive increase in operations, hit us really hard. The watchword truly became "survival": people were doing whatever was necessary to keep their units alive under enormous financial and operational stress. We were dealing with budget cuts introduced in 1994 by the new Liberal government, under Jean Chrétien, on top of the cuts and underfunding of previous years, accompanied by a simultaneous massive increase in deployment of soldiers in large numbers into areas where we often didn't even have maps, much less support facilities or cultural awareness.

Somalia, where the Canadian Airborne Regiment was deployed as part of a United Nations mission, eventually turned into one of the most traumatic experiences in our military's history. Two Airborne soldiers, Clayton Matchee and Kyle Brown, captured a Somali teenager and tortured him to death, making the front page of newspapers across Canada. This tragic episode opened a floodgate of other dirty stories on wrongdoing by the Canadian military from years past—some of them true and some incorrect or wildly exaggerated.

Our soldiers were already facing huge demands for their services in operations far from home and were trying valiantly to contribute to the success of those missions, despite the fact that they had to do it with equipment that was old, shoddy and ill suited for the mission, the environment or both. We sent vehicles like the Cougar tank trainers or the Grizzly armoured personnel carrier—equipment designed only for training—into combat zones, and paid a price for it. This was as close to criminal in the eyes of our soldiers as one can get.

Morale was low to begin with, and coupled with the growing number of overseas operations, the scorn we saw from Canadians in the wake of stories about the Somalia scandal, pay freezes, equipment removal and steadily eroding funds for training, it sank even lower. We took the Canadian Forces to, and in some cases past, the breaking point. Under those conditions, perhaps it wasn't surprising that we didn't make the needed changes to our structure and focus, because the country had no long-term plan for its military, just a short-term focus on saving money (which devastated our budget) and on the Canadian need to contribute to UN operations everywhere, despite the shrinking pool of soldiers with which to do it. What change did take place in those years was consistently for the worse. Units were shut down. Our numbers were reduced, leaving us with fewer soldiers and a smaller footprint on the ground. Training exercises (where you really can turn lessons observed into lessons learned) were cancelled, particularly at the battalion or brigade level. It went on and on and on. These troubles were a big part of the reason that we never did learn those lessons in the 1990s.

In the incredibly negative conditions at that time, we also had a lot of things forced on us, in part because we had no solutions ourselves, but also because the Canadian Forces was on its heels, lacking in institutional self-confidence, suffering from low morale, high stress, little funding and absolutely no public (and, therefore, political) support. It seemed as if every special interest group got to push something on us, whether it was to change our legal system, how we should be educated or how we should train. In fact, a lot of what we have been trying to do over the last four to five years was simply to recover from some of that negative change. We could have handled any one of these enormous stressors well, several of them easily, but all of them together proved almost fatal. Social experiments became the order of the day. Because of human rights challenges, we lost the ability to demand that everyone wearing a uniform be fit to fight: while we had requirements forced upon us that required every one of our leaders to have a degree, be bilingual and be allowed to serve regardless of gender or sexual orientation, we couldn't demand that they be fit enough to do their job. That would have been a tough sell for any institution, but having these pressures occur when troops were developing the "thousand-yard stare" because of operational exhaustion from multiple overseas deployments for which they had to cobble together equipment was almost too much.

In the summer of 1992 I left Petawawa and what I assumed would be my last posting in that hidden jewel on the Ottawa River, bound for the nation's capital kicking and screaming all the way. I did not know the Ottawa bureaucracy well, did not know National Defence Headquarters, and after having already served at what I thought was a large headquarters in Montreal, I didn't really want to do it again: I just wanted to be a soldier, command a unit and stay with troops, but that wasn't in the cards.

I handed over command of the Royal Canadian Dragoons to Matt Macdonald, my old roommate and friend from Staff College in Toronto. Matt and I had been following each other around the regiment, Staff College and the army since we had been lieutenants and joked that we could plan our next post-

My great uncle, John Clark, was killed August 14, 1917, in Flanders at the age of twenty, while serving with the Royal Newfoundland Regiment. His story motivated me to become a soldier.

Mom and Dad, whose strong belief in education and in family shaped us all.

Always a Leafs fan.

A very "green" trainee at basic, in Chilliwack, B.C., 1974.

My good friend Dennis Hartnett and I ham it up a little for the camera during basic training.

Well camouflaged, minus the berets! Life as a Tank Squadron Commander in Germany during the mid-'80s was enjoyable and satisfying, from both the work and the family perspectives.

Finishing the Special Service Ironman competition when I was CO of the Royal Canadian Dragoons. Joyce was concerned that the demanding event was really going to finish me, but the coin I earned for it was worth the effort.

In 1993, with Lieutenant-General Patrick "Paddy" O'Donnell, who became a mentor and friend. He was one of the true heroes of the "decade of darkness."

Delivering humanitarian aid, sent to me by the church ladies in my home-town of Campbellton, Newfoundland, to Bosnian shelters, 1996.

In Bosnia, as Division Commander, with ever-present interpreter Elizabeth. We visited with a Bosnian Serb woodworker who bemoaned the fact that the end of fighting meant a significant drop in his business—making coffins!

One of our jobs was to take lethal weapons from Bosnians. Here, the Green Jackets, a British regiment, hit the motherlode as a result of their brilliant and imaginative approach to dealing with the population. I wished I'd had another ten units like them.

The ice storm, Ottawa, January 1998. The PM was low maintenance and straight to the point—unlike the host of hangers-on who followed him (a dozen of whom would fight for three seats in the helicopter).

Chris and Caroline's wedding in the Dominican on January 9, 2004. Left to right: Steven, our younger son, Caroline, Chris, Joyce and me.

Welcoming the Commander of ISAF in Afghanistan always meant flowers, usually presented by children, like these girls in traditional dress—and we often had poppies tossed at our vehicles.

The little girl is making a scribbling motion on her hand, asking for pencils and paper so she can go to school. Most Afghans believe that education is the way out of the chaos.

Taking command—February 4, 2005.

A true privilege: representing the CF at the annual Remembrance Day
ceremonies in Ottawa on November 11, 2005. As a kid, I had dreamed about
just being there one day.

With (left to right) Minister of Defence Bill Graham, John Ralston Saul and Governor General Adrienne Clarkson.

Tim Murphy, me, Prime Minister Paul Martin and Joyce at the gala to welcome our new Governor General, Michaëlle Jean.

ings based on where the other guy was. We were to run into each other again a few years later: he went to the former Yugoslavia for a year, and as he left I arrived. I then came back and took over as commander of a brigade and my replacement was, guess who? Matt Macdonald. Walt Natynczyk, who would eventually succeed me as Chief of the Defence Staff, was commanding officer of the RCD while I was his brigade commander, and when I went to Bosnia as Division Commander, Walt was the director of international operations and staff back in Canada, so I ended up dealing with him often. That's what invariably happens with a small Canadian Forces: you keep seeing the same folks all the time, especially the ones with talent.

Reporting to work in late July, I became the executive assistant for one of the senior civilians responsible for all the non-military employees of the Department of National Defence, the Associate Assistant Deputy Minister of Personnel. It proved an opportunity to get to know the Department of National Defence and, specifically, the civilian component. During that time, I also met an officer who shaped a good chunk of my career from that point forward: Lieutenant-General Patrick "Paddy" O'Donnell, Assistant Deputy Minister for Personnel, responsible for all personnel management in the Canadian Forces and the Department of National Defence. His offices were just two doors down from my little cubicle. I had not met Lieutenant-General O'Donnell before, but over the next seven or eight months or so I really came to respect him for the kind of leader that he was. And he was a leader. He knew where he wanted to take an organization, always had the thought process laid out and always knew all the pieces that needed to get done to achieve the vision. He was very highly thought of by all the people around him, military and civilian alike—in fact, by all who knew him, which made him something of a rare commodity at that time.

There was great speculation that winter about who would make up the next command slate in the Canadian Forces and what moves would take place, but it was pretty much assumed that General O'Donnell was going to become Vice Chief of the Defence Staff (VCDS), the second in command of the Canadian Forces, with responsibility for running the Canadian Forces day to day and with particular responsibility for resource management.

I used to go running during my lunch hour, and in wintertime I would skate on the Rideau Canal. Paddy used to run and he liked to skate too, so we had something in common. One day in early March, I was in the office at lunch hour working while everybody else was out, looked up, and there in my door was General O'Donnell. We started chatting about running and he saw my skates in the corner of my office. And I told him about how I would run with my skates in my little backpack down to the end of the canal at Dow's Lake, then lace them on and skate back to the office. He then leaned into my cubicle and said, "You know, Rick, that I'm probably moving."

I said, "Yes, sir, I understand that you're going to be VCDS," and told him I thought he was the right man for the job and all that stuff. "Yeah," he said, "but I'm going to need a new executive assistant. How would you like to be my executive assistant?"

I thought about that for a second and said, "You know something, General? I'd be trading in long hours and a lot of work for longer hours and more work. I don't think I'd like that at all."

"No, no, no. I phrased that question incorrectly," he said. "How are you going to like being my new executive assistant?"

I paused, kept a perfectly straight face and told him, "This is going to be a fucking great job, sir—there's no doubt in my mind. Can't wait to get at it."

So in early July 1993, I became his executive assistant and worked with him very closely for the next year. That was around the time when the Somalia revelations and speculations occupied all, so I was a fly on the wall watching the Deputy Minister, the Minister, the Chief of the Defence Staff and the senior commanders, who were all still based outside of Ottawa, try to deal with the fallout.

That was one of the things that made a big impression on me: seeing how the army commander in Montreal was really divorced from the key decisions that were being made in Ottawa about the army he supposedly commanded. It was likewise for the navy and air force commanders. I realized that many of these generals and admirals were out of touch. The Vice Chief of the Defence Staff was running things from Ottawa, while the Chief of the Defence Staff, who was out of town an enormous amount of the time, and the army, navy and air force commanders just weren't effective players.

I had worked hard for Paddy O'Donnell for a year and my reward, which I desperately wanted, was supposed to be an operational job—a posting to Croatia/Bosnia with the UN mission. In May, the small team that worked with Paddy hosted a little farewell for me with a couple of pops in the Navy Officers' Mess near National Defence Headquarters. On the way out the door, Paddy grabbed my elbow and said, "You know, Rick, there's a possibility you might get promoted to colonel, and if so, I'd really like you to stay and run the NDHQ Secretariat here. What do you think?" This question was as rhetorical as the one he had asked me a year earlier about whether or not I wanted to be his executive assistant.

The National Defence Headquarters Secretariat was a real hub of activity at the senior commander and bureaucratic level within NDHQ. The officer running it worked in equal parts for the Chief, the civilian Deputy Minister and sometimes the Minister, and reported to the Vice Chief. As that officer, I would have responsibility for coordinating all the necessary senior-level meetings, passing on the relevant information and doing anything else that was needed. It truly was a window into how senior leaders actually made decisions within the headquarters—a chance to watch how they would think strategically and to see the give and take of running the entire Canadian Forces. I knew officers who would have loved that job, simply for the profile it would give them with the generals and admirals who would eventually decide on whether or not they got promoted, but not me. I still wanted to go on an overseas operation. I said to the general, "I'll soldier wherever you tell me to soldier, sir," as if I really had a choice, "but I'd love to go on operations: that's what I really want to do. But I'll soldier anywhere."

A couple of days later Paddy phoned me at home and said, "Look, you're going to be promoted to colonel, and I'd like you to stay and be the head of the Secretariat."

So I did. And as a consequence, Walt Natynczyk was promoted to lieutenant-colonel, filling the vacancy left by my promotion, and went to Bosnia instead of me; he took my enviable spot on operations.

By the time I became director of the NDHQ Secretariat, Somalia had blown into a full-scale mess for the Canadian Forces. The military Board of Inquiry on Somalia had reported back and convened a press conference in September 1993 to announce its findings. The turn of events at the press conference, including the focus of the reporters' questions and their unending skepticism, resulted in what most watching viewed as an appalling outcome, with the board losing credibility and its report being dismissed as unworthy. Admiral John Anderson, the Chief of the Defence Staff, was in front of the media, announcing the findings of the board, and, sadly, he appeared surprised by the tone and direction of many of the questions put to him and ended up offering a *mea culpa*. Admiral Anderson was trying to say that what had happened in Somalia had been an isolated incident, but the reporters clearly didn't believe him. There had already been more revelations about problems in the Airborne Regiment, and Anderson was clearly caught unawares by the tack that the questioning took. The credibility of the Board of Inquiry took a beating, and, along with it, so did that of the entire Canadian Forces.

Personally, I had been around the Canadian Airborne Regiment for some time and thought that it certainly had disciplinary problems. The tone that was set within the organization definitely led to the soldiers there, at times, thinking of themselves as renegades within the CF. While there were many fine soldiers and officers in the Airborne Regiment—in fact the majority were exactly that—the attitude that prevailed led a few, who were then not constrained, to believe they were above the rules, and that inevitably led to problems.

That news conference led to demands for a full public inquiry into the affair, which in turn resulted in the creation of an equally appalling inquiry. If there was anything that was guaranteed to drive our morale lower, that public inquiry, led by those with a complete lack of understanding of the CF, its leadership and its men and women, and what many of us perceived as contempt for us and our efforts on behalf of Canada—accomplished it. Those who had never borne the burdens of command and had never held responsibility for putting the lives of others at risk now stood in judgment on those who lived with it every day. The headlines and news reports were dominated by their remarks.

Retired general John de Chastelain was brought back from his job as Canada's ambassador to the United States to become the Chief of the Defence Staff for a second time in an attempt to stabilize the situation and lead the CF forward. The day of that announcement was almost surreal. Rumours that he was coming back started to circulate late that morning, which happened to be the day that the Canadian Forces' senior leadership were all convening in Ottawa. Upon hearing the news, people were saying, "No, no. That won't happen. That won't happen. It would be an insult to all those serving in the senior ranks—senior people wouldn't let it happen. Even if the government was stupid enough to do something like that, John de Chastelain wouldn't have anything to do with it." Those commentators were wrong, however, and at noon hour the news broke: John de Chastelain was indeed coming back to be CDS again, bringing what was a solid credibility, based on his handling of the Gulf War and the Oka Crisis, to an organization in desperate need of such credibility.

It was equally interesting—and surreal—to watch Defence Minister David Collenette hold his news conference to announce the disbanding of the Canadian Airborne Regiment in 1995. It was clear to me that the senior military commanders did not know what the Minister was going to say at that news conference until he stood up and started speaking. To me, that meant he was really standing up in front of the media to announce that he had little faith in his own military, did not accept their advice, and had little confidence the chain of command could resolve the issues around the Airborne Regiment. I thought that showed the complete lack of respect that politicians and political leaders had for our military. As a result, we had virtually no ability to influence events. We had been marginalized. Canadians did not recognize us as their armed forces and apparently couldn't have cared less about us. Politicians read the public-opinion tea leaves, realized there were no votes in sticking up for the Canadian Forces and began to pillage and burn our budget. Those ministers and bureaucrats trying to correct our dismal national economic health by slashing the federal debt and budget deficits knew they had a free hand to cut us savagely, and all those whose ideology made them distrust or hate anything to do with the military cheered them on.

It wasn't that we had bad or incompetent people leading the Canadian Forces at the time; in fact, I think we had some pretty decent guys. I had a lot of respect for so many of them, including John de Chastelain, an incredible officer. And I obviously thought very highly of Paddy O'Donnell. But I would not have wanted to have been in their shoes. It was a dark period, the start of the Canadian military's "decade of darkness." There was almost no way that anyone could have turned the tide of public opinion that was against us at that time.

The news of the torture and murder of Somali teenager Shidane Arone by members of the Canadian Airborne Regiment was followed by allegations of a cover-up and the release of videos of the hazing of new recruits. It was just one thing after another. Collenette made the political decision to take action himself and disband the unit. I watched him do that on national television and then come into the meeting of the Armed Forces Council, made up of all his senior generals and admirals, including the Chief of the Defence Staff, with Deputy Minister Bob Fowler, to try to explain why he had taken this action.

In my view, as soon as he said, "I'm going to disband this regiment because they've got disciplinary problems and we can't fix those," he was saying that he had given up completely on his military chain of command. In fact, I believed that by saying so publicly he'd seemed to almost be expecting that chain of command to resign. That didn't happen. I sat there listening to him talk to the senior commanders from across the Canadian Forces as he told them, "Well, you know, we had to make a political decision." The commanders just sat there and took it. Everybody said, "Okay, we'll carry on." It was a very short meeting: the decision to disband the Airborne Regiment had been made, and there was nothing anyone in uniform could do about it. Nobody had been consulted. The politicians had ignored the military advice of the army commander and operational commanders. And while everybody else in the Canadian Forces found it appalling, few in the top ranks seemed to be able to really come to grips with the impact throughout the CF: they just could not deal with it.

Once the whole story became front-page news, it helped to prolong a long, sordid and difficult journey that just seemed to go on endlessly, and continued to get worse. When those infamous pictures of Clayton Matchee posing with the young Somali he tortured to death hit the front pages, those of us in the Canadian Forces living in Ottawa felt like we were trapped in a never-ending nightmare.

On the day that those photos came out, one of Joyce's co-workers, knowing that she was the wife of a soldier, said, "Anybody in uniform or anybody who was associated with the army should be ashamed to come out in public today." Joyce was devastated and so was I. I thought, "Oh my God. Do we really want to be a part of this anymore? Do we really think this can actually change? Can we recover?" A lot of people left the military during that time because they didn't think it could change. They could see no light at the end of the tunnel and did not want to be a part of something so demoralizing and depressing anymore. They didn't have any faith or confidence that things would improve, and I admit there were periods when I also lost hope.

During the months that followed those pictures becoming public and the disbandment of the Airborne Regiment, revelations of misconduct by senior officers simply got worse. I remember watching the Somalia inquiry on TV and seeing Jean Boyle, who had taken over from General de Chastelain as Chief of the Defence Staff, being grilled on the stand by the inquiry lawyers. The senior-ranking military officer in Canada was treated with absolute stunning contempt. It was so clear that we had no standing in Canadian society and were viewed as a bunch of robots in uniform who were getting what we deserved. This was at the time when many people in uniform were having to take second jobs because they couldn't make ends meet on military pay, and the public's attitude seemed to be that we had all volunteered, so if we didn't like it, we could leave. I found that attitude appalling.

Everywhere I looked around me I saw incredible young Canadians in uniform—men and women who were willing to do anything to serve Canada, even to the extent of laying their lives on the line. What a way to treat them!

I looked at the officers and soldiers working around me every day and could see from the looks on their faces that they were absolutely dejected. Up until then, I wasn't sure I wanted to continue to be a part of this devastated Canadian Forces, but I started to realize that the problem was that we had lost contact with Canadians, and if we were going to survive, the Canadian Forces had to win back their respect. We needed to recruit the entire nation and get the Canadian people back on our side. That recruitment had to be done from a basis of credibility. Average Canadians and our country's leaders had to have complete confidence in their military and its leaders. Credibility was our centre of gravity and had to be built and protected at all costs. That would sometimes mean publicly correcting the record if others said something wrong, but our integrity as leaders had to be beyond question. Those were my biggest lessons out of the Somalia affair, but it was only later that I found out how difficult they were to implement.

The entire Somalia scandal and its painful aftermath just go to prove that, as I've said before, perception is reality. John Ward, a reporter from the Canadian Press, told me after the scandal broke that he was astonished to return to Canada after seven years overseas and find that Canadians had so little regard for their own soldiers.

"Wherever I went in the world, Canadian soldiers were held in the highest esteem. Their credibility was huge. People valued them, wanted them. Canadian soldiers were like gods," he said. "I came back to Canada after being away for an extended period, and I couldn't believe it. Were these the same Canadian soldiers that I had heard about from so many nationalities and people around the world as being a god? I came back here and find they're lower than dirt? Quite incredible."

The public perception was that the entire Somalia mission had been a dismal failure. The fact that the mission, or at least our piece in it, went as well as one could expect in a mission without a clear goal, without a clear vision, without a clear strategy, without a clear plan, was lost. The politicians sent us in there thinking, "We must do something, and therefore we've got to do something." I think that set our soldiers up for failure. The troops did the best job they could. Then we had the breakdown in discipline and breakdown in the command and control structure that allowed something like taking a detainee and torturing him so badly that he eventually died to occur, which is absolutely unforgivable, absolutely unacceptable. And that's the only thing that people remember about that mission. So one thousand people went, worked their asses off under appalling conditions in an ambiguous, unclear mission, without much support from the Government of Canada, and all that people remember is that one episode. Even though what happened was a major failing and led to some badly needed

127

changes, the perception of the mission was that it was an absolute disaster. Somalia became a failure because in the eyes of Canadians it was.

That marked the beginning of a new, even lower tide for the Canadian Forces. That was the year, 1994, that the wheels came off, the beginning of years of despair—even if we didn't necessarily realize it at the time.

From 1993 to 1997, we were overstretched, underfunded and under-resourced, and at the same time we were in the midst of the debacle over Somalia. All this was at a time when the pay of our men and women in uniform was abysmal relative to that of every other profession in our society. We had soldiers working at part-time jobs, not because they were energetic and industrious and wanted more money, but because they had to do that to feed their families. We had military families lined up at food banks, and people in uniform who had difficulty making their rent.

With the federal budget of 1994, and the massive cuts to defence spending, it seemed like the only work we were doing was that of deciding which bases to close or garrisons to shut down and what budgets to shrink. For six weeks in January and early February of 1994, prior to the budget, the Canadian Forces' senior leadership team sat down every night after normal working hours and walked through preparations for what the budget announcements were going to entail in terms of closures. All this was going on at exactly the same time as Somalia was breaking in the news and at exactly the same time as operations in the former Yugoslavia were ramping up into major and dangerous commitments. So in addition to the stress of those issues, every night for six weeks straight, all the commanders sat down and spent three to four hours getting briefed about what was going to go next. Someone would say, "Okay, we're going to close CFB Calgary," and somebody else would comment, "Well, that'll teach them to vote Reform out there." That was the kind of black humour and cynicism that was in the air.

The guy who did all the work and then stood up in front of the commanders to talk about those closures was Brigadier-General Gordon O'Connor. This work led up to budget day and the big announcement of up to 25 per cent in defence funding cuts, huge personnel cuts, force reduction programs, infrastructure cuts and closures of bases in Toronto, Calgary, Chilliwack and London. Two of our military colleges ended up closing their doors, despite the fact that everybody felt that they were sacred cows. In hindsight, there were no sacred cows in the military at that time. When you face a budget cut and you've still got to continue carrying out certain operations, then suddenly sacred cows take on a whole different meaning. In truth, three military colleges were far too many for such a tiny Canadian Forces, which would shrink further, and clearly we needed to get rid of at least one. Everybody involved in the discussions felt that if we tried to close Royal Roads Military College, in Victoria, B.C., without doing something else, the blowback from the western provinces would be enormous, and rightly so. The thinking was to throw in Collège Militaire Royal, in Saint-Jean, Quebec, as one of the cuts because it was a francophone institution and would never be closed.

Prime Minister Chrétien took one look and said, "Close it!"

Suddenly, something that everyone had anticipated would not get approval was a done deal, and we closed CMR as a military college. That was a dramatic error, one that we're just rectifying now in reopening the college.

It was a tough time to be a soldier. The Canadian military was in crisis, divorced from the population and being used as a punching bag by the government. We went through five chiefs of the defence staff in four years: John de Chastelain from 1989 to '93 and again in 1994–95, John Anderson in 1993, Jean Boyle in 1996, Larry Murray in 1996–97 and Maurice Baril from 1997 to 2001. It was as if the Canadian Forces had been deliberately set up to fail: our critical leader had changed six times while we were being hammered by the budget cuts, personnel reductions, massive increase in operations, the Somalia scandal, the closure of bases, underpaid soldiers and sailors and airmen and airwomen, military families who were in rebellion because of the low pay and long hours we were demanding of our troops, and Canadians' rejection of us.

It continues to amaze me that the Canadian Forces didn't break completely, or cease to exist between 1993 and 1997. Probably the only thing that saved the CF from complete collapse is that the Canadian economy during those years was slow in recovering from a recession. The economy didn't really take off until the late 1990s: if it had done better sooner, we would have seen a mass exodus of our people.

I wanted to get away from National Defence Headquarters, from Ottawa, from the daily headlines and the crises over the latest dust-up during Question Period, to get away from the contempt of Canadians and go where the only danger would be somebody shooting at me. I still wanted, as I had reminded Paddy a year earlier, to go on operations. The massive UN mission was underway in the former Republic of Yugoslavia, with thousands of Canadian troops on the ground, and the feeling in the army was that if you hadn't been, you just didn't have credibility. This was soldiering, and if you did not want to be there, you should not have been in uniform. I wanted to go, not to collect the medals and the ribbons, but because I simply wanted to be a soldier and be part of a significant mission. So in early June of 1995, Paddy let me know that I would be posted to the former Yugoslavia in the next few weeks. I was on cloud nine!

CHAPTER 8

BOSNIA

So after two years of working for Lieutenant-General O'Donnell as his executive assistant and as the Director of the NDHQ Secretariat, I was to go on operations to the former Yugoslavia, to be director of plans and policy at the UN headquarters in Zagreb. The job was supposed to begin in the first week of August, and I handed my work off to Colonel Dennis O'Brien, from the Royal Canadian Regiment, in mid-June and went on leave.

Six weeks of leave would be the most I had ever taken since putting on the uniform, and I anticipated much golf and relaxation. I had had precious little time to myself or with the family the previous several years, because the Vice Chief of the Defence Staff simply works all the time, which means his staff work most of the time, leaving them very little opportunity for annual leave. But now I was finally going to have six weeks to myself and, with my wife working and our boys still pretty young, I promised Joyce that I was going to spend that time working my way through her "honey-do" list, which had become pretty long by that point.

I wanted to leave Joyce comfortably set up while I was in Croatia so she wouldn't have to worry about any household maintenance (but no new Chrysler this time). I came home after finishing my last week on the job, all set to have a relaxing weekend golfing, and told Joyce, "Right! On Monday I'm going to start in on your list. I'll do five things a week, golf in the morning and work in the afternoon around the house doing this list." This included everything from doing the electrical connections for our pool, digging the trench across the garden to sink the wiring, to minor stuff around the house, whether it was painting, tidying up the basement and garage or throwing out things that we had accumulated over the previous years. So I had my weekend off and went golfing Monday morning.

When I came home, my phone rang. It was Colonel Cam Ross, the Director of Peacekeeping Policy, and a good friend. "Rick, how are you doing?" he said.

"Good, what's up, Cam?"

"Look, we just had a call from UN headquarters. They would like you in Zagreb on Monday."

"This is Monday. You mean they want me there next Monday?"

"Yep, they need you there on Monday."

"Okay," I said. "Always ready to go."

As I hung up the phone, my mind was racing: Joyce was still at work and I looked over her "honey-do" list. I spent the rest of the day on that list, and when Joyce came home I sat her down and told her the news.

She was devastated. We'd had no time together really for several years. She was going to take a couple of weeks vacation time from her job, and we had planned on enjoying the summer together. Now those plans were shattered and she was going to be left with the things I couldn't get done, like usual.

So I said, "Look, I'll work Tuesday, Wednesday and Thursday and I'll finish that list and at the same time I'll do my packing so we can have a long weekend together before I head off on Sunday night."

So I worked like crazy to get everything on her list done: I mean, I was up at five in the morning and I never got in a single round of golf. I worked Tuesday, Wednesday, Thursday, did all of the things on that list, packed up my kit and was ready to go. By late Thursday afternoon I was ready. I'd checked everything off the list, and everything was packed.

Just before Joyce came home, Cam phoned me again and said, "Good news, Rick: they don't need you in Zagreb now until the sixth of August."

In hindsight, it was the best thing that could have happened, because it had prodded me into getting the things on that list done in record time. I had nothing left to do: the list was finished, my kit was packed and my travel arrangements were all set—I just had to push the departure date back. I had the next five weeks free and clear, so I golfed thirty-six holes a day for three of those weeks, and when Joyce took her two weeks of vacation, we had a wonderful time together. I went on mission well prepared and with peace of mind knowing that Joyce did not have to worry about household maintenance. If I hadn't had the pressure of that first phone call from Cam, I would have procrastinated and ended up cramming all that work into the last week that I was home. As it was, I gave a great sigh of relief when I got that second phone call.

———————

When I arrived in Zagreb, home of the United Nations Peace Forces Headquarters, Lieutenant-Colonel Chris Davis, a friend from Phase IV Armoured Officer training in 1976, who was already on the ground, met me at the airport, helped me sort out a place to stay and walked me through the local geography and basic security procedures. For the first couple of weeks, the job was fairly uneventful. In fact, there really wasn't any work to be done in setting policy, and there was only a small amount of planning work to do, so I had lots of time to meet people and assess the headquarters and the job it was doing.

The UN mission in the former Yugoslavia was very much in transition, as was the mission headquarters in Zagreb. There were three separate UN missions, in Croatia, Bosnia and Macedonia. In theory, Zagreb ran all of them, but the reality was that they were completely independent and usually didn't even refer to the large, heavily staffed headquarters in Zagreb. They often took direction straight from UN Headquarters in New York or, just as often, the commanders in each location got it from their respective national capitals. After the first two weeks, that all changed. This was shortly after the Serbs had overrun the UN enclave in Srebrenica. They had brushed aside the Dutch battalion that had supposedly been protecting it and, as we discovered later, massacred thousands of Bosnian Muslim boys and men inside the town, while brutalizing the women in unspeakable ways.

With the changes, I became the Director of Operations for the United Nations in the former Yugoslavia and took over the operations centre, with both current operations staff and future planners working for me. We were involved in almost all the events—those happening at the time and those we were planning or expecting to happen.

It was good to have a demanding job, as opposed to sitting around with nothing to do. Although based in Croatia, I spent a lot of time in Bosnia: up in Tuzla with the UN sector there; in Bihać, where the Serbs had isolated a large Muslim population; in Mostar, where the hatred was largely between the Croats and Muslims, with the Serbs trying to kill both; in Sarajevo, which, like Bihać, was still under siege from Serb forces that had encircled it; and in Gornji Vakuf, where the British commander had his headquarters and a number of other units under him, including a Canadian battle group.

This job was a great opportunity to see the whole mission in Bosnia, from the strategic to the tactical levels, and to improve on what we were doing. It allowed me to look around the southern and western parts of Croatia, which were called Sector South and Sector West, and to get down to Macedonia. It was an awesome opportunity, and I piled on, building relationships at every level, working hard, trying to reduce my operations staff in the overstaffed headquarters, assessing those who worked for me (eighteen different nationalities and cultures did not always work together smoothly) and simply learning as much as I could in order to be as effective as I could.

The Srebrenica massacre had left us with enormous numbers of refugees to deal with, tens of thousands of them left homeless during a viciously hot summer. I went to Tuzla and landed by helicopter at the airstrip just outside the UN sector headquarters on a hot afternoon, with temperatures hitting 40 degrees Celsius. There must have been 35,000 refugees on the runway, most of them old men and women and some very young children, but almost nobody in between. They were on that runway in the hot sun with precious little water, almost no food and no shelter. Almost all were in deplorable condition because of the traumatic and severe hardships they had faced during the attack and afterwards, when they were forced to make their way into Muslim-controlled territory, over hills and through forests, on foot. That tarmac had now become their home.

The United Nations, representing the will of the international community, had failed. The UN just couldn't handle that many refugees and was incapable of looking after them, let alone helping them recover and get on with their lives. By then we were starting to learn the details of what had occurred during the preceding days in Srebrenica. The reason there were so few young adults in that flood of refugees was because the Bosnian Serbs had murdered them, and those who had escaped were on the run, hiding or fleeing for their lives.

We were trying to get the Dutch battalion that had been in Srebrenica back into Zagreb and out to the Netherlands. The Serbs wouldn't let any of the Dutch vehicles or their equipment out of the town, so we concentrated on getting the soldiers out of harm's way.

It was quite moving to see and talk to, first-hand, the elderly refugees, with small children in tow, and to realize that we were looking at the most vulnerable parts of a society, the old and the young who normally pay the biggest price, first and longest, when a society falls into chaos. The youngsters recovered quickly. If we gave them a little something to drink, got a little bit of food in their bellies, gave them a chance to sleep in a warm, safe place and maybe even somebody to love them, they would get better overnight. Without a doubt they would carry these traumatic events with them for the rest of their lives, but in the short term they got on with life; kids are resilient.

For the older people, however, that tragedy often became their last memory of life. I went to one refugee camp that the United Nations was helping run for people seventy-five years of age and older. It was as pathetic as it was appalling and tragic. All these elderly people were living twenty-five to a room in a tiny, decrepit schoolhouse that had only a partial roof. Each of them was sleeping on a thin blue rubber mattress and had a little bag containing food or clothing from the United Nations High Commission for Refugees, which was now everything they owned. They had been driven out of their villages, their families killed or dispersed to God knows where, and this was what they had to look forward to for the rest of their lives. One very old lady, with eyeglasses so dirty I could not see her eyes, wanted to know if I had a couple of cigarettes to give her (I did, and they disappeared into her pockets quickly), and she told me she appreciated Canada sending people to help. She had expected nothing less, she said, because the people in the next valley had always been good neighbours—it turned out that was where she thought Canada was.

Within several weeks, in late August, Croatia, which had been building its army and methodically retaking its own territory with the help of U.S. privately contracted military advisers and equipment, launched Operation Storm, knocked the Kyrenian Serb military forces out of the Serb-held Krajina area on the west coast of Croatia and pushed them back into northwestern Bosnia, away from the Dalmatian coast and the major towns of Split and Dubrovnik. The Croatians had decided what they were going to do, and the UN, up to and including the Secretary-General, could not change a single thing. Within four days the Croats had won an overwhelming victory, re-establishing the integrity of their borders, while the UN looked on helplessly as another tragedy unfolded.

Within days, we assumed responsibility for organizing the evacuation of the Krajina Serbs, who had been bypassed by Croatian military forces and were now refugees, living in a hostile area and fearing retribution from angry Croats. Many had fled ahead of Operation Storm, but a lot of them were still trapped behind the Croatian front lines. In what became a showcase of human tragedy and the viciousness of human nature, this motley collection of tens of thousands of impoverished men, women and children left Krajina by motorcade, on tractors, bikes, carts, horses or whatever vehicles they could find, with as many of their household possessions as they could carry, and travelled through parts of Croatia to other, Serb-held areas. All of this was carried live on TV around the world. Despite the supposed protection of Croatian police and UN forces, those convoys of old women and children, riding in the back of hundreds of tractors and carts, were pelted with rocks, eggs and anything else people could get their hands on all along the route out of Serb Krajina. It was a travesty and, again, the UN was powerless to prevent it.

In the aftermath of Srebrenica it became overwhelmingly clear that the United Nations' approach to the crisis was dysfunctional and that its presence was tolerated by the warring parties only as long as each could manipulate it for partisan gain. The UN could do nothing to change the dynamics that were tearing the country apart and was usually completely ignored, with only the occasional local success to cheer about.

The commander in Zagreb was a French general, Lieutenant-General Bernard Janvier, who, unfortunately, was not a visionary. As his senior operations officer, I was with him often, and he frequently appeared out of touch with what was going on on the ground. Janvier was the United Nations commander for the entire former Republic of Yugoslavia, operating from the headquarters in Zagreb. He was theoretically in command of the United Nations Peace Forces, with the peacekeeping forces in Croatia, which were also based in Zagreb, the Bosnian mission, with its headquarters in Sarajevo, and the United Nations Preventive Deployment in Macedonia, which was based in Skopje. In Zagreb we had two contingents: the civilian UN staff and the military side. Our top civilian was the senior representative of the Secretary-General (the SRSG), Yasushi Akashi, who, based on controversy over earlier air attacks on the Bosnian Serbs that had gone awry, now had very little play in military operations. Within the headquarters and between staff, there was little confidence that he was going to bring anything to the leadership team to increase the chances of mission success.

It was an organizational nightmare. No one had any clear understanding of who had what authority or which responsibility. When you threw in the multinational mix of soldiers and commanders, it became clear why so little was accomplished. We had something like sixty different nationalities serving under the UN in the former Yugoslavia, everyone from Malaysia to Pakistan to Bangladesh to Russia, as well as Canada, all the Western European nations and more. That caused problems. None of those nations had trained together, and each had different operating procedures, values and approaches that varied enormously from one nation to another.

Sector East, for example—the eastern Slavonia district of Croatia, bordering on the Danube River and run by the Russians—became known as an organized-crime sector because the Russian commander was running a good chunk of the Balkan underworld from there. He eventually got fired by the United Nations for corruption, went back to Russia and two weeks later was back in eastern Slavonia, continuing as the organized-crime boss, minus his UN hat. The Ukrainians, on what was one of their first UN missions, had already developed a well-deserved reputation as an organized-crime gang unto themselves, selling UN fuel, supplies and vehicles on the black market and running prostitution rings in their operational area. This reputation was reinforced in subsequent missions, to the point that the UN declined to accept any more Ukrainian units until their behaviour improved.

English was the working language of the headquarters, but many of the officers and soldiers working there neither understood nor spoke it. Janvier himself spoke no English at all and, alone among the senior military and civilian staff that I used to brief each morning, failed to comprehend the jokes that I invariably worked into my daily spiel. It also became a bit of a challenge to, for instance, deal with the Egyptian battalion in Sarajevo or the Russian battalion in Sector East. We didn't have that problem with the Pakistani battalions because all their officers spoke English.

Complicating everything were the mandates of the different UN missions, which were as ambiguous, complex and unfocused as they could possibly get. Nobody understood the mandates within those missions. The mix of this complicated organizational structure was a recipe for chaos. We faced a diversity of languages and disparity of language skills, different orders from every national capital to their own troops, often bizarre directions from UN headquarters in New York (which varied from micromanagement to no direction at all) and bullets flying in all directions, leading to what could be interpreted as total chaos. I actually caught myself one day yearning for Canada, Ottawa and the NDHQ!

Things were changing, however. As a result of the debacle at Srebrenica (the scale and brutality of which was not widely known, either inside the Balkans or out) and of the prospect of attacks on other supposed UN safe havens by the Bosnian Serbs, we began planning, in conjunction with NATO headquarters in Naples, Italy, air strikes against Serb positions around Sarajevo and throughout Bosnia. Our goal was to force them to comply with the numerous UN Security Council resolutions that they had blatantly ignored, so far without any consequences.

To plan and coordinate the air strikes, General Janvier held teleconferences with General Rupert Smith, the British UN commander in Sarajevo, and U.S. Navy Admiral Leighton Smith, who was the NATO commander in Naples and the man responsible for the air power that was going to carry out the strikes. Once we started each call, Janvier would say something and then the conversation would continue between Rupert Smith and Leighton Smith, in English, discussing how we were going to implement measures necessary to protect both blue-beret troops and local civilians, what the desired effect was and how we would know when we had achieved it. General Janvier was left listening to an interpreter who was always well behind the current conversation. After the teleconference had finished, Janvier would then take out his frustrations on us, screaming because he didn't understand what was going on and had essentially no way of influencing what was happening. As a commander, he was powerless, with nothing to bring to the table: no authority to make significant decisions, no additional troops, no tactical plans, no equipment. He had no levers to actually shape the fighting that was going to take place, so his sense of helplessness was incredibly frustrating and he took it out on us, the people around him.

General Smith, by contrast, was one of those guys who brought considerable intellect to his job. He understood the business of how to stop a civil war, how to rebuild a country and how to soldier in what was termed "asymmetric warfare." This guy understood what key battles needed to be fought, who the critical leaders were and which important areas needed to be struck. He knew, in short, what needed to be done.

In early September 1995, we were all up in Janvier's office in a teleconference between Janvier, Smith in Sarajevo and Smith in Naples to discuss the final aspects of the NATO air strikes that would commence at midnight. As usual, the French-to-English translation was not going well. The decision was finalized: NATO would strike the Bosnian Serb positions at midnight and continue until they had forced the Serbs to comply with the UN directives. Immediately after the teleconference, I briefed Janvier and shared with him some of the detailed analysis we had done for the region, particularly the Sarajevo Sector, given that that was what the world heard about whenever the Balkans were front-page news.

Most of our work again came compliments of the Canadian "old-boys' network" that we were fortunate enough to have scattered throughout the UN structure: me and others in UNPF, Colonel Norris Pettis and Colonel Andy Leslie in the Croatian mission, and Lieutenant-Colonels Matt Macdonald and Rick Hatton working for Rupert Smith in Sarajevo. We talked every day and often accomplished more, because of the Canadian connection, than any other part of the organization.

I briefed Janvier on what we believed were the Bosnian Serb forces inside the Sarajevo exclusion zone, the twenty-kilometre area around the city within which they were not supposed to have any forces. The Bosnian Serbs had routinely ignored that exclusion zone for more than two years, however, and I said exactly that. Our information was that they had fifty to fifty-five tanks inside the zone, mostly T-55s and some T-62s, well camouflaged and difficult, if not impossible, to find from the air. Janvier interrupted and said, "No, no, you're absolutely wrong. You must have made a mistake. You guys had no one that could tell you that. It's four or five tanks is what your people probably meant to say, and you guys took five or four and transposed it into fifty-four."

"Well, you know, General," I said, "this is our best analysis and we're pretty confident, but I hear what you're saying and we'll recheck it to verify our level of confidence in what I'm telling you, but I'm also telling you we have done that already and have a high degree of confidence in those numbers."

We had done a pretty good job. After the air strikes, the Bosnian Serbs capitulated and began moving everything they could out of the exclusion zone around Sarajevo. We had teams of observers posted at the agreed upon exit points they were permitted to use, and sure enough, they counted exactly fifty-four tanks driving out of the zone!

The general in charge of the Croatian mission was a Jordanian two-star who we never saw. After the Croats had retaken their territory during Operation Storm, that mission was in desperate need of refocusing and restructuring, but it never happened. That Croatian mission was carried almost entirely on the backs of its Canadian chief of staff, Norris Pettis, and, later on, Andy Leslie. Both made sure that whatever needed to be done by the UN mission in Croatia got done, and without them it would have failed.

The Croatians had returned to their borders—or what they considered their borders—with Bosnia, and the Muslims had driven the Serbs back from Bihać in the northwest of Bosnia and broken the stranglehold around that town. By middle to late September everything had reached a stalemate and the Dayton peace negotiations began, driven by Richard Holbrooke as the U.S. President's special envoy on Yugoslavia. The Dayton

Peace Accord, a 180-day detailed plan to lead to a more lasting peace, was signed in Paris on December 14, 1995, and was
subsequently implemented by NATO, commencing on December 20. Our headquarters in Zagreb was swarming with NATO
officers even before the peace accord was reached, and we were
already planning to shift the mission from UN to NATO command. The NATO Implementation Force, or IFOR, was made
up of many of the same UN forces already in the country, which
would simply shift to NATO command; with an infusion of new,
external forces, particularly from the United States, IFOR would
drive the process.

Everyone who had served in the former Yugoslavia realized that a lasting peace was a long way off. In January 1996 I
went to visit the town of Prijedor, in northwest Bosnia. Prijedor
had a pre-war population of about 130,000, a well-balanced and
integrated mixture of Bosnian Croatians, Bosnian Muslims and
Bosnian Serbs. Within weeks of the outbreak of fighting, it was
ethnically cleansed, one of the worst instances of the practice
in the whole former Yugoslavia. The Bosnian Serbs set up the
Omarska concentration camp right up the road from Prijedor.
It was a death camp, pure and simple, established in and around
an old gravel pit.

Prijedor was in the Canadian area of operations for the
Dayton Peace Accord implementation, and we had put the
reconnaissance squadron from the Royal Canadian Dragoons
(the regiment I had grown up in) in this area. Under Major
Lowell Thomas, the squadron was located in an abandoned
schoolhouse outside the town. The school hadn't been used
for many months, the power was off and it was cold and wet.

I went there, stayed the night and had a meal with the troops, just to get a feel for what was going on in their area. Soon after I arrived, Lowell, who I had known since he joined the regiment as a young officer, said, "Hey, sir, come with me," and led me back into what had been the school library. He started showing me the textbooks that were still stacked up on the shelves. "I've got to show you this one," he said.

To this day I wish I'd kept the book he showed me. It said more about the conflict in the Balkans than anything else I've read, heard or seen since. It was an illustrated history book for junior grades, the sort of book that kids under ten would have used in their history classes. It was all about how the tough Bosnian people (the partisans) had beaten the Nazis in the Second World War. It showed the stealthy and bloodthirsty "Huns," with their distinctive German helmets, attacking the innocent people living in Bosnia. The Huns had fangs, with bright red blood dripping from them, and were pictured bayoneting babies and decapitating old people. According to the book, the tough, resilient Bosnian population retreated to the forests and caves and survived despite the terrible times. It then went on to show them attacking the German soldiers and shooting and bayoneting them, with all of it depicted in colour pictures!

As I read through I thought, "Oh my God—this is what they were teaching to seven-, eight- and nine-year-olds. No wonder they're on a constant cycle of death, murder and destruction." I put it back on the shelf.

When I went back to Bosnia as multinational division commander four years later, I visited one of the local schools that had been reopened, and it quickly became apparent that not much had changed. When I arrived, these little tiny girls and boys, about four years old, were all gathered together in a group dressed up in their traditional costumes to greet me. They were all singing a song in their sweet little voices, and I thought it sounded just beautiful. So I asked my interpreter, Elizabeth, "What are they singing? What's the song?"

Elizabeth listened for a moment, then started translating it for me, and said, "It's a song about when the Chetniks came, they killed my grandfather and my grandmother and now when I grow up I can't wait to kill them."

I said, "What?!"

It was incredible, almost unbelievable to a Canadian what was being played out in front of all of us. The hatred was being promulgated from one generation to the next through their education system. It was a stark lesson in how hatred can perpetuate itself, and it made me appreciate Canada even more.

Despite the frustrations of UN service, we worked hard with some satisfaction that year. One of the "truths" about multinational missions is that 95 per cent of the work is done by 10 per cent of the people. That was certainly true in the Balkans. That 10 per cent or so included several outstanding British officers, a few really capable Danes, one or two out of the very small number of Americans there, one notable Ukrainian officer and many, many Canadians, including Peter Atkinson (a good friend who was living just five houses away from us in Ottawa), Andy Leslie, Rita LePage, Andy Wojnockski, Sean Myers and Stu Beare, all great Canadians who, in tough and stressful times, did our country proud.

The Ukrainian officer was Major Andre Ponakarovski, a prince of a man and an excellent leader who had adapted from the Warsaw Pact system to the UN easily. He was completely dependable but, after eighteen months in theatre, needed a break, so we sent him home for three weeks' leave with his family over Christmas 1995. He departed, and four days later, when I went into the Operations Centre, there he was. He could

not afford financially to stay at home. The Ukraine stopped his UN pay while he was there, and he had received no Ukrainian military pay for six months. As he said, if his three daughters wanted food and shoes, he had to stay and work. I again thanked God for being Canadian.

I enjoyed every moment of the operations, particularly the camaraderie of the Canadians in theatre. We worked hard, supported each other, socialized together, drank the occasional pop together and often formed friendships for life. The changes early in 1996, after the Dayton Peace Accord, led to my becoming the Chief of Staff of a much-reduced UN headquarters in Zagreb as we started to focus on eastern Slavonia. The Serbs still occupied most of that devastated region, and a separate UN mission was established there until the area could be returned to Croatian control. In mid-January of 1996, I got a phone call from Brigadier-General Bruce Jeffries, the brigade commander in Petawawa, Ontario, telling me that Canada was going to join IFOR. The government had not, until then, made any commitment to participating in the NATO mission, so we had extracted our three thousand soldiers from Bosnia and Croatia, packed up all of their kit, and now had those hundreds of sea containers on the docks in the Croatian port of Sibenik, awaiting shipment back to Canada.

Now Bruce was telling me that Canada was going to send a brigade headquarters and some combat troops, a total of one thousand soldiers, to Bosnia. He was going to be the commander of a multinational brigade made up of those Canadian troops with some British and Czech soldiers, to be based somewhere in northwest Bosnia, probably near Bihać, an area I knew well.

"How intense is your job right now?" he asked me. "Do you think you could get out of it without causing undue problems? I'd really love to have you come in as my deputy commander."

I said, "The job is not intense. For all intents and purposes, the UN military mandate has been fulfilled here. I'm getting bored and I'd love to come and do the job for you. If you can make it happen, I'd be delighted."

About twenty-four hours later I got an early morning phone call from Andy Leslie, who had gone home to Canada at the end of his tour in December. "I'm back in Edmonton," he told me. "I've been back three weeks and I just got a phone call saying I'm coming back to replace you. What's going on?"

We talked it through, although I really wasn't completely sure at that point that he was coming back, but Andy eventually returned and took over from me as UN Chief of Staff for about six weeks to help set up the UN mission for eastern Slavonia. I moved to the NATO mission in Bosnia and became deputy commander for 2nd Canadian Multinational Brigade (2 CMNBG), with headquarters just north of Bihać, in a small Muslim town called Coralici. The brigade was responsible for overseeing implementation of the Dayton Peace Accord in northwestern Bosnia and was made up of Canadian, British and Czech units. We worked in a British-led NATO division, commanded by Major-General Mike Jackson, a straightfor-ward, tough, whiskey-drinking soldier who later became Chief of General Staff of the British Army. That last appointment as CGS was made while I was commanding that same division of NATO troops in Bosnia in 2000 and 2001, and the relation-ship that had developed between us in 1996 sure made life easy when dealing with British issues.

Working for the NATO-led organization was a completely different experience from working under the UN. The ideal of UN peacekeeping is beautiful, but after my time in Zagreb I con-cluded that the United Nations itself couldn't run a one-man rush to the outhouse. Pragmatically, it was almost criminal to put Canadian troops under UN command in missions that were anything but absolutely benign because the UN was fundamen-tally incapable of running effective military operations. The UN Security Council, a large and dysfunctional committee based in New York, cannot provide effective vision, strategy and guidance to a UN military commander in the field. It certainly could not respond to dynamic and rapidly changing situations, particularly on weekends and holidays.

There were good people in the UN, some of whom we saw in Bosnia and Croatia. But as an institution, every time it has tried to do a job that it is just not set up to do, like run major peace support or peacekeeping operations, the effect has been difficult to determine. The United Nations had no concept of how to build multinational forces into one effective team for a mission and, worse than that, it usually had no concept of what kind of mission it would be asking that team to do. We were doing things in the former Yugoslavia that no one had been prepared for, and even though it was dawning on some of our military and civilian leaders that UN peacekeeping operations were a thing of the past, there was no way that we could get past that mantra of "peacekeeper, peacekeeper, peacekeeper."

So whenever the United Nations was in, Canada was in. The vast majority of people in the Canadian Forces, at every level, realized the futility, frustration and danger of what was occurring, and yet there was no way that we could break out of that peacekeeping bubble. With Canadian, British or French troops fighting all-out battles with extremist and radical militia forces, how could anyone not realize that this was not peacekeeping?

Yet our soldiers were sent into the Balkans under Chapter 6 of the UN Charter, a peacekeeping mission where they could use their weapons only to protect themselves. As a result, we put soldiers and sailors and airmen and airwomen, who served on the ground, in positions where they saw brutal acts that they were powerless to stop. That was a scar that a lot of our people brought back from the Balkans, and a scar that the entire Canadian Forces, particularly the army, brought back as an institution. With the UN mission in the former Yugoslavia so ineffectual, it became difficult for those of us who were part of it to put the best face on things.

During the peace talks leading to the Dayton Accord, we would get what the Americans called "codels," or congressional delegations, coming through the region on fact-finding trips. When they came through Zagreb, one of my jobs was to brief them. Invariably, they would ask me, "Okay, so what has the UN accomplished?"

Wanting to put the best light on the mission, I would say, "Well, first of all, we think we've played a part in helping keep people alive, by sending through some humanitarian assistance that otherwise wouldn't have gotten through." In fact, sometimes the local people were being held hostage, used as levers by one side or the other in the civil war to push and pull the UN, and the aid it delivered, whichever way they wanted. So you have to wonder, if the UN wasn't there, would people have found food more easily from other sources?

The second thing I told them was, "We think the UN might have helped in containing the conflict within the borders of the former Republic of Yugoslavia." I'm not sure that's true at all, but we used to say that we believed we played a part in keeping it that way.

The third thing I told them was that we played a role in helping set the conditions for the Dayton Peace Accord by providing a way for the different factions to communicate back and forth, either with us as intermediaries or facilitated by us. But we were never really sure that was true either, because the Bosnian military would often open up their radio channels and talk to the Serb military. They'd talk back and forth all the time, either throwing insults and shouting at each other or, on occasion, having serious conversations that then led to things like the exchange of prisoners or bodies.

So we put Canadian soldiers, as part of the UN mission, on the ground in the former Republic of Yugoslavia without a clear mandate, without a clear plan as to how we were going to accomplish anything, and constrained them to be peacekeepers in a region that had no peace for them to keep. Once we got there and realized what we had gotten ourselves into, nobody seemed to be able to do anything about it. We had soldiers on the ground getting shot at, and sometimes killed, in Bosnia, Croatia and all the other parts of the former Republic of Yugoslavia. The concept of peacekeeping was meaningless in practice. In fact, it was worse than meaningless: it was farcical, and far too many of our young men lost their lives there for no discernible effect.

That effect only started happening when NATO went in under Chapter 7 of the UN Charter (peace*making*, as opposed to peace*keeping*) and was given the responsibility and the authority to implement the Dayton Peace Accord. Of the agreement's 250 paragraphs, every second one said, in essence, "If you don't do what we said in the previous paragraph, we're going to knock you upside the head."

Guess what? Everybody got in line and complied, because NATO had the combat power and the determination to use that muscle. That's what led to Croatia's being an increasingly stable nation and a member of NATO; to Macedonia's being an increasingly stable nation and a future member of NATO; and even to Bosnia's improving, although it's still fragile and vulnerable. There's hope that Serbia can also eventually become stable and democratic enough that it too can join NATO.

The other lesson I took home from my first Bosnian tour was that if Canada wants to maximize the effects of having its soldiers, sailors, airmen and airwomen involved in operations, we have to work together as a Canadian Forces, under one flag. Under the UN mandate, we had Canadian troops scattered all over Bosnia and Croatia—an abysmal way of doing business. We had a battle group of about 1,200 soldiers in Croatia, in Sector

South, and we provided much of the Sector South headquarters. We also had a battle group of 1,400 soldiers in Bosnia as part of Sector Southwest, in the British sector, as well as a lot of people in combat support units throughout the region. We had Canadian pilots, airmen and airwomen providing air support from NATO bases in Italy, and we had ships and submarines that were part of the NATO naval flotilla in the Adriatic Sea. Our people were split up among different commands without any synergy. So even though our total numbers were enormous—we deployed over 4,000 troops every six months for three years—none of those individual parts was big enough to give Canada the clout among the NATO allies that would give us any real influence or voice on how the former Republic of Yugoslavia was going to develop.

We deployed our people piecemeal, and despite the enormous investment, enormous cost, enormous amounts of work and tragic loss of life, we got almost zero credit for it internationally. We were not invited to the table when the Contact Group met to discuss the future of Bosnia, because of the way we did our tactical business. If our troops had been deployed in one block of 4,500 Canadians working under one Canadian flag, by God, that would have given us a say in how things were done in the Balkans. Instead, we were frittered away, and as a result we really never got a say in what went on in the former Yugoslavia.

This situation, of course, runs contrary to our history, going back to the First World War, when we insisted on keeping our soldiers under Canadian command in one Canadian Corps and as a result got our own signature on the treaty that ended the war.

We were part of the deciding process because we had credibility. More importantly, our determination as a young country to command our young men led to the strategic, country-changing victory at Vimy Ridge at Easter 1917. What we achieved there as a result of our insistence on unified Canadian command still continues to shape our country, over ninety years later. A decade after our major commitments to the Balkans, nobody remembers we were there, much less that we were present with so much of our nation's youth.

I insisted on a Team Canada approach, combining the military, diplomatic and other departments. We would fly our Canadian flag high wherever we went and would have a unified approach going into any mission. Of course, that unified approach became difficult to implement once we tried to include the Canadian civilian and government officials working abroad, but eventually we'll get there if we have enough people that can see the benefits. Sadly, as of this moment, other than those in uniform, we don't. Canada has never articulated its national interests. We've always talked about Canadian values, but we're a nation, and like it or not, nations have interests. If we put our military forces in a place where they don't have a clear mandate or mission, don't have a clear strategy or the right tools to do their jobs, including rules of engagement, leadership and equipment, Canada can easily discredit itself and therefore significantly harm our ability to realize our national interests, not only where we are operating, but elsewhere around the world.

Those battle groups on the ground in Bosnia, in spite of being in a UN mission without clarity, intent or purpose, still could have achieved so much if they had operated boldly. They were, however, enormously constrained in what they were able to do because of the risk-averse approach of both the government and the military in Ottawa. We had been promoting folks to senior ranks through thirty years of a risk-averse environment: in other words, we promoted bureaucrats over combat leaders. We put battalions in place on the ground, but because of the nervousness in Ottawa, those units were, more often than not, reluctant to take on missions, slow to carry them out or unable to get approval for them, despite the fact the soldiers would see how necessary they were. That discredited our country and the Canadian Forces, and harmed us internationally.

Monty Meigs, a retired four-star general from the United States who had commanded in Bosnia, told me, "Rick, the Canadian troops were the most proficient under my command in the NATO mission. It was a pity that Canada would not let them do anything, because their effect was minuscule. The rogues trying to stop the peace process were aware of Canada's approach and knew what they could get away with in your sector, but not in others. It was a shame, really, to use great troops like that."

I knew exactly what he meant, as did any one of us who had served in the Balkans. Although we had great soldiers at every level, who wanted to do what was needed to save lives and actually effect change, they couldn't. The most telling sign was the names given each of the national battalions in UN. Each battalion was given a common abbreviation, so the Russian battalion became "Rusbat," the British battalion became

"Britbat" and the Canadian battalions were "Canbat 1" or "Canbat 2." After several months of operations, with the Canadians constantly saying no to jobs because Ottawa had refused permission for them to participate or to allow our commanders on the ground to make decisions, because they were more concerned with what was happening in Ottawa than getting something done in Gornji Vakuf, the Canadian battalions were quickly and cynically renamed by other nations "Can'tbat 1" and "Can'tbat 2."

We paid the price in late 2001 and early 2002, when the Europeans were putting together the International Security Assistance Force mission in Kabul, Afghanistan, and wouldn't let us participate. Canada desperately wanted to join ISAF at the start of the war in Afghanistan, but we were shunned. Part of the reason was that the Europeans, the British in particular, remembered our risk-averse approach in Bosnia and had no faith that Canada would pull its weight, especially if things got tough. They did not want us as part of their alliance.

Bosnia and Croatia was also my first experience with the media covering military operations, and it quickly became clear to me that when you talk about a complex issue with journalists, they'll sometimes turn out a sound article, but some headline editor will turn what you said in two hours into a four-word headline that relates not at all to the sophisticated discussion about a complex issue. But I also realized what an important lever the media could be for us. Major-General (Ret'd.) Lew MacKenzie, who deserves huge credit for this, recognized that if you want to get something done, you have to bring pressure to bear. One of the best ways to do this is through public opinion, and you get that public opinion working for you by telling a story and then using the media to help tell that story widely. The media is your pipeline to Canadians.

I left Croatia and the UN in January 1996 and joined 2nd Canadian Multinational Brigade to work for Bruce Jeffries for the next six months. We had not really worked together closely, but we had both grown up in the Armoured Corps. When he phoned me to ask if I'd be his deputy commander, I was delighted. In hindsight, it was one of the greatest things that ever happened to me, because I had got to know all those soldiers from Petawawa, which is where the Canadian contingent to his brigade had originated. I was a newly promoted colonel, relatively junior in the hierarchy after fourteen months in that rank, and I had thought my next posting after the former Yugoslavia would be to Halifax, to become the chief of staff to the commander of land forces in the area. Although it wasn't a done deal, Joyce and I were nonetheless looking forward to going back to the Maritimes that summer of 1996.

Then on February 14, Jean Boyle, the Chief of the Defence Staff, arrived in Zagreb on his way to visit the brigade in Bosnia. Bruce Jeffries stayed on the ground commanding and sent me up to look after the Chief and the VIPs who were travelling with him. I met General Boyle when he landed, and travelled with him to the Intercontinental Hotel in downtown Zagreb. I still remember going into that swank hotel armed to the teeth and booking rooms for all of us. (I sometimes wonder what would happen if we tried that in Canada.) I took him out to a little restaurant for dinner that night, with Andy Leslie, Colonel Pat Sansom, who later became our Director General of

Intelligence and our senior Provost Marshal, and Lieutenant-Colonel Peter Atkinson, now Brigadier-General Atkinson in Fort Hood, Texas. The Canadian ambassador to Croatia, Graham Green, a man we all knew well and were friends with, also tagged along.

Halfway through an enjoyable dinner, General Boyle tapped on his glass to get everybody's attention and said he wanted to announce that the next day the list of new general officers was coming out for the Canadian Forces for 1996. In the car travelling from the airport to the hotel, he had asked where I was going after completing my tour in Bosnia, and I had gone on ad nauseam about the joys of living in the Maritimes and how that would offset the boring staff job I would be given. At the dinner, he reached over his chair, put his arm around me and said, "One of the things we are going to do in that new general officers' list is start to change our leadership, and we're going to start by promoting this young colonel here to brigadier-general and give him command of 2 Brigade in Petawawa."

That was a big, big surprise to me. I was not expecting promotion or command of a brigade any time soon, if ever, so all I could say was, "You are?"

Ambassador Green leaned over and said, "You didn't know about this?"

I said, "Graham, no. This is an absolutely a complete surprise. I certainly wasn't expecting anything like this. If I had ever hoped to get command, it would have been several years down the road at the very earliest."

"So your wife doesn't know anything about this?" he said.

"Well, obviously not, since I didn't know."

"Okay," he said, "let's phone her then and break the news."

So he grabbed his cellphone and we dialled Canada. When Joyce answered the phone, I said, "Joyce, we're posted."

"Okay, where?" she asked.

"Well, guess," I said.

"Halifax?"

"No. Petawawa."

"Oh, we're going to go be the base commander, are we?" she said, because the base commander was a colonel's job. "We'll have our married quarters there."

"No, Joyce, we're not going to be the base commander."

Now she was stumped. "Well, what are we going to do?"

"I'm going to be the brigade commander, and oh, by the way, I'm getting promoted to brigadier-general."

She didn't believe me. So Boyle said, "Hey, Rick, let me talk to Joyce."

He took the phone and said, "Joyce, this is Jean Boyle. Thank you for what you've done too, and yes, we're going to promote Rick and send you guys off to Petawawa and I'm sure you'll make a great command team." Then we passed the phone around the table. Peter Atkinson spoke next. (He and his wife, Charlene, lived just down the street from us and were good friends of ours.)

In hindsight, the fact that I got to know those great troops from Petawawa and soldiered with them for six months in Bosnia was absolutely perfect. When I arrived in Petawawa in July 1996, I already knew a lot of the people in that brigade, particularly the service battalion folks, engineers, signallers, medical staff and others who were among the most difficult to get time with, and therefore get to know, in garrison. The relationship we had already developed on operations would put me in great stead for the next two years.

163

A Flood of Affection

I returned from Bosnia in June 1996, and by then Joyce had already sold our house in Ottawa, so within a few days of my arrival in Canada we were on our way to Petawawa, a couple of hours' drive northwest. We were in Petawawa a week before the handover of command only to discover that Bruce Jeffries was still living in the designated brigade commander's house, so we had to stay in temporary quarters for about seven weeks. In that short time I learned an incredibly valuable lesson about unpredicted implications, and how you can inadvertently piss people off without meaning to or worse, without even knowing that you're doing it.

While I had been away Joyce had bought me a small speedboat, something she knew I'd always wanted. She had seen one for sale, second-hand, and had asked Peter Atkinson, who was now at home, and Walt Natynczyk, who lived near us in Ottawa, to take a look at it. They went over to kick the tires and said to Joyce, "This is a great deal." She bought it as a coming-home present for me and in preparation for our new tour.

A few days before the change-of-command ceremony, I went down to the marina in Petawawa, put the boat in the water and met the guy who ran the place, a retired warrant officer from the Artillery named Stan Shaw. Stan introduced himself, knowing I had a boat and that I was the new brigade commander. "Sir," he said, "do you know the river?"

The base yacht club was right on the Ottawa River and I hadn't been out on it. "You got any charts of the river?" I asked. "I don't know it at all. I've never actually been on it—I've got the boat now and I'm going to run around, but I don't want to do anything stupid."

"Tell you what, sir," he said, pointing out his boat, a thirty-five-foot cabin cruiser that made mine look puny. "You pick the day and come out on my boat. You and I'll go for a drive upriver and I'll show you all the points to avoid, points to find—give you a full orientation."

I didn't want to put him to any trouble and told him so, but he just said, "I'd love to do it." I asked if he was available two days from then, and we agreed on a time.

Joyce was already working in Deep River, just north of Petawawa, and Chris, our older son, was going to college in Ottawa. He came up for the weekend, and even though I hadn't yet had that promised orientation trip with Stan, I decided to take Chris and Steven out for a short cruise in the boat. It was a sizzling hot day and eventually I realized that we needed gas. I headed back to the yacht club, which is one of only two points on the river where you can get gas, and there was a line of about six or seven boats waiting to fill up, with nobody running the pumps.

It was two o'clock in the afternoon, about 37 degrees Celsius, and out on the water it seemed even hotter. We could hear the people in the boats ahead of us grumbling about the delay until finally this kid came running down the dock and started pumping gas. The boats began moving and people continued to grumble about the lousy service. As we got closer, I could hear the teenager who worked part-time at the yacht club apologizing to the people in one of the boats in front of us.

"We would have been down earlier, but Stan is taking the general out tomorrow to show him the river, so we had to spend all day cleaning his boat. The reason you got screwed around at the gas pumps and had to sit for two hours in the hot sun is because General Hillier is going out on Stan's boat."

We were all in shorts and T-shirts and I had my straw hat and sunglasses on, so when I heard that I just slowly sank down into the cockpit, hoping nobody recognized me. Making all those people wait, pissing them off, had been the furthest thing from my mind when I'd accepted Stan's invitation to go out on the river.

The incident has stuck in my mind ever since, and I came to realize how often my name gets used, without my ever knowing it and in ways I never intended. The lesson was that my actions could cause ripple effects down the road, effects that I didn't know about or foresee. Some of those effects could be extremely negative. As CDS I figured the best way to keep this from happening was to go out and tell everybody, numerous times, what we were going to do, as clearly, frankly and memorably as I could. This led to an initial spate of "town halls" across the CF—meetings during operations, in aircraft, on ships at sea and in every conceivable place where I could find uniformed men and women. (In fact, I spoke so much that it became automatic. One night I woke from a deep sleep and found myself briefing Joyce. Her response, at 2 a.m., is not printable!)

While I wasn't completely successful at keeping people from invoking my name for their own purposes, every time someone claimed "The CDS said he wants this," there were hundreds of people who could judge for themselves the validity of that comment. They had heard directly from me our vision, our approach and their part in it.

Nevertheless, I was constantly hearing, usually long after the fact, that I had supposedly made some wild demand. I would say, "Really? I don't recall saying anything like that, ever. In fact, I didn't even know about the issue." I kept relearning the lesson from that story about every two months: people take your name and use your anticipated or assumed wishes as an excuse to do things their way.

When I took over as brigade commander, the Canadian Forces were still suffering from the fallout of Somalia and hiding from the public, fearful of doing anything except what was perceived as being absolutely essential but at the same time unable to articulate what actually was essential. Among other things, that meant we were not permitted change-of-command parades, so when I took over 2 Canadian Mechanized Brigade Group (2 CMBG), the occasion was marked only by a twelve-soldier quarter guard, the brigade staff officers and a handful of invited guests.

I took the brigade from Colonel Walt Holmes, a very good officer who had been acting commander while Bruce Jeffries was away in Bosnia. We were not permitted to have the outgoing commander thank all the soldiers, sailors and airmen and airwomen who were part of our brigade or to let them get a look at their new boss and hear what he had to say. It was quite remarkable that we would be barred from doing something so basic, so traditionally military, and so efficient at ensuring that everyone knew a new person was in command. It came down to money—all this was happening at a time when we had to justify, ludicrously, every nickel of spending. The fact that we might spend $1,000 in hospitality funds for a reception to have the people on base and the local community leaders get to know the soldiers and the commanders in the brigade was seen as a waste of taxpayers' money.

When the Canadian Airborne Regiment was disbanded, the media focused almost entirely on the $5,000 in hospitality costs for the event. In response, the senior commanders in the army ran away and hid from the controversy. Nobody stood up and pointed out that commanders need to be seen by their troops, or that a little of the military pageantry that is part of our tradition and history has an enormously positive impact on those soldiers, sailors and airmen or airwomen. Nobody pointed out that a bureaucratic methodology of counting dollars was leading to the demoralization of our forces. We simply weren't allowed to do it. Fortunately, we've managed to do our work despite this foolishness.

I had more fun commanding 2 CMBG than almost any other job I've held. It wasn't the general's rank I wanted, although the CF made a bit of a fuss with the news release about my promotion (perhaps trying to take away a little pressure over the flood of bad publicity the Canadian Forces had been getting), saying that this guy Hillier had been promoted to general while he was just forty years old. To me that was irrelevant. In fact, I told General Boyle that he had missed an opportunity to save some money: he could have had me in that job as a captain instead of as a brigadier-general. It was a great challenge and it offered me the chance to continue soldiering. All I wanted was the opportunity to meet that challenge.

When I took command, the brigade was tired: they'd been used hard—going and coming for more than three years, most recently to the former Yugoslavia—and needed rejuvenating. I saw a really good chance to try to lead in a very direct way, with simple little things to bring the brigade together as a team. We conducted a brigade rucksack march, with all the soldiers in the brigade putting on those big, heavy packs and going for a 13-kilometre hike together. We went out on a brigade snowshoe march that winter, held a brigade sports day, and did a host of other things. We faced a lot of resistance at first, from the soldiers and some of their commanders, but I kept the inconvenience to the individual units to a minimum, and once that teamwork started to develop, enthusiasm for the events spread quickly.

We spent the rest of that year in team-building exercises combined with low-level training, which turned out to be a good thing given the events that followed. One of the things I did was hold a formal orders group every four to six weeks for all the commanders of the units that made up the brigade and their senior soldiers (sergeants major or regimental sergeants major), bringing everyone together and kicking it off with an enjoyable event. In the winter, we met at my house and went cross-country skiing together. When we came back, the brigade cooks had whipped up breakfast for us, over which we discussed all the issues relating to the brigade and our soldiers. Another time we took snowmobiles and rode them in a long circuit around the training area, about 75 kilometres in total. The COs made a big deal out of it. Steve MacDonald, the head of military police, showed up on his military police snowmobile, complete with siren and lights!

That particular orders group was memorable because my old friend Walt Natynczyk, commanding the Royal Canadian Dragoons, went for an unscheduled swim on a freezing February morning. There was one narrow spot toward the end of the route where you had to scoot between the road and a creek that fell down a fairly steep slope. What you were supposed to do was stand up on your machine, get it moving and keep it moving, because if you stopped and lost momentum, you were going to slide down that bank and into the river. Walt, unfortunately, was not entirely comfortable on a snowmobile, and he released the accelerator. I was in front and when I looked back, Walt and his Ski-Doo were in the river. We fished him out and went the last couple hundred yards to the yacht club, where we were prepared to have breakfast, so he could get himself partially dried out.

These get-togethers were fun, but also important for building a team. After the first six to nine months of socializing, training hard, working together, getting frustrated with each other, trying new things, living with the enormous constraints imposed on us and being shocked at the environment of mistrust for the military in Canada, my commanders in the brigade and their senior enlisted advisers were a cohesive group who knew and trusted each other. The talent in that group was enormous, with most of the commanding officers, then lieutenant-colonels, eventually becoming general officers. We had all internalized a command philosophy, four things I talked about all the time: assess your situation; use your common sense; work hard; and look after your people. We were all thinking, in similar ways but with our unique experiences and abilities, about how to approach any problem and resolve it. We knew each other, we built on that knowledge to create trust among us, and with that trust came the makings of a phenomenal team. From commanding officers, regimental sergeants major and company commanders right down to the most junior or newly arrived soldiers, we built a four-thousand-strong team of "battle buddies." It was quite a significant achievement and, as it turned out, a powerful tool. Everything that we did together as a brigade came from that great base of trust.

Almost as soon as I took over the brigade, I began to talk to my commanders and soldiers about the importance of their families. The brigade was tired. They had worked hard for three years, and some of the units were particularly fatigued from overseas deployments and seemingly endless training exercises. People had been away from home a lot. The soldiers would come back from an exercise on Thursday or Friday, be involved all weekend in more training and by Sunday they would be gone on another exercise that would keep them away from home until the following weekend, when the cycle started all over again. They had been doing this constantly, and they were starting to ask why. As soon as I arrived, I said to the unit commanders, "Boys, we're working Monday to Friday—that's the workweek. Saturdays and Sundays are days off, like most normal people in our country have. They're not field time, they're not standard workdays and they're not deployment times. So sort out plans to achieve the necessary results using that as a basic principle. Now, if we're on a two- to three-week exercise, deployed away from Petawawa, then obviously we're going to have to work those weekends; sometimes we'll have to do that. But we're not going to leave for those long exercises on the Saturday or the Sunday. We're going to deploy on the Monday, and when the exercise is over, two and a half weeks later or whatever, we'll come back on the Friday. We'll work hard, we'll train from Monday to Friday. We'll do it during what is meant to be a standard workweek."

The feedback was incredible. After the first four or five months, I couldn't go anywhere in Petawawa without someone's wife or husband grabbing my elbow or tugging at my shirtsleeve and saying, "General Hillier, I just want to thank you for what you did." That one little change made a huge difference in their lives. This was back in the days when soldiers weren't getting paid enough to make ends meet, when morale was low and equipment was horrible. So even a little bright light in what was then a pretty dark tunnel had a huge impact. A simple thing like reducing the workweek became one of the memories that everyone in that brigade still speaks to me about whenever we meet and reminisce.

The team building, direct leadership, trust and support for families paid off in the spring of 1997, when the Red River flooded from southern Manitoba up to Winnipeg, causing the Flood of the Century. The brigade was almost out the door on our way to a large-scale spring exercise in New Brunswick when it became apparent that the flooding in southern Manitoba was a national disaster. We turned around, changed some of the train packets to take off the tanks that were heading to New Brunswick, replaced them with engineering vehicles like bulldozers and headed west.

When we arrived, nobody was quite sure how big the flood was or when the Red River would crest, and for the first couple of days things were pretty low-key; we were just another agency among many, including the RCMP, fire departments, paramedics and the provincial emergency measures organization. Then, at one particular briefing, a provincial hydrological engineer stood up and told us that they'd been following the course of the flooding upstream, in North Dakota, and that not only had the flood waters not yet crested, but they were already literally off the charts.

"When will it crest?" he said. "We don't know. The water levels we're at now are beyond our water-table data for how it will respond. We don't know how far, wide or deep the flooding will be, but it will be beyond what we've seen before." He sat down to stunned silence. Nobody had realized until that point just how serious the situation really was. Nobody knew if the diversion ditches would work or if the dikes would hold. People realized for the first time that major parts of Winnipeg, one of our nation's larger cities, were in very real danger of going under water, and that literally hundreds of thousands of people in the city were at increasing risk.

We were the one organization on the ground that could lead the way, whether it was by directing planning efforts to evacuate the city, commanding operations, building or reinforcing flood barriers, doing mobile lifesaving patrols or checking on people in isolated farmhouses in case anybody was in trouble. In fact, we could do almost anything. We were self-sufficient; we had our own communications net, our own supplies of food and water, our own command and control structure and, most importantly, an incredible team of trained and motivated men and women who were ready to do whatever it took to help their fellow countrymen and women. All of a sudden we became very popular.

We divided up the province between my brigade, which took responsibility for the city of Winnipeg itself, and 1 Canadian Mechanized Brigade Group from Edmonton, commanded by my old friend Brigadier-General Bob Meating, which had the southern part of the province. We were dealing with the Manitoba government, including Premier Gary Filmon, but mostly the senior bureaucrats, the Deputy Minister for Emergency Relief and of course the local members of the provincial legislature, who were always around. We worked with civil engineers, police, medical health authorities, water and sewage folks and any others who had a role to play or something to offer. We established a solid relationship with Winnipeg's mayor, Susan Thompson, who was intimately involved in every aspect of protecting her city. We got to know this energetic lady well. City councillors representing their respective wards, federal government officials, Cabinet ministers and members of Parliament for the area were all also involved. Then, just to complicate things, a federal election was called during the flood. Throw in non-government groups like the Red Cross or St. John's Ambulance, which were running shelters for flood victims, and a host of local non-profit organizations like the Lion's Club, Rotary Club and Kinsmen, and flood relief became almost like a multinational operation abroad. And we were right in the middle of it. Our experience in these multidisciplinary approaches to an emergency gave us an edge and made me feel comfortable in our ability to help.

We often ended up with the Premier, provincial ministers and members of the provincial legislature, and members of Parliament showing up at one time. Before the flood, I don't think any of them, like most Canadians, could even have even spelled "CF." It was a slow process for them to awaken to who we were and what we could do for them, but at least it had started.

Over the next ten to fourteen days, we sent out boats to patrol flooded areas, looking for people who needed help or just generally keeping an eye on things; combat engineers built massive flood containment ditches with their heavy equipment; our quick response forces handled sudden collapses of dykes or ditches and our medics helped those who needed help. Civil authorities saw how we could coordinate and control massive operations easily. And they saw us fill sandbags—we filled lots and lots of sandbags to help keep the flood waters back.

I filled my share. Soon after we arrived I told my commanders that everyone in the brigade was going to fill at least one sandbag. "Look, we've got every soldier out here, part of our country's history in the making," I told them. "And what do you do in a flood? Fill sandbags. That's the thing that most folks think about. So we're going to make sure every single individual in our organization gets a chance to directly participate in helping people. Whether you're a medic and you get an opportunity to help folks who've sprained their ankles, a cook keeping everybody fed, or an electrical engineer making sure the generators are working and providing light and heat, I don't care. I want you to get a shovel and fill sandbags."

Everybody in the brigade got a chance to help directly, for at least a few hours. That gave us a close connection to what was happening, above and beyond our primary professional responsibilities. It also gave us a few chuckles.

One of our many visitors during that operation was General Maurice Baril, the Chief of the Defence Staff, who happened to find me while I was down at the river holding a sandbag for one of the soldiers to fill. We had been trying desperately to shore up one section of the riverbank because it looked like it was going to fail, causing a good chunk of southern Winnipeg to be inundated. He and I we were standing around talking to some of the troops, watching them fill sandbags and pass them along in a line to pile up against the bank. Baril turned to me and said, "You know, Rick, I've been watching this, and let me just tell you something. It appears to me that if you fill those sandbags completely full, and if the guys in the line stand a little farther apart, you could do the job a lot more quickly."

I said, "Sir, get in the line."

He and I both got in the sandbag line and started throwing them onto the riverbank like everyone else. After about seven minutes, General Baril said, "I see what you mean." We stood close together when we were passing those sandbags along the line and filled them half-full because when you spend up to eighteen hours a day doing it, filling sandbags can be pretty demanding. If you start filling right to the top and standing farther apart in the line, you'll be lucky to last for a couple of hours a day. The soldiers were amused that the Chief had learned the same little lesson on sandbags that they had also learned on their first day. That connected him to them, and that was good.

General Baril later sat down with us for a meal and noticed that we were eating American MRE rations (short for "meals ready to eat"). He asked me, "These are American rations. How come?" I just laughed and said, "Sir, it's a long story. You don't want to know."

What had happened was that at the end of the previous fiscal year, we had managed to build up a small surplus in our brigade budget and wanted to stock up on supplies for the coming year as a way of reducing current-year costs. We would stockpile items like vehicle parts, fuel or rations. Our complicated contract procedures, however, meant that we could not quickly buy Canadian rations, known as IMPs (individual meal packs). We could, however, go across the border to Fort Drum, New York—this is how complicated and how silly military contracting can be in Canada—and buy rations there. So we bought 50,000 American meals, all within regulations, the spirit and the letter of the rules. It was just a lot simpler to buy American rations than to get the meals that were supposedly made uniquely for the Canadian Forces, in Canada. I did tell General Baril about this later on, about how stupid our contracting system is. As I write, our contracting procedures are, if anything, more complicated and cost us millions more than we should be spending for almost any single thing we acquire.

There was a lot of news coverage about our work in Manitoba. Most reporters initially stayed pretty much to themselves, often asking questions that appeared, to us, to be trying to put a negative spin on our efforts. We distrusted them enormously, and they didn't seem to be sure who the heck we were exactly, because most journalists hadn't dealt with the military for such a long time. In fact, most, never. But once they were out for a few days with the troops working on the embankments or on the floodways, or going out in boats to help people stranded by the flood, their attitudes seemed to change.

We hosted an open-line radio show one day with some of our soldiers, from the back of an M113 armoured personnel carrier, which went over well. We had a French Canadian battalion with us, out of Valcartier, Quebec, and we put some of them in St. Norbert, with its large francophone population. They were able to communicate to the residents through a lot of local radio and television shows. By the end of the first two weeks, journalists and soldiers had gotten to know each other and started to develop a much more comfortable relationship. It didn't get in the way of objective coverage or of the journalists' telling a story, but that relationship went from a deep freeze to slightly thawed and became a part of the trigger for the much more significant thaw that we saw later in relations between the military and the media.

The Winnipeg flood changed the way many individual journalists and some news organizations viewed the Canadian Forces. They saw that we weren't an organization of ogres, bloodthirsty demons and ill-disciplined thugs. We were their men and women in uniform; their soldiers; their Canadian Forces; their sons and daughters. That's how they responded to us, and that's what they communicated to Canadians.

It all started to come together at the end of nearly two weeks in southern Manitoba. The people of Winnipeg were very appreciative of the efforts. My brigade saw a lot of gratitude from local residents, perhaps because we were in the city while the other brigade was spread out in more rural areas. As the days went on, our soldiers couldn't go into the local Tim Hortons without somebody buying them a coffee. One group of six soldiers stopped off at a restaurant on their way back from a task and sat down for a meal. When they got up to pay the bill, the waitress said, "No need—the guy who just left took care of your bill for you as his way of saying thanks for your work."

On the last day of the operation, we were preparing to move our hundreds of vehicles to the railroad yards to be loaded onto trains for the return trip to Petawawa. It's a long and tiring road from Winnipeg to eastern Ontario, particularly if you're driving the Light Support Vehicle Wheeled (LSVW), our boxy little light truck. When we moved to Winnipeg, our drivers were exhausted by the time they showed up, and a couple of kids actually had to see a doctor for physical exhaustion after driving that distance for four days in that vehicle. I said to Major-General Bruce Jeffries, who was now the army commander in western Canada, "Look, I want to fly the brigade back. We ain't driving back. Send the vehicles back by train and fly the troops home." He agreed, pushed hard up the chain of command and that's how we went home.

On the last day of our major efforts, we stopped work and

moved all of our vehicles from the southern part of Winnipeg, where the flooding was the worst and where we did most of our work, up to the rail yards in the northwest end of the city, so we could load them on the trains. We were moving in a convoy, and had to coordinate with the Winnipeg Police to provide traffic control. When Mayor Thompson found out we were moving, she and the city councillors ended up redirecting the route to take our vehicles past City Hall, in effect, turning the move into a massive parade. Schools along the route let their kids out of classes, and the children lined the road, waving along with thousands of others who came out to say thanks and farewell. We rolled four hundred vehicles past a little stand set up at City Hall. Bob Meating and I were standing next to the mayor and city councillors as all those trucks and soldiers rolled past. Soldiers were telling stories for months after that day, about how many young ladies had written out their phone numbers and tucked them into their pockets as they went by, something always good for morale!

It became an awesome, stirring event, and it turned what we had thought was going to be just a routine move to the railhead into something that got everyone in the brigade excited and fired up. It was a wonderful, coalescing, appreciative and very enjoyable moment. The reconnection of Canadians with their armed forces had started. People began to realize what great young men and women serve our country in the CF; that they are our sons and daughters and that they need to be appreciated.

The most powerful lessons for me included the fact that our best spokespeople in the CF are our most junior young men and women in uniform, and that once ordinary Canadians started showing their appreciation for us, they simply kept building on that genuine desire to look after "their" soldiers. In fact, what we saw in Winnipeg was a light at the end of a long, dark tunnel, a light that made us squint because we had been in darkness so long.

After that last big day in Winnipeg, we got the vehicles onto the trains, loaded the troops onto the air force's Airbus transports and flew them home. We managed to get everyone home for the Victoria Day weekend and gave the whole brigade extra days off to go with that long weekend so they could enjoy their success with their families. They had earned it.

People saw for themselves what I'd been saying for some time: that 98 per cent of our soldiers are decent, admirable and dedicated young men and women—a message that nobody had heard over the previous years of Somalia and other difficulties. The municipal officials, provincial officials, general public and even the media, for the first time in a long time, started to realize this; our soldiers made an instant and powerful impression on everyone. That was a key element in, and certainly one of the triggers of, the rejuvenation of the Canadian Forces and the re-establishment of our link with Canadians. The Winnipeg flood became the turning point. The flood was a dark cloud, causing massive property damage, turmoil, insecurity and fear in so many people's lives, but there was a silver lining: people bonded together and conquered adversity. The men and women of the Canadian Forces were a fundamental part of that experience. Canadians concluded that, hey, this is a pretty good organization and they've got some pretty great people out there. Although it took a while to see, that flood was the start of change for the CF.

CHAPTER 10

THAWING THE ICE

Fighting the Winnipeg flood allowed my brigade to do about 60 per cent of what we were trying to achieve in our training, short of actually fighting a battle—we set up our command and control system, ran our organization and had everybody working together. We had done all that, and done it, in my view, exceptionally well. The whole experience really helped bring my brigade headquarters together as one efficient team, which was to prove invaluable a few short months later.

The summer of 1997 was fairly uneventful. I took my little speedboat out on the river at every opportunity, and the soldiers got much-needed summer vacations. New soldiers joined the brigade, while others left for jobs elsewhere in the army, including Mike Jorgensen, who was promoted from being my operations officer to commanding one of the infantry battalions in Petawawa, the 3rd Battalion of the Royal Canadian Regiment.

That fall we began training in earnest to get one of the units ready to go to Bosnia as the deployed Canadian battle group. In preparation for the upcoming six-month tour, the 1st Battalion, Royal Canadian Regiment, now started training seriously for the deployment, which was to begin in January 1998. Their commander, Lieutenant-Colonel Peter Devlin, made a positive impression on me from the moment I met him. I had heard good things about him from others, including Bob Meating, and knew he had worked in Sarajevo for U.S. General Ric Shinseki, who later went on to be Chief of Staff of the U.S. Army and to clash with Donald Rumsfeld about the number of troops needed in Iraq after the 2003 invasion. Shinseki warned Rumsfeld that more soldiers would be needed on the ground after Saddam Hussein was defeated, a prediction that turned out to be entirely right and one that caused Rumsfeld to undercut him at every opportunity thereafter. The general left all of us in uniform with a new appreciation of what moral courage means and how important it was to give clear and blunt military advice to the powerful, no matter whether they wanted to hear it or not.

It was his own soldiers, however, who paid the greatest compliments to Peter Devlin. Since becoming brigade commander, I had been trying to address what I saw as a major problem with the Canadian Forces' failing to recognize in a reasonable amount of time the good work our soldiers did. Medals and commendations were handed out only sparingly and often years after the fact. I said to my brigade staff, "This has got to be fixed." Coincidentally, at about the time Peter Devlin was due to take command of his battalion, a subunit commendation (an award given to an entire group of soldiers) had finally worked its way through the system and landed on my desk at brigade headquarters. It was to be awarded to N (November) Company, one of the four companies that made up the 3rd Battalion RCR, for their work in Bosnia and Croatia in 1992. November Company had gone into the region as part of the first Canadian battle group and pushed through Croatia and Bosnia, confronting rogues, criminals and mass murderers time and again, to open up Sarajevo, which was under siege by the Bosnian Serbs. Now, five years later, the commendation for this company of 140 infantrymen showed up. The commander of November Company when this recognition was earned happened to have been one Peter Devlin.

I said, "Look, we're going to do this right. We're going to have this company parade in front of everybody in the brigade to get this commendation."

That's what we did. There were only about sixty soldiers who had been in Sarajevo in 1992 left in November Company, the rest having been posted to other units or, in some cases, already retired. We lined them up and recognized their bravery and achievement, even if it was five years after the fact. After everybody else on parade was dismissed, I said to that company of soldiers, "Stay right there—I want to shake everyone's hand."

I went down the line shaking their hands, laughing and talking with them. A couple of the guys said to me, "Hey, sir, we hear that Major Devlin's coming back to command 1st Battalion."

There's a healthy rivalry between the two battalions even though they're both part of the same regiment, so I expected them to be rolling their eyes or making a few jokes about him changing battalions. I said, "Yes, it's Lieutenant-Colonel Devlin now, but he's going to command that other battalion."

All those soldiers just smiled and told me, "Ah, sir, don't worry about that. He'll be over to see us."

That made a massive impression on me. For these young soldiers to be excited that their former commander was coming back, years after he served with them, and for them to be certain that he'd drop by to say hello, said a lot to me about what an impression Peter must have made on them. Never mind that he was now commanding their sister battalion—they were confident he would not forget them.

When I got to know Peter, that first impression was validated: he was one of the best officers and best leaders I've ever met. That fall he led his battalion through a preparatory exercise for Bosnia that turned into another step in connecting Canadians with their military. We decided to run an exercise that involved almost the entire brigade out in the civilian area, as opposed to in the big training area at Petawawa. We had already gone to Wainwright, Alberta, about three hours southeast of Edmonton, to watch an exercise for another unit going to the former Yugoslavia. The staff, under Bob Meating, had built a replica of their area of operations in Bosnia right on the Prairies, inside the training area. We took that idea and decided to go it one better, and turned the area around Owen Sound, Ontario, into a miniature Bosnia. We took over an old industrial plant and made that our base, set up our brigade headquarters in another little town nearby and used the entire Bruce Peninsula, an area of about 130 square kilometres, to train our soldiers. The area featured civilian traffic, children going to school, and treacherous road conditions, as did Bosnia, and we made all of those elements part of the exercise, to get the soldiers used to what conditions were really like in the former Yugoslavia.

Peter performed superbly, and the exercise was extremely well received: it became one of the most successful we ever held, not only because it helped the soldiers realistically prepare for what they would see and do in Bosnia, but because it also introduced the local population to the soldiers, who they would see driving around their streets and highways or walking through their towns. The folks around Owen Sound loved having the troops. At the end of the exercise, we held a small reception for all the region's mayors and aldermen. A couple of pipers were playing, and I got the chance to talk to the local representatives and hand out certificates of appreciation. It worked out really well.

We were on our way home the last night of the deployment, driving back to Petawawa in a small convoy that included most of my commanding officers and regimental sergeants major, when we encountered a small preview of how we'd be spending the next month. It was snowing and dark, a typical December night in Ontario, when we came upon an accident and stopped to help. A vehicle had skidded off the highway and was down in a deep ditch. A woman and her two young sons were inside. She told us her husband had gotten out of the vehicle and had left to walk the five kilometres to the nearest town to get help. There were about twenty of us, so we decided to see if we couldn't get her out of that ditch. I stood by her window and got her to slide over into the driver's seat.

"Look, just straighten the wheels and add a little bit of gas," I told her. We all started pushing, and within a few minutes we took her right up onto the road. Just as we were getting back into our vehicles, her husband returned and spent the next few minutes running around to our vehicles trying to thank us before we drove off.

The brigade got an extended Christmas break that year. The troops had been working hard and needed a little extra time off, and so, as it turned out, did I. We had a phone call from my family saying that my dad, who had been previously diagnosed with terminal cancer, was going downhill fast. One of my sisters showed up that night from Toronto. The next morning, Christmas Day, we made the decision to head back to Newfoundland on Boxing Day. We landed in St. John's at midnight, and right away I sent my exhausted mom and sisters to the hotel. I stayed at the hospital and sat up with Dad all night. He died at seven that morning. It was a tough Christmas for the Hillier family.

My dad, despite his initial reluctance to have me join the army, was extremely proud that I was a soldier. His proudest moment, I think, came after he had been told he had terminal cancer, when Joyce phoned to say I would be promoted to general. Since he was home alone when he got the call, he took great delight in getting my mom and sister to guess what news he had to tell them. I've thought about Dad every single day since he died.

No sooner had I returned to Petawawa after the funeral than heavy snow started falling, followed by icy rain. I was reading a book in front of the fireplace, Joyce was puttering around the house and our youngest son, Steven, was in the bedroom watching TV. After a while, he came out and said, "Dad, on TV, they're saying the army is going to Ottawa. They need help because of the storm."

The problems with freezing rain and ice across eastern Ontario and parts of Quebec had been in the news for a day or so, but my brigade was essentially the entire regular army in Ontario. If there had been anything happening, I thought we'd at least know about it. So I told Steven that if there was any truth to that I would be the first to know, so obviously there wasn't, and went back to my book.

About an hour and a half later, he came back out, saying, "Dad, the Prime Minister is on TV saying that the army's going to Ottawa."

This sounded a little more definitive, so I phoned my brigade staff. They hadn't heard a thing from headquarters in Toronto, but I decided that maybe we should call the command group together anyway. About 10:30 that night I called in all my commanding officers and said, "Let's have a look at this."

By then we were starting to get indications out of Toronto, where Land Forces Central Area and my superior headquarters were based, that they might need some troops, a fairly limited deployment of about 200 soldiers to Ottawa. That was enough to start us thinking, and, based on our recent experience with the Red River flood, all of us felt that if we were needed, the entire brigade would be required, not just a few soldiers.

Walt Natynczyk, the commanding officer of my old regiment, the Royal Canadian Dragoons, Kevin McCloud, the commander of my engineers, Stu Beare, the commanding officer of the Artillery regiment, and Mike Jorgensen, who was now in charge of the 3rd Battalion, Royal Canadian Regiment, sat down to brainstorm, along with Ryan Jestin, who coordinated brigade logistics, Bruce Pennington, who synchronized operations, and my regimental sergeant major, Bruce Prendergast. I left Peter Devlin, CO of the 1st RCR, out of the planning process because in the next days, he and the first troops were due to leave for Bosnia. As we talked over the situation, it quickly became clear that Ottawa and much of eastern Ontario would need our help.

I decided to recall the rest of the brigade. In my view, it was a low-risk decision to make, because the Ottawa area was in dire straits and you can't do much with just 200 people. The brigade was still scattered, quite literally, around the world. Many of my soldiers and officers were on extended vacations across Canada, and some were abroad, as far away as Malaysia. So we started the process of recalling the troops while my command team and I headed to Ottawa to show the city how well prepared the Canadian Forces were to handle these kinds of emergencies with forethought, preparation and planning.

The fact was, though, we didn't know exactly where to go. We didn't know where Ottawa-Carleton Regional Headquarters was. A few of us had lived in Ottawa before, so we had a rough idea of where it was, but we didn't know exactly, or where its emergency measures organization was based.

We drove down that ice-covered highway from Petawawa to Ottawa, at a crawl, in what was a memorable trip. The highway was slick, with sheer ice the entire way, with tree after tree on either side broken or bent almost double by the weight on the branches. When we got to Ottawa, we drove around the city trying to find our way to the Ottawa-Carleton Regional Headquarters. Here also there were trees everywhere, covered in ice and bent into the centre of the road, or broken and blocking traffic. Telephone poles and electrical towers were smashed because of the weight of the ice on the wires, which were now lying across many streets. Many, it appeared to us, were still live wires, and therefore dangerous. Hydro crews were out, trying to make sure those wires were safe, and city workers were putting in a massive effort to clear streets. Ambulances and police vehicles couldn't get anywhere because of the blocked roads. Electricity was off in most places, leaving people on the upper floors of apartment buildings, particularly the elderly and the handicapped, trapped. The power had been off for quite a while in many locations, and the temperature was down to minus 30 degrees Celsius.

It took until about three o'clock in the morning, but we finally found our way to what is now Ottawa City Hall and hooked up with the emergency measures organization there. Bob Chiarelli, who was the chair of Ottawa-Carleton Region and later mayor of Ottawa, was running the show, and we got a briefing from the regional emergency measures organization, which seemed to have a pretty good handle on the situation around the city. There were a lot of communities, however, just outside the region that were apparently in a bad way, and for which nobody had any details of what help they needed. Ottawa was running well, but Emergency Measures Ontario, responsible for the rest of the region, was nowhere to be seen.

After the first briefing, I sat with my commanding officers and, based on the information we had, designated the areas that each unit should take as its responsibility. The soldiers in the brigade were slowly making their way up that icy highway from

Petawawa and I told my operations officer that we would meet them at the Corel Centre, now called Scotiabank Place, in suburban Kanata, where the NHL's Ottawa Senators played. "Hold the brigade there," I told him, "and then we'll have them rendezvous with their commanding officers. We'll start moving out from there."

The police then took the commanding officers out to the areas that I'd designated for each of their units, while the staff set up my headquarters right in the Ottawa-Carleton Regional Centre. When the commanders came back from their three-hour reconnaissance with the police, we held a second, quick confirmatory meeting and changed the boundaries of a few of the areas to reflect the political realities. For instance, we initially had no idea where one municipality started and another began, so once we had that information, we realized it would be easier to conduct operations by adapting to it.

My commanding officers were really taken aback at the scale of the damage and destruction. There are three main power lines going into Ottawa, and two of them were down. All those massive steel hydro towers had been crushed, just one after the other. They'd broken under the weight of ice. Wires were down in hundreds of places across the region, some of them buried in the ice and snow, difficult to locate and even more difficult to recover. We did everything we could to help get the power back on.

This was clearly going to be a massive undertaking, but we had learned a lot of lessons in the Manitoba flood and applied them as soon as we hit the ground in Ottawa. My command team was all thinking along the same lines, and so was the rest of the brigade, right down the chain of command to the individual soldiers. It was incredible, particularly when you consider that while we were in eastern Ontario, we continued to deploy that battle group of some 1,200 soldiers to Bosnia. It was a magnificent effort by my officers and soldiers. We treated the operation exactly as if we were deploying into a foreign theatre, setting up areas of responsibility and dividing up the work. My operations officer laid out a map of eastern Ontario and started drawing lines, telling each battalion or regiment which area they were responsible for and what their tasks would be. We turned that plan into formal brigade orders and reinforced those units if there was a need for specialists, whether those were military police, engineering detachments or extra electricians.

What made all this work was the fact that we were going with the same team that we'd been building for eighteen months, the same team that we had taken to the flood. We'd done all our training together, were a team, knew each other and had all those lessons fresh from Winnipeg.

Walt Natynczyk and his Royal Canadian Dragoons were given responsibility for the Cumberland/Navan and Orleans area, to the east of Ottawa. When he first went out to tour his area, he brought a group of his young officers with him, all equipped with cellphones, which were still a novelty. Wherever he went during that first day, he left one of those officers, so that by the end of his first visit, he had that communication structure right across his region—somebody at every municipal level could tell him what was needed and could respond to any questions or requests. Thanks to Walt, and the other commanders, we moved the troops out of the Corel Centre and within twenty-four hours had the brigade deployed across eastern Ontario.

From the start, life and limb was our number-one priority. Number two was to stop the damage from getting worse. Number three was helping people recover from the storm. We reached a couple of Ottawa neighbourhoods early, helping the hydro and emergency crews get electrical wires off the roads so emergency vehicles and residents could get in and out. Then they started to get some phone service back, and pretty soon all that was left for the troops to do was help clean up some fallen trees. In other words, we had moved from emergency aid to beautification, not sticking to our fundamental priorities.

That's when I stepped in and said, "Let's get these guys out of here and get them to somewhere else where they're needed badly." One or two of the residents of those neighbourhoods said, "Oh no, we want them to stay and help us clean up this mess." I said, "Stop. We've got people whose lives are at risk in the next community." They all quickly realized that we'd established the right priorities and supported our move to implement them.

We had a great working relationship with the emergency measures organization in Ottawa. They would take the city's salt trucks and run them out as far as Petawawa—not part of their area of responsibility, but they did it anyway because they knew we were driving down this very slick road and they didn't want anything to happen to us en route.

Bob Chiarelli told me, that first day as we sat down to go through details of our plan, that he wanted to have a media briefing later that morning. Bob said he had been doing regular briefings every morning at about 10:30 to let the citizens of Ottawa-Carleton, and all of eastern Ontario, know what was going on and what their local government was doing about the crisis. Then he added, "There may be some interest in the fact that the military is here, so would you come and be prepared to answer any questions, Rick?"

We had been talking all morning about how we could work together, how to command and control the relief efforts and what the Canadian Forces could offer. I thought that with all the lessons we'd learned from Winnipeg, and my guys being so well organized, it would be a good opportunity to bring the work of our soldiers to the public domain. So I said, "Sure, I'd be happy to participate." Naively, I walked into a room full of media with the EMO guys and sat down with Bob, his Chief of Police, the head of Emergency Services, the Chief Administrative Officer for the region and a variety of officials from across the city and eastern Ontario.

There were dozens of media outlets represented from across Canada, as well as a crew from CNN, and with all of those important people there, the only person they wanted to talk to was the man in uniform. Unfortunately, it was like going back to the first couple of days of the Red River flood: the journalists seemed to feel that there was something negative going on and their job was to find and expose it.

One of the first questions was "How many soldiers are you bringing here?"

"Up to a couple of thousand," I said. "I'm going to flow the brigade in and then see what's going on before we decide if more are needed."

"Well, the Defence Minister said there were 894 coming. So you're saying something different than your Minister. How do you explain that?"

I just shrugged. "I don't know, I can't tell you how many soldiers are going to flow here. I want to bring in the right number
to do the job, and I'll keep my chain of command and obviously
the Minister informed of what we're doing. He'll provide me any
direction that he needs to, through the chain of command." That
was my first experience talking to the national media in Ottawa.
Within two days, however, their skepticism largely disappeared

and, as in Manitoba, we developed a warmer relationship.

We were still bringing troops in. We'd discovered that the
volunteer organizations and emergency workers who had been
doing most of the work in the early going were exhausted after
working non-stop for three, four or five days. We had a role to
play in trying to stabilize the situation and offering psychological
security, which is perhaps the most important element that we
brought to the relief effort. Of course we offered real and direct
help in cleaning and opening up streets, helping hydro crews
to get electricity back on or relieving stressed-out paramedics
or staff in shelters where people were going because their heat
wasn't on. Mostly, though, we were out there in the communities, providing a presence that reassured people.

I wanted everyone in my brigade to make the same kind of
hands-on contribution that they had filling sandbags during the
flooding, but we had a different challenge during the ice storm. I
thought that we could have all the soldiers clear up some downed
wiring, but my command team quickly told me, "No, no, sir—we
shouldn't have the boys touching electrical wiring." There wasn't,
unfortunately, any one specific thing that everyone could do,
because it was a whole different kettle of fish. So we simply did
everything necessary.

We had a huge issue with generators, for example. They were in short supply, and we searched everywhere to find more. Our electricians at one point worked with the railroad to move a locomotive into a small town southeast of Ottawa, hook that big train engine into the local electrical grid, and power that community from the massive diesel engine sitting there chugging away.

As always in those kinds of events, what really counted was people. Not organizations, or systems or bureaucracy or process—people. Stu Beare, Mike Jorgensen and Walt Natynczyk brought confidence and assurance with them to spread wherever they went. Lieutenant-Colonel Hilary Jaeger, the commander of my field ambulance unit, now a brigadier-general and Surgeon General for the Canadian Forces, did just incredible work coordinating with the regional health authorities to send her young medics, doctors and nurses to provide badly needed emergency medical support around the communities. Hilary's medics weren't providing major health services; it was just that people were stressed, and sometimes slapping a Band-Aid on somebody made all the difference in the world to reduce that stress. That's often all they needed, and those actions usually kept a molehill from becoming a mountain.

Our soldiers saved lives during the crisis as well. Two of them were making their way into the town of Hawkesbury, north of Cornwall, Ontario, during the storm, and as they passed a farmhouse, one said, "There's a flicker in that window."

They went up to the house to check. No lights were on, but there was still a flicker. The older couple that lived there had gone to bed and left some candles burning on the coffee table. By the time those two soldiers passed by, the living room was on fire and these folks were still sound asleep. The soldiers kicked the door open and managed to put the fire out, all without waking the couple sleeping upstairs.

A couple of other soldiers were out doing a standard patrol through one of the Ottawa neighbourhoods that were without phone coverage. They stopped at one home and could hear a generator going inside the house somewhere, but couldn't see it. One of the guys, a mechanic, realized that the generator was inside the garage that was attached to the house. They went and tapped on the door, rang the doorbell, pounded on the door—nothing. They finally kicked the door open and found the entire family lying unconscious, knocked out by the carbon monoxide from the generator exhaust that had seeped through the walls from the garage. They got the windows open, got the family out and saved their lives.

I talked to the media on a regular basis to make sure that they and the rest of Canada knew what those young soldiers were doing. Of course some of them were always trying to dig out the dark lining in the silver cloud. One reporter said to me, "Rumour has it that the Canadian Forces are trying to blow this emergency into something greater than it is, just for your own benefit."

"You know something?" I replied. "I don't have an answer for that question, beyond the fact that I consider it ridiculous. Look, don't ask me the question, ask the people around this region, the ones who haven't got electricity, don't have their stove on, have no heating system in their house, don't have phone communications and haven't been able to get out of their neighbourhood or their street or their farm for days. It's still 30 below. It's going to be 30 below for quite a while, and that electricity is not going to be restored for a long time. If you've heard something like that, I'll bet it came from somebody in a nice warm apartment here in the centre of Ottawa who doesn't have those worries. It certainly wouldn't come from those folks, but ask them anyway."

That rumour died right there, because the people around the Ottawa region were quick to say, "Actually, we want those soldiers here. We don't want them to go anywhere."

Our soldiers had arrived in the dark, literally and in terms of our organizational knowledge. There were no Canadian Forces plans or preparations for this situation. Very few relationships existed between the military and the civil authorities, and those that did were superficial. There was no obvious involvement from the Ontario government. It was just us, working with the people on the ground in eastern Ontario, and everything we did—however well it was done—was ad hoc. It was our people, incredible and talented, using their initiative, training, common sense and ability to deal with chaos, who brought first psychological comfort to stressed residents, and then real pragmatic assistance.

Every night I brought all my commanding officers together, talked through the situation in each region and then gave them any additional direction. During the day, I visited them in their areas and saw first-hand the challenges and how they were being handled. One night I brought in a group of Ontario deputy ministers and other officials, including Jim Young, the Chief Coroner. They sat in on the briefings along with Bob Chiarelli and by the end were astounded at how quickly and efficiently the Canadian Forces can work. We were showing them what my brigade command team could do, with focused briefings, offering solutions as part of the discussion of problems, discussion of future issues and then orders from me, confirming what we would be doing next. They found it quite incredible and, I think, started to develop an appreciation for what we could actually bring to the table.

What was still missing from that table was the Ontario government. We got almost nothing out of the provincial government in Toronto in supplies or assistance. Emergency Measures Ontario was simply not a player, because they tried to do everything from Toronto, and as a result were out of touch with what was happening in eastern Ontario. After the first few days, Premier Mike Harris came to visit with a half-dozen of his ministers and deputy ministers and I sat down to talk to them. We were still facing significant challenges: icy rain falling, electricity still off in many places, communications not working, heat off in many homes in the area and temperatures continuing to hover around minus 30 Celsius. We were still trying to get to people in apartment buildings or in isolated farmhouses, particularly older people. The military and the Ottawa-Carleton Region command teams expected that people might still be dying as a result of these problems, and I thought the provincial government could be doing much more. I gave a short, off-the-cuff briefing and at the end of it Mr. Harris asked me, "What do you think, General?"

I said, "Mister Premier, let me just tell you something. Unless the Province gets its act together and gets us more resources to do certain things, like medical services and paramedics, delivery of food, delivery of water, additional generators and all of that kind of stuff, you're going to have people dying needlessly. People dying who could otherwise be saved."

I was being blunt, but I thought it needed to be said. A

bunch of his ministers were sitting around the room, and from the looks on their faces they had obviously told him something very different. So Harris said, "General, would you excuse us for a couple of minutes?"

"Yes, sir," I said and went outside the room and drank my fiftieth coffee of the day.

A few minutes later, the Premier asked me back inside, turned to me and said, "General, we're going to do all that we can do."

The next day representatives from EMO began showing up at our brigade headquarters and started to bring their resources into the region to help.

One of the things complicating our lives was the new Municipal Act in Ontario, which had abolished the old munici-palities and set up new ones, merging a lot of city councils or regional governments and doing away with others. The act had gone into effect on midnight of December 31, just days before the ice storm struck, so we were caught in a governmental limbo. There were fifty-three municipalities in the region in a state of crisis because of the storm, and fifty-two of them did not yet have elected municipal councils because of that new law. Most of the councillors showed up to help anyhow, but they did so with-out any legal mandate or regulatory powers. In some cases our commanders ended up filling the gap left by the new law.

By the end of two weeks we were deployed across every part of eastern Ontario. The people in Perth wanted to adopt Stu Beare and his unit of gunners. Those in Alexandria, where 3 RCR was operating, wanted Mike Jorgensen and his Royals to stay, too. They wanted to keep those guys forever. The relation-ships between the brigade and the people in these towns became incredibly close. I walked into the emergency operations centre in Alexandria and discovered that 3 RCR was running the whole show. Soldiers were taking calls from residents about fire, water, town services and everything else. People were showing up in their trucks and two or three soldiers would load up fuel or some water or whatever they needed. Their operations officer was running it all: he was effectively the town administrator. I had to grab some of my commanders, these incredible Canadians, and tell them, "Hold on, you guys are not the mayors of those towns. You've got to support these people and help them out, but you are going to have to start backing out of here."

When we tried to go home after two weeks, nobody wanted us to leave. Every politician in the region was afraid to be the one who let the Canadian Forces leave, but by then the situation had improved so much that we were becoming part of the problem. A lot of soldiers were living in schoolhouses, for instance. Now that the power was back on, kids needed to go back to school and we had to move out to facilitate that. We had troops living on City of Ottawa buses, which sooner or later would have to return to service. We had a great relationship with the bus drivers, who quickly became part of our team. A couple of OC Transpo drivers even took their buses all the way to Petawawa with their thirty or so troops on board, without the permission of the transit authorities. They just wanted to make sure their soldiers got home safely and comfortably in the middle of winter. (It remains hugely satisfying to see the OC Transpo buses serving Ottawa, each with a large "Support Our Troops" yellow ribbon displayed.)

The reaction of the people across eastern Ontario and in Ottawa was phenomenal, so positive and from a broad spectrum of the populace. It became another step in the rejuvenation of the Canadian Forces. I went on an Ottawa radio talk show with Lowell Green while we were deployed, just talking to people and telling them what "their" soldiers were doing to help them. The response was just incredible. The Ice Storm of the Century gave us the chance to say to Canadians that the Canadian Forces are here and, if you need help, we'll be there for you.

We even had the opportunity to get that message out across the country. I had about 150 soldiers of the Royal Newfoundland Regiment come in to be part of our brigade effort, and I said on TV, "This is awesome. Every dark cloud has a silver lining. Here I am, a Newfoundlander who has always wanted a Newfoundland unit under my command, and the ice storm is the vehicle that allowed me to do it." The Royal Newfoundland Regiment saw that on television while they were forming up in the armoury at St. John's and were even more excited to come to Ottawa. The people in Ottawa were certainly excited to have them.

At the same time as we were doing this operation, I was constantly going back and forth to Petawawa. We had decided to let the deployment of 1st Battalion, Royal Canadian Regiment, to Bosnia continue, and we were sending out 170 troops a day. I was flying to Petawawa by helicopter for the most part, and whenever I returned, my helicopter would land in front of Ottawa-Carleton Regional Headquarters. In order to make that approach, we had to fly by National Defence Headquarters at just the right height to look straight into the Chief of the Defence Staff's office. I would land, walk into my brigade headquarters and, within ten minutes, General Baril, the Chief, would be over to find out what was going on. He'd see the helicopter come in and stop by the first opportunity he got. He didn't interfere, but he wanted to keep in touch with events on the ground.

I was only about 750 metres from Parliament Hill, so we had visits from senior military officers, members of Parliament and more VIPs than we knew what to do with. Prime Minister Chrétien came and, of course, as soon as he showed up so did sixty-five toadies, all trying to get into the same helicopter with the Prime Minister or have their picture taken with him. There were members of Parliament, former members of Parliament and wannabe members of Parliament, all jockeying for position, a spectacle we found entertaining.

There was a little going-away event the last night the brigade was in town, with the staff at Ottawa-Carleton Region, who we worked most closely with. After we were back in Petawawa, the region held a concert at the Corel Centre, and at their insistence we sent down several hundred troops. We marched the soldiers into the centre of the arena to the applause of what must have been twenty thousand people. I was on my way to Bosnia, to visit the battalion that had just arrived there, so I stopped in the Corel Centre on my way to the airport and wound up on stage with Max Keeping, the popular Ottawa television news anchor, and singer Wayne Rostad and had the chance to talk to all those ordinary people in the crowd. I told them how proud all of us in the brigade were to be part of what turned out to be a great community effort. I told them that what the Canadian Forces had done for them during the ice storm was all part of our mission and the whole reason we were in uniform in the first place: to look after Canadians when things go wrong. It was another great day, in a string of great days, to be a soldier.

CHAPTER 11

FORT HOOD, TEXAS

After the ice storm, planning for the promotions and careers of the senior officers in the Canadian Forces began to culminate. I expected to be sent to Kingston. The idea was for me to get a postgraduate degree, probably at Royal Military College, in military science, political science or business administration. Sure enough, a posting message arrived in early February 1998 from Bill Leach, Commander of the Army, saying exactly that and indicating, privately, that after I'd completed my studies, I would go to Division Headquarters in Kingston, get promoted from brigadier to major-general and command the army's field forces. Joyce and I started to prepare for that move, but for some reason I never actually got around to applying for a postgrad program. Doug Bland, a retired officer occupying a research chair at Queen's University, called me, saying, "You'd better get your ass in gear and get enrolled in the program, because the deadline's upon us." However, I still procrastinated and, before

I was forced into doing the administrative work necessary, Fort Hood, Texas, beckoned.

The Fort Hood posting resulted from work begun by Leach, who had recognized that the United States is the one country in the world whose relationship with Canada is fundamentally important to our economic and military security. Bill felt that the Canadian Forces had a part to play in reinforcing that relationship, and knew that such relationships are not built in a day, a week, a month or even a year. They're based on mutual respect and credibility that develop over a long time. During the 1980s and 1990s, Canada had been lacking in the eyes of the Americans, and the Canadian Forces, in particular, had become a less than credible allied force. To help rebuild our credibility, Bill started the process of reconnecting us with the United States military. He wanted to do it at the most senior levels, with a general, because there really is a distinction in the U.S. Army between general officers and those below them in rank. As a U.S. Army general, a leader in their nation, you get unparalleled access and opportunities, and the chance to make an impact at a level undreamt of in Canada.

It took a long time to set up, but in the spring of 1998 we reached an agreement with the U.S. Army to send a Canadian general to the Third Corps (III Corps), United States Army, in Fort Hood, Texas. The officer would become the deputy commanding general of III Corps, which was an enormous organization of close to 100,000 soldiers, nearly half of them based at Fort Hood itself. The Corps was responsible for operations around the world and was at the cutting edge of military technology.

As this program was being agreed upon, I was mentally preparing to leave the brigade after a two-year command, which had zoomed by. I went to visit a squadron of the Royal Canadian Dragoons that was training in Fort Hood, spent two days with them and then flew to Toronto to attend the General Officers' Seminar, where the CDS had all his general and flag officers together to discuss the major issues for the CF. During a break, Bill Leach grabbed me and said, "How flexible are you about your posting?"

I said, "What do you mean?"

"It looks like you might be getting the Fort Hood posting, and it's coming together very quickly. Would you be interested, and could your family move with you?"

I was pleasantly surprised, and said I would be interested, which was perhaps the understatement of my career. In fact, I was trying hard to hide my enthusiasm. I had been enthralled by the "Great Place," as Fort Hood is nicknamed in U.S. Army circles, when I was there on the small unit exchange in 1978 and had enjoyed my recent visit immensely.

My promotions had come quickly, and I was still considered young to be a general. There had already been a little jealousy from some officers who had been colonels at the same time and it was expressed to me, in a variety of ways, by several of them. Two or three made comments to General Baril after news of my promotion to brigadier-general came out, asking why I was promoted. To them, I wasn't even eligible; I'd been a colonel for only a short time and the eligibility for promotion was twenty-four months.

One of those colonels, who left the Canadian Forces shortly afterwards, asked me the same question and told me he had also put it to Baril. I was a little disappointed in him and the few others like him, but I never saw or heard it anywhere else. The soldiers seemed pretty comfortable with the idea of my promotion. In Bosnia the troops went out of their way to congratulate me, unsolicited. They were really happy to see that promotion come through and were happy I was becoming their commander back in Petawawa, all of which was heartwarming. There was no better compliment I could have received.

I got the official word three weeks later, near the end of March 1998, that the Texas posting was on, so Joyce, our younger son, Steven, and I left the snowbanks in Petawawa for a house-hunting trip to Texas. We drove to Toronto, flew out during a full-scale blizzard (it's a miracle the army wasn't called in to help!) and arrived in Dallas to 29 degrees Celsius temperatures and sunny skies. I had been a little worried about how the family would react to the change, which was more than just moving to a new town or province—this was a completely different experience. On top of that, we didn't know anybody there. Our first thought, sitting in the garden at the guest house in that warm sun, was "Yup, we could live here."

We—and I stress *we*, because the family was all-important to the U.S. Army and particularly in III Corps—were welcomed warmly by Lieutenant-General Tom Schwarz, the Corps commander, and his command team. The U.S. Army really reached out and wrapped its arms around us. I mean, they looked after our housing, getting us moved in, hiring staff and everything else needed. They brought us into the fold completely and made it clear they wanted to have us there. The relationship was important to them.

Over the next several days we got a chance to see the housing and the community and to meet our neighbours, which in

our case included the Corps Chief of Staff and the garrison commander, and to familiarize ourselves with this enormous military
city. The garrison commander in particular, Colonel Dave Hall,
and his wife, Sue, spent lots of time with us, starting a friendship
that gets stronger every year.

Meanwhile, I got an introduction to the Corps command
structure and the different divisions and brigades that were part
of it. The fort itself was massive, with lines of tanks and fighting
vehicles, artillery and engineering vehicles that ran for 11 kilometres. The population on the base on any one day was about
250,000 people, including the soldiers, civilian employees and
their families. This was slightly different from Petawawa!

After about three days, Joyce and Steven told me to go back
to Petawawa and organize the move; they'd stay in Texas. This
attitude probably had something to do with the fact that it was
still snowing in Petawawa. We all went back anyway, packed up
our things and left Petawawa in July, four months later. True to
form, I handed over command of the soldiers in Petawawa to my
good friend Matt Macdonald. We reluctantly left those awesome
young men and women and, less reluctantly, left Ontario and
headed south. We drove first to Washington, D.C., then to Ten-
nessee, where we had a chance to reconnect with friends from
Fort Knox all those years ago, and then on to Texas. The first
day we crossed the state border gave a new meaning for us to
the words "warm welcome." Temperatures near Texarkana were
hovering around 43 degrees Celsius, which was unbelievably hot
for this boy from Newfoundland.

I started work right away, trying to carve out a niche for
a Canadian officer as a deputy commander of III Corps, which

now had two deputy commanders, one responsible for support and the other for training and operations. I was charged with training, most of which was focused on getting ready for Bosnia and Kosovo, where the Corps was deploying units as part of the NATO force. My previous experience there was invaluable.

III Corps was twice the size of our entire regular-force army, and those were just the elements located in Fort Hood. There were other units in Fort Carson, Colorado, throughout the state of Texas and across the U.S. Southwest. The sheer scale and scope of the Corps' assets were incredible. At one point I was in Fort Polk, Louisiana, with responsibility for running the validation training exercise for the units getting ready to deploy overseas (similar to what we did near Owen Sound for Peter Devlin's unit, just on a much grander scale). I was in charge of the Corps headquarters, most of 10th Mountain Division out of Fort Drum, New York, a good chunk of the 49th Texas National Guard Division, the 2nd Armored Cavalry Regiment (which provided opposition forces for the training) and support teams from Fort Leavenworth and Fort Polk itself. It all made me just stop and marvel at what an incredible opportunity it was to get to lead so many soldiers. I had expected command of 2 Canadian Mechanized Brigade Group in Petawawa to be my last chance to "soldier." Instead, I found myself in command of more soldiers than the Chief of the Land Staff in Canada. It was sheer enjoyment, and though it was lots of hard work and much time away from my family, it was immensely satisfying. You just couldn't go anywhere in Texas as a soldier without someone patting you on the back, shaking your hand or simply saying "thank you." Joyce and I remarked numerous times that it would be incredible if something like that occurred in Canada.

I stood out on that post, the only Canadian in uniform among tens of thousands of soldiers in III Corps. A couple of American generals had trouble with the idea of a Canadian as a deputy commander at first, but Joyce and I very quickly became well known in the Fort Hood area and everyone soon accepted us as their own. It helped that Dennis Reimer, the Chief of Staff of the U.S. Army at the time, had personally pushed the exchange program through to fruition. I attended a video teleconference with almost the entire command structure of the U.S. Army, including division commanders and Corps staff from every corner of the world appearing on twelve different TV screens. I happened to be sitting in one corner, minding my own business, when General Reimer interrupted the briefing to say how glad he was to see Rick Hillier, a Canadian officer, as part of the team. He went out of his way to welcome me into the fold. His personal leadership and attention helped ensure the exchange was going to work. It re-emphasized for me a simple fact of leadership: what the commander or boss is interested in, the staff, units or bureaucrats will be interested in.

Having a Canadian exchange officer so high up in the command structure did cause a degree of concern in other quarters, however, and some of the right-wing militias in Texas who liked to go off the deep end on what they called "patriotism" went on a rant about having a foreigner in such a sensitive job. Soon after we arrived in Fort Hood, a late-night radio talk show in Austin, Texas, had a vitriolic, over-the-edge diatribe (it sounded a bit like Fox TV!) about how alarming it was that this Canadian general in Fort Hood was getting access to all of their military secrets. It all seemed a bit silly to me, but it turned into something of a serious security concern when the FBI reported that some groups on the far right were thinking about how they could get at us, the foreigners, somehow. It got to the point where we had to install significant security in our house, with alarms and a plan for how the military police would respond to those threats, just in case anything ever came from them.

The Military Police brigade in III Corps took its job very seriously and had a well-rehearsed plan for responding should anyone ever show up intent on harming us. They were going to seal off the neighbourhood and then move in to surround our house and deal with whatever intruders were present. They were ready to respond in minutes, as we found out for ourselves a few months after arrival.

One day while both Joyce and I were away and Steven was home alone, a massive thunderstorm was making its way through the area. Steven was fifteen and a very independent young man. He had been at the back of the house, in his bedroom, reading, when he heard a pounding on the door.

I was out in the middle of the desert in California on a field exercise when my cellphone rang. It was Steven. "Dad," he whispered, "there are guys with guns trying to come through the doors. What should I do?"

The storm had triggered the silent alarm system, and all Steven could see out his bedroom window was bunch of guys with guns at the front door and a bunch more guys with guns coming over the backyard fence headed for the back door. "Dad, what should I do?" he asked a second time.

"Steven," I told him, "move very slowly. Speak loudly, clearly, tell them who you are and keep your hands in view at all times. Beyond that, you're on your own and I'll see you Friday."

The military police response team quickly figured out that it had just been a false alarm and let Steven return to his book. It happened again several months later, when we had some friends from Canada as dinner guests. One, Brigadier-General Ed Gosselin, the Commandant of the Canadian Forces Staff College, went to use the washroom. When he came back he said, "You know there's this switch in there that wasn't working. I kept hitting it and it wasn't turning on the light in the bathroom." What he thought was a light switch was the "panic" button that triggered the alarm.

"Okay, boys," I told them. "Everybody stay quiet and I'll go down to the driveway and explain what happened." I got to spend a few minutes explaining to a group of heavily armed military policemen that no, we were not being held hostage by a far-right militia, and that these scruffy-looking individuals were all my friends.

Because of, or perhaps in spite of, all the precautions, nothing ever happened. People in the Fort Hood area and Texans in general welcomed us with open arms, wrapped them around us and made us feel welcome. We met people from every part of society, from judges and sheriffs to senators and congressmen to the workers who mowed lawns and ran the routine operations around the post that kept us all functioning. I met the Lieutenant Governor and most of the state Cabinet, and had the opportunity to teleconference from Bosnia with the Governor of Texas, George W. Bush. Joyce and I were both made honorary citizens of Bell County, where Fort Hood was situated, and honorary citizens of Texas.

I also got to meet and work with most senior commanders of the U.S. Army and National Guard as well as FBI, State Department, USAID and Department of Defense officials. This job was in the middle of their army, filling one of their senior appointments, and I was engaged in everything.

It was an invaluable experience, not just in how to train, operate and deploy a big formation of soldiers, but also because of the people we met, befriended and served with there. Ten years later, I'm still tripping over them, now in appointments in Europe, Korea, Bosnia—all of those folks were the same ones that I was dealing with when I commanded the army and later when I became Chief of the Defence Staff. David McKiernan, former ISAF commander and later overall commander of coalition forces in Afghanistan, was one of the division commanders when I was in Fort Hood.

It also turned out to be two of our best years as a family. Our older son, Chris, was attending college in Ottawa, but came down a couple of times a year to stay with us, and he and I would overdose on golf. Steven, who was with us, participated in many activities in the local community, including the Junior ROTC program in high school, summer camp in San Antonio, leadership seminars and charitable drives for numerous causes. All the while, he remained an army cadet back in Canada and spent six weeks at cadet camp each summer in Borden, Ontario.

We came to love Texas and Texans, the Southern states and the United States of America. In June of 2000 we had one of our more memorable experiences, when I was asked to represent both III Corps and Canadian army commanders at the opening of the D-Day museum in New Orleans. The ceremony was held on the anniversary of D-Day, June 6, so Joyce, Steven and I spent five days in New Orleans along with twenty thousand veterans and celebrities who were in town for a massive parade to mark the occasion. We met many of the participants, those who had driven this project to remember, including Tom Hanks, Steven Spielberg, Tom Brokaw, the military historian Stephen Ambrose and George McGovern, the former presidential candidate, who had been a bomber pilot during the Second World War. Most enjoyable was meeting hundreds of veterans, including those who had gone ashore on Omaha and Utah beaches on D-Day. Getting celebrities onside and using them, in the most positive sense, to achieve things for your country, was something I made a mental note to remember.

Working as deputy corps commander taught me lesson after lesson about how to run a large military organization, but more importantly, how to be a better leader. The U.S. Army and III Corps in particular did everything possible to enable their people to be successful. They planned seriously for international and domestic operations, gave their soldiers the right equipment, maintained an operational focus and made sure their leaders were visible to their soldiers. They had commanders who backed up their words with actions.

One of the things that most impressed me was how they looked after people, especially families, through housing, community programs and school support. One small but important example was that on the first day of school every year, the Corps started work late in order to give every soldier the opportunity to take his or her child to school for that important day. During each quarter of the year, schools would send the Corps a list of soldiers who had not been present for parent-teacher meetings at their children's school. Those soldiers were called in and asked why they hadn't gone to that parent-teacher interview. An alternate time would then be arranged when the soldier, spouse and child could go to meet the teacher. Attention to detail was phenomenal: they really kept a close eye on the welfare of their soldiers and their families.

It was a stark contrast to what was happening in Canada at the time. This was the year when the House of Commons Standing Committee on National Defence and Veterans Affairs was completing hearings across the country and listening to family after family of our soldiers, sailors, airmen and airwomen talk, and in some cases scream, about the many problems they faced. The pay we gave our troops was miserable, the housing on bases was pathetic, the training was visibly inadequate and the feeling among soldiers and their families was that their country cared not a whit about them. I looked around me at what was being done in Fort Hood and asked myself why it could not be the same in Canada.

Joyce and I were involved with so many events linking the Corps to local, state and national leaders that we developed an incredible appreciation for the importance of tying the military into the community. We participated in junior leadership programs in the towns outside the fort, and attended businessmen's lunches, ice-cream socials, hail and farewells, military committee discussions in various communities and what seemed like thousands of parades and rodeos across Bell County. Fred Latham, the mayor of Killeen, and his wife, Rene, became close friends, as did city councillor Kathy Gilmore and her husband,

Wayne. In addition to its focus on families and connecting to the community around them—and in part because of this—III Corps also focused on training and operations to a degree that the Canadian Forces just couldn't match. We were still a bureaucracy, putting much more of our time, resources and attention on process and little on product—getting soldiers out the door and carrying out missions, both at home and abroad on behalf of Canada. The Americans made product the priority. It was mandatory in the U.S. Army that their front-line units maintain 95 per cent readiness, having their soldiers trained, vehicles ready to go, units tested and prepared for overseas operations. That rule drove everything.

In Canada, it would have been a miracle if we'd achieved 50 per cent readiness in any of those categories. What I saw in III Corps was an organization that could do what it was designed to do without trying to carry everything on the backs of their soldiers. They had the right equipment, the right training and the right support to do the job. It was an incredible learning experience to sit and absorb and to be part of it while we were there.

Physical fitness was a priority in the Corps, and the leaders at the most senior levels understood the importance of doing that fitness training together to build camaraderie and teamwork. Every morning at 6:30, soldiers in the Corps would come to attention while "Reveille" was played over loudspeakers across the base, followed by the U.S. national anthem. Then all the units would go on a run together. It was a big deal, with the Corps and division, brigade and battalion commanders in front of their soldiers, setting an example. To celebrate the official birthday of the

U.S. Army in 2000, during our last few weeks in Hood, we had a Corps run, led by the commanding general himself, with me and the Corps staff right behind him and every unit in the Corps following us. It turned into a huge community event. The 1st Cavalry Division band was at the starting line, playing music through the whole run. The ladies in the local grocery store stayed up all night making a twenty-four-square-foot birthday cake saying "Happy Birthday U.S. Army." There were almost 40,000 soldiers on the 8-kilometre run, so many that by the time we finished— and the Corps staff finished first because we'd started first—the last units still had not left the starting line. That event produced an incredible energy and gave all of us the feeling that we were part of one big team.

The other major lesson I drew from Fort Hood was the importance of recognizing people and rewarding them for a job well done. When they recognized soldiers in III Corps with medals or commendations, they made sure everyone was there to be a part of it. The Corps commander, people from the community, the soldiers' families—everyone came out to watch and participate in these parades. When I compared it to how the Canadian Forces had handled the subunit commendation for N Company that I had presented in Petawawa, it was night and day. "Compared to these guys we've got a recognition system for our soldiers that's based in the '90s," I told my Canadian colleagues who came down occasionally to visit me. "Unfortunately, it's the 1890s."

I saw an example of the American approach while I was in Bosnia with 1st Cavalry Division, one of our units, in the spring of 1999. I had trained the brigades going in and visited frequently to validate the training and refresh my knowledge of the situation for future workups. On the first night I was there, a special forces team snatched a PIFWC (pronounced "Piff-Wick"), a person indicted for war crimes, who happened to be the senior Bosnian Serb commander for northeastern Bosnia. He was grabbed from his home in the wee hours of the morning by an American commando team, brought into the U.S. base at Tuzla and hustled onto a plane, and was in The Hague at the International Criminal Tribunal for the former Yugoslavia literally before breakfast. Due to a communications screw-up, word about this operation wasn't passed down to the U.S. battle groups in the area. Later that morning an American major and his driver headed to the Bosnian Serb headquarters, unaware of what had occurred. They arrived to find a very angry group of Serb soldiers and officers, all of them agitated that their "innocent" commander had been forcibly abducted.

The situation had all the potential of a major confrontation and could even have gotten these two Americans killed. If American soldiers had died, it could well have caused the Dayton Peace Accord to implode, but the major's young driver, a private, displayed incredible coolness and composure, even though he must have been scared to death, and managed to defuse things over a period of three or four hours. Despite the death threats from the Serbs, their weapons pointing at him and the physical abuse he took, that young man calmed everybody around him, kept the situation sufficiently peaceful that there were no shots fired and got both himself and his major out of there in one piece.

All of that happened before noon. By six o'clock that night, his division commander, Major-General Kevin Byrnes, was awarding him the Medal of Bravery in front of the headquarters staff. He stood that young soldier up in front of two hundred people he worked with, told them what a great man he was, what a great American he was, what a great soldier he was, what a great job he'd done, how brave he was, how proud he was of him, and pinned the medal on his chest. That kid must have felt fifteen feet tall.

In contrast, about a year later I tried to get a Deputy Chief of the Defence Staff Commendation for one of my officers in Bosnia. When I asked Ottawa to approve the commendation quickly so I could award it to him while he was still in theatre among the people he had achieved so much with, the answer was "No, we're going to follow the normal process." The normal process took months, sometimes years, and I thought, "You know something? That is not the way to recognize soldiers. Process is for bureaucrats."

Two years in Fort Hood also gave me the chance to soldier with and become friends (sometimes very good friends) with some of the best future generals and leaders in the U.S. military. Many of the colonels and brigadier-generals I worked with in Texas have gone on to become Corps commanders, running operations around the world with the U.S. Army or on behalf of NATO. Dick Cody, for instance, became the Vice Chief of Staff of the U.S. Army. He and I golfed together, and worked and trained hard together as well. Dave McKiernan, the general who became the overall NATO commander in Afghanistan, was a division commander at Fort Hood when I was there. I got to know him very well and to appreciate what an incredible guy he is, so much so that when I heard that Dave was to be given command of ISAF, I had confidence that our troops there were in good hands.

Building on those relationships was an important step for everything that I did afterwards. I had personal links to the U.S. Army's entire chain of command, from the very top almost to the bottom. We weren't just peers; we were also friends who could talk frankly to each other on the key issues. After my time in Fort Hood, they viewed me as one of them. I had had the same responsibilities within III Corps that their own generals had.

This is not to say that I became "Americanized." In fact, my experiences in Fort Hood confirmed for me that the most important thing about being a leader is to be yourself, and in my case that meant being a Canadian, the lone Canadian uniform among a sea of American uniforms. I learned a lot from the way the U.S. Army did things, but when I came to apply those lessons, I put a Canadian thumbprint on them. For instance, the Americans insisted upon keeping the arrival of the bodies of their fallen soldiers from Iraq or Afghanistan completely out of the public eye. We did exactly the opposite and made everything as public as possible. I felt quite strongly that Canadians needed to see the sacrifice their soldiers had made, needed to show their appreciation and needed to be part of that public grieving process. The families of the fallen soldiers needed that public support to help them cope with their loss.

The relationships I fostered in Fort Hood paid off for the Canadian Forces and Canada in some significant ways. When we were trying to get helicopters that we so badly needed in Afghanistan in the last year of my term as CDS, I reached out to Dick Cody. I asked him, "Can we get six Chinooks flying in Afghanistan?"

Dick made it happen. Within two days, they had laid out a purchase plan and a transfer agreement, how they could help train our pilots to fly them, how they'd flow our guys into an operational unit to give them some front-line flying experience—and all that came about because of the credibility and the relationships that we had built with them. Without that, we would not have gotten those helicopters, the true workhorse for operations that enables success and reduces risk, flying in Afghanistan.

CHAPTER 12

BACK TO BOSNIA

When I left Texas in 2000, I was asked by Bill Leach to command the Multinational Division Southwest in Bosnia. This was partly because of the experience I had in Bosnia already, but also because a big part of my responsibilities in the U.S. had been training the units III Corps was sending over there. It all happened quite quickly. We moved out of Fort Hood and occupied our new house in Ottawa on August 4. On August 5, I left to spend three weeks training my headquarters and was then deployed to Bosnia. As I was going out the door, knowing I was going to be away for more than a year, Joyce looked at me over the pile of unpacked boxes crammed into the entrance. It was not a pleasant look!

Commanding a division in Bosnia gave me the opportunity to put some of the things I had learned in Fort Hood into practice, with a Canadian twist. Because my division was made up of so many different nationalities, I had to develop significant relationships with the British, Dutch and Czech militaries and had to build my headquarters from the ground up.

We broke new ground in training that division headquarters. Up until then, Canada had little experience in training, equipping and organizing any units bigger than a battle group (about 1,000 soldiers) for an overseas operation. Training was now viewed almost as a luxury in the Canadian Forces since so much had been cancelled due to budgetary concerns. What training we did get to execute was always at the very lowest levels: usually individuals and occasionally, for a very specific mission, something greater. Now Canada was faced with the monumental task of pulling together a large organization, a division headquarters for Bosnia, and setting it up with soldiers from nine different countries in a fairly short time period. If we did not get it right, and failed, it would be seen as Canada's fault, and our flag would fly low in embarrassment. I felt that we had to get it right. A multinational military organization can be a force multiplier all by itself. All those flags flying outside my headquarters building told the Bosnian Serbs, Croatians and Muslims that the international community was there and operating with one voice that said, "We are going to do this." That can be a powerful force to have behind you.

If it's not done right, however, having a multinational unit can be a weakness. If that division came across as disorganized or discordant, those who wanted to stop the progress we were trying to bring to the Balkans could use it to cause major problems. The troublemakers can exploit rifts between the countries making up that multinational division, treat every nation differently and play one off against the other, which had happened more than once in the former Yugoslavia. It seemed to me that we had to build that multinational team *before* we went into Bosnia. If we weren't prepared, we were inviting chaos and failure.

I had to come up with a plan to bring a headquarters together that could enable my command of the division, representing those nine different nations, and build about 250 people who had never worked together, who didn't know each other and hadn't trained together, into a team. I wanted us to be ready the day I took command, so that if we ran into something that went terribly wrong in the early days, we would be able to handle it. I came up with some proposals and submitted them to Walt Natynczyk, who was now working for the Deputy Chief of the Defence Staff, in charge of international operations. I laid out for Walt what I thought was a fairly modest two-week program.

Creating and training a headquarters staff is a difficult task at the best of times, but when faced with a multinational headquarters staffed by representatives from the different armed forces, we had to work that much harder to establish the kind of working relationships and the camaraderie that make everything work the way it's supposed to. Training my staff was critical to the mission, in my view, but some in NDHQ didn't understand why we needed to do it. To them it was just a simple matter of putting those 200-plus people on a plane together and sending them to Bosnia.

I pointed out that while all the parts were in place, the people weren't trained to work together. If the shit hit the fan two days after I took command, without a properly trained headquarters we would have been just leaving it to chance that we would actually be able to do something about it.

I had gone into the Balkans, from Texas, to get a look at the situation on the ground early in the summer of 2000. As I prepared to return, I received a message from Walt: "There's some resistance here at NDHQ to doing this training, because it would cost something like half a million bucks. Everyone's asking 'Why?' You really need to get back here and spend a day talking to the key players and get them on side."

So I changed my travel plans and rerouted my trip home from Kosovo via Ottawa. My aide-de-camp from Fort Hood, Captain Troy Otto, flew up to join me and brought along some material I could use for a presentation of the plan. I got in at midnight, met him in the hotel room, and we spent a couple hours squaring away what I wanted to articulate. I briefed the Deputy Chief of the Defence Staff the next morning and the army commander, Bill Leach, immediately after that and got their approval to proceed.

After that approval, I then took the chance over the last several weeks of June, while Joyce was getting us ready to move back to Canada, to go and visit each of the nations that were contributing to the division. That was key: establishing a relationship with senior operational commanders and their staff in the Netherlands, the Czech Republic and the United Kingdom. That relationship made a huge difference over the next year. I made a point of going to each country as division commander two or three times throughout the twelve months, just to maintain those contacts, have an eye-to-eye discussion about the issues and ensure I had their support for what we were trying to accomplish and how we were going about it. That way, when things went right or wrong—and both happened—I had a relationship with the commanders of each of the nations that made up my division and was able to talk with them directly and frankly, and deal with anything that arose.

After all the training and preparations were complete, I arrived in Bosnia in September 2000 and assumed command of the multinational division on the eighteenth. The entire command team from the Texas National Guard, those soldiers that I had worked with for over eighteen months and who were just finishing off their mission in northeast Bosnia, came to my change of command ceremony in the northwest. This truly was a reunion of old friends, and I was touched that they made the trip. We had a great laugh when I hoisted my combat shirt to show the Texas 49th Division belt buckle they had presented me a year before, during their last preparatory event.

Most of my division staff officers were on six-month rotations, with only a small core group staying for the entire year. It was winter weather for the first months of our mission, so we spent most of our time maintaining the status quo and getting our feet underneath us. Once we started to really understand the environment, we were able to start to change the dynamic. The situation had reached a stalemate in Bosnia, without much progress visible after the first actions during the implementation of the Dayton Accord.

We knew there were many obstacles to the implementation of the accord, especially after the eventful first 180 days following December 20, 1995, which included the withdrawal of Bosnian, Serb and Croatian forces from the front lines, consolidation of their units and the handing in of their heavy weapons. It all went down largely without incident, mainly because almost every second paragraph of the agreement said, in effect, that the NATO implementation force (IFOR) reserved the right to enforce the agreement with Chapter 7 rules of engagement. That is, lethal force.

All the warring factions moved pretty quickly to do everything the Dayton Accord required, but after the first months, everything seemed to hit a plateau: the Bosnian government was being built very slowly, and the Bosnian Serbs, Bosnian Croats and Bosnian Muslims were all manoeuvring to try to shape it the way each group wanted. The Serbs, for example, were trying to keep their Republic of Srpska entirely separate from the rest of the state, dragging their feet at every consolidation initiative. There was also some very active resistance to the implementation of the accord, most of it funded by money that was being channelled through a variety of criminal networks.

In western Bosnia, the Bosnian Croats had established a very strong shadow government, trying to run the western part of Bosnia themselves, with the aim of eventually uniting with Croatia. This caused significant challenges to the UN and NATO and was affecting, very negatively, the implementation of the Dayton Accord. Based on some good intelligence work, we determined that this group was getting significant financial support through the Bosnian Croatian Hercegovacka Bank, really just a money-laundering operation, spinning millions of dollars in illegal funds and directing it to support people who were essentially criminals masquerading as Bosnian Croatian nationalists. Some of them held political appointments, some were in the military or police and all were doing their best to slow or subvert the implementation of the accord. They considered themselves to be above the law and unaccountable for their actions. As always, average men and women, Bosnian Croats, were paying the price with unbelievable levels of deprivation, missed opportunity, loss of rights and violence.

Finally the high representative in Sarajevo said, "Enough. We need to stop this. We need to get that money and stop it being used against the peace accord, to the detriment of all Bosnians." We also wanted to get the financial records of those banks in order to help prosecute those criminals under Bosnian law.

My boss, Lieutenant-General Mike Dodson, the American commander of the NATO Stabilization Force, or SFOR, was given the job of going after those Bosnian Croatian banks, seizing their assets and handing over the financial records to the Bosnian government. There were three banks in my division's sector, and Denis Thompson, who later became the Canadian brigade commander in Afghanistan, led his battle group to take out one. The idea was to roar into the town with complete surprise, surround the bank, seize its money and assets and then take the records to special auditors in Sarajevo, who would do a forensic analysis and support criminal prosecutions by the legal government of Bosnia. Any money seized would be used by the Bosnian government to benefit the entire country.

At eight o'clock in the morning, Denis's battle group headed out of their base and drove into the town of Livno. They achieved complete surprise, setting up their armoured personnel carriers and sections of soldiers to establish a cordon around the bank building. They sent more troops in to take control of the bank itself, followed by a team of civilian auditors who were to collect all the cash and records inside. Unfortunately, one of the civilian auditors wanted to produce computer labels for each of the dozens of boxes of seized records and slowed the entire operation. In the meantime, a crowd of local Croatians had gathered, egged on by some of the local criminal element, and Denis's company began getting hammered by rocks, bottles and other projectiles. To their credit, no one started shooting and the operation was a success. Every soldier in that Canadian battle group could tell their grandchildren that they had robbed a bank!

Similar operations took place across Bosnia, with the Dutch taking down another bank and the Americans and the French doing several as well. In Mostar, one of the operations in the French sector went badly. A Spanish battalion got into a bad situation when the local Bosnian Croatian militia grabbed some of the civilian auditors as they were going into the bank to help identify the important records. The hostages included a Canadian woman who'd come into Bosnia from Vancouver on a contract to carry out what she thought was going to be a simple audit. She ended up in a bathroom in the bank with somebody holding a gun to her head saying, "We're going to kill her if the money and the files aren't returned."

The Spanish unit caved and gave back the money and records to this branch in Mostar. That was a black eye for SFOR and would have undermined our credibility immensely, so Dodson asked if I would put together a unit to go into the French sector and get that money and those records back. We put together a battle group, based mostly on the British units, and conducted a march into Sarajevo—the opposite direction from Mostar—to fool anyone who might have been watching. At nightfall the battle group turned and headed toward Mostar, following a route that would have gone past the city, or so we wanted them to think. Then, at one o'clock in the morning, the units veered off the line of march and raced into downtown Mostar and, with the full battle group of about 1,000 soldiers, threw a cordon around the bank, completely surrounding it. We had inserted some special forces commandos into the neighbourhood around the bank several days earlier to keep an eye on things, and sent in other undercover soldiers—Italian *carabinieri* in civilian clothes—to blend in with the local population, so we knew the situation on the ground before the first troops arrived. There would be no surprises.

We blew in the door to the bank with explosives (unfortunately, somebody coming through after that decided to try the doorknob and discovered it was unlocked!) and sent teams of snipers onto nearby rooftops to watch over the area around the bank.

During that entire operation only one local civilian came up to try to challenge us. At about 2:30 in the morning, one Bosnian Croat, who had had a few drinks, walked toward the bank from outside the cordon, belligerent and defiant. He had only seen a couple of the troops placed around the bank, but when he got closer he realized there were about a thousand, all armed to the teeth. He looked around for a second, then turned and made a beeline in the opposite direction.

There were three safes in that bank. The two smaller ones were blown by experts in explosives and coughed up about 50 million Deutschmarks, along with records. The third safe, about the size of a small car, posed a problem. The walls of the safe were so thick and the lock mechanism so complicated that the commandos felt that to blow it open would require enough explosive that we would probably destroy whatever was inside. The solution was to take a British Warrior vehicle, a 30-tonne tracked beast, and bring it around to the side of the building where the safe was located. A thick chain was wrapped around the safe, run out through a small window in the basement and hooked onto the back of the Warrior. When that vehicle hit full speed and took up the slack from the chain, the safe came flying out the window, taking most of the bank's wall with it. The troops lifted it up onto the back of a truck with a crane and took it to Sarajevo. The soldiers who went inside the bank had gathered up a few keychains with the Hercegovacka Bank logo as souvenirs. I made sure I got one.

This was a great operation that moved the yardstick significantly in the implementation of the peace accord for Bosnia. All four of those "bank jobs" went superbly, and the amount of intelligence we gathered allowed us to break the back of the Bosnian Croatian resistance and led to much of the progress Bosnia has made in the past few years. We freed up a lot of money, which had been made illegally on the black market, or skimmed from UN or humanitarian relief funds or through a variety of other criminal activities. That money now allowed the Bosnian government to fund some of the projects the population critically needed. These actions, coming after a couple of years of relative inactivity by NATO in Bosnia, also convinced the entire country that the international community was still serious about doing whatever it took to make Bosnia a secure and stable nation. All three sides in the civil war had signed on to that Dayton Accord, and those bank operations made it clear to all of them that no excuses were going to be accepted for not living up to their agreements. It was all pretty exciting. I still have the scarf that one of the snipers on the operation gave me as a souvenir, and I kept the keychain as a reminder of the excitement that the profession of soldiering has brought me.

We spent a lot of time getting a grip on the heavy weapons and ammunition that were still in the hands of the various militias in Bosnia. We wanted to get them into safe storage facilities and out of reach of the militia forces, who were extremists and had started much of the ethnic cleansing and the fighting in the first place. We had to get soldiers from the Bosnian Serb army, the Bosnian Croatian army and the Bosniak army into their garrisons and their heavy weapons into storage areas where the Dayton Peace Accord said that they should be. The garrison and storage sites had to be well separated.

There were hundreds of thousands of tonnes of heavy weapons and munitions stored all over Bosnia. The accord had specified that they had to be put in safe and appropriate storage places that were not easily accessible to any armed or militia force. During that plateau after the first 180 days of Dayton Peace Accord implementation, nobody had really followed through on the ammo-storage issue. We had ammunition supply depots right next to apartment buildings or near schools. In the Bosnian Serb areas of our zone, ammunition and weapons were stored on the same bases as some of their brigades; in other words, the extremists—pretty scary people—still had complete access to weapons and ammo. What we were accepting was really not acceptable, and we determined that it had to change.

The division staff, led by Lieutenant-Colonel Chris Simmons from Canada, began a detailed reconnaissance and planning process, sending out officers to look at every single weapons storage site in the division area in Bosnia. From there we made our own plan on how weapons should be stored. We did such a good job locating and identifying these weapons stockpiles that when we went to the local army commanders to get them to do what they were required to do under the Dayton Accord, we knew the status of the storage sites better than they did.

One Bosnian Serb corps commander claimed, "Oh, I can't put weapons into storage in these sites because they're already full." I was able to come right back at him and say, "Yeah? Well there are twenty-one shelters there, and nineteen of them are full of spare tires, grey blankets and empty cans, none of which needs specialized storage. Meanwhile, you've got 5,000 tonnes of high explosive right next to apartment buildings over here. Just switch them around."

We were able to put a lot of pressure on all sides to live up to their side of the accord and dramatically changed the situation by removing much of the ammunition and weapons from the hands of those most likely to cause a return to hostilities.

We conducted those operations and had that impact in the last three months of my tour. It had taken us nine months to build our database on the armed forces, do the planning and recces, visit those storage sites and record everything, to get a full picture of what was going on on the ground. It was a clear lesson that we needed to keep commanders in theatre for a full year on similar missions because it takes that long to get to know the lay of the land. That also taught me that you need to learn how to play the game better than the locals if you want to be successful.

The mission in Bosnia also gave us the chance to figure out a lot about how to rebuild a nation after catastrophic events like civil war, ethnic cleansing or mass murder. That's where the idea for what eventually became the Strategic Advisory Team in Afghanistan took root. The former Yugoslavia was a much different place than Afghanistan, but we needed to achieve the same result in the end. After working with the overall NATO headquarters in Sarajevo in trying to help the Bosnian government, the United Nations adviser and the high representative figure out what had to be done to rebuild Bosnia, it was obvious to me that a team of dedicated military and civilian professionals working with the local leaders could accomplish great things.

Bosnia taught me some important lessons, once again, on the incoherence of the United Nations and its inability to accomplish anything other than to use resources and get in the way of the people who were actually trying to do something. The UN seemed to be all about organization, structure, ego, power and good living, and very little about doing the job. Nothing during my time in Bosnia frightened us more than having UN personnel show up and start a discussion by saying, "I'm on my sixth continuous mission," or "I've been here since 1992." We immediately dismissed such functionaries as useless, self-serving, allowance-drawing bureaucrats who were more interested in keeping their jobs and mission allowance than accomplishing anything. The UN could not have performed more dismally than it did in Bosnia.

Despite all of the challenges, my experience in Bosnia was incredible, albeit at times frustrating because of what we saw as missed opportunities to effect potential changes. Fortunately, there were small mercies. The food was one. I was living in the British camp, where our headquarters was located, and, for a Newfoundlander, their food was like dying and going to heaven. I mean, it was fried food for breakfast, french fries with lunch and dinner, and for dessert they had bread pudding. It all tasted great to me, although my wife and doctor were not as happy about the diet as I was.

236

In early September 2001, in the last two weeks of my mission, I made one more trip to each of the capitals of the nations that had contributed troops to my division. I went to Prague, spent some time in Amsterdam and then on to London. On the morning of September 11, we were in a taxi going to Heathrow Airport, on our way back to Bosnia. Over the radio we heard that a plane had run into the World Trade Center. I thought it might have been a small plane or some freak accident and, like millions around the world, dismissed it. As we were waiting to check in at Heathrow, I heard one of the airport staff whisper to another that a second plane had run into the twin towers. We then boarded our flight to Germany, and as soon as we had taken off, the captain came on the intercom and announced that Heathrow Airport had just been closed, transatlantic traffic had shut down, but he thought we could make it to Frankfurt before it closed as well.

We did make it to Frankfurt, where we made a mad dash to the gates for the Croatian Airlines flight into Zagreb. We got airborne, and a few minutes after we took off the captain came on and said that Frankfurt Airport had closed. We got into Zagreb at ten o'clock at night and were met by my close protection team and one of the division's helicopters. By midnight we were back in Bosnia.

I'd spent 9/11 in total ignorance of what had actually occurred. It was not until I got back to headquarters and the staff gave me a briefing that I realized the scale and scope of what had happened, that the World Trade Center had been hit by passenger jets and had collapsed with massive loss of life, that the Pentagon had been struck and air travel worldwide had been brought to a standstill. I started to realize that this attack was a strategically destabilizing move that would dominate our lives for the immediate future.

Unlike most people in the rest of the world, I never got a chance to talk to my family that day. It was at least another day before I got to talk to Joyce. Everyone was concerned and shaken and just wanted to talk to family and make sure they were okay. Fortunately, no one in my family was anywhere within the area hit by the 9/11 attackers or was affected by any of the subsequent fallout effects, but it was still reassuring to talk to them and confirm that they were all fine.

Almost every nationality that lost people in the World Trade Center attacks was represented in division headquarters. A couple of days later we held a small memorial service in remembrance of those who had died. I was shaken, as was everyone else, and it reminded me yet again that everything we do is about people. It's not about organization, structure, process or management: it's people who accomplish things, and they need to be inspired, informed, enabled and supported. In this case, they needed to be comforted, and that's what we did.

That first day after the attacks I asked myself what was going on, and thought hard about where we were and how it would affect us. Bosnian Muslims, Croatians (who were mainly Catholic), and Orthodox Bosnian Serbs were all working in and around us, and God knows they'd just come through years of bloodletting. As well, inside of Bosnia there were still several hundred extremely fanatical Muslims, jihadists or mujahedeen, who had settled there after the fighting and tried to blend in to the population. We were trying to figure out if they had been a part of the 9/11 attacks or if they would be a part of any further attacks, and how the Serbs or Croats would respond if that happened.

Over the next few days some of the Serbs, even those we considered forward-thinking and open-minded, came up to me, put their arm around my shoulder and said, "What did we tell you? It's us [meaning them and us] against the Muslims."

Some of the more reasonable Bosnian Serbs, guys that we had thought we could work with, said similar things, and I just politely told them all, "You know something? It's not us against the Muslims. It's not us against anybody, buddy."

I came back to Canada a week after the attacks, flying into London from Bosnia, then on to St. John's, where I was going to meet Joyce. The Canadian High Commission in London told me that I had to be in Heathrow Airport at least three hours early because of all the security checks after 9/11.

My flight was scheduled to leave at noon, and we decided to arrive three hours before, as requested. We showed up at 8:25 in the morning, and by 8:45 we were through security and eating breakfast. Almost nobody else was flying. The long lineups we'd anticipated never materialized, and the guard at the security gate apologized to me for patting me down and running his hands up and down my legs. "Buddy," I told him, "I've been away from home for a year—go ahead and take your time with that."

A few hours later I met Joyce in St. John's. We spent a week in Newfoundland on vacation and then went home to Ottawa. I took four weeks' leave, which I spent golfing and puttering around the house, then went back to work in National Defence Headquarters as Deputy Commander of the Army.

I was surprised that no one had a real sense in the days after September 11 that everything had changed. Even in the military, there was no appreciation that we had all witnessed one of those pivotal moments in world history. On my very first week back at work, all of the senior leaders of the army met in Cornwall, Ontario. Lieutenant-General Mike Jeffery, who was Commander, asked all of those attending to come up with answers to a few key questions, including whether or not the strategic situation had fundamentally changed because of the actions on 9/11.

All the senior officers, including many generals, broke into small groups and discussed the questions. When we reconvened after a long discussion on a variety of issues, all the other groups said that no, things had not changed fundamentally, that this was just a blip, just another attack.

I was the last to present, outlining first my small group's discussions and then our conclusions. "Here's what we think: Fundamentally, this is a strategic shift in the international environment. The situation has changed, and therefore how we're going to work within this new international environment has changed. Canada and its place in the world is fundamentally different now than it was before 9/11."

Clearly, it took a little while for all of the implications of those attacks to sink in. Just weeks after 9/11 we were still unable to see the big picture of what was happening in Afghanistan, what the Americans were trying to do there and elsewhere, and to start thinking about where this would all go. The prevailing emotion in Canada, in every department and organization, after September 11, was to try to get back to September 10. But that was just not possible.

CHAPTER 13

FRIENDLY FIRE

Deputy Commander of the Army, with Lieutenant-General Mike Jeffery as my boss, was a great job. Mike was excellent—a visionary leader who always thought about the big strategic picture but who wasn't afraid to get down into the nitty-gritty detail with the rest of us. He was also one of the smartest officers I've ever worked with (I used to tell everyone that he was so damn smart he gave me a migraine trying to keep up) but also a very friendly and down-to-earth guy. I thought the world of him and was delighted that he picked me to be his second in command. On my first day on the Land Staff at National Defence Headquarters, I said to him, "I guarantee you my best effort and my complete loyalty. You focus on the issues you have to focus on, and I'll tend to the day-to-day business of running the army."

That was late October 2001. One of the first things on our agenda was the potential deployment of the 3rd Battalion, Princess Patricia's Canadian Light Infantry (PPCLI) to Kandahar in early 2002. I was just coming back to Ottawa when the decision was being made to send the PPCLI to Afghanistan, and while I wasn't directly involved in that decision-making process, as deputy army commander I was a fly on the wall for a lot of the discussions. There were a lot of meetings and even more chatter back and forth between NDHQ and Foreign Affairs over whether or not we should go and, if we did go, *where* we should go.

Obviously, Canada wanted to be seen as contributing something to what everyone was calling "the campaign against terrorism," or, in the less politically correct U.S., the "War on Terror"—we all used different words for it, that's for sure. The Liberal government's overwhelming desire was for Canadian troops to serve under the International Security Assistance Force (ISAF), which was being formed to take responsibility for the area around Kabul, the Afghan capital. But when we put out feelers about a possible Canadian contribution to the force, we did not get a warm response. The British, who were leading the charge to put ISAF together, were clearly stiff-arming us, diplomatically but firmly fending off any suggestion of Canadian soldiers' joining their force. They just were not interested in having Canadian troops participate. The supposed reason was that this ISAF was to be a European force, rather than a NATO mission or an American mission, and they wanted only European nations to contribute.

There was a strong negative undercurrent to this refusal, however, that quickly became evident to all involved. Canada was not being invited because the Brits believed we had lost our ability to be a war-fighting nation. The British felt that ISAF might have to fight its way into, around and out of the Kabul area, which was still unstable, with various militias and armed factions controlling large parts of the surrounding countryside. ISAF might even be asked to surge into other parts of Afghanistan. As far as they were concerned, Canada could not be relied upon to do the tough stuff and was therefore of no use. The British command structure remembered the years in the former Yugoslavia when "Can'tbat"—Canada's contribution to the UN, and later to NATO, forces—needed days or even weeks to get approval from Ottawa before we would take on an operation, assuming we were even allowed to do so. The Canadian government, which desperately wanted to join the ISAF operation, was paying the price for its risk-averse, micromanaging approach to military overseas operations.

The discussions in Ottawa over which mission Canada would join went on interminably, with our diplomats, politicians and senior military officers trying to talk our way into joining ISAF and the British firmly saying no. Foreign Affairs was chattering to officials in other countries; various Cabinet ministers would talk to their counterparts in other governments; and the policy analysts, advisers and senior military officers were talking to a whole bunch of different people around the globe. The discussion went back and forth from Canada to the U.S., Canada to Britain, Britain to the U.S., and Britain to its European allies. Clearly, Canada was not going to be a part of ISAF. It just wasn't going to happen.

The government really wanted to contribute to some kind of anti-terrorist operation and to be seen as supporting the Americans in the aftermath of 9/11, so they jumped at the chance when the U.S. offered an opportunity for a Canadian battalion to join an American division in southern Afghanistan, filling one of the battalion slots in the 101st Airborne Division that was going to Kandahar. The government had so little understanding of things military that I don't believe it truly comprehended the mission to which it had just committed our soldiers, our first combat mission since the Korean War.

Those detailed discussions and plans around what became known as Operation Apollo, Canada's contribution to the War on Terror, were not my prime responsibility, but as Deputy Commander of the Army I was responsible for running the day-to-day business of preparation. That included ensuring that 3 PPCLI would be ready for any scenario it would encounter in Afghanistan. I was busy trying to set conditions for success in everything from leadership to training to equipment to finances.

The decision to go into Kandahar was made at the political level—at the very top, by the Prime Minister and his Cabinet. It soon became clear that we were sending a battalion to serve with the 101st Airborne, commanded by Major-General Dick Cody, one of my battle buddies from Fort Hood, Texas. Dick is a war hero, having flown one of the first Apache attack helicopter missions into Iraq during the Gulf War in 1991. He later became the Vice Chief of Staff of the U.S. Army, and was credited with having set the conditions for the growth that they're going through right now and the fact that they've turned an enormous demand on them into an opportunity to rebuild. I had several conversations with Dick in the fall of 2001 about exactly what they were looking at for the mission, so I could make sure that our soldiers were as ready as they could be before we deployed them. Because I knew him well, I could call and say, "Look, if we did do this mission, how would we best set ourselves up for success?" On the other side I was able to go to my boss, Mike Jeffery, and tell him that if we were going to put a battalion into Afghanistan in a combat mission under American command, we could have no better commander than Dick Cody—he's that good. To me, that was just one example of the huge benefits of having established those sorts of relationships.

One of our biggest issues in getting 3 PPCLI out the door was that the Canadian Forces had failed to keep troops at high readiness to deploy overseas and we had to make up this ground in very short order. We had no units able to move on only a few hours' notice, and the concept of bringing units to such high readiness and then maintaining them at this level, prepared to move anywhere in the world when they were ordered, was foreign to us. The Americans, on the other hand, had been doing this for years. At Fort Hood, for example, a tank or a mechanized brigade would be ready to deploy on twenty-four hours' notice—a formation of thousands of soldiers, equipment, weapons and heavy vehicles. This meant that the first company of that brigade had to be on the move within four hours of getting their orders. They would go on these cycles for six, nine or twelve months, ready to roll even if most of the time that order never came. In Canada, the culture was quite different.

In late fall 2001, 3 PPCLI stepped up to a higher level of readiness because it appeared as if they might have to deploy imminently. We wanted to have a unit ready, and the battalion under Lieutenant-Colonel Pat Stogran was the "go-to" unit. They were brought to a higher level of readiness in November, and spent several weeks sitting in Edmonton ready to move. This caused severe headaches higher up the chain of command, and several senior officers insisted that this battalion had to deploy somewhere, anywhere, now that they were at high readiness. We had not mastered high readiness as a concept and were unable to keep a unit at that level over a period of weeks or months. Yet in my view, we had a responsibility to our nation to be ready at very short notice to deploy anywhere in the world, even if the order to go never came.

Up to that point, we hadn't needed to worry about such things. As we started going down that road in 2001, we faced what amounted to a significant cultural change. Pat Stogran's battalion was getting ready to go on operations, while a second unit was "on deck" getting ready to become the high-readiness battalion if 3 PPCLI deployed. That battalion was in Valcartier, Quebec, almost literally sitting on their rucksacks waiting to go. After ten days, they started asking when they were going, to which we replied, "Hopefully, never."

This culture shock was building in the days before 3 PPCLI was sent to Kandahar, but we were very much focused on coordinating details like getting whatever training and equipment might be required by Pat Stogran's battalion. My job was to ensure that that unit had conditions set for success no matter where it deployed.

Running the day-to-day business of the army for Mike Jeffery kept us all busy. Key to our future, and something that would serve the army and the CF well in the next years, was building a successful planning model for senior leadership succession, considering the criteria we needed in our future leaders. How would we give them a chance to realize their potential, continue to validate it all the way through their career and make sure each individual got the right education, experience, command and staff time to enable him or her to develop fully? When we brought in the senior commanders for a week in the spring, I remember saying to them, and to Jeffery when we briefed him, "You know, it's probably going to take about five years for this to mature and to work people through the system using this framework as our guide." It did take five years, and now the army's system for producing leaders and planning the succession of senior officers is generating one outstanding senior leader after another, with all the right credentials, the right characteristics and the right qualities.

The Patricias deployed to Kandahar early in 2002, augmented by specialists such as combat engineers and a reconnaissance squadron from the Lord Strathcona's Horse, in their Coyote armoured reconnaissance vehicles. The battle group worked superbly with the Americans, hunting down the remnants of the al Qaeda leadership that had turned Afghanistan into their home base for the 9/11 attacks and defending the Kandahar Airfield base from sporadic attacks by the handful of Taliban that had not fled the American-led coalition attacks. They earned credibility and respect from every individual they encountered, particularly Dick Cody, who had a special place in his heart for Pat Stogran and his regimental sergeant major, Joseph Comeau. Dick was impressed by our soldiers, who were living on the main coalition base under pretty harsh conditions.

Unlike the current base, which has a Burger King, a Pizza Hut and fairly comfortable accommodations, Kandahar Airfield in 2002 was a horrible place to live. The soldiers were living in individual tents, in brutally hot, dusty conditions and eating hard rations. There weren't many amenities.

I talked to Dick Cody several times during the mission. He told me, "You've got some great guys there." He talked to the Canadian soldiers every chance he got and said, "You guys are warriors. We love you. God bless you." To this day, every time I see or talk to Dick, he mentions the Patricias and asks how they're doing. He thought the world of Canadian soldiers, and he said later that after that tour in Kandahar with the PPCLI, he'd never be found sitting on his backside when the Canadian flag went by.

Dick had confidence in our soldiers for any mission, but unfortunately there was a cumbersome process to allow them to carry out an operation, similar to what had happened in Bosnia. As with Bosnia, there appeared to be an aversion in Ottawa to allowing our troops to do anything risky or significant, very quickly. Pat Stogran's comment to me when he came home was "We'll never be able to fight this way." As simple as that. The process of getting operations approved and the details that the bureaucratic machine back in Ottawa demanded before giving approval, coupled with the constraints placed on a battalion in an operation, really would not work in any kind of fast-flowing mission. As a result, in Pat's view (and mine), the Canadian battle group sat on guard at Kandahar Airfield much more often than it probably should have.

Then, on April 17, I got a late-night phone call from Mike

Jeffery. "We've had a terrible incident in Afghanistan," he said. "I'm not sure yet what the toll of casualties is. We do know we've got one or two dead, but it could be quite a few more."

I told him, as always, that my rule in such cases was that first reports are always wrong. Second reports are also wrong, and third reports are usually wrong. I had, unfortunately, all kinds of experience to back that up.

Mike agreed, but he said, "I just wanted to give you a heads-up that we're going to have to start looking, down the road, at boards of inquiry, and trying to learn some lessons from this. And one of the first people I'll look to will be you, as one of my commanders with more operational experience than most."

We found out soon enough that we had lost four of our soldiers—Sergeant Marc Léger, Corporal Ainsworth Dyer, Private Richard Green and Private Nathan Smith—and that eight of their comrades had been severely wounded. They and their company had been out late at night firing their weapons at the Tarnak Farm range just south of the base and a flight of U.S. Air Force F16s patrolling over Kandahar Airfield mistook the fire on the ground for a Taliban attack. Despite not having clearance to attack, one of those F16s dropped a 1,000-pound bomb into the midst of the Canadians practising on the range, killing and wounding our soldiers.

An hour later, Mike phoned back and said, "Looks like we've got four killed and a larger number wounded. Over the next forty-eight hours we'll resolve how we're going to deal with all this. I just want you to start thinking about it, pronto." I actually pulled my rucksack out of the closet and packed it that night at midnight, just to make sure I was ready to go if Mike asked me to fly out to Afghanistan on a moment's notice. My place was in Ottawa, however, as the Minister of Defence and the Chief of the Defence Staff asked Maurice Baril, the former CDS, to lead an inquiry. We found the right people to go with him, and they did an excellent job in determining what had occurred, why, and what we could do to reduce the probability of another friendly-fire incident in the future. One of the things Baril said in his final report was that combat operations are fluid and you cannot guarantee perfection. That was, though, of little comfort in 2002, or when we lost another soldier in a similar incident on the Labour Day weekend in 2006.

Instead of sorting out what had gone wrong and how it could be prevented, I concentrated on organizing, at the army level in Canada, what was really our first handling of combat casualties of this kind in any of our memories. As soon as the wheels of the plane carrying those four bodies touched down in Trenton, our fallen soldiers and their families became the army's responsibility. We had a lot of details to sort out, including how we were going to handle everything from the death certificates to the funerals and memorial services and the medals given out to their families and loved ones. We discussed how we would look after the families of those four soldiers, what we were doing for them, what the arrangements were, where funerals were going to be and who was responsible for what. We held video teleconferences twice a day for nearly two weeks with commanders across Canada to make sure we had all the details straight: we were going to get this right.

We had to figure out who would get the Memorial Cross, the medal given, since the First World War, to mothers and wives of soldiers who have died in the line of duty. Initially, we said the mothers of each of the four from Tarnak Farm should get it, but it quickly became more complicated that that. The mother might be estranged from the rest of the family; she might have a new husband, or the father may not have been on speaking terms with her son who's fallen in battle, so how do you decide who gets those medals? We had to discuss whether or not we were just going to give out *one* Memorial Cross per soldier. The reasoning used to be that the mother got it, because nobody could argue the fact that she was the mother of the child. (Somebody might argue over who was the father, but with DNA testing that's not necessary anymore.) We had to work through some significant changes to our accepted policy, which had stagnated since the Second World War. (Now, the Memorial Cross is for whomever the serviceman or servicewoman designates, to a total of three.)

We had to bring four young men's bodies home, honour them with all the dignity and respect they had earned, and look after the families while doing it. We had learned some pretty horrible lessons during the Bosnian operations. The legacy from that mission included parents and wives who had been all but abandoned by the CF, and we were determined not to allow that to happen again. Kevin McLeod, the commanding officer of 2 Combat Engineer Regiment while I was brigade commander in Petawawa, had lost one of his soldiers in Bosnia. He built up a relationship between the regiment and the family of that soldier which I'm sure exists today, and the way he handled that became, for me, the model for what we had to do to support the families of the friendly-fire casualties.

I also got to see just how powerful—and inspirational—the

families of our fallen soldiers could be. Marley Léger, the wife of Sergeant Marc Léger, made a statement on television about her husband that was emotional, strong, sad and, at the same time, inspiring. I said, during one of our teleconferences, "Somebody go and tell that great lady how inspirational, how courageous and how powerful she is, and make sure she understands that we all stand in awe of her strength and dignity."

I didn't have the opportunity to meet her and tell her that in person until about three years later, at the farewell ceremony for Adrienne Clarkson, the Governor General, who was leaving office. A variety of people were invited to the ceremony on Parliament Hill, all of whom had been touched by Ms. Clarkson during her time as Governor General. Marley was one of them, along with the entire Léger family and the families of some of the other soldiers who had died. Marley and I were almost the last two people left at the reception, and I finally got to tell her what a hero she was for me and how incredibly inspired I was by her courage during what had to have been the worst day in her life. She started crying when I told her that, so I said, "Don't you be doing that or pretty soon I'll be crying too."

It was tough to deal with those losses.

For two weeks our command group was consumed by the monumental task of making sure everything was not only done, but done right. It was a huge organizational and logistical challenge to get the bodies home and identify all the members of all the families, because our systems weren't as prepared as necessary when troops are off to war. We returned the bodies, gave all the support we could to the families and got them to Trenton in time to see their loved ones' remains land in Canada. We had to do the hundreds of things that were necessary to take those bodies through mortuary affairs in Toronto, then support the families in making the decisions for burial, whether in a military cemetery, cremated or not, and then get the bodies to the selected locations. Appropriate respects had to be paid. Our message to those families was that we were going to support them until they were through this, and there was no time limit on that support. Fortunately, good people rise to the occasion, and one of those was the commander in western Canada, Brigadier-General Ivan Fenton. Ivan's professionalism, compassion and command ability were the key elements to doing what was right, and doing it well.

That commitment to the families continued for years after the incident and the deaths of those four soldiers. We later brought in the assisting officers from the friendly-fire deaths and gave them commendations—formal recognition for them—because they had stayed on the job for such a long time and shown such incredible dedication. Those assisting officers had to be present or with the families during the courts martial for the two pilots who bombed that training exercise at Tarnak Farm and caused so much death and pain. The hearings into the case went on for a long time down in the U.S., and thus so did the assistance. Some of our officers were actually suffering from stress themselves because of the time and effort they put into helping the families.

When the funerals and memorial services began across Canada, Canadians came together with these soldiers and their families. From the looks on some of the faces in the crowds that gathered near Trenton to pay their respects when the four bodies were flown in, they were shocked that their soldiers might actually be in danger, but the reaction across the country to the deaths at Tarnak Farm took me completely by surprise. These were the first Canadian casualties since 9/11, and that played into it, but the public response still was almost completely overwhelming to everyone in uniform. For so many years, we in the military had been ignored or at times even scorned by the Canadian public, so it was surreal to see thousands of people lining Highway 401 when the bodies were driven from Trenton to Toronto in what was a spontaneous outpouring of affection and grief. People were stopping soldiers in uniform in the streets and talking to them. There was such immense public interest in the deaths of those four young men at Tarnak Farm that their memorial service in Edmonton was televised live on all of the major networks. The media—whether CBC, CTV, Global, the newspapers or radio stations—were also surprised by the public reaction to the deaths of those four soldiers and weren't entirely sure how they were going to cover potential future casualties.

During a media interview about a year and a half later, I was asked about the mass grieving that swept the country. My response was that it was obviously touching and also helped not only the families but all of us deal with the loss of these great Canadians. The families felt as if the whole nation were grieving with them. They could be certain of, and take comfort from, the fact that the sacrifice of their sons and husbands had been seen, remembered, appreciated and mourned. That response really shaped how we look at death on these missions and how we handle our losses, like that of Corporal Robbie Beerenfenger and Sergeant Robert Alan Short, killed in Kabul a little over a year later.

When the PPCLI battle group finished its tour in Kandahar in July 2002, they came home to beautiful summer weather in Edmonton. They weren't replaced by another Canadian unit, as it had been decided even before they left that this was going to be a one-shot affair. All the rotations of troops in and out of Bosnia, combined with this Afghan mission, had put the army under a lot of stress, and most of us thought that the war in Afghanistan was going to be over quickly. The Taliban had crumbled, the new government had been formed under the Bonn Accord, and it seemed simply a matter of carrying out the last few operations to clear the remnants of the Taliban and al Qaeda and maybe, just maybe— everyone was quietly crossing their fingers over this one—get the opportunity to lay hands on Osama bin Laden himself. The expectation in 2002 was that Afghanistan was going to be largely wrapped up by the summer. It didn't work out quite that way.

When the battalion returned, I went to Edmonton on behalf of Jeffery to welcome those soldiers home. Mike had gone to visit the battalion in Kandahar during Easter weekend of 2002, but I hadn't had the opportunity to do that, so I wanted to shake the hand of each and every one of those returning soldiers. There were three planeloads, all of whom had been to Guam for their post-tour decompression period, and they were flying in on Malaysia Airlines 747s chartered for the purpose. The troops were all happy to be on those planes because they were relatively decadent compared to the air force transports. These guys had been constrained to Kandahar Airfield for a significant period of their deployment and as a result had spent an enormous amount of time lifting weights, getting fit and preparing to go on an instant's notice. The first 250 of them came off the aircraft and I stood at the door greeting them. Unfortunately, I had forgotten to take the ring off my right hand. Now, no soldier wants to give a wimpy handshake to a general waiting to welcome them home. These guys were incredibly fit and strong after five months of working out, so by the end of that line of 250 soldiers, imprints of my ring were cut through to my outside fingers. So, lesson learned: take off your ring when you shake hands with soldiers, because nobody gives you a weak handshake—not if you are a general and, as I found out later, especially not if you are CDS.

When those soldiers went into the terminal at Edmonton International Airport, they saw the first demonstration of how much Canadians' appreciation had grown for their sons and daughters serving as Canada's soldiers, sailors, airmen and air-women. When the first plane arrived, there was a bit of a screw-up in the airport's baggage-handling system, and it took two and a half to three hours before the troops were able to collect their bags and go outside into the waiting area to clear customs. At one point, we had soldiers walking up into the luggage conveyor belt to try to get the baggage, which was blocked for some reason. So the anticipation was all the greater. When they got out of the baggage area and into the main part of the airport, they saw crowds of people with yellow ribbons and signs welcoming them home, all of whom had waited, with incredible patience, through the long delay. The cheering and screaming when they caught sight of the soldiers was startling to all and signalled a distinct change in the relationship between Canadians and their armed forces.

That signal was evident everywhere in Edmonton. When the soldiers boarded the buses that took them up the highway and through Edmonton to the garrison, people with signs and yellow ribbons were lined up for miles. There were police and firefighters, paramedics and ordinary men, women and children lining the road in the thousands to cheer "their" troops. Because of the delay in the baggage area, many had been standing there waiting for almost four hours. The soldiers themselves just stared in amazement and asked themselves, "My God, what is this?"

The buses carrying the soldiers rolled along behind an Edmonton City Police motorcycle escort past people out on the streets saluting them, waving and shouting, "God bless you!" or "Welcome home," or "We love you!" When they arrived on the base, there was a huge crowd to welcome them like the heroes they were. The soldiers will tell you that the impact of that welcome on their lives was enormous.

Although the battle group had done an excellent job on that Afghan mission—the first of many Afghan tours of duty, as it turned out—not everything had gone as smoothly as it could have from an army perspective. Pat Stogran and I had a long talk after he came home. He said, "Sir, this just won't work. Not if we're into agile operations and heavy shooting matches. It just won't work with the way things are set up back here. The length of time it took us to get approval from Ottawa for operations and the details that they needed to approve stuff—it was simply unsustainable."

That made me stop and think, look at our system for running overseas missions yet again and conclude that we were just not set up to run operations effectively. That impression was confirmed when I deployed overseas myself and had to deal with Ottawa. As Commander of ISAF two years later, I did not turn to Canada as my go-to nation when I wanted a job done, because of the complex and cumbersome system in Ottawa and bureaucratic approach to operations. When we had missions that had to happen quickly, I went to my British contingent, I went to the Norwegian company and occasionally I went to the French battle group to get them done. Very seldom did I go to Canada.

The time, detail, pain and agony to get something done, and the hand-wringing over it, were so extensive that I concluded it just wasn't worthwhile to even ask Ottawa, through the contingent commander in Kabul, Colonel Alain Tremblay, to approve an operation. When I had intelligence that placed a cell of Hezb-e-Islami Gulbuddin (HIG) terrorists in a certain compound on the outskirts of Kabul planning a suicide car-bomb attack, I needed to be able to send troops into that compound within two hours. If I went to the Canadian battle group, it would take twelve to twenty-four hours to get Ottawa to approve their participation in the raid, assuming that they did approve it. If I went to the British contingent or the Norwegians, they'd have that operation not just approved, but carried out in less than two hours.

That talk with Pat Stogran confirmed for me that we desperately needed to change how we ran operations from Ottawa. More specifically, we needed to change the level of operations that we ran. In other words, we didn't need to reach into downtown Kabul and tell a commander that he needed to wear his ballistic vest, and his tactical vest on top of that and carry fifteen magazines of ammunition. We needed to tell our commander on the ground, "Here's your mission. Here are the guiding parameters for it. Here's the materiel that we've got for you. Here is what I want you to accomplish. Now go make your plan, back-brief us so we are comfortable, and then we will launch, assessing changes as they come." The key lesson here was, the soldier on the front line is always right, but sometimes that was not entirely obvious to NDHQ in Ottawa.

We did learn one other important lesson from Operation Apollo and the PPCLI mission in 2002, and applied it pretty quickly when next deploying. We had a unit in Kandahar, fighting a war, commanded by a lieutenant-colonel, Pat Stogran, who was also the senior Canadian officer in the theatre and therefore the only guy responsible for dealing with Ottawa and national concerns. We needed to have Pat Stogran focused on the fight with the Taliban and al Qaeda, not looking back over his shoulder toward Ottawa and answering endless questions from there. We never really got the command structure right in Kandahar to allow that to occur with the first battle group. We had a national commander who was co-located with CENTCOM (the U.S. Central Command, responsible for Afghanistan and the entire Middle East region) in Tampa, Florida, who was in charge of both the naval forces in the Gulf and the battalion in Kandahar, and we had NDHQ, a voracious maw demanding more and more information, back in Ottawa. Both NDHQ and Tampa were trying to command and direct operations more than 10,000 kilometres away in southwest Asia. Both were trying to get information from and issue directions to Pat Stogran, who was just trying to fight a battle. We had put the weight of the world on the shoulders of one admittedly capable, but still one, lieutenant-colonel.

That's why, when we moved back into southern Afghanistan in 2006, we put a general with a command team in Kandahar. He had the dual job of commanding NATO forces in the southern provinces but also—as the senior Canadian in Afghanistan—being responsible for dealing with the command structure back in Canada. We had that largely right, but in planning the transition from Brigadier-General Tim Grant to the next commander, the recommendation came to me that we not put a general officer there: we were going to put in a colonel. I said, "Stop, stop, stop. No, we're not. We've got to have a general officer there, for a whole variety of reasons, working with all the different nationalities, working with the Afghans. He's carrying the weight. We're going to have a full command structure on the ground there, and we're going to make sure that the individual has sufficient rank and sway to keep Ottawa off the backs of combat units and allow them to focus down-range." We didn't have that right in 2002, because we hadn't done command at the more senior levels for a long time in the Canadian Forces, but we fixed it and we did get that part right in all our future deployments to Afghanistan.

On December 1, 2002, I got called to the CDS's office. The Chief, accompanied by Mike Jeffery, told me I was being promoted to lieutenant-general and would stay on as Deputy Commander until May and then take over the army when Mike retired. We were watching the Americans build up for an Iraqi invasion, seeing our own government's feet get colder and colder over participation in that invasion and hearing more and more about a second Afghan mission with the countries comprising ISAF. The Europeans had suddenly warmed to the idea of Canadian participation after realizing the challenges of generating the ISAF force, which was so far still confined to the relatively small and quiet area around Kabul. All of a sudden, the Europeans were making overtures to Canada to participate. I had no idea then just how much of an impact those overtures would have on the country, the Canadian Forces and me personally.

CHAPTER 14

FOUR STARS

In late 2002 we watched the Americans begin building up to the invasion of Iraq, and by early in 2003 it became clear that the question of whether or not Canada would, or even could, join the U.S.-led coalition was being looked at on a senior level, in military, diplomatic and government circles. There was very little discussion inside the army about what roles we might play in Iraq or in Afghanistan, because the military options, always designed to offer a government as many different alternatives as they could imagine, were handled by a very small group centred on the Deputy Chief of the Defence Staff. Sensitivity of the information they were dealing with, and the political impact should it become public, demanded this. The team considered how they might use air, land, sea and special forces elements in Iraq or elsewhere, and analyzed the impacts of their possible use for the government. Everyone in uniform, however, recognized the intense desire of Prime Minister Jean Chrétien's government to stay out of the invasion force, that the American actions in Iraq were politically charged and that how we dealt with this might affect our long-term relationship with the United States. The view in the halls of National Defence Headquarters was that the Canadian government would do anything, commit troops anywhere, on almost any kind of mission, as long as it meant we could stay out of Iraq. That was certainly the cynical point of view in the army.

At the same time, the serious and challenging conditions under which our land forces were operating had become increasingly clear. Still in the "decade of darkness" and its perfect storm of budget cuts, scandals and neglect, the army's ability just to survive, let alone execute a major overseas mission, was in doubt. Our equipment was tired: we were still in the early stages of deliveries of the new Light Armoured Vehicle (LAV) family of modern fighting vehicles, and most of our other equipment was either worn or wearing out. The Leopard tank was completing a significant upgrade program, but it remained an old tank, with belly armour that had been scraped over the ground during years of exercises and operations until it was paper thin. We knew we faced major challenges just to keep those beasts running. The number of people in our units was down—way down—so that to get a battalion (normally about 800 soldiers) ready to go on operations, we required two battalions to make up the necessary numbers. Morale was at an all-time low; we had not recovered from the challenges of the 1990s, when it had bottomed out. Those of us in senior command positions weren't certain that the army could take on a major role in Afghanistan or Iraq—or anywhere else, for that matter—though it was clear we were going to have to have a major role somewhere.

So the details of our commitment came as a major surprise to me and most everyone else in the Canadian Forces when John McCallum, the Defence Minister, stood up in the House of Commons and announced that we would be sending 2,000 troops to Kabul for a six-month rotation starting in August 2003 and would assume command of the International Security Assistance Force (ISAF) there in February 2004. Surprise is a well-established principle of war, but we soldiers like to surprise the enemy, and in this case we were surprised by our own minister. Suddenly we were committed to a brigade-level operation, and that sent significant shock waves across the land forces. People were saying, "Oh my God, we're going to actually go out and do this?" The shock was somewhat mitigated by the widespread cynicism within NDHQ, so that we had been prepared for almost anything from the government. The driving force behind the decision was clearly not our readiness or ability to carry out the mission, but the political cover needed to allow Canada to say no to the U.S. when asked to participate in Operation Iraqi Freedom, the name the United States gave their mission in Iraq when they invaded in March 2003. The government wanted to stay out of Iraq but at the same time wanted to be seen as contributing to something Washington saw as important.

Personally, I didn't feel strongly about whether or not Canada should have participated in Operation Iraqi Freedom. Iraq did become much more of a distraction for the U.S. than anyone had expected, and that distraction had a profound effect on the mission in Afghanistan.

The Iraqi invasion and the months upon months of insurgency that followed took troops and resources away from

Afghanistan at a crucial time. It wasn't just the Americans who diverted forces to Iraq—the British, Spanish, Italian, Czech and Polish forces were also drawn into that long and demanding fight. This diversion resulted in a "minimalist" approach to Afghanistan that severely constrained the mission there. NATO planners had determined from the beginning that the force needed to defeat the Taliban in Afghanistan was significant, somewhere in the vicinity of 70,000 to 80,000 troops, most of them required in the southern provinces. The war in Iraq left the coalition with only a fraction of that total, and it was only with the American troop surge into Afghanistan in 2009 that we started to approach those optimal numbers. The closer we got to that number, the more effective we became. Iraq significantly diminished what we were able to do as an international community elsewhere. The international community, including the countries of NATO, was simply was not willing to commit enough troops, equipment, UAVs (unmanned aerial vehicles), special forces or money to fight in both Iraq and Afghanistan.

Perhaps more importantly, the war in Iraq gave the Taliban heart at a time when it was largely beaten. They had been thrown out of their country and driven into hiding in Pakistan. Their leadership had been almost entirely killed or captured, they were being soundly beaten in battles with the U.S. forces and they weren't getting money from their usual financial supporters in the Muslim world. The Taliban were licking their wounds. Then, in late 2002 and early 2003, military resources began shifting out of Afghanistan and into Iraq, where a bunch of ragtag insurgents were having some success taking on modern U.S. and international forces. The Taliban saw from the fighting in Iraq that Western military forces could be hurt and maybe even have their will to fight destroyed. They watched, learned and soon began applying the tactical lessons from Iraq in successfully attacking Western forces. As often occurs, success begat success, and in 2005 and 2006 a resurging Taliban started to attract seasoned veterans of the fighting in Iraq who came through the safe havens in northern Pakistan to reinforce them. Combat-experienced leaders from years of fighting the Russians or each other were still around in sufficient numbers to direct these fighters. Others began aggressively coercing young, jobless Afghan men to take up a weapon and attack the Americans. This renewed sense of purpose triggered money to start flowing from around the world again. The attacks into Afghanistan against the "great Satan" increased these funds and, combined with the drug production of northwest Pakistan and Afghanistan, provided sufficient dollars to fund the renewed offensive.

All that started to coalesce just about the time the first Canadian troops hit the ground in southern Afghanistan. Whether the Iraqi invasion was good or bad is irrelevant to me: all I know is that it took troops and resources away from Afghanistan at a time when they could have made a significant difference to that country. Iraq gave the Taliban hope at a time when they had just about given up. The most valuable asset missing was intelligence—no Western country, or indeed any country, predicted the resurgence, because the intelligence flow from on the ground was skimpy. Most of the people who did that kind of work were focused on Iraq.

In 2003 we didn't have an inkling of what would occur. Meanwhile, we had our hands full trying to get ready for our mission with ISAF. Land Forces Central Area, the part of the army based in Ontario, was tabbed as the lead on that first rotation in Kabul, but we didn't necessarily prepare them very well for all aspects of what was going on in and around the Afghan capital. In tactical terms we were doing it right: the battle group under Lieutenant-Colonel Don Denne was training in Wainwright, Alberta, going through their paces with great success. Major-General Andy Leslie was running that training and it was all going well. I talked to Andy a number of times about what I wanted him to get the troops to practise, thinking ahead to a possible worst-case scenario, in which major fighting broke out in Kabul. "Andy, you get your soldiers to practise pulling out and conducting a fighting withdrawal from Kabul to the massive U.S. base at Bagram," I told him. Nobody knew how shaky or fragile the situation was, or when the city—indeed, the whole country—might once again turn into a free-fire zone, and I wanted Andy and those soldiers to be ready no matter what occurred.

Despite the experience I had gained from training my headquarters for Bosnia, and how valuable that had been, we did not send Leslie off to Germany to train with Lieutenant-General Goetz Gliemeroth, the German who was the overall ISAF commander, and his ISAF command team. We looked at Andy Leslie almost exclusively as the commander of the Canadian contingent, whereas when he got on the ground in Afghanistan he spent almost all of his time working at the job of being Deputy Commander of ISAF. We did not understand very well how to set up this kind of command structure, and consequently we did not prepare as well for it as we could have. Andy had only two days to coordinate with his international command team before he flew into Kabul to become the Canadian commander and Deputy Commander of ISAF. This higher-level operational set-up was not well thought out from our perspective.

The soldiers themselves were trained and ready as individuals or teams, and we were scrambling to get all the necessary equipment to ensure success. One equipment challenge reared its head immediately: we had not resolved the shortage of desert kit and still had green camouflage uniforms as opposed to the lighter-coloured desert-pattern camouflage. When we ordered the new Canadian pattern digital camouflage uniforms, which made us one of the first military forces in the world to design this state-of-the-art camouflage, nobody thought that we'd have such a large number of soldiers operating in a desert environment any time in the immediate future and, given both lack of money and the stage of the program to deliver the uniforms, we had only the green. The shortage of available fabric made it simply impossible to get Canadian desert-pattern uniforms for our soldiers in time for this mission. We didn't have the right uniforms until the second rotation. The media made a fuss, with what seemed like every reporter in Canada coaxing almost every politician in Canada to weigh in on the issue. In the end it was a fairly minor problem, but all that media attention probably kept many of the other shortfalls in equipment or mission planning from being aired.

We were determined to get this mission right. After a lot of hard work by a lot of people, we did get the battle group, based on the 3rd Battalion, Royal Canadian Regiment, trained and ready to go. Don Denne, a tough, no-nonsense leader who I knew well, had been a company commander in the brigade when I was commanding the Royal Canadian Dragoons in Petawawa, and we worked together often. We ran exercise after exercise and built good combat teams, so I knew how capable he was and was very confident that we had a good commander. The designated brigade commander, who would command tactical forces from twenty or more nations in Kabul, was Peter Devlin, who had impressed me so much while I was commander of the brigade in Petawawa. So, again, I was confident that our troops were in good hands.

It really was the army that built that organization and got it out the door to Afghanistan, with support from the logisticians and airlifters. The rest of the Canadian Forces was facing its own enormous pressures: the navy had rotated almost every ship in the fleet through the Persian Gulf for Operation Apollo and had put more than 90 per cent of its available sailors to sea in operations in 2002 and 2003, many of them for a second and third tour, while the air force was struggling with aging aircraft, an expensive modernization program for its CF-18 front-line fighters, and trying to open a supply bridge to Afghanistan with forty-year-old Hercules transports, replace the antique shipborne helicopters and deal with massive attrition of its very best pilots and ground crews.

I had been promoted to lieutenant-general and was obviously headed for a senior appointment sometime in 2003. The logical choice was that I would become army commander, and that soon became clear: I was going to take over the army from Mike Jeffery, who had already said he was going to retire in late spring 2003. Mike and I had worked closely together and had some frank discussions about the state of the army and how it had to be shaped for the future.

Before I took command in May, Mike and I spent a fair bit of time discussing the ISAF mission. Leslie had not yet deployed, but we were doing all the preparations for the first phase of the mission, where Canada would contribute a battle group and the Deputy Commander, plus the brigade headquarters and numerous other staff officers, under General Gliemeroth. Canada was going to have the majority of the forces on the ground, and we felt that we were eventually going to command ISAF. There was no way Canada could have such a large commitment and not end up getting command—that would have been ludicrous.

As Mike and I assessed how we were going to ensure that Canada could get and execute that command, we realized that we were going to have to nominate at least a three-star general as our candidate. It would have been very difficult to propose that a major-general take command of ISAF and then promote him to a three-star if he got the job, because other NATO nations would have pre-empted us by putting forward their most senior and experienced three-star generals. We felt that we had to make a decision immediately to allow that commander-designate time to prepare himself and build his headquarters. It really came down to one of two people: Mike Jeffery or Rick Hillier. Either Mike would stay on as army commander and I would go to command ISAF, or Mike would go to Kabul and I would take over the army. We were running out of time and couldn't get a decision in Ottawa. Canada might not take over command of ISAF and, if somehow we did, a two-star might be put in charge, so we would wait and see was the prevailing view.

269

In May, Mike retired and handed over command of the army to me, eliminating one of two options. In September 2003 the decision could not be put off any longer. If we wanted command of ISAF, Canada had to put forward the name of a lieutenant-general in order to get the Secretary-General of NATO and the Supreme Allied Commander Europe (SACEUR) to support us. It had to be an army three-star, and that three-star had to have credibility—that is, operational experience. It really came down to one option: I would go to Afghanistan to command ISAF.

I sat down with Henault, the CDS, and scribbled out a list of our generals who could handle that command. We named five or six officers who could do the job capably, but only one of them was a three-star general. So I said to the Chief, "Are we serious about trying to get a Canadian in that job? Because if we are, there's only one name at the top of the list: Rick Hillier." Henault agreed. He told the Minister our choice, and the Minister eventually took it to Cabinet and announced it in the House of Commons.

While this was taking place, we in the army had our hands full. We were focused on the strategic planning for the future land forces, assessing what kind of army Canada would need against what kind of threat. Enormous budgetary challenges could no longer be ignored and we were getting hammered by that combination of financial constraints, old equipment, personnel shortages and the push to transform the army from a Cold War organization into a modern, flexible and responsive force. The situation was exacerbated by the deployment to Afghanistan. Clearly, our very best equipment, sustained by our few spare parts and replacements, was going to Afghanistan, and the older, often broken equipment would remain in Canada. Yet I would sit in meetings with deputy ministers and assistant deputy ministers within the Department, along with other senior military officers, and have to listen to them tell me that we had enough money for transformation, growth and operations.

I got yelled at in some of these meetings when I said, "No, we don't."

The response, incredible as it seems, was "Well, if you can't transform an army with this amount of money, we'll take it back, find a better use for it and the army will be screwed." My confidence that I had support at senior levels, and my faith in the senior levels of the public service, was at another all-time low!

We had barely enough money to survive, let alone grow or transform into a more modern force. The total Department of National Defence budget at this time was between $10 and $11 billion, and that could not even begin to address the challenges we were facing, challenges that people even within the Department failed to recognize. There had not been increases in the defence budget, and we had to now go to Cabinet to gain approval for urgent operational requirement funding for the Afghanistan mission, funding that would enable us to provide the needed equipments to our soldiers. We had to buy infrared patches to put on the soldiers' uniforms to identify them in their comrades' night-vision sights, and new counter-mortar radars to locate any incoming bombs or rockets aimed at our base, and we needed a UAV (unmanned aerial vehicle) for surveillance. Buying when you urgently and desperately need things, however, is not a wise policy. In this case, when we went to buy a UAV, the only model available was the French-built Sperwer, which quickly proved to be an atrocious vehicle for the mission. It just wasn't capable of performing well in the heat and high altitudes of Afghanistan. But we needed the capability, it was the only one available and so we bought it.

The Canadian army was in shock. We did not have nearly enough soldiers, and the ones that we did have were fatigued from the Bosnian experience, the constant rotations in and out of the former Yugoslavia and the sense that nothing was going to change for the better. We had "ghost" units—battalions or regiments that were supposed to have 750 or 800 people on strength but which instead could muster maybe 450 soldiers, and out of that 20 per cent or more would be unavailable for deployment for one reason or another. Our buildings and facilities on bases across the country were in appalling condition. An incredible amount of money had been scooped from infrastructure budgets to pay for unfunded training or equipment programs. The soldiers were working and living in buildings that in some cases dated back to the First World War and that had been stables during the 1920s. The troops swore they could still smell the horses! The majority of our equipment was past its expiry date. We were still running inadequate vehicles like the Cougar tank trainers and personnel carriers like the Grizzlies, while the new LAV vehicles, just being delivered, were present in only minuscule numbers.

Those challenges were being felt throughout the Canadian Forces, not just in the army. We had enough money in the Canadian Forces for maybe two out of the army, navy and air force. There was just not enough money to go around for all three, and the battles for dollars were brutal. We did not know what Canada wanted for its armed forces; we did not have a strategy for how the army, navy and air force would work as one, and every day seemed like it was survival of the fittest. The army was not going to get "voted off the island" if I had anything to say about it, and so my elbows were up in every meeting. I never met a fight I didn't like, and I always wanted to win every fight 100 to nothing.

When I suggested that we had to have a strategy, stop trying to do everything for everybody and focus on one area of expertise for Canada, some of my colleagues became defensive. I got beaten up regularly by the head of the navy, Vice-Admiral Ron Buck, and the Commander of the Air Force, Lieutenant-General Lloyd Campbell, because they had their own views of what had to be done and defended their branches as vigorously as I stuck up for the army. Ron is one of my closest friends and a guy that I really admire and respect, but we got into loud debates because of the survival atmosphere in NDHQ in those days.

The army, navy and air force commanders over the previous few years had carried an incredible weight on their shoulders as all sought to survive. It was dog eat dog. Budgetary discussions became heated every time we sat down. To simply have survived as a fighting force after those challenging times is enormously complimentary to incredible Canadian leaders who commanded at that senior level. Guys like Ron, who became Vice Chief of the Defence Staff and made the job of running complex organizations seem easy, and who presided over the first year of the dramatic transformations that we made in the Canadian Forces, are the unsung (and unrecognized) heroes of our country. They kept the CF from breaking, when by any reasonable measure it should have.

On my first working day as head of the army, I went to the Minister of National Defence, McCallum, with Henault, the CDS, and walked him through why we needed a break in our overseas missions the following year. I drew a stick-man diagram representing the army's field force, with each stick man representing roughly 1,000 soldiers. I left one stick man out of battle: that stick man was either getting out of the military, was sick or injured, on parental leave or otherwise unavailable. A second, larger group of four stick men represented those soldiers who had just returned from operations and would not be available for another tour for at least a year. I drew another group of stick men to represent those training to go on the next mission and so on. By the time we got through the year-long mission in Afghanistan, I had more stick men than we had soldiers available, and I pointed out to the Minister that all of this was happening while the army's personnel strength continued to slide. I said, "Look: we can do the mission in Afghanistan until August of '04, but after that you've got essentially nothing, unless you're prepared to carry it on the backs of the soldiers. If you're not willing to grow the army, and it appears we're not going to do that here in Canada, then here are your options: (a) don't do anything past August of '04, or (b) recognize if you do that you're doing it on the backs of soldiers, and it will become pretty clear to you, quickly, what that will do to those men and women and their families, or (c) inject large amounts of money right now and authorize up to another land brigade to be recruited, trained and made ready."

McCallum clearly wasn't happy with what I had to tell him, and said so, but the message got through. "I don't like this, but I understand it," he responded. As a result, after August 2004 the Canadian presence in Kabul dropped significantly. We were still there, but our presence was minuscule.

Although I believed this to be the absolutely right approach at the time, in hindsight I believe I made a major strategic error. With the break in operations, starting in late summer 2004, any urgency or pressure to resolve manning, equipment or budgetary problems disappeared. Additionally, the government got used to not having to cough up additional money for operations and, consequently, caused the CF to bear many of the extra costs when operations reconvened. In short, I believe the army was in worse shape after the pause than before.

These were intense months with enormous demands on all. We were executing the first deployment into Kabul, fighting for more funding and equipment, and taking the first casualties in Afghanistan. I was hosting the Conference of American Armies (CAA) at the Westin Hotel in Ottawa (I was the president of that institution, comprising all the land forces in the hemisphere save for those of Cuba, for a two-year period), and at the same time I was training a headquarters team and preparing for command of ISAF in Afghanistan. It would be an understatement to say it was a busy and challenging time.

On the morning of October 2, 2003, I was on my way to Cabinet with the Minister (the Chief wasn't available so I was filling in for him) to sit in on the discussion concerning a billion-dollar project to purchase new armoured vehicles for the army. I'd pulled myself out of the CAA meetings, leaving the Deputy Commander, Major-General Marc Caron, to carry on, and while I was driving up to Parliament Hill I got the phone call saying that we had lost two soldiers in Afghanistan, Sergeant Robert Alan Short and Corporal Robbie Beerenfenger. The families had not yet been notified, and so their deaths were not public knowledge.

I met McCallum in the waiting room outside the Cabinet meeting room, and he and I got on the phone to Leslie in Kabul. Leslie told us what he knew so far: the Iltis jeep they were riding in had hit a mine or improvised explosive device (later determined to be several anti-tank mines stacked one on top of the other) that destroyed the vehicle, and that we had a couple of other soldiers wounded but that they were expected to survive. Meanwhile, the army was striving to locate the families of those soldiers in a race against time to ensure the families did not find out about the loss of a loved one from a news report.

Finalizing the discussion, I said, "Andy, here's how we're going to handle it from this end. We're going to treat those fallen soldiers with respect. We're going to return them with dignity and with the honour they have earned, and we're going to grieve with, and support, their families. And we're going to do it all the right way."

We went into the Cabinet room and McCallum told his colleagues that we had lost those two soldiers. There was a palpable sucking in of breath around the table, and it was obvious that the ministers were shocked by the news. Then he said that when Parliament resumed that afternoon he would go into the House of Commons and break the news of the deaths there. He felt it was appropriate for Canadians to hear the news of the two casualties in this manner.

We were concerned about having time to notify the families before the deaths went public, and the Minister's determination to announce the deaths in the House increased our urgency to do so. We always resisted releasing the fact that we had lost soldiers until we finished notifications, so that we could also announce, publicly, that next of kin had been notified. We had nearly 2,000

The first CF Heroes' Ball, hosted by Governor General Michaëlle Jean at Rideau Hall, June 2006. (In the front row: Joyce and me with Their Excellencies, as well as Audra and Paul Franklin.)

It wasn't all work. While participating in the Changing of the Guard ceremony in July 2005, I felt even prouder to be Canadian—but it was *hot*!

The commemoration on the 90th anniversary of Vimy made me proud, yet again, to be Canadian. The ceremony featured 3,600 children, one to represent each soldier killed in battle. What an emotional day.

Talking with Peter Mansbridge on the Vimy Memorial site, Easter Monday, 2007.

Having a laugh with Prime Minister Harper in Parliament at the 2007 throne speech.

The Calgary Stampede offered a rare opportunity to build relationships with those important to Canada. Left to right: our host and friend, Guy Buchanan; Commander of NORAD, Admiral Tim Keating; me; and Peter Pace, the U.S. Chairman of the Joint Chiefs of Staff.

The Prime Minister's arrival in Kandahar, in March 2006. Left to right: me, Minister of National Defence Gord O'Connor, Prime Minister Stephen Harper, Dave Fraser (the Canadian Commander) and Ambassador David Sproule. I awarded the PM a CDS coin for his foray into Taliban country.

With President Hamid Karzai of Afghanistan, in his office. During our very first meeting, the President told me that the greatest threat to Afghanistan was the Afghans' own lack of capacity to do anything—and that was the area in which he thought the international response could help most. The conversation led directly to the creation of the Strategic Advisory Team.

Some awesome Canadians at a change of command in KAF (Kandahar Air-field). Left to right: me; Tim Grant and Dave Fraser, who both commanded in Kandahar; George Petrolekas, who kept us in the loop on all things inter-national; and Fred Lewis, a combat engineer who managed things so easily.

Working with "warlords," like the one on my left, was part of the daily business in Afghanistan.

Those on our side weren't any easier to work with. I thought Donald Rumsfeld was a grumpy old man at this meeting in Kabul, 2004—and my impression was confirmed each time I met him afterwards.

Afghan Defence Minister Rahim Wardak (right), me, Ambassador Chris Alexander (to my right) and Canadian Contingent Commander Colonel Walt Semianiw. Minister Wardak and I worked closely together on intense and risky issues and became good friends. Immediately after the meeting we adjourned to the garden for a cigarette (him) and a cigar (me). We have both since quit.

Canadian philosopher and icon Don Cherry, who has a special place in the heart of every man and woman in uniform—and of everyone in their families—for his support and appreciation for their sacrifices. Left to right: our son Steven, Don, Joyce and me.

Enjoying a "Timmy's" with Tim—Tim Grant, our Commander in Kandahar, that is. Tim Hortons was a visceral connection to home for all those deployed. God bless Tim's.

With Team Canada, Christmas Eve, 2006, on board HMCS *Ottawa* in the Persian Gulf. Newfoundland singer Damhnait Doyle leads in singing "O Canada."

There's nothing more important than pouring the gravy. Rick Mercer, Jay Hill and Laurie Hawn (face partially hidden) serve the troops Christmas dinner at Strong Point West, in 2006. The sign on the wall was to the point.

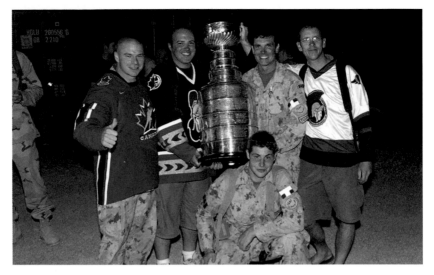

This silver Canadian icon connected Canadians around the world to Canada in a powerful way. Master Corporal Tom Charette (standing, in uniform), knowing I was a Leafs fan, informed me that having the Cup in Kandahar meant the Taliban had been closer to it over the past forty-two years than the Leafs!

Arriving at Kandahar Airfield, Christmas Eve 2007, with Ambassador David Wilkins from the U.S., a true friend and supporter, and Minister of National Defence Peter MacKay.

soldiers in Afghanistan, and if we had sent out a notice saying that we'd lost two soldiers and didn't mention anything about notification, instantly we would have 2,000 families across the country going into shock, refusing to answer their phones or their doors, or calling, with trepidation, for information. In this case, I felt that the news was going to come out very soon whether we wanted it to or not—media were already querying our public affairs people. We reached the last members of the families ten minutes ahead of the Minister's announcement. McCallum had heard my comments to Andy, and when he stood up in House of Commons early that afternoon to announce the deaths of those two men, he used the exact words that I had: "We're going to return those soldiers with respect; we're going to treat them and their families with dignity and honour and we're going to grieve with and support those families." We both felt that was the absolutely right approach.

I had to carry on briefing Cabinet on that billion-dollar vehicle purchase, deal with a Minister who wanted to be able to break the news of the deaths in Parliament before it became public and then go back to the Conference of American Armies—twenty-six army commanders from the U.S., Latin America, Central America and the Caribbean, all with spouses and entourages in tow. I walked out on Parliament Hill to a cold October day in an early snowfall and the deaths hit me all at once. The snow, and the fact that winter was arriving very quickly, depressed me further. It was not a good day.

Shortly after the bodies were returned to Canada, I went to Petawawa to meet the Beerenfenger and Short families—great families who were obviously devastated. I presented the mother and the widow the Memorial Cross at the Officers' Mess on the base, in a smaller room, with just family present, to try to relieve some of the stress that accompanies large ceremonies. We had decided we didn't want a massive, national memorial ceremony as had been held for the Tarnak Farm soldiers, but instead a more private, community-based event.

All of us felt that it was better to make these ceremonies smaller and more intimate. Every one of us in the command structure realized that we were going to take more casualties in Afghanistan. We were determined to do all the right things, with appropriate dignity, respect and ceremony, but we knew we couldn't do something like the Tarnak Farm memorial every time one of our young soldiers died. We just couldn't go full-throttle and engage the nation in that way every time we lost someone. Even if we had wanted to, after a while the nation would grow tired of it.

The service for Short and Beerenfenger was done in a smaller regional hockey arena in Pembroke, near Petawawa, where the local community turned out en masse to show their support. It may have been smaller, but the service was powerful. There must have been 3,000 people packed into that arena, and when we arrived, after presenting the Memorial Crosses at the Officers' Mess, we lined up at the main entrance to the arena, the spot where the Zamboni drives onto the rink. As we were getting ready to go in, I stood there with the regimental sergeant major of the army, Greg Lacroix, ahead of Beerenfenger's wife, Tina, and two of their three children, all very young. Immediately behind them was the Short family.

While we were waiting to move into the arena, Tina's oldest boy said, "Mom, Mom, look! This is the place where I played hockey two weeks ago. This is where I played hockey!"

My heart sank. I thought, "Oh my God. He doesn't know how his life has changed." That's how a child responds to a tragedy like this: he recognizes that this is the place where he plays hockey. So I went in there with my heart in my throat and participated in the service to remember those two incredible men, soldiers, husbands, fathers and Canadians.

One thing I did learn that day was not to talk to the media following such an emotional situation. Before the service started, I had agreed to talk to the reporters afterward, and answer a few of their questions. I wanted to talk about the soldiers we'd lost, but of course all they wanted to ask about was "Are the vehicles that our soldiers use any good?" Well, I had left that memorial service quite moved, after having poured my heart out in public about how I felt about my soldiers, in front of those families, 3,000 other people in the arena and thousands of others watching on TV. The video message from Don Denne in Kabul was enough to cause anyone to cry, and then, to go out to a media event where people are badgering you with questions about whether the vehicles were any good or not—well, I had no time for that, none whatsoever. I thought to myself, "You should not be in this situation. This is not the time." I wrote that down in my little book to remember: don't do this again.

The army's handling of the deaths of Corporal Beerenfenger and Sergeant Short was appropriate and dignified, just exactly as it should have been. The communities in the Upper Ottawa Valley, the police, the emergency services, the local mayors and municipal politicians really looked after those families and paid respect to the fallen soldiers magnificently. The families of our two fallen heroes were indeed wrapped in their arms. What Joyce and I had seen in Texas was becoming reality in Canada.

In the midst of all this, I was trying to hand off my responsibilities as army commander to my deputy, Marc Caron, so I could focus on what we needed to do to build a headquarters for Kabul. Because I was taking command, a significant portion of that headquarters was obviously going to be Canadian, and I wanted certain key players—my "go-to" guys—to be Canadian. So far, we had put little thought into how we were going to build and train this headquarters, who would be a part of it and how we would prepare and test it, particularly given the fact that some twenty-five or more nationalities would be included. We were already behind the curve; it was now October, and I was still trying to hand responsibility over to Marc, who had just been promoted to two-star. He was focusing on training the battle group that was going into Kabul after the Royal Canadian Regiment, making sure that everything was done much as I had done the previous spring for Andy Leslie and Pete Devlin.

It helped that Marc had just come from command in Montreal with responsibility for the brigade in Valcartier, Quebec, and the Royal 22nd Regiment (the Van Doos), which would generate the battle group that was going to Kabul with me. Marc knew the units and soldiers well and, most importantly, knew exactly what they needed to do and what equipment they had to have in order to be ready.

I also had to take into account that ISAF had been a European mission, largely run by the Germans with the British, French, Belgians and a few others participating to lesser degrees, but that this was changing. There had been huge pressure from many countries for NATO to take over ISAF, but particularly from the United States, Canada and Germany. The Germans wanted to expand into the northern provinces of Afghanistan, but the only way they could do that at the time was under American command, which was unacceptable to them. Canada wanted NATO to take command of the mission so that when we took charge of ISAF, Canada would be working for the alliance, rather than for the Americans. That was an important distinction to the Liberal government. Both Germany and Canada also wanted to expand the ISAF mission beyond the 60 to 80 kilometres around Kabul that were its present limitations. NATO itself was looking for something, anything, to do that would allow it to prove that it was still a worthwhile organization in the new, post-9/11 world. The United States, of course, wanted NATO to take responsibility for more in the world, but particularly in Afghanistan, as a way of getting Europeans and others much more involved in the War on Terror.

Lord George Robertson was the NATO Secretary-General, clearly an extroverted leader of an alliance that had lost its reason for existence when the Soviet Union crumbled and the threat to Western Europe vanished. He was not the type of a man who would take no for an answer, and he believed that without the ISAF mission, NATO would wither and die. The trouble was that NATO was being pushed into the Afghan mission without any strategic plan or, indeed, any substantial troop commitments from its member nations.

NATO ended up taking an incremental approach into the mission, agreeing to take responsibility for ISAF and then trying to get member nations to deploy the troops and equipment to do it. One result of this was the idea of provincial reconstruction teams, which were seen as a way for the alliance to expand the ISAF mission throughout the rest of Afghanistan without any need for the large numbers of troops that it didn't have committed. Some NATO members were already leery of sending their soldiers to Afghanistan, and many were not eager to allow their soldiers to engage in anything resembling combat.

The context made my job exciting, but it led to some long days at work trying to juggle so many priorities while planning how to get to Afghanistan and successfully run a mission there. To do all of that by February 9, 2004, with now some thirty-seven nations each having a say, occupied me fully!

I should have paid more attention to preparing Joyce for what was coming, since I had not really talked about any of this with her. About a week after our casualties in Kabul, I came home from work, sat down to a late dinner and watched *The National* with her. There was Peter Mansbridge, saying that Canada would be taking command of ISAF, as announced by the Secretary-General of NATO, and that one of our army three-stars would be commanding the mission. Joyce looked at me and said, "How many army three-stars are there, again?"

I said, "One, and yes, it's me!" The look on her face made me realize I had been remiss in my duties as a husband, but, strong and loving wife that she is, I got away with it. Within minutes she was already thinking ahead about what my absence would mean to the family and how we would deal with it. I have said many times that if I had to live my life over I'd for certain do two things: become a soldier and marry Joyce. Few others could have been so supportive, much less that forgiving.

CHAPTER 15

KABUL

I had gotten my first look at Afghanistan in the summer of 2003, during a visit to Kabul, the surrounding region and Mazar-i-Sharif (in northern Afghanistan) in order to see where our brigade would be working. The regimental sergeant major, Greg Lacroix, and I spent three days on the ground and got the chance to visit ISAF headquarters, where I met the German commander. I also met Major General Karl Eikenberry, the U.S. general responsible for training the Afghan National Army, who would, several years later, become the Coalition Force and ISAF commander, then, in 2009, the U.S. ambassador in Kabul and, throughout those years, a friend. We had a chance to see the lay of the land at Camp Julien, the massive camp under construction for our troops between the King's Palace and the Queen's Palace in the southwest corner of the city, and the chance to talk to brigade commanders, drive around Kabul and see quite a bit of the city. We rode around in soft-skinned vehicles because the security threat was low. I have always believed that a low profile (in other words, trying to look as much like everyone else as possible) was the best security. In Kabul, at least, we had not yet seen the dramatic change in the threat resulting from the American surge into Iraq.

The first thing that went through my mind when I landed in Kabul was "Man, it's hot." Even in Kabul, which at some 6,000 feet above sea level is a lot cooler than the south, it was still 40 degrees Celsius, which is especially warm if you're wearing a flak vest and combat kit.

The destruction from the Russian invasion and the numerous civil wars was striking, but so was the energy evident in the incredible amount of construction going on around the city. The signs of war remained visible everywhere, however, whether it was in the old Soviet fighting vehicles that had been burned and left where they were destroyed or in the buildings that had been bombed from the air, shelled by artillery or blown up by car bombs. The roads were in terrible shape, not from bombing, but from neglect during the Taliban's rule and twenty years of constant warfare before that. Public and municipal service in Kabul had been effectively destroyed.

When we first flew into Kabul International Airport, we could see all the wrecked airplanes along the side of the runway. The pilots had all been told that if they started to get into trouble on landing and had to go off the runway, they were to make sure to go off to the south, because the north side was a minefield laid by the Russians to protect the airfield from mujahedeen attacks.

Despite the destruction and the abject poverty, I was struck by the obvious dignity and pride of the people. Every Afghan I spoke to wanted to have something better for their families than what they had now. I was enthralled by those people. Soldiers spend a lot of time in many countries where the impression we have—rightly or wrongly—is that locals are often quite willing to sit back and let us do everything for them. In Afghanistan, on the other hand, the people told us, "We'll rebuild our own country, thanks very much. We need some help, but we need a hand up, not a handout."

Their resourcefulness was astounding and at times even caused us some difficulty during the mission. ISAF launched a program to get Afghan kids to bring in their toy guns, because in Afghanistan a toy gun is often a real gun that is broken beyond repair. Everybody was nervous that some child was going to point a "toy" gun at a soldier and get shot. Nobody wanted to see that happen, and the consequences for the mission would have been severe. So everything possible was done to encourage the kids to turn in their guns for kites, toys or school supplies. What we hadn't counted on was the entrepreneurial spirit of Afghans, who realized that the kites, pencils, pens, notebooks and toys they were getting in return for a toy gun were far more valuable than the gun itself. All of a sudden there was a surge of imports from Pakistan of toy guns, so much that the program had to be curtailed and eventually cancelled.

I was surprised by the many young people and large numbers of children crowding the streets of Kabul. When I came back to Canada at the end of the mission, everyone seemed old and grey by comparison. In Afghanistan nearly 55 per cent of the population is under fourteen years of age and the average family has nine children, of which six or seven would survive past the age of five. Those children were everywhere, and their energy was infectious. Their incredible beauty added to the tragedy that was their lives.

I was most deeply affected, however, by the overwhelming poverty and destitution. Most kids had no shoes, even in the deep snow during winter. Half of them were covered in parasites or had skin diseases, and all of them, because of severe malnutrition, appeared about a third of their real age. I saw one tiny girl, happy as can be, running around and playing on a gravel path, without any shoes. She looked about eighteen months old but somebody told me she was four. She was playing with something she'd found, chewing on it, and when I got a little closer I could see it was the filter of a cigarette that somebody had thrown into the ditch.

I thought then that with some security, a little bit of health care, some basic education, hygiene and a little better nutrition than what they're getting now, the incredible potential in that population could be harnessed for their country. It would be great to have a population with that youth, and hence that energy and work ethic, here in Canada.

There was no doubt that the scale and scope of the challenge before us was massive. Nothing in Kabul or indeed anywhere else in Afghanistan had been working for decades: not the government, the economy, local services, the military or the police. Everything seemed to be broken or destroyed, and it was obvious that we could start the work of helping Afghans fix it but we would not be able to finish the job for a long time. It would take at least a generation to complete a task so monumental.

I spent the two months before I was to take command of ISAF training the officers and men who would make up the headquarters, setting all the pieces in place for a successful mission. At the same time, I was trying to ensure that the army continued to run successfully back home. Marc, my deputy army commander, took over most of that before I left Canada because I needed to focus on the Afghan operation. After all, we were trying to prepare ourselves to run a mission with tasks from the tactical to the strategic level in the midst of a live enemy. That is to say, on any given day we could be orchestrating our troops' response to rocket attacks on Kabul, working with President Hamid Karzai to shape his government, delivering positive programs for the population or setting conditions for future expansion of the NATO area of operations. There did not seem to be enough time to do it all. To help, I had reached out to an incredibly capable officer and old friend, Colonel Bill Brough, who was on the army staff. I phoned him one night at his home right after I was designated ISAF commander and said, "Bill, I'm going to need someone with me to help shape all this, to focus completely on it while I'm still trying to balance running the army with getting ready for ISAF. Will you do that for me and then deploy with me on the mission and act as my executive officer?"

Bill signed on immediately for what would be a year of complete involvement and time away from home, so for a while after that I avoided his wife, Marnie, just in case she blamed me for his absence. Likewise, Colonel Mike Cessford, who had been my strategic analyst and planner in the division headquarters in Bosnia, came on board for an interim period and helped develop the training program for the headquarters staff. The experience and ability levels in our colonels in the CF were without peer.

It was quickly evident that NATO was going to be both our main support and our biggest headache during the mission. In

October, three months before I took command of ISAF, I visited the NATO Joint Forces Command (JFC) headquarters in Brunssum, Netherlands, the headquarters to which we would report (the commander of JFC had responsibility to SACEUR—the Supreme Allied Commander Europe—for the ISAF mission). I met with the staff officers at that headquarters and with a variety of other commanders from the countries that had been designated to provide forces to ISAF. It was crystal clear from the start that there was no strategy for the mission in Afghanistan.

ISAF had a brigade in Kabul, more troops outside the capital and a German provincial reconstruction team in the northern half of the country that was to come under NATO command during our tenure. So there was a huge area, all of northeast Afghanistan with just one provincial reconstruction team in it. That entire quarter of the country had no international security forces, leaving NATO with no ability to influence events. People at the NATO headquarters were talking about all kinds of pie-in-the-sky ideas for Afghanistan, but they had no strategy, no clear articulation of what they wanted to achieve, no political guidance and few forces. It was abysmal. NATO had started down a road that destroyed much of its credibility and in the end eroded support for the mission in every nation in the alliance. Sadly, years later, that situation remains unchanged.

NATO also seemed to be dominated by jealousies and small, vicious political battles. When I arrived in Brunssum, I met the officer who was supposed to become my deputy commander, a Danish general. He and I started to build a solid relationship over the next couple of weeks, which included flying him to Canada to work with us for a period of time. Then he was summarily pushed aside because the Germans wanted to fill that deputy commander spot, since they had such a large number of troops on the ground. Suddenly, I had a German general as my deputy. That general trained with us and was working out well, and then on the last day before we were to start deploying into Kabul, I was informed that he wouldn't be going. The Germans designated another two-star general to be deputy commander instead. By happenstance it all worked out well, because the guy who came in with us, Major-General Wolfgang Korter, was superb. He and I got along very well, and became good friends.

At the front end of our preparation, however, NATO's lack of cohesion, clarity and professionalism was ominous. This was my first, hard lesson in how NATO worked: it was more important within the alliance that every nation get to build up its own little fiefdom than it was to put together a solid team for a successful mission. Some nations were meticulous about selecting the best people for the job, preparing them well and making them available for the pre-deployment training. Many did not, and some of my headquarters officers didn't show up at all. Others arrived with only a few hours' notice that they were going to Afghanistan, and still others had to deploy to Kabul without any training. I once said to the chief of staff in Brunssum on a Wednesday, "You're telling me that somebody is going to the mission in Afghanistan next Monday who hasn't even been told that yet?" It was unbelievable. There is a great saying that it is not the journey of a thousand miles that is so daunting, it is the pebble in your shoe at the start. My pebble was NATO, specifically the approach at the various NATO head-quarters in Europe.

NATO and ISAF by now had completed the expansion into northeast Afghanistan through the German provincial reconstruction team in Kunduz. They had done that without a long-term plan, without a united political front and without any military strategy beyond somebody saying, "We're going to expand through provincial reconstruction teams." NATO had backed into the mission, taken over ISAF and then expanded it outside of Kabul without clearly articulating what they were trying to achieve or how they would do it. In other words, without any of the things needed to be successful.

NATO had become an enormous military bureaucracy. Its headquarters in Brussels prepared intricately detailed plans inside a massive and ponderous bureaucracy but would not or could not take responsibility for laying out broader military strategy. The Supreme Headquarters Allied Powers Europe (SHAPE), in Mons, Belgium, commanded by SACEUR, with enormous numbers of high-ranking civilians and military—general officers were a dime a dozen in all of these headquarters—tried to stay at the strategic level of planning but were constantly getting end run by headquarters in Brussels, who were into the tactical level and often dealing directly with forces on the ground. Then there was Joint Forces Command (Brunssum), another four-star-level headquarters, which was theoretically in charge of the ISAF mission and, with some 1,500 people on staff, including at least another platoon of generals and admirals (all carefully divided by nationality), had no idea what its real job was. JFC Brunssum couldn't send more troops if requested, couldn't approve risky or important operations, couldn't change the mission or articulate a strategy and couldn't provide more money or equipment for construction projects, because that was either SHAPE's or NATO headquarters' role.

So I was reporting directly to a headquarters that had no role but that was still in my chain of command—a situation that caused huge problems for every commander in that mission, and continues to do so. Brunssum was constantly getting into the details of the mission on the ground, trying to control everything going on in Afghanistan. They behaved like GM headquarters trying to repair motor vehicles across the world from Detroit—with a 7,000-kilometre-long screwdriver that is put into the correct spot by looking through a straw the same length. It was a situation ripe for disaster.

To complicate command, there was a new commander of JFC Brunssum, a German general, Gerhard Back, who had just replaced General Jack Deverell. Deverell was an operationally experienced, flexible and forward-looking British general who was focused on getting results. Back, on the other hand, was a typical Cold War bureaucrat. I knew as soon as I met him that we were not going to work together well. Back was interested in following procedures, in attention to details and micromanagement—in short, he was a control freak and, based on my experience, had bullied his way through those who did not agree with him. It was obvious that our styles would not blend well. In our initial meeting I was seeking some clarity as to what my mission would be and the way ahead. I was not interested in hearing how he thought we should run patrols in downtown Kabul, which is what he was focused on—that was why I had brigade, battalion, company and, particularly, platoon commanders. In fact, I wasn't much interested in how we ran patrols in downtown Kabul.

We ended up yelling at each other over the phone just two days after I took command of ISAF, and the relationship went downhill from there. He told me it was his job to ensure that I knew how to obey orders, and I told him that as soon as I received some intelligent ones, I would. It got worse, and the relationship between his headquarters and mine became strained. We looked at almost every single issue from opposite ends of the spectrum. I believed that we had to shape the international support to Afghanistan and that there was no distinction between military or non-military tasks: we just had to get things done. To say something was non-military, and therefore something I shouldn't be involved in was ludicrous. If half of the things that Back deemed non-military jobs had not been done, the mission would have failed. So we ignored him and continued to do what we felt was necessary to ensure success. Back saw my mission as running those patrols and taking intimate control of detailed tactical operations at the street level, while he did all the rest from back in Europe. Obviously that did not fit at all with my view of the mission, and we remained at loggerheads.

My biggest concern, however, arose long before I took command of ISAF, and continued to be the lack of strategic approach. NATO had not given me a clear idea of what my mission was and what exactly they wanted me to do. So, in December 2003, I took my key staff into Afghanistan about a month before I was to take command and spent four days on the ground, getting the lay of the land, seeing the work done at ISAF headquarters and meeting the major players from the UN, international aid organizations and others. During that time I had the opportunity to meet President Hamid Karzai for the first time, along with some of his ministers. When I first met the President, he told me, "You know, General, the greatest threat to Afghanistan is us—our own lack of capacity to do anything. It's not the Taliban, it's not al Qaeda—those are threats, but if we had a capacity to handle our own security they would no longer be threats to the country's stability and future. The greatest way to help us overcome the threat to us is to help us build our ability to govern ourselves: not just build our army or police, but a functioning government structure. And the greatest threat to that is the lack of coherence in the international assistance that's coming to us. It's an incomprehensible mess."

293

Karzai said most international donors used "drive-by" assistance, sending in money, aid projects or consultants and then leaving town without any follow-up. That, I thought, was where our focus should be, where we could help.

My key staff and I had taken more than twelve hours to get into Kabul on that reconnaissance trip. The flight stopped twice before we landed in Afghanistan, once at a German resupply base in Uzbekistan, just north of the Afghan border, and once prior to that, for refuelling at an airport in the Russian steppes. That airstrip had been built on the bare Central Asian plains: it was so flat and treeless you could've watched your dog run away from home for ten days. It was winter, and we were not allowed into the only building on the strip, so we stood out on the tarmac while the jet was being fuelled, freezing because our jackets were on the aircraft and imagining that this was how the Germans must have felt in 1941 when they hit their first Russian winter.

We finally got into Afghanistan, met with Gliemeroth and Andy Leslie, and spent four days walking through everything they were doing and meeting the major players. After we were through, winter weather set in and the Luftwaffe couldn't make it into Kabul to pick us up for the flight home. So I sat with my team in Kabul International Airport from eight o'clock in the morning until about four o'clock in the afternoon on December 15, when an RAF C-130 finally made it through the weather, picked us up and took us to Uzbekistan, where we could catch a Belgian air force jet back to Brunssum. That long layover turned out to be the most valuable day in our preparation. As we sat in a lounge in the back of the airport, I found an easel and stood there drawing, in schematic form, what we were going to do and my thoughts on how we were going to do it, articulating our mission and commander's guidance for implementation. I thought our main effort had to be rebuilding the Afghan government and walked through this with my nineteen key leaders. By the end of that waiting period, we had sketched out our mission. We had to help build a government, or, more accurately, help Afghans build a government that could deliver what their population wanted and needed, and help deliver it. Our mission, we felt, would be judged on what we could build, not destroy.

That six or seven hours of airport brainstorming allowed us to talk things through, summarize all we had been able to learn in our training to date, particularly from our recce on the ground, and lay out our mission with our main effort. We all got into what I can only describe as a mind-meld: it was one of those rare and really powerful examples of a group working together as a seamless team. One result was the idea of establishing a strategic planning cell that would be part of my headquarters, working for the Afghan President and government.

Thus the Strategic Advisory Team, or SAT, concept was born; it became one of the most successful programs ever introduced to help rebuild Afghanistan.

The twenty officers who made up the strategic planning team got their direction: "Your job is to help develop a program and process that lays out how we can help build a better Afghanistan: how we help get to a stable and democratic Afghanistan, and what the Afghans need to do accomplish this." The team had to develop the concept prior to deployment; ensure it was what the Afghans were comfortable with; help me sell their program to other international organizations, such as the UN, the United States (the U.S. ambassador particularly), Great Britain, Canada and others; and then help implement it. The work they did was not purely military—often not military at all—but it was absolutely crucial to building on any success that we had in military operations. Otherwise those patrols being run by platoon commanders in Kabul had no purpose whatsoever.

Officers like Lieutenant-Colonel Ian Hope, my strategic planner and later the first battle group commander when we went into Kandahar in 2006, knew what we needed to get done, and I turned Ian loose on the many problems facing the Afghan government. He looked at problems in a strategic and geopolitical way. He, and the other officers on the team, just went out and got things done, whether it was helping Afghans shape themselves to deliver, with international community assistance, medical, transportation, economic, budgetary, counter-narcotics services or, indeed, anything else. Ian would lay out what steps needed to be taken and who should be doing them, whether Afghans or internationals.

We used those planners and those strategic plans to help Afghan government officials walk through what they had to do, so they could develop, prioritize and implement their finalized plans. It was most important that we were not doing the work but helping Afghans do it for themselves. We walked them through what they wanted to do and then, with them, laid out the steps they needed to take to reach their goals: what their budgetary process would be, what resources they needed, how those resources got where they were needed and so on. It was basically teaching them the ABCs of responsible government. Few of the skills to do that were in place, since most of Afghanistan's competent public servants were either dead or living in exile after twenty-five years of chaos and violence. So we were using these twenty officers, from the various nationalities in my command, as a tool to get things moving.

One key leader who had a huge positive impact on this process was Chris Alexander, the Canadian ambassador. Chris and I became good friends very quickly, and we saw many things in a similar light. We challenged and supported each other, and our skill sets complemented one another. Once in a while we would also gently knock the other, but we were able to build an excellent working relationship, one that has unfortunately not been repeated. There was a great synergy in having a Canadian officer commanding ISAF at the same time as we had an ambassador who quickly gained immense credibility with both the Afghans and the international community because of his intellect, decisiveness, personality and ability to understand what was going on in that country.

When Chris would go to see President Karzai to talk issues, I was able to support him in a variety of ways. Equally, when we were working on the process to make the ISAF mission more coherent, more effective for Afghanistan, Chris was one of our key supporters. Our work led naturally to the creation of the SAT team to help the Afghan ministers organize and deliver some of the basic functions of government. Again, the officers didn't do the work and didn't offer political advice—they simply helped build a process of planning, finance, coordination, work and validation. We did it because nobody else could. Chris understood the needs, including the need to continue the SAT from Canada when different ISAF commanders had headed in other directions.

Before that final step to assume command of ISAF, I went home for Christmas and for our son Chris's wedding, which was held in the Dominican Republic right after New Year's Day 2004. I had met the commander of the Dominican Republic's army during the Conference of the American Armies the previous October. He had met our future daughter-in-law, Caroline, and when she told him they were getting married in his country, he insisted on getting her e-mail address and keeping up to date on the wedding plans.

It was a small wedding at a beachfront resort with about a dozen family and friends present. Caroline had planned to have it right on the beach at a certain time so the sun was just right for taking pictures. On the morning of the wedding, a Black Hawk helicopter came swooping down and landed right on the beach, scattering sunbathing tourists. Out came a uniformed army officer, the executive officer for the commander of the Dominican Republic's army, followed immediately by his boss, the army commander, with a big package under one arm. We invited him into the resort for coffee, and while the resort staff were running around, going crazy over all this, he handed Chris and Caroline the present. It was an oil painting of a typical scene in a Dominican Republic village. "This is a gift, but it is not your wedding gift," he said. "My wedding gift to you is that tonight, at your wedding, the Dominican Republic army orchestra will play for you."

At 5:30, half an hour before the wedding, a bus pulled up and twenty-six musicians got off with their instruments, formed up on the beach and began to play. The wedding went ahead and they played throughout, including singing Latino love songs during the signing of the register. We, during a surreal evening, danced on the sand grass to the music. It was quite a night.

Two nights later I landed back in Canada in the middle of a stormy, cold January evening. I went home, grabbed another suitcase and two hours later was in the air headed for England for a two-day seminar on ISAF and then onwards to Germany to do the final build of our command team.

From there, after a quick return visit to Canada, I headed to Afghanistan, but, before taking command, visited Pakistan and got an up-close look, from the other side of the fence, at the long, volatile border they share with Afghanistan. In hindsight, my visit to Pakistan was an incredibly positive move. I got an eye-opening education on the challenges along that border, which we knew the Taliban and al Qaeda were crossing regularly to mount attacks in Afghanistan. I had the chance to meet with the senior chain of command of the Pakistan Army, including their Chief of General Staff, and the Director General of Inter-Services Intelligence (the ISI, their version of the CIA, which helped create the Taliban, and some of whose members still maintain ties to them), and received detailed briefings from their perspective on events in Afghanistan and the challenges. From there it was on to Peshawar, into the FATA (Federally Administrated Tribal Areas) to South Waziristan, North Waziristan and, eventually, on to the Khyber Pass.

I visited the Pakistan Army brigade commander on the ground in South Waziristan and went up to the Durand Line, the border between Pakistan and Afghanistan, which the British drew in 1893. The brigade commander had been deployed there for eighteen months when I saw him and was a Pathan (as he called himself), or what we would call Pashtun. He had grown up in the border area and knew it well; it was his home. He showed me a sketch he had started, outlining the tribal relationships and territories in the region, and said to me, "I grew up in this area but I'm still discovering things that I had no idea existed, on the tribal level, or sub-tribe, or sub-sub-tribe, or district sub-tribe. It's quite incredible how complex this is and how everything goes back centuries, all complicated by the Pashtunwali [the Pashtun code of honour] and the fact that you never forget a slight. Two generations after a perceived insult, somebody will walk up and kill a person because of that remembered affront to family honour."

In that harsh, tough part of the world, a man's honour is everything. Without it he becomes a pariah, scorned by his tribe. Thus every insult demands revenge, an eye for an eye. We needed to remember this code.

We flew to the Khyber Pass by helicopter, a Russian-built Mi-8, reaching altitudes of over 12,000 feet. I became a little nervous when the pilot opened his window to get, as he described it, sufficient oxygen from the thin air to avoid blacking out.

On landing we were met by the commander from the Pakistani Frontier Corps. He brought out soldiers from the Khyber Rifles to demonstrate their war dance. These guys were all young men, with longish hair compared to our troops, all quite good-looking, and as we watched them whirling and slashing the air with the two sabres they were each carrying, I thought, "My God, I wouldn't want to meet these guys in a dark alley!"

Our host sat us down on a hilltop near the Pakistani end of the Khyber Pass and said, "See that numeral 1, there?" Three kilometres away was an enormous numeral 1 painted on the side of a hill. "That was where the first artillery engagement took place in 1842 during the British retreat from Kabul, and if you can see that big numeral 4 down there, that's where Dr. Brydon came through the Khyber Pass."

A plaque saluted Dr. Brydon, the British Army surgeon who was the only survivor of the British retreat from Kabul in 1842. He rode in badly wounded, on a horse so exhausted that it dropped dead as soon as he'd cleared the pass. I had a copy of *Flashman* with me, the first in the series of humorous historical novels by George MacDonald Fraser. I had read the series multiple times, but I brought the first one with me because it was about Flashman's misadventures during the First Afghan War. As I looked over that forbidding landscape of hills and mountains, filled with the warriors I had seen doing their ritual war dance an hour before—perfect defensive terrain, ambush alley and definitely bandit country—all I could think was, "Poor Flashman, chased up here by a bunch of dervishes."

The ancestors of those Khyber Rifle soldiers I had seen twirling those swords so effortlessly were the people who had chased the British and (in the book, anyway) poor old Flashman out of Afghanistan. We had dinner with the commander of the Frontier Corps in Peshawar, who gave me another book, *The Frontier Scouts*, which tells the frontier story of the period from the late 1800s through to the 1940s, focused on the British officers who became the officers in charge of the frontier scouts who had responsibility for securing this wild country. It was enthralling—about the tactics, the operations they mounted, the cunning and natural warrior ability that are native to the people of that area and the number of weapons that they manufactured. It proved educational reading indeed going into Kabul, and every once in a while I still dig it out and peruse a portion of it.

The Pakistanis had invited me to visit, and the fact that I had accepted was well received in Islamabad. That I, as commander designate of ISAF, would come into Pakistan before going to command in Afghanistan particularly impressed them. They gave me the full tour and detailed briefings at army headquarters and the Frontier Corps in Peshawar, followed by the chance to see their forward troops. The lack of equipment and training and the incredible challenges of the terrain were obvious.

The visit gave me a real appreciation of the Pakistani side of the problem: one look at that geography and you could tell how easy it would be for a terrorist group to live up there forever and move with impunity. Everyone knew that the Taliban were using the area as a safe haven, and it was already becoming clear that the early wins against the Taliban in 2002 and '03 were distant memories. The Taliban were still present and still a threat. That threat was reflected in the suicide-bomber attacks in Kabul in 2004 and the continued low-level attacks across Afghanistan's southern provinces.

I flew out of Pakistan and into Kabul, compliments of a U.S. Army C-12 aircraft, directly from Peshawar. I was sick with a virulent flu, sweating with a high fever and missing my bags, lost on the way from England. They never did catch up, but I had one day to get up to speed before assuming command and so got to work.

Despite the discomfort, I was on show and had to give a speech after accepting command of ISAF, in front of President Karzai and most of his Cabinet; David Pratt, the Canadian Minister of National Defence; the Secretary-General of NATO; and the military chain of command from NATO, the Afghan army, and the American Coalition Forces, along with numerous hangers-on and lots of media.

As usual, I started with a joke. "You know, I think I am the perfect example of multinationality, and so I feel confident in stepping into this multinational appointment," I said. "I am Canadian, but I've served with the United States Army, had British, Czech and Dutch battle groups under my command in Bosnia, and I've worked with soldiers from most of the nations represented here, including those from the Federation of Bosnia-Herzegovina, who make up the ISAF fire department.

"But it's more than that," I continued. "Even in the way I'm dressed, I represent multinationality. I'm wearing a watch that the Dutch gave me so I could always be punctual, a belt that the Americans gave me representing the great state of Texas, and I'm wearing Turkish combat boots. The reason I'm wearing Turkish boots is because the British lost my luggage."

That got a pretty good laugh, particularly from the British soldiers, who went around chortling about it for the next month, because they thought I was poking fun at the Royal Air Force. They were somewhat disappointed when I told them it was actually British Airways that had lost it, somewhere between London and Islamabad.

Chris Alexander said, "You know, Rick, if you can get a chuckle out of this group, with all these different languages and levels of understanding, well, you're off to a good start."

It *was* a good start, but I also included some serious words in that brief speech. "There is no greater privilege or responsibility that a commander can accept from a nation than command of their soldiers," I said. "I accept and commit that they shall be my troops and everything I do will be designed both to increase their chances of success in the mission we have and reduce the risk to them as they do it." That too went over well with the ambassadors and senior national commanders of each contributing nation. I meant every word.

Just before the change-of-command ceremony began, however, I had one very nervous moment. I was taking over from Lieutenant-General Gliemeroth, the German commander, and, as the incoming commander, I had no say in planning the change-of-command ceremony. We had done a good reconnaissance of the Kabul area, all of my key leaders had met all of his key leaders and the main players in the Afghan army, the Afghan government and the international community, so I didn't think I needed a long handover. We had already gone through all the major issues and I was ready to go to work. The Germans, however, had a different view. They wanted a ceremony, and they wanted it at a high school in the north end of Kabul that they had just rebuilt, because, naturally, they wanted to showcase one of their high-profile projects and make a big deal out of it.

There was a significant security presence because of all the VIPs in attendance. We had dozens of potential targets for the Taliban in one little building and all I could think as I looked around the area was "This is a juicy target indeed."

I arrived with my British regimental sergeant major and we stood next to the honour guard as we waited for President Karzai to arrive. As soon as he got out of his motorcade and began walking toward us, I heard, in the distance, the distinctive thump of mortars firing. "Oh, Christ," I thought. "We're going to have incoming fire right in the middle of this parade."

For a fraction of a second my heart was in my throat. What I didn't know was that nobody had bothered to tell the troops to shut down the artillery ranges at Poli Charkhi, a few kilometres away. The mortars that I heard firing were ISAF, completing some practice firing on the range.

Doing such a large ceremony didn't seem right to me. My comments to the staff as we prepared to depart theatre months later were "This was stupid. We shouldn't be doing this kind of thing. This is an operational theatre, there are major security risks and so we'll do a small handover ceremony with the appropriate folks from here in Kabul, but that's it." The change-of-command ceremony was small. We invited the ambassadors from the countries that had troops in ISAF, the Afghan Chief of General Staff, General Abdul Rahim Wardak, the coalition commander and one or two others. There were about fifty people for a simple ceremony where the Commander Joint Force Command, the incoming commander and I all spoke. Then we handed the flag over and went on our merry way. And I made sure the range at Poli Charkhi was closed during the ceremony!

Surprisingly, I did not get any flak from NATO over that, which was unusual because we got flak on almost every other thing that was not pre-approved by Brussels. I confirmed yet again: it is better to beg forgiveness than permission, particularly when dealing with bureaucracies.

The threat in Kabul was building. The Germans had been attacked by a suicide car bomb just before the Canadian battle group surged into the area; in October 2003 we had lost two soldiers to roadside bombs and we expected more casualties. Unfortunately, we did lose soldiers on that mission, but we had gone into it with the full understanding that this mission came with significant risks. While we tried everything humanly possible to minimize those risks, there was always the possibility that terrorist organizations—al Qaeda, the Taliban or others—would launch attacks against us or other coalition troops. Andy Leslie, who was rotating out of the mission, had updated me on the threat levels regularly, particularly after a British soldier was killed in January 2004 by a suicide bomber in Kabul itself just two weeks before my arrival.

Although we in the CF appreciated the risks involved in our deployment to Kabul, as did Canadian politicians—John McCallum had visited Afghanistan and had seen and heard for himself that there was a substantial threat—apparently not everyone got that message. Right after that British soldier died in Kabul, the

North Atlantic Council, composed of all the ambassadors who represent the NATO nations and who sit in permanent session in Brussels, decided to visit. Gliemeroth was out of country, so Leslie, as the acting commander, decided that the threat level had gone up significantly and nobody was certain that this one attack was not a precursor to more. He determined that this was not the time to have sixty visitors, including twenty-six high-profile (and often egotistical) ambassadors, in a big mob going around Kabul. So he diverted their aircraft into Bagram and said no, they couldn't visit—the threat level was too high.

The ambassadors and the various NATO officials had flown all the way from Brussels. Andy's decision, however absolutely correct, left us with twenty-six permanently angry ambassadors and an equally upset deputy secretary-general—angry at military commanders in Kabul and at Canadian commanders in particular. Eventually they were able to come into Kabul, later that year, but they were still disgruntled. When they did get on the ground, we had a whole program planned, with briefings, visits to key facilities and a chance to get a feel, taste and touch of the mission, all within a secure environment because of that continuing, very real threat. Their reaction shocked me. A lot complained because they couldn't go shopping in downtown Kabul or could not visit all the well-known spots, such as the famous Kabul bazaar or the old fortress of Bala Hissar. Several accompanying officials were perturbed because they could not get access to duty-free booze.

Finally, I had had enough. I said, "Wake up. This is the real world we're talking about. I don't give a shit about you getting killed, but if you do get killed here that's a strategic blow to

NATO, and we can't allow that." They probably still dislike Canadian commanders!

So we had to live with them having their noses out of joint. Andy made absolutely the right call, and if I'd been the commander I would've done the same thing.

Those NATO dignitaries weren't the only ones unhappy with Canadian commanders. About halfway through my tour, Donald Rumsfeld, the U.S. Secretary of Defense, came to Kabul, and I was asked to meet with him. Obviously, I agreed, since he was the Secretary of Defense for the superpower in NATO and I was the alliance's senior commander on the ground. Rumsfeld struck me as a grumpy old man. He was very complimentary to Canadian soldiers and, during an earlier visit, had told Leslie, "You Canadians are great. The problem is, there are not enough of you. We'd like to have double, triple or quadruple the number of Canadians around."

This time as he visited, the United States was pressuring NATO to do more in Afghanistan, in large part because the American military was so tied up in Iraq. Almost immediately Rumsfeld began peppering me with questions: "How many troops do you have?" and "How come you're not doing operations in the south, or out in the east [of Afghanistan]?"

After a few minutes of this kind of stuff I finally said, "Actually, you know, Mr. Secretary, I operate under the rules that NATO gives me. The last time I checked, the United States of America was a member of NATO. If you don't bloody well like the way NATO is working, then sort it out."

That brought the meeting to a pretty abrupt end. I had pushed back, because in my opinion the U.S. was beating NATO up without actually playing the role they should have playing been in order to straighten out both NATO and the ISAF mission in Afghanistan. Rumsfeld didn't like people pushing back, and I wasn't invited to come visit with him anymore.

The Afghans and allies had a high opinion of Canadian soldiers, but as the mission went on it became clear to me that the Canadian battle group in Kabul was not going to be my "go-to" guys. The Canadians were not my first choice of the units under my command when I had a dangerous or time-sensitive mission to accomplish. As had been the case in Bosnia, that was not a reflection on their commander or on the soldiers in the battle group, who were, without exception, terrific. But for any missions beyond a routine patrol, Alain Tremblay, who commanded the Canadian contingent, had to go to Ottawa for approval of almost every detail. By then it was far too late.

After the first time or two, when it took anywhere from twelve to seventy-two hours to get a mission approved by Ottawa, no matter how crucial, we stopped asking. We let the Canadians carry on with their normal routine and went to the British or the Norwegians instead—they were much more capable of responding quickly.

The Norwegians had contributed a company to ISAF. They were superb, professional, well trained and well disciplined, with very good leaders. Overall, they had a robust and well-equipped force of about 185 soldiers in Kabul that wasn't micromanaged by their national government in Oslo. So when we needed something done quickly, we very often reached out to the Norwegians. They had an effect far beyond their relatively small numbers.

I made a point of getting out with the different contingents at least twice a week to do something on the ground. I wanted to see what it was like out on the foot patrols in the various regions around Kabul, witness how the locals reacted to the troops and see first-hand what the relationships with the police, the army or other internationals were like. Personal experience is the only way you can learn those things, and going out was the only way to get personal experience, so I was out with the Turkish battalion in their region of Kabul, with the Germans quite a bit, with the French and of course with the Canadians in the west and northwest of Kabul. (And, as I mentioned previously, I'd been out with the Norwegians a variety of times, and they had impressed me.)

In early May I joined one of the Norwegian foot patrols in the centre of Kabul. We did all the rehearsals and preparation in their camp before heading out. I had my own little team of Canadians with me, and we headed off in the Norwegian Land Rovers, a stripped-down Land Rover with the driver and me in the front, one guy in the back facing to the rear with his machine gun and another guy, Corporal Tommy Rødeingsby, standing in the centre manning a heavy .50-calibre machine gun in a ring mount. Rødeingsby was a cocky and funny young man, all of twenty-nine years old. We drove out to the area we were patrolling, dismounted and spent about four hours on the ground, moving through the bazaar, talking to folks, gathering intelligence and seeing what the state of affairs was—all those kinds of things that you do on patrol (and I could only imagine how happy Back must have been, back in Brunssum, knowing that I was on patrol myself). Then we came back and mounted the vehicles, which had moved from where we'd been dropped off, and got ready to drive back to the compound. I saw that we were only about 500 metres from ISAF headquarters, while it was about 10 kilometres to the Norwegian base. So rather than travel all that way only to come back again, I said, "Hey, just drop me off."

We rolled by my headquarters, and I got out and thanked them all for their great work and for taking me along. I shook hands with my crew, Tommy last. They drove out of the ISAF compound headed back to their camp and within five minutes were hit by a rocket-propelled grenade ambush. One of the grenades hit the vehicle I had been riding in and exploded, tragically killing Tommy.

I went out to the Norwegian camp the next morning and talked to the platoon that had been on the patrol. They knew by then that two of them were going to be going home with the body and would be talking to the parents, so I had the chance to tell them what I wanted Tommy's parents to hear. He had truly been a great credit to his country and his family.

We were pretty certain, after the intelligence analysis, that the attack had not been aimed at me and that the risk to that patrol had not been increased by my going with them. It was just one of those unfortunate coincidences. If it hadn't been them, it would've been the next ISAF patrol to come along that road: that was our best assessment.

Every day in Afghanistan was exciting, but the latter half of our mission became interesting because of the upcoming presidential elections. We kept busy with security preparations for registration and voting and generally keeping a lid on things in Kabul and the northern half of the country. During early July,

President Karzai was deciding who he would name as his vice-presidential running mate. His initial choice had been Fahim Khan, a famous warlord, now Minister of National Defence and Vice President and also an extremely wealthy man with a sizable armed militia that was loyal to him alone. He was the successor to the "Great Massoud," Ahmad Shah Massoud, in the Northern Alliance and was seen as Karzai's de facto running mate, but there were a lot of downsides to that from Karzai's point of view. There was huge pressure from the international community to show that those leaders who were "warlords," still maintaining their own forces, could not be involved in politics. Fahim, who styled himself a five-star general or field marshal, was viewed as a warlord by pretty much the entire country, who felt that if he stayed as the vice-presidential running mate, Karzai was going to discredit himself significantly, not only with the international community but also among normal Afghans who wanted the warlords, with the attendant corruption, gone. As well, there was no question that Fahim was involved in illegal activities and certainly had a very checkered past, which is how he became so wealthy.

One of the risks of not naming Fahim as his vice-presidential running mate was that Fahim could go offside and bring the Northern Alliance, or at least a significant chunk of it, into Kabul to decapitate the Afghan government and take over himself. He certainly had a large number of troops and equipment, including heavy weapons, which he had not yet handed over to the Afghan National Army, ISAF or U.S. forces.

Over four days, I was in the palace two or three times a day, along with the special representative from the UN, Jean Arnaud, the British ambassador, the American ambassador and the U.S.

coalition force commander. We went to dinner with the President on one of those days, then out onto the lawn for tea and a fruit dessert under the stars. President Karzai was using this group as an international sounding board as to whether or not Fahim should be his running mate. Out of the blue, he turned to me and asked, "General Hillier, what do you think? Should I keep Fahim Khan as my running mate or not?"

I had known Karzai since December, had been working with him since February, and I think he had a lot of confidence in ISAF. And he clearly viewed me as his commander, albeit of the international forces. That was a powerful thing, so he wanted to bring me into that decision-making process. My advice was to walk through each part of the pros and cons carefully, use our help as needed, consult widely—and that, whatever decision he made, it would be the right one. There was no way I was going to be telling him who to take on as his Vice President!

Karzai decided that he was not going to take Fahim Khan as his running mate, so the coalition commander, Lieutenant-General Dave Barno, and I went to work to try to keep everything stable.

Dave and I met Fahim Khan at the Ministry of Defence with one interpreter and one of Fahim's lackeys. We had discussed our approach and Dave asked me to take the lead in the discussion. We articulated all the arguments that we could to keep Fahim onside, within the political process, and from doing anything to destabilize the country. We emphasized the positive aspects of his keeping faith with the democratic process, but at the same time we alluded to the possible implications of his causing any unrest. Fahim was not a well man; he used to travel to Germany regularly for medical treatments. We had talked to the Germans and so we could tell him that the Germans were quite willing to say, "You will not be going to Germany for treatment again if you become violent." Fahim had millions of dollars scattered around the world; we had talked to a variety of intelligence, banking and accounting experts and were able to tell him, "If you want to be able to access and enjoy that money, you don't want to turn to violence. If you do, you're going to find that that money's going to be tied up in ways that will take you until long past your deathbed to resolve."

Mostly, however, we appealed to his place in history. Fahim Khan believed that he had been the victor that freed Afghanistan from the Taliban ogre. After Massoud died, at the hands of Osama bin Laden's suicide bombers on September 10, 2001, Fahim had stepped in as leader and had liberated much of Afghanistan, including the capital, Kabul. He saw himself as a significant figure in the history of Afghanistan, and we reinforced that, telling him that he had a chance to make history again by showing the men and women of Afghanistan that the political way was the way of the future. He remained peaceful, although he said to us that the real reason he would not run as Vice President was that he did not want to give up his rank of Field Marshal in order to stay in politics (he had five stars on his licence plate), and that he might fight, but he'd fight in the political arena.

Then he changed the topic slightly, and asked Dave and me what happened in American and Canadian politics: were our general officers allowed to hold political office or belong to political parties? I told him no, serving generals were not allowed to hold public office, and in fact, I said, "I don't think we've had a retired general officer elected to Parliament for years, and I don't think we're going to have one for quite a while." Little did I know that Gord O'Connor was running for Parliament in Kanata that very month and that our paths would soon cross when he became Minister of National Defence in 2006. An interesting footnote to our work was that in May 2009, President Karzai announced that his running mate as Vice President in the presidential elections of August 2009 would be none other than Fahim Kahn. I wondered if Fahim had resigned himself, like me, to being a former general!

The 2004 presidential elections happened shortly after my tour ended. We had done all the preparation with all the various organizations, from the United Nations, which had the responsibility to set all the conditions for the vote, to the Afghan electoral commission and the NATO nations that were part of the ISAF mission. President Karzai was very comfortable that he had all the right support mechanisms in place with us in ISAF and the coalition forces under Dave Barno. Then he realized that the guy that he had confidence in, me, was going to be leaving in August, six weeks before the elections were to take place. "Absolutely not," he said. "You're staying."

That decision was up to NATO, so I said, "Okay, Mr. President, but you need to resolve this with NATO."

He asked NATO to extend me and the current ISAF headquarters for a few weeks, and lined up the support of several international groups working in Afghanistan—including the European Union ambassador, who was hugely supportive of this idea—to help him. It did make little sense to change the command structure of the main security force right before the first elections in Afghanistan in decades, but when President Karzai made his request to SecGen and it was considered by NATO's military committee, where all the military decisions were made, one country said, "We don't think the decision needs to be revisited." The issue died there.

It was indicative of how ineffective NATO had become, particularly when asked to do something quickly. A French general was due to take over command of ISAF from me that August, and the North Atlantic Council simply heard, from one country, "We don't think this decision needs to be revisited." That's all that had to be said to kill the idea, despite the request of the President of Afghanistan.

Everything was arranged for the elections and the security preparations around them, and it all went smoothly. I went home in August, took some time off and went back to work in late September in Ottawa.

A week before we were to depart, though, I went to see the President to ask him for a small favour. I saw Mr. Karzai pretty much every day and felt we had a very good relationship. I said, "Mr. President, you know I've got this great staff that's been with me ever since November of last year and the vast majority of them have toiled in obscurity. They rarely see anything or get to meet anyone outside the headquarters. Do you think that if I brought them over to your palace and we organized ourselves outside, that you could take thirty seconds of your time, come down, sit in the centre chair and have your picture taken with them?"

So the day before the change of command, all twenty of those in my key leadership team went to the palace. President Karzai had some of his Cabinet ministers there and had a meal set up under a grove of trees on the palace grounds, and we had lunch together. The President met everybody, thanked them personally, told them all how much he appreciated their work and spent about two hours with us. Then, at the end, we sat down for a group photo. I thought that was incredible of him, to take that much time and trouble when all I had asked for was a picture. President Karzai then stood up and said, "We're especially proud of General Hillier and what he has done for us. He has been a real friend of Afghanistan. So we want to recognize General Hillier with a medal, but the medal is of such significance to our country that we want it to be presented to you by the father of the country, the *baba,* who is the former king. So, General, if you would come back tonight to the palace we'd like to have a small ceremony, and the father of the country, the former king who lives in the inner palace, will preside."

I said, "Certainly, no problem," and the last night before I left Afghanistan, Chris Alexander, Bill Brough and I went to the palace and were ushered into an ornate room, where we were presented to the former king. He was ninety-one years old, sitting next to his son-in-law, who was eighty-two and in a wheelchair. Chris, Bill and I sat down and talked to them for about half an hour in English, French, Dari and Pashtun. The former king was very articulate and interesting, and talked about how he'd seen the country change over his lifetime, how they'd been on a real high in the '50s and '60s and then things went straight downhill in the '70s, into violence and civil war. Then the Russians came, and he talked about his frustration at being outside the country, in Italy, during that time and his joy, now, at being back home. Then, on a signal, the doors opened and in came the local media. The former king got to his feet, I stood in front of him and, witnessed by Chris Alexander and Bill Brough, he pinned Afghanistan's highest decoration on me to show the appreciation of the people of Afghanistan. It was surreal, but a lasting and fond memory of Afghanistan.

The last act belonged to Dave Barno. We had formed an incredible relationship with the Coalition Forces that he commanded, and Dave and I had become solid friends. Immediately following the change-of-command ceremony in the garden of ISAF headquarters, as we were quite literally heading to the door for the airport, Dave entered with his aide and presented me a framed Canadian flag as a memento. He had had that Canadian flag flown over the Coalition headquarters the day prior to honour both Canada and me personally. The impact that one person can have was brought home to me yet again.

CHAPTER 16

CHIEF OF THE DEFENCE STAFF

Coming home from Afghanistan took a little bit of a mental adjustment. Every time I came back from a place that had been almost entirely destroyed and landed in what is the most afflu-ent country in the world, I was always jarred by the silly, petty little things that dominate life in Canada. I flew into St. John's, met Joyce and spent a couple of days there just relaxing before we flew back to Ottawa. After we landed we sat in the airport lounge waiting for our luggage, which was—story of my life—lost. I picked up the newspaper and saw a story about a couple in Kanata complaining that the sidewalk was not wide enough for two people to walk side by side. These people went on about how terrible it was that with inline skaters or skateboarders coming up the sidewalk they couldn't walk beside each other. I thought, "What sheer lunacy."

If I've heard it once, I've heard it a billion times: every sol-dier who's been deployed has wished that every single Canadian could spend a week in a place like Afghanistan. If they did, goes the line of reasoning, they'd come home far more appreciative of our awesome country, just as soldiers do. They would understand what things are really important, and that sidewalks not being wide enough don't even rate.

When I was on my way out of Afghanistan and heading to Europe, a reporter asked me about the human rights situation. "You know what?" I said. "I've never seen a place in my life that is more focused on human rights than Afghanistan," I told her. "They spend 99 per cent of that focus on the most fundamental human right of all: the right to live. When you're dying from disease, hunger or violence, that becomes very much your focus."

I came back tired and with little patience for the mundane routine of the Canadian Forces, particularly the endless process at National Defence Headquarters. It was the same every time I came home from a mission: I would go back to work, sit down and get the first set of briefings or attend the first meetings, trying to focus on the task, and by a quarter to nine of the first day I just wouldn't give a damn. This was not what I wanted to do after having just done something so important, so satisfying and so very real in people's lives. Instead I was worrying about stuff like whether or not the sergeant in a LAV section should be sitting up in the turret commanding the vehicle or back in the rear, in charge of his section of eight soldiers. It always took a while to get over that impatience and back into the swing of things.

Major-General Marc Caron had been doing a good job running the army in my absence. I had told Henault that I would be retiring in September 2004, but when he asked me to give him a final answer and confirm my intentions, I decided to stay on until the following summer, 2005. So I knew that I wouldn't be back as the army commander for an extended period. I didn't want to start taking back more and more of the job from Marc, because I'd be retiring in the very near future and he was the most likely permanent successor. Certainly he had *my* vote, and I was trying to avoid another handover or switch in leadership at the top.

Then, in early October 2004, the process of finding a replacement for the outgoing Chief of the Defence Staff began. Once I threw my hat in the ring, it became easier to keep Marc as point man, running the day-to-day business of the army with my support. I had no expectation of becoming Chief, knowing that incredibly capable people like Vice-Admiral Ron Buck and recently retired Lieutenant-General Mike Jeffery were potentially available. The dynamic of picking this Chief was different than it had been in the past, because the first step—deciding that the incumbent Chief of the Defence Staff would step down—had been already taken when Henault was selected to be the next chair of the NATO Military Committee during the November 2004 meetings in Brussels. Chiefs of the Defence Staff do not serve for any fixed time period—they stay as long as the Prime Minister wants them in the job and they want to keep working. Usually their terms run to three years and toward the end of that period there is always a time when everyone in NDHQ is wondering when the Chief will retire and the job will be up for grabs. When Henault accepted the NATO job, the field was open to all candidates. Those up for the job were aware that the interviewing process was going on but rarely mentioned it, although we all looked at each other once in a while and wondered what it would be like to work for that individual.

I had my first interview with the Minister in the last week of November, and after I had managed to be late because of the misunderstanding over where the interview was to take place, I had pretty much written off my chances to become CDS. I never really thought that I stood much of a chance anyway, because I had insisted that even if offered the job, I would accept only if there was a real commitment to support the changes necessary to rebuild the Canadian Forces. When more than two weeks went by after my initial interview with the Minister, with no word, I pretty much decided that was that and started thinking seriously about retirement from the military the following spring.

Then Bill Graham called in early December and I found myself at 24 Sussex, sketching and doodling for Paul Martin, describing the changes I wanted to make to the Canadian Forces. I knew at the end of that breakfast meeting on December 10 that I was going to become CDS, and by mid-January the whole country knew.

I had already started working with Ward Elcock, the outstanding deputy minister at DND; Ken Calder, the assistant deputy minister of policy; and Vice-Admiral Ron Buck, who was now and would continue to be Vice Chief of the Defence Staff. I was trying to get all the pieces in place for the defence policy review, with the assistance of a number of the DND policy analysts, most notably Vince Rigby, who later became an assistant deputy minister. I wasn't yet Chief, however, and did not want to undercut Henault, who I was replacing, or step on his toes by jumping into his job before he actually left. But at the same time I had been given a mission by the Defence Minister, with the Prime Minister looking on and very much involved in the process. We had to get a new defence policy paper drafted to reflect the vision discussed at Sussex Drive in that pre-Christmas interview, and articulate the significant changes that needed to be made in the Canadian Forces. This would be the first Defence Policy Statement produced by a Canadian government in more than ten years. It was important to get it right, so there was a flurry of activity in the weeks before my change-of-command ceremony as we burned the midnight oil shaping one draft and concept after another.

We needed to transform the Canadian Forces completely, from a Cold War–oriented, bureaucratic, process-focused organization into a modern, combat-capable force, where the three elements—navy, army and air force, enabled by Special Forces—all worked together as one team to protect Canada by conducting operations effectively at home and abroad. I envisioned a flexible, agile and quick-thinking military that would be able to bring exactly the right kind of forces to accomplish whatever mission they were given, whether it was responding to a natural disaster like a tsunami or an ice storm or fighting a counter-insurgency war in southern Afghanistan. My team wanted the new Defence Policy Statement to reflect that. The key words I wanted to see reflected in the policy statement were "effective," "relevant" and "responsive." This differed fundamentally from what Graham had seen when he first asked for a new policy statement and was handed what he considered a rehash of existing documents. In other words, no change, but change was what he—and the PM—wanted!

To accomplish our work in the post-9/11 world, we needed to make that change, in the way the Canadian Forces was organized, the equipment we gave our troops and the number of people we

323

had at our disposal to carry out the missions that the government gave us. We had to get these changes started, and thus many of our decisions were made even before I took over as Chief.

Our change of command took place February 4, 2005. It gave me a good chance to set the tone for my term as the CDS. "Never underestimate the soapbox you have" is one of my beliefs, and I did not intend to waste this opportunity. We held the parade in a hangar called the Canada Reception Centre at CFB Uplands in Ottawa. Henault spoke first, and although I strained to hear what he said, I couldn't understand a single word. I was sitting next to Governor General Adrienne Clarkson. She leaned over to me and said, "The acoustics are terrible. This is appalling." The building had bare metal walls and, with a crowd of people, a band and an honour guard, all you could hear when someone got up to speak was, "Wah wah wah . . ."

She was right of course, but there wasn't much that could be done about it then. We all cringed. There was a huge crowd, it was an important event and I was afraid we were going to be embarrassed in front of all those dignitaries and media. Then Paul Martin, who was sitting right behind me, leaned forward and said, "You know, General, I think if you put your mouth right up close to the microphone, that'll work."

I said, "Yeah, I think you're right, Prime Minister. I'll give it a shot!"

So when I got up to speak, I leaned right into that microphone, articulated clearly (and loudly enough that I probably didn't need the speaker system) and it worked. The key messages I wanted to communicate included that we needed to recognize the incredible treasures in uniform who protected our country.

I had the good fortune to have several of the men and women who had worked for me in previous missions in attendance and was able to introduce them to the crowd. I also introduced some of our military families and was able to assure them that they would be a priority. My team from Afghanistan—Canadian, British and American—was there, and I put an emphasis on allied operations by introducing all of them. Lastly, I asked for money. "We'll probably never be able to give these men and women enough money to have all the equipment that they need to do what we ask them," I said, "but we sure can give them too little, and that's what we're doing right now." I then turned in the general direction of the Prime Minister and said, "Remember them in your budgets."

The reporters covering the ceremony made a fuss out of that, interpreting it as a direct challenge to the Prime Minister. In fact, it was just about exactly what I'd told him during that job interview at 24 Sussex, so he wasn't bothered by it in the least. I'd told them I was going to be frank during the change-of-command parade, and I worked in that message not to browbeat the Minister and the Prime Minister, but just to say we all must recognize this reality. I had not taken the job to preside over continued downsizing and reduction in capability while the demands kept growing, so why not get it out there? I knew that Martin was planning a huge increase in the size, funding and capabilities of the Canadian Forces as part of the budget that was due to come down later that same month, so what I was really doing was setting him up to be successful.

Martin, Graham and I got along superbly, right from the start, without any large disagreements or clashes in the relationship.

We discussed issues all the time, and while we didn't always completely agree on everything, that was to be expected.

It was exhilarating, later that afternoon, to drive home from the hangar with the Chief of the Defence Staff's pennant fluttering from the front hood of the unfortunately bright blue Canadian Forces staff car. "This is it," I thought. "The responsibility is mine."

As Chief of the Defence Staff, I was at the top of the chain of command for the entire Canadian Forces and all 85,000 men and women in uniform, both regular and reserve force. It was an enormous responsibility and a very humbling one as well: I was responsible for the lives and well-being of so many of Canada's finest men and women and for ensuring that they were capable of protecting Canada and Canadians by executing successfully a myriad of missions. Of course I wasn't doing this alone. I had three-star commanders who ran the army, navy and air force, with responsibility for training and preparing people and units, commanders who ran operations and a staff that coordinated and synchronized all the activities. The breadth and scope of our activities were enormous. We used to tell each new Minister of Defence that if there was an issue in Canada, we dealt with it in the CF. It didn't matter whether that was paternity care, environmental law, the Geneva Convention, Arctic treaties, air-space control or the Law of the Sea, we would be involved. Our men and women, on a daily basis, did an amazing variety of exciting and sometimes dangerous tasks—boarding other vessels at sea, sailing below the oceans, search-and-rescue missions under the most extreme circumstances imaginable, interdiction of passenger aircraft by high-performance fighters, and anything else, up to violently preventing good people from being abused. Every day more than ten thousand of those wearing Canada's uniform toiled, without fanfare, in Canada to do those jobs, and thousands more put themselves at risk overseas. Their families lived, usually in obscurity, with the stress from that on a daily basis.

I had help from all those 85,000 but also help from the Minister of Defence and the Prime Minister, who I worked for, and an entire government structure that should have set the CF up for success.

A large number of family and friends were gathered at the house when I arrived, none more important to me than that team of officers from my command of ISAF, some of whom had flown in from around the globe to attend the ceremony. Joyce and I celebrated with Texans, Newfs, Brits, French Canadians, English Canadians, long-time friends, family, sons, one daughter-in-law and one potential daughter-in-law, a four-month-old grandson and many others. I could not have guessed the incredible rollercoaster ride we were about to go on and how tumultuous the next months and years would be.

In the first couple of weeks after the change of command, I launched into a series of activities to build on the momentum for change that followed my appointment. Within days of taking over I ended up in France with Graham, attending the NATO Ministers of Defence conference in Nice. I spent a lot of time on the phone there, conferring with folks back in Ottawa, particularly Ron Buck, trying to offer as much guidance as I could on urgent issues. I took Ron's invaluable suggestions and began the long process of steering the Canadian Forces into the significant changes planned from afar.

First in the batting order was a three-day meeting with all my generals and admirals in Cornwall, Ontario, along with the senior officials in the department, to walk through our vision of how we were going to shape the Canadian Forces, with a view to setting up action teams to carry out some of the changes, study other options and get the process started. That same week, however, there was a NATO summit in Brussels with the heads of government attending, including our Prime Minister, and the CDS was expected to go. Since we were so busy starting the transformation of the CF, continuing to run daily operations and simultaneously working on a new Defence Policy Statement, I decided not to attend. My belief that it would be more productive to stay than go was confirmed by our military representative in Brussels, Vice-Admiral Glenn Davidson, who said, "The meetings are endless, outcomes are decided before the summit commences and you are not even invited into the room most times." It was good enough for me, and yet another confirmation that NATO meetings were a waste of time. Invariably the limited number of seats for each country at meetings became a classic bureaucratic bun-fight, with the civilian bureaucrats sniping at each other over who sat where and trying determinedly to keep the Chief of the Defence Staff out. I've never, ever heard anything innovative come out of the meetings and didn't think attending them was a good use of my time.

The Canadian media felt otherwise and made a big deal out of my absence, deciding that the reason I hadn't gone to the NATO summit was because I had spoken out at the change-of-command parade and therefore the Prime Minister and I weren't on speaking terms. Martin and I both found that pretty amusing. I had a lot to do and actually got much of it done because I didn't go to the summit.

I arrived back in Canada from the NATO Defence Ministers meeting in France on a Friday, after having been Chief of the Defence Staff for exactly one week, and the CBC, a couple of newspapers and some television stations interviewed me on the Saturday morning. They were the first of many media appearances I made during my time as Chief, and an important part of my plan for the Canadian Forces. I thought of it as our "Recruit the Nation" strategy, although we never formally gave it that name. I wanted to rebuild the relationship between the army, navy and air force within the Canadian Forces and, equally important—perhaps more so—build the relationship between the CF and the public to connect Canadians to their military. We wanted to re-establish ourselves in the Canadian psyche as *their* armed forces and educate Canadians about how we did our operations, what we needed to do them and how we would use their support to achieve more.

Tom Ring, the assistant deputy minister for public affairs, understood strategic communication better than anybody I've ever met. He was superb at laying out a way to tell the Canadian public that there were folks out there trying to kill us and here is what we must do about it. Tom, who was marginalized by the Prime Minister's Office after the election in January 2006, knew more about strategic communications than all of the prime ministerial communication advisers combined.

One of the first things we did was set up some roundtables with journalists, which allowed relatively in-depth conversations

on issues of significance while at the same time building relationships with journalists themselves. They used us to sell their
newspapers, television or radio programs, and we felt no qualms
about using them to enable us to get our messages out. The first
of those roundtable events, a free-ranging discussion, took place
in July 2005, an informal lunch with about ten reporters who
had been covering defence issues and the military, with another
half-dozen listening in via telephone from around the country. I
led off with a short assessment of our vision—what we intended
to accomplish and how it was going so far—and talked about
equipment purchases and our plans for the transformation of
the Canadian Forces. At this time, the Department of Foreign
Affairs and International Trade, the Department of National
Defence and the Canadian Forces were holding extensive discussions about the potential deployment into southern Afghanistan, and naturally the question came up about that deployment.
Although I hadn't planned what I was going to say specifically,
nobody in the room had any doubt that my view of the men who
were killing, or trying to kill, my soldiers—Canada's sons and
daughters—was pretty low. I called them "detestable murderers
and scumbags."

Right after I said that, I joked, laughing as I said, "You guys
aren't going to report that, are you?"—knowing of course that all
of the reporters were rushing out right away to do just that. I said
to Tom afterwards, with a bit of a grin, "What do you think? Are
they going to report that one or not?"

He replied, "Yes, it's already happening."

I said, "Okay. I needed to say something to make Canadians
wake up and something significant to make my mark with our

servicemen and servicewomen, and that was probably it. I'll live with what I said."

I didn't plan to say exactly those words, but I've never regretted them. As it turned out, the response couldn't have been any better. All of a sudden the people of Canada got a wake-up call, which was truly what was needed. I had gone on to say that the Canadian Forces are not the Public Service of Canada, and our job is to kill people. I admit to being stunned by the reaction of some segments of our society to that idea, which seemed pretty obvious to me. They said that killing isn't our job, but I asked myself, why do they think we spend millions, even billions of dollars a year on equipping, training and building air, land and sea combat units? Why were we attracting, enrolling and training to a fever pitch so many fine young Canadian men and women, equipping them with the best weapons systems that we can find, putting them together as teams and leading them? Why did they think we have artillery, automatic cannon and precision-guided bombs and missiles on our ships, aircraft and vehicles, if not for when our country orders us to go and kill bad people? I guess that came as a shock for some, certainly to those politicians, academics and others who were leading us down this path of so-called soft power, or of keeping Canadian soldiers in an exclusively peacekeeping role and hence, in my view, keeping Canada's impact soft and small. We can't have much of an impact in the world using soft power when the rest of the world is hard!

There was quite a to-do in the media about those words over the next few days, but what pleasantly surprised me was the reaction from the rank and file in the Canadian Forces. The day after I'd made those comments, I went to Edmonton to say farewell to a group of soldiers from the Princess Patricia's that were headed to Afghanistan. I accompanied Bill Graham and Anne McLellan, who was Deputy Prime Minister, and whose home riding was in Edmonton. The two of them were overwhelmed by our soldiers when we arrived. "It's about time that we had a soldier as CDS!" they said. The soldiers piled on to Anne and Bill, one after another, and all of them were pleased as can be at what I'd said. Those comments did more for my credibility with the people I led than almost anything else. All of a sudden people were taking note of what was actually happening in their own organization. Soldiers, sailors, airmen and airwomen lined up to shake my hand.

The Year of the Veteran, 2005, tremendously aided our reconnection of the Canadian public with their military. I had, unfortunately, missed the commemoration and celebrations in the Netherlands for the 60th anniversary of VE Day (Victory in Europe) in May and asked Henault, who was in transition, to represent me and the CF. He graciously agreed, and I stayed in Canada with the Prime Minister for the opening of the new Canadian War Museum and for the Veterans Day celebration on May 8, marking the end of the Second World War. That day, with the crowds, excitement, emotion and proud veterans, must have been just a taste of what VE Day was like in 1945. First we went to the National War Memorial in downtown Ottawa for a service of remembrance and wreath-laying ceremony and then Joyce and I left and headed down Wellington Street, to the reviewing stand in front of the Supreme Court where the parade of veterans was to march.

We were going to walk the kilometre or so between the War Memorial and the War Museum on that beautiful, sunny day that had downtown Ottawa packed with people—there must have been 150,000 or more there—but people started saying, "Oh look, it's General Hillier!" and reaching out to shake my hand. I never blow by people who just want to speak to me or shake my hand—I always worry about inadvertently insulting someone or giving an impression that I'm pompous—but when you stop and shake one hand, all of a sudden you're trapped in the crowd. Every step we took, there'd be five more people wanting to shake my hand and get their pictures taken with Joyce and me. I was even handed babies to kiss. This was looking bad, much as if I was trying to usurp the Prime Minister or run for political office, and I wanted out. We had to call up my driver to come and get us, just so we'd be able to get to the saluting base in time to take the salute from the veterans.

We finally got to the small stage prepared as a saluting dais, and while Joyce watched from the sidelines with Cabinet ministers and dignitaries, Prime Minister Martin and I took the salute as the veterans marched past, or rode in their wheelchairs, on vehicles or in buses. Thousands of veterans participated, and the excitement was contagious. Some of them were riding in antique military vehicles that had been restored by private collectors or hobbyists, and even though all these veterans were in their eighties, on this day they were again just like the seventeen-year-old kids who had gone to war. After the first few vehicles passed, traffic started to slow, then stopped, and we started getting groups of veterans in front of us for several minutes until the parade moved on again.

Four veterans all in their eighties in an open-topped Willys jeep from the Second World War stopped right in front of us.

The Prime Minister was kind of shy about talking to them, which surprised me a little. So I said, "Hey, Prime Minister, why don't we go down and chat with these guys?"

We jumped down from the dais and went to take a look at their restored vehicle. While we were chatting and laughing with them, one of them said, "Prime Minister, I've got to show you this." He pulled out a weathered piece of paper and showed it to the Prime Minister, careful to keep it out of my view. When I bent to look at it, the vet grinned and said, "No, General, you're too young to look at this. You're too young." I finally got a peek at the page and saw a hand-drawn sketch of a nude woman, from 1944, that he had obviously hung onto for all these years. The Prime Minister and I got a chuckle out of that and I thought, "Man, soldiers will be soldiers."

After the parade we went to the new Canadian War Museum for its official opening and toured the museum itself, which is spectacular. At one point Joyce and I found ourselves going down a long corridor, the entrance to the main exhibit hall, which is lined with pieces of fuselage from bombers—Lancasters, Wellingtons, Mosquitos and Halifaxes—from the Second World War. Each of those aircraft remnants displayed the paintings that the flight crews had put on the noses of their planes. Underneath one of those pieces were three older veterans, with their rows of medals on their chests. They recognized us and waved us over. "General! General! This is Bill," one of them told me, "and this came from his plane."

We were all looking up at a bomber's nose with a cartoon of a wolf on it. "Look, look at all these other planes here!" The noses of the planes all had a picture of a semi-nude or nude woman somewhere on them, which was common at the time. "That's the second plane we were shot down in," Bill said. He told me that the first plane his crew flew had had a nude woman that he had painted on the nose and they had been shot down on their first mission in North Africa but managed to get home alive anyway. After that, however, the boys in his crew wouldn't let him paint any naked women on their plane anymore. They thought it was a bad omen, so he put the wolf on instead.

The crews of the first Canadian Griffon helicopters deployed to Afghanistan in 2008 started painting pictures on the nose of their aircraft as well, of skeletons, hockey sticks and even a few naked women, although they weren't as big and gaudy as those painted on the sides of those old bombers. It wasn't so long ago that it would have been unthinkable for pilots or aircrew in combat to show a little esprit de corps, pride in what they do and the aircraft they fly. Regulations and procedures would have ensured that it never happened. This rebirth of the tradition signalled the rebirth of pride.

I spent hours that day with the Prime Minister, standing on the saluting dais, chatting with him and sharing laughs, celebrating being Canadian with the veterans and those who came to fete them. Mr. Martin was interested in the restored vehicles and equipment in the parade, and during our tour of the War Museum kept asking, "What kind of gun is that?" and "What kind of tank is that?" Martin is inquisitive, and during the whole time he was Prime Minister asked about the equipment and weapons systems the Canadian Forces were using. I wanted to get him up for a ride in a CF-18, but he was getting a lot of pressure to not go up because of the fear for his health under those arduous conditions and a smaller fear that the jet would crash, so it never happened.

That day was phenomenal, memorable for me. It was the anniversary of the end of the Second World War, the Year of the Veteran, the opening of the War Museum and a fitting tribute to all those veterans from that "Greatest Generation." It was one of the most magnificent events that I've ever had the opportunity to participate in, and it all helped to push our "Recruit the Nation" strategy, because that great day—and the whole year—was really a celebration of our military, past and present. Anyone in uniform got sucked into that joy and celebration. Those who weren't in uniform could not help but notice those who were and get some appreciation for their value to Canada.

On August 3, 2005, Sergeant Ernest "Smokey" Smith, the last surviving Canadian recipient of the Victoria Cross, passed away at the age of ninety-one. Smokey won the VC in a fight over a river crossing in northern Italy, when he single-handedly held off nearly one hundred attacking Germans and two tanks to save one of his wounded buddies. As it was the Year of the Veteran, I saw an opportunity to get support for an event that I thought would bring the whole country together and, most importantly, do something incredibly right. We decided to honour Smokey as one of our great heroes and believed that the country should do it, not just the CF. I said to Mr. Martin, "Prime Minister, I believe that we should pay tribute to this man in the way that a hero of Canada should be commemorated. We should have a full military funeral, with Smokey lying in state on Parliament Hill and we as a nation paying him all the appropriate respect. This is the Year of the Veteran, and it's the perfect opportunity to really allow Canadians to show their appreciation to Smokey and, through him, to all those others who gave so much for Canada."

I had met Smokey half a dozen times, usually at Remembrance Day ceremonies. He was certainly a character, even in his advanced age. I speak of him publicly now as an example of how you can't stereotype people: Smokey was certainly not the stereotype of a model soldier. In his time in uniform, he had been promoted to corporal and then busted back down to private nine times, and when he was sent from Italy in 1945 to Buckingham Palace to be presented with his medal by King George, two military policemen accompanied him to the gates of Buckingham Palace to ensure that he did indeed get there for his audience with the king instead of taking a detour to the nearest pub.

The army had developed, years prior, what we called Conplan (Contingency Plan) Victoria: our plan for Smokey's funeral. We had already gone through the details with Smokey and his family members and had been constantly updating it. We monitored Smokey's whereabouts and his health so closely that every time he'd get a cold, we all went on high alert until we were certain he was going to make it. Smokey knew that and joked about it.

When he died in August the plan was ready, but the Prime Minister was getting a lot of conflicting advice, mainly from the staffers in the Privy Council Office who told him that someone like Smokey shouldn't lie in state in the Parliament Buildings. That honour was reserved for governors general and prime ministers. They didn't want him to set a precedent. Mr. Martin and I went through it several times. Eventually I told him, "I'd be quite glad to argue precedent the next time we have a Victoria Cross winner who dies, but that will be forty years or more from now."

The Prime Minister's real concern, as I discovered later, was that not many people might show up if Smokey lay in state, and it would end up inadvertently being an insult to his memory. I assured him that wouldn't happen. I said, "Prime Minister, we're going to truck in men and women in uniform from Petawawa, Kingston, Trenton, Montreal and Ottawa to pay their respects to this Canadian hero, because we want to do that. Let me tell you, there are going to be a lot of people lined up."

The Prime Minister decided to go ahead with our plan for Smokey's funeral, and everyone involved had enormous pride in being part of the event. Smokey's body was flown to Ottawa on one of our Airbuses with the call sign "Smokey One." His body was brought into the Parliament Buildings by senior non-commissioned officers from his regiment, the Seaforth Highlanders. They carried him to the foyer of the Centre Block, where he lay in state for a full day. The Governor General, the Prime Minister and Cabinet ministers passed by the casket to pay their respects, followed by the Canadian Forces' senior enlisted man, Chief Warrant Officer Danny Gilbert, and me. Then the long line of members of the public began filing past. Ordinary Canadians lined up for four hours or more to bid farewell to Smokey. Even though we had bused in a lot of people in uniform, it turned out that we didn't need their numbers to ensure that proper respect was paid to this great Canadian. It was incredible. People lined up all day and late into the night to say goodbye, and thank you, to Smokey.

The next day the body was flown back to Vancouver, with a small honour guard and the pallbearers also on board. When the aircraft carrying Smokey was getting ready to take off from Ottawa International, the pilot called into the tower to get clearance for takeoff. Air traffic control responded, asking, "Are you Smokey One? Are you carrying the body of Sergeant Smokey Smith?"

The pilot said, "Yes, we are."

The tower responded, "Right, you have number one clearance."

Every other flight waiting to take off was moved aside so that the Airbus could go first. The air force captain who was commanding that flight told me later that every air traffic controller across the country cleared a path for them. "You know," he said, "we had the most direct route I've ever seen to go from Ottawa to Vancouver. They gave us priority over all the other air traffic because we were Smokey One."

The funeral procession in Vancouver started at the Seaforth Highlanders' home armoury in downtown Vancouver, proceeded to the church and then returned to the armoury for a reception for hundreds, which Smokey had paid for as his final gift. His body was cremated and his ashes were scattered at sea from one of our warships, HMCS *Vancouver*. I was an honorary pallbearer, and it was a beautiful day. Thousands of people packed the streets. Smokey's casket was carried on top of an old gun carriage that some of the local soldiers had been polishing and getting into perfect working order for days. A two-hundred-strong guard of honour marched in front; the family was immediately behind, followed by a small contingent of twenty decorated servicemen and servicewomen, another two-hundred-strong guard of honour, the RCMP guard, resplendent in their red serge, and then members of the Royal Canadian Legion. The soldiers marched with their white gloves swinging in perfect unison, their bayonets and brass glinting in the sunlight. As we crossed the bridge over False Creek, a flight of five CF-18s came screaming very low over the water, and one pulled up to complete the "missing man" formation, where one plane pulls into a vertical climb to signify the lost man. People on the sidewalk applauded and yelled out, "Thank you!" It was one of the most inspiring ceremonies, one of the most emotional moments I think I've ever seen, and a truly fitting way for our nation to say farewell to one of its heroes.

After the church service, Bill Graham passed me a note from his wife, Cathy, who was watching at home in Toronto. "Bill," she said in an e-mail, "you tell the Chief that the CF sure knows how to do it right." She was correct—despite much opposition from bureaucratic mandarins, we had done what was right, and we had done it well. Smokey, with that glint in his eye, may have even given us a thumbs-up from wherever he was.

Smokey was the perfect example of what a difference one person can make. And Smokey sure did make a difference, not only in that terrible campaign in Italy where he won the Victoria Cross for single-handedly beating off enemy soldiers and tanks, but for his six decades of service to his country—in uniform and out. We all hoped that he would live forever, but obviously he could not. Even in death, however, Smokey Smith served our country. He died while Parliament was in recess and there was little else going on in the country, the perfect time to allow the nation to take the time to say its collective thanks, show its appreciation, say farewell to a real hero and bring those serving veterans that I now commanded into the public's consciousness. His funeral brought more focus to the Canadian Forces and what we were trying to do than anything that we could have done by ourselves. Thank you, from the heart, Smokey!

CHAPTER 17

FIRST YEAR ON THE JOB

Not long after Smokey Smith's funeral, the Prime Minister was having a Cabinet meeting in Winnipeg and I was asked to attend to talk about the Afghanistan situation and the rationale for our involvement. I arrived the day before, and as I was sitting in the lobby, waiting for my room, in came the Prime Minister and his wife, Sheila. They both came over to talk. Joyce and I had become friends with the Martins in the short time we'd known them. Whenever we went to the same functions, Sheila would rearrange the chairs at the table to make sure we were sitting somewhere around her. The Prime Minister said, "Maybe we'll get together for dinner tonight."

"At your beck and call, Prime Minister," I said.

Bill Graham joined us and we all ended up at 529 Wellington, a restaurant in Winnipeg. We sat at a small table and had a little wine to drink over a magnificent meal. We talked for about three hours, discussing the transformation of the

Canadian Forces, what effect the budget was having, how the process of building up and growing the Canadian Forces was going and what we had to do next. We also spent a fair amount of that time discussing the Afghanistan mission and what we were trying to accomplish there.

It had already been largely decided that the Canadian presence in Afghanistan was shifting to the southern half of the country. Even before I returned from commanding ISAF, NATO had announced its intentions to expand the ISAF mission beyond Kabul in 2006, and planning was already well on its way for a move into Kandahar province by the time I landed back in Canada that fall.

NATO had wanted us to take over in Herat, in western Afghanistan, by sending a provincial reconstruction team there, but the Canadian government was resisting that idea. Soon after I returned from Kabul in November 2004, I had sat in on a video conference with Ray Henault, who was in Brussels at NATO meetings, and the Deputy Chief of the Defence Staff, Vice-Admiral Greg Maddison, in which Henault said the Supreme Allied Commander Europe (SACEUR), NATO's top military commander, had been advising him to send a Canadian provincial reconstruction team to Herat, and that pressure to do this was extremely high.

My suggestion for a future Canadian mission in Afghanistan had been for us to take over responsibility for Kabul International Airport, the country's main military and civilian air link with the outside world. The airport was a mess in 2004, with land mines still a hazard near its sole, broken runway, wrecked planes littering the landscape and few modern facilities for passengers or air freight. I had envisioned a project wherein the Canadian Forces would take over responsibility for security around the airport, with RCMP and Canada Customs training Afghan customs and immigration officers, Transport Canada helping to set up proper airport facilities and air traffic control while building an Afghan capability in air traffic controllers, and the Canadian International Development Agency (CIDA) helping to rebuild the airport infrastructure and maybe even add another runway. It would have been a real Team Canada approach at a cost I estimated at approximately a billion dollars. Such a high-profile mission would have given Afghanistan a modern, fully functioning gateway to the rest of the world. "We could paint a huge maple leaf on the middle of the runway," I told everyone. "That way it would be the first and last thing everyone saw when they came to Afghanistan."

Nobody in Ottawa was interested, so the idea died. The government had already signalled its intent to go into Kandahar province, and the Department of Foreign Affairs, CIDA and National Defence were well into their planning of that mission by the time I came back to work at NDHQ after my time as ISAF commander.

I agreed completely with the choice of Kandahar over Herat, because that western Afghan city was a backwater and sending a Canadian mission there would have been costly and given us little visibility, credibility or impact internationally. What I did insist on was that a full battle group should be sent to Kandahar along with a reconstruction team, because two or three hundred Canadian soldiers in that team could make little impact on their own. If the security situation in Kandahar became dire, as indeed it did soon after our arrival, those soldiers would be stuck out in vulnerable positions with no easy way to ensure their security or rescue them from the extreme risk they would face every day. So the Kandahar mission was pretty well set. The Prime Minister, Bill Graham and I were discussing the details at that restaurant in Winnipeg.

We talked until the wee hours. I thought that this was the way that all CDS's should work, sitting down with the Prime Minister and the Defence Minister and walking through key issues, in good detail, so that we all understood the Prime Minister's broad intent and so that any concerns would be aired and discussed. Martin told me over that dinner table that he wanted to bring the Canadian Forces back to the levels and capability that it needed, and he wanted to know what I was doing to make that happen and how he could help it along. He had a lot of questions about Afghanistan, no doubt about it; he just wanted to be absolutely certain that he understood what this mission would entail and how we would go about it.

Graham said, "We're going to fight in the hills and make love in the cities. We're going to make sure the population's getting development and aid in the cities; we're going to make sure that the Taliban are going to be kept off-balance, and let the population start to rebuild their lives, families and communities with our assistance." We walked through the mission, what we thought might happen and how things could develop. It was an extraordinary chance to really discuss issues in detail with a Prime Minister, without fifty onlookers all taking copious notes so they can run back after the meeting and debrief their fifty bosses. No issues of substance are seriously discussed in meetings of that size, so what was happening here was incredibly valuable and, unfortunately, all too rare between a Prime Minister and a CDS.

It didn't happen while Jean Chrétien was Prime Minister. Chrétien had political acuity second to none, and the Canadian Forces didn't have a constituency: we didn't have the votes. Nobody in Canada thought of us as their armed forces. Nobody even gave us a second thought. We had disappeared from the landscape except for the events that had given us a black eye. As a result, when the budget cuts took place in 1994, there were no protests, nobody saying, "Hey, wait a minute." It was quite clear that there was no support for us. Chrétien realized that and cut money from our budget, with all the resulting implications. It is the government's prerogative to make those decisions. My beef was that while all that was occurring, they were continuing to ask more of us; in fact, they were asking a *lot* more of us. We were being asked to do everything we had done before the cuts of the 1990s and to do it all over the world with less money, fewer soldiers and outdated equipment. The Government of Canada and Canadians wanted their cake and wanted to eat it too, and we paid the price for it. If the government decides to have a Canadian Forces of only ten people, it's their right to make that decision. You can agree or disagree with it, but when a government decides to have an armed forces of ten and wants that armed forces to continue to do the work of ten thousand, that's a different kettle of fish. That's what really caused the decade of darkness.

My relationship with Paul Martin was, I thought, exceptional. He had said, "I like what you have proposed in the vision, how we articulated it in the policy statement, and now I want to do it." He put the weight of the Prime Minister's Office behind me, and I tried to give the same kind of support to him within my role as Chief.

Obviously, because Prime Minister Martin had selected me, we had a good rapport, but the relationship became stronger as we went through that first year. The people around Martin helped strengthen that working relationship too, whether it was Tim Murphy, his Chief of Staff; Scott Reid, the Director of Communications; or Bill Graham himself, one of the smartest and most thoughtful people I know and an excellent Defence Minister. Graham really understood the strategic level of what the Canadian Forces could do and how it could affect Canada's role in the world.

When we were drafting the Defence Policy Statement, Graham, Elcock and I went back and forth with the Prime Minister several times, sitting down for blocks of two to three hours to talk over the issues. The meetings with Martin were kept small, with the three of us, plus Pierre Pettigrew of Foreign Affairs (with his deputy minister); Alex Himelfarb, Clerk of the Privy Council; Eugene Lang, who was Chief of Staff to Graham; and usually Scott Reid or Tim Murphy. We would sit down with the Prime Minister and go over the draft of the statement. Martin would have already read it thoroughly and would ask detailed questions and dig for clarification on many points. We would respond, explain why we had done things a certain way or why we had taken a certain approach, and the discussion would continue until the PM was satisfied. Sometimes there were no answers to the questions asked, and at one point I just said, "Hey, Prime Minister, give us a break. We're shaping this thing the best way we can; this is what we believe will work."

Martin and the folks around him were satisfied after our two-way discussions and, in the end, we walked out of those long and intense meetings with a 90 per cent "go" on the Defence Policy Statement. We left the last meeting with that seal of approval and the feeling that we were helping the Government of Canada articulate to Canadians what their country was going to do in the war-torn world in which we were living. That was a pretty good feeling; we had already come a long way.

What we didn't see at that point in time was much coming from Foreign Affairs on their half of the policy piece: the International Policy Statement. That was, consequently, shaped to a large extent by the Defence Policy Statement; there was significant overlap in what both documents were talking about—our role internationally and a focus on failing or fragile states around the globe—because that's the place where you get a chance to make an impact, particularly in this post-9/11 world.

The Defence Policy Statement was released in the spring of 2005, and we immediately started working on the detailed planning for the implementation of the vision it laid out for the Canadian Forces while simultaneously starting to look ahead to the shift of mission in Afghanistan from Kabul to the south. That was what we were discussing in the restaurant in Winnipeg. The next day I had the opportunity, at the Prime Minister's request, to go into a meeting of the full Cabinet and walk through everything we had discussed for all the ministers. Mr. Martin wanted me to tell his ministers the same things I had just told him, and because it was a full Cabinet meeting, there were a lot of folks around the table who got the full gist of the changes we were making.

During that first year we were on a climb, generating excitement within the Canadian Forces for everything that we were doing and excitement around Canada for their men and women in uniform. The Year of the Veteran events and all the positive public support we were starting to get that first year were just a remarkable start to my time as the Chief of the Defence Staff.

The year ended in a frustrating manner, however, despite having a prime minister and a defence minister with a vision for the Canadian Forces; a chief of the defence staff selected because of that vision; and defence and international policy statements articulating that vision. The budget gave us the big money to get the projects going that we needed to make this all happen. Yet when we went to Cabinet to finalize the approvals to actually acquire the equipment referred to in the budget and policies, it all came to a crashing halt.

While we were working out the detailed plan of how we were going to implement the vision, we wanted to get specific equipment projects off the ground because we needed many basic requirements filled immediately. We desperately needed to replace the fleet of C-130 Hercules, most of which were older than the pilots who flew them; we needed heavy lift helicopters to move our troops around southern Afghanistan and anywhere else we sent them; the army had to replace its old and worn transport trucks, and the navy had a critical need for new replenishment ships to refuel and resupply the fleet, because the old ones were literally rusting away.

We had money for all of these projects, so we went into Cabinet with a proposal for what I called the "Big Four": buying the C-130J, the newest model of the Hercules; a fleet of new heavy- and medium-weight trucks; transport helicopters; and fixed-wing search-and-rescue aircraft. Despite all the meetings and briefings we'd given Cabinet, suddenly they became a bunch of worrywarts. Clearly ministers had heard concerns from their staff, because all I heard in that meeting was objections: "Oh my goodness—you know, this is big money"; "We can't do this, can't do that"; "We've got to do it another way"; "We've got to avoid sounding like we're sole-sourcing."

The proposition was rejected. I walked out of that meeting three feet off the ground, I was so angry, and went back to my office. Scott Reid, the Prime Minister's Director of Communications, called and I told him, "We've got a problem, Scott. What's the good of saying yes to a vision of the Canadian Forces, yes to the money in the budget, yes to the Defence Policy Statement and then no to actually doing it? I'm fucking pissed off."

Everything was in place. We were well into planning for the mission into Kandahar, and we needed to get these pieces of equipment. I found it infuriating that bureaucrats, prompting their ministers with objections and obstacles, could so completely sidetrack a major government initiative.

Scott got the message loud and clear. The next morning I met with Anne McLellan and Minister Graham. Anne said, "I understand that you're a little bit upset over what happened in Cabinet yesterday."

"Well, you know, Minister, actually I'm not a little bit upset." I said. "I'm pissed off."

The point I made was that if we couldn't do this with the Prime Minister's support, with Cabinet onside, with the policy in place and the money in the budget, then we were sending a clear message to the entire Canadian Forces that we were not serious—we were all talk and no action.

I don't know what Anne and Bill did with that information, but the next day the C-130s were back on the table in Cabinet, and within a couple of weeks we made the announcement of that project.

By then it was too late. It was certain that an election would be called in December, within days of the announcement, for January, and any project that was not already in contract would have to restart with a new government. So the proposal, approved at Cabinet and announced publicly, died as soon as we went into an election—like every other government purchase that wasn't already in production.

There was a lesson here on how *not* to do business that I'm not sure was learned. Allocating money to accomplish things as a government and then being incapable of spending that money gives enormous opportunity to your opposition. In this case, the Liberals allocated $13 billion to defence, couldn't organize themselves to spend it to achieve their goals and left it for the Conservatives to utilize. The Conservatives, on election, were presented with this plum, organized themselves to spend it and branded themselves as the party to support the CF. Dollars and decisions must work hand in hand.

In the interim, during that pre-election period and into the actual election campaign, we continued moving quickly on the changes needed in the Canadian Forces' command structure. We had dismantled the Deputy Chief of the Defence Staff organization, which had been in charge of all operations, both overseas and in Canada, and replaced it with a much more focused command, Canadian Expeditionary Force Command (CEFCOM), under newly promoted Lieutenant-General Mike Gauthier, with responsibility for all overseas operations. Mike immediately got to work setting his small team up to run the international side, particularly working the Afghanistan mission. Meanwhile, Vice-Admiral Jean-Yves Fortier was setting up Canada Command, with responsibility for all domestic operations by the Canadian Forces, whether search and rescue or a response to domestic situations such as the Manitoba floods or the central Canadian ice storm. All of this was done with Bill Graham's approval and support, as I had walked through the command and control issues with him in the preceding months. At one point, he turned to Eugene Lang and said, "I hope the Chief stays in his job a long time. With all the changes, he should get the opportunity to see them through and enjoy the fruits of his labour."

351

This new structure was complete, but the formality of changing the commands publicly so others would be aware of what we had done had yet to take place. We did that in early February 2006, but since, after the election, we had a government-in-waiting, I took a beating—some felt that I took advantage of the transition period to do whatever I wanted. In fact, we had made the changes the previous fall and the ceremony was just the public announcing of what had occurred. We had dismantled the old structure and had to have command and control structure in place to run that more intensive operation in Afghanistan while being able to respond if events requiring the CF occurred at home. The public change became, however, a burr under the saddle of the new minister when the government took office.

Still, in that first year, we had brought an energy back into the Canadian Forces and the Department of National Defence, to some extent to the entire Government of Canada and therefore to the country, by rallying them behind their men and women, their sons and daughters in uniform. We had gotten traction, even within the first months, on the changes needed to reorient the organization dramatically. The perception from those in uniform, in government circles and in the general public was that the Canadian Forces were changing for the better. A key part of that was the incredible relationship that we had with Prime Minister Martin, first and foremost, his Cabinet and, most importantly, the Department of National Defence.

Bill Graham was confident, incredibly smart and sage. He didn't know much about running military operations and he didn't worry about it, but he understood the political dynamic—that was his bailiwick. Ward Elcock, the Deputy Minister, had accomplished an incredible amount as the head of the Canadian Security Intelligence Service (where he had been before moving to become the top civil servant in the Department of National Defence), and having lived in the defence and security world for a decade or more, he understood strategy and the fact that we were operating in a very different world after 9/11. He knew what we needed to do, and he understood the department and the public service side of it. Ward is a very quiet guy, but when he speaks he makes a lot of sense, his arguments are eminently logical and everybody listens. Then you had me, a new Chief of the Defence Staff who had taken the job to actually do something different in the Canadian Forces.

Our triumvirate worked very well for the department and the Canadian Forces because our roles were all beautifully defined.

Ward and I had a partnership in how to rebuild the Canadian Forces, get the operations done and reshape DND and the Canadian Forces to make us truly effective. Graham wanted all that done for the government and he was working the political piece of the initiatives we were pushing through. The three of us would show up at meetings either for the acquisitions of the Big Four or to brief Cabinet on whatever was going on, and we were unassailable. Nobody could come at us from any angle and win, because if they came at us politically, Bill Graham was more than a match for them. If process or procedure got trotted out, as it did all the time in the great bureaucracy we have in the public service of Canada, then Ward Elcock could handle all that with his eyes closed. Few could take me on over the military aspect because what we said was fundamentally logical from the military perspective. We could, together, articulate exactly what was needed to accomplish our mission: how we needed to carry it out and what we needed, whether personnel, training, leadership or equipment.

Individuals make a difference, and when you get three individuals, each focused on their area of expertise but working toward one vision, who complement each other so well, anything is possible. When the Liberals were kicked out and Graham left as Minister, that cohesion started to break down and we never did have that sort of triumvirate again.

In that first year we began to get what Lieutenant-General Angus Watt, the Chief of the Air Staff, started calling "a shine" on the Canadian Forces. That shine became one of our most important enablers. I have always believed that perception is reality. Canadians perceived from very early months that we were an organization that was changing for the better, changing to be what they thought the Canadian Forces should be, and becoming the flexible, agile and responsive armed forces that they needed. We were looking forward, not back; we weren't dinosaurs.

Politicians reacted to that shine and started trooping to our side. They perceived popularity, and with popularity comes votes, so elected officials and those who wanted to get elected started paying attention to what we were doing. Even those who criticized us, or criticized what we were doing or how we were doing it, always started off by saying, "Now, it's not that I don't support the troops . . ."

Men and women started walking through the doors of our recruiting centres in increasing numbers—so many that we soon realized we had to revolutionize our way of recruiting people. We were taking months and months to get a young man or woman from that recruiting centre into uniform. We were actually turning people away at the door, where in the past we often had difficulty attracting enough good recruits. At a time when we were trying to increase the strength of the Canadian Forces, our pedantic and risk-averse recruiting policy was a problem.

I got a personal look into the challenges we were facing in our recruiting system during that first year. A young lady walked into a recruiting centre and said she was considering joining the Canadian Forces. She was a dental hygienist, one of the trades that we desperately needed, in her early twenties, physically fit, fluently bilingual, well educated and very smart—in short, she was perfect for us. She went to the recruiting centre and asked some questions. They went through the whole program for dental specialists with her. Then she said, "I'm here in Ottawa and this is my home now. So if I apply and join, once I've finished my training, is there any possibility of getting posted back to Ottawa as my first operational posting? There are dental units here."

The recruiter's response was "Absolutely not. In fact, if you're from Ottawa, well, we'll probably take somebody from Vancouver and post them to Ottawa and post you to Vancouver."

That story got back to me because the young woman was my daughter-in-law, Caroline. I didn't send her to that recruiting centre as a test, she went on her own; and when she came home that night she gave me an earful! The phone rang, Joyce answered it and said, "Here, take the phone, your daughter-in-law wants to talk to you!" Caroline said, "Let me tell you what just happened."

I realized then that we needed to fundamentally refocus how we attracted, recruited, enrolled and then trained people. Here was a young woman who had everything that we wanted, and we turned her off completely. I called the head of military personnel for the Canadian Forces into my office the next day and told him we were going to set some goals for how we did our business, including how quickly we got people enlisted and into uniform. I wanted to empower recruiters to take the top 30 per cent of their recruits—people with all the qualifications, no criminal record or other problems—and tell them the day they sat down to apply that we were going to make them an offer on the spot. I wanted the next 50 per cent enrolled within a month. So 80 per cent of our recruits—assuming their grades or qualifications checked out and they didn't have any complicating issues—would be in uniform and ready for basic training within a month of signing up.

Of course, a red flag always goes up for 20 per cent or so, and we would take our time to make sure we got those right. (Marc Lépine, the murderer of the fourteen young women in Montreal in 1989, had been turned down by the Canadian Forces after he failed a psychological assessment; we did not want to miss weeding out someone like that in the future.) We would also offer people their choice of first postings and enrol recruits in the job categories that we were really searching for within a minimum of a week from when they first applied. That was like a bombshell going off in the recruiting group. Everyone in recruiting told me it would involve taking some risks, and many were petrified at the idea. Fortunately, others were already in front of me and quickly seized on my direction to radically change how we approached the entire process, from how we attracted Canadians to, finally, after long service, how we said farewell to them.

My response to those who constantly worried was simple. "Yes, we are taking risks," I responded. "But we're going to take even greater risks if we continue to take eight to twelve months to enrol somebody in this shrinking demographic of young people that we have in Canada, with a huge demand for more people in uniform and the fact that other organizations have all kinds of offers to make to the folks we're trying to attract. We will not have the soldiers to do the job in the army, or the airmen, or the airwomen, or the sailors if we continue the way we are. Without people, we will fail. Which is the greater risk?"

We did it. We're still fighting some of those issues because there are still people in recruiting and in their chain of command who rely too much on process and bureaucracy, so we had to put a senior officer in charge of recruiting as a signal that commanders right up to and including the Chief of the Defence Staff were focused on this incredibly important issue.

Walt Semianiw became the new commander of the recruiting group. We sat him down with all the general officers and flag officers, walked through what we had to do and gave him his marching orders: recruit 7,000 more soldiers, sailors, airmen and airwomen into the regular force and another 5,000 into the reserves. We met those recruiting goals every single year, even when we increased the goal by another thousand people halfway through the first year. We made some mistakes and got some things wrong, but we met our goals and got the people we needed.

We also revolutionized the training system at Saint-Jean, Quebec, where all of our recruits go through basic training, increasing the amount of time they spent training and putting an emphasis on physical fitness: we had relearned from operations in Afghanistan and elsewhere that our overall fitness levels were not good enough to facilitate success on our missions. I went down to Saint-Jean to demonstrate that I was paying attention to what was going on there, and went for a morning run with the staff and the entire class of recruits. There were about a thousand of us out running and doing exercises. Claude Bachand, the Bloc Québécois MP for the area, joined us, took a tour of the school and actually enjoyed the heck out of it.

There's an old adage in the military: what the Commander pays attention to, others focus on. Because I was paying attention to recruiting and training, people were actually making changes instead of talking about making changes. We got the kids in the door, got them enrolled and into the training system, a system we adapted and changed dramatically to produce people who were the complete package: fit, well trained, better educated and ready to become the backbone of the Canadian Forces.

It was all part of the "Recruit the Nation" strategy, waking people up to what great young men and women they had in uniform. I think there was always a base of support for us among our population, but the public needed a wake-up call. It always amazed me that Canadian moms and dads were content to let their sons and daughters who served in the Canadian Forces be so ill prepared, ill equipped, and sent on some of the ill-conceived missions that we gave them. Mostly, it was because they didn't know.

Canadians by and large knew nothing about the armed forces, so that was the part we needed to change. It wasn't as hard as it seemed at first, because once you actually start talking to Canadians, you realize that everyone in this country, almost without exception, has a military connection of one kind or another. Whether it was a father who was in uniform or a grandfather who served in one of the world wars, like my great-uncle John Clark, or whether it's a brother who's serving in the military, or a sister in Afghanistan, a third cousin once removed on one of our frigates or whatever, almost every single Canadian has that connection. Once we began to point that out to them, people started to open their eyes a little bit and see other connections all around them—a soldier who lives in their neighbourhood or a naval reservist in their workplace. Suddenly they started to get a full appreciation of the width, breadth and positive impact of the CF.

We had to build to that from the almost zero knowledge about people in uniform, what they did as individuals and what the armed forces, as a collective of those individuals, did for us, but once we started that education process it developed a momentum of its own.

After the first few months, everywhere I went young soldiers, sailors, airmen or airwomen would thank me for what they perceived I was doing. Each time I would say, "Don't thank me. If I had some little part to play with turning the spotlight on you, okay, thanks. But if I had done that and you weren't doing your job in the incredibly professional way that I know you do, that spotlight would be hurting us, not helping." So I'd turn it around and say thank you to them. The spotlight shone on them while they were carrying out search-and-rescue efforts, conducting counter-piracy operations off the Horn of Africa, fighting terrorists on the ground in Afghanistan or helping the destitute in Sudan, and that's what led Canadians to love them. That was an important part, maybe the most important part, of that "Recruit the Nation" strategy and became a fundamental part of what we were doing. Our best spokesmen and women were our front-line troops, in the air, at sea and on the ground. Every day I would be astounded by how another one or several of them could articulate so eloquently, with such passion, their role, work, commitment and belief in their county. My own faith in Canada was revitalized as a result.

Clearly, Canadians were beginning to look at us through a different lens. All of a sudden people were coming up to us and telling us that they liked what we were doing. It happened hundreds, thousands of times. We participated in the festivities around the Grey Cup game in Toronto in 2007, and at one point during the game I sidled out the door to have a quick cigar. It was late afternoon, cold and almost dark, and I was standing outside the stadium when two punk rockers came along. They looked to be in their early to mid twenties, wearing leathers, chains, earrings and tattoos and hoping to bum a cigarette from us. One of them said, "Hey! You're the guy that runs the military, aren't you?"

His friend piped up, "Yeah, we know about you. We know about you!"

Man, I thought, this young punk rocker lives on the street, obviously, yet he not only knows about the Canadian Forces, he knows that we have a Chief of the Defence Staff and he recognizes who the Chief of the Defence Staff is. That, to me, was a sign that we had come a long way.

That didn't mean there weren't issues we still had to resolve or that everything was perfect. We faced lots of significant challenges, but none that affected the broad strategy of what we were trying to achieve and where we were going.

That strategy also included making Canadians aware of the next part of our mission in Afghanistan, in the southern half of the country, and what that meant. We had to be clear that there was a changed and increased risk—things were not going to be like they had been in Kabul, and Canadian servicemen and servicewomen were going to be at significantly higher risk. I refused to say that we were going to have people coming home in coffins or body bags; those were not words I would ever use. I simply said, clearly, that the risk was going to be high, and while we were going to take every step possible to reduce that risk, we couldn't reduce it to zero.

All that aside, any success that we had in changing the Canadian Forces for the better—and there had already been a lot—grew out of that triumvirate (of Bill Graham, Ward Elcock and me), who were so personally engaged in defence and foreign policy, and was augmented by the support of Canadians. We were on track, on course, and honestly, it was a hell of a lot of fun. All in all, not a bad first year: I gave it a C-minus and hoped for better.

361

RECRUITING THE NATION

I've always believed that if you're doing a job right, you should really be enjoying it. I loved being a soldier, enjoyed doing all the things associated with soldiering, and when I became CDS I had the perfect opportunity to do them all and enjoy the heck out of the job. Of course, my work was all for a purpose: I used the appointment as a soapbox to educate people as to what the Canadian Forces needed, to get us out there in the public's view. I considered one of the perks of being Chief to be that I got the chance to do all these great things, visit all these amazing young men and women in uniform, which made my life perfect.

For example, I had always watched the Ceremonial Guard on Parliament Hill with pride and a touch of envy, looking at those tall, fit men and women who performed as such a synchronized team. On my first posting to NDHQ, working for the head of the department's civilian employees, the window of my small cubicle looked down on Cartier Square Drill Hall, where the

Governor General's Foot Guards and the Cameron Highlanders started their Changing of the Guard parade every morning in the summer. I would hear the band start playing and I'd be up with my nose pressed to the glass, watching the troops march out of the drill hall toward Parliament Hill for their daily spectacle.

The parade, a great tourist attraction in Ottawa, has been going on for more than a century and is one of Canada's great military traditions. It's based on the Changing of the Guard at Buckingham Palace, where the soldiers who guard the Queen parade through London to change one group of guards for a new group. It dates to when the Guards regiments really did provide bodyguards for the royal family, and here it was adopted for the governor general, our representative of the monarch in Canada. During the summer months, the guards march through downtown Ottawa every morning to Parliament Hill and parade on that vast lawn in front of the Parliament Buildings, carrying on the centuries-old tradition.

I would watch them march out of the drill hall on their way up to Parliament Hill and then see them come marching back down Colonel By Drive when the ceremony was over, in perfect unison, in those impressive scarlet uniforms with the tall bearskin hats. I loved it. It was a beautiful part of the face of Canada, and judging from the crowds of tourists who watch it every day, a lot of other people love it too. The keen young men and women in the ranks demonstrating the work ethic, discipline, teamwork, cohesion and symmetry that went into that show every day represented everything good about our country. When you looked at the faces under those imposing bearskins, they reflected who we are as a country. Whenever I got an opportunity, I'd slip out of the office, walk the two or three blocks to watch the ceremony on the Hill and go back to work, motivated and inspired. I had a chance to talk to a lot of those young people and one day said to Daniel Gilbert, the Canadian Forces' Chief Warrant Officer, "Let's go out and do that. We'll be privates for a day and do the Changing of the Guard."

He said, "Oh no, sir. We couldn't do it." He was too polite to say it, but he had done a lot of drill and ceremonies and figured that it would take the whole summer to work the "old man" up to a decent standard.

Since I was the Chief, and can sometimes be a little stubborn, we did it anyway. We made arrangements with the Guard and in late July went out to Carleton University, where the soldiers who perform the ceremony live during the summer and train for the parade. Gilbert and I spent one afternoon with the soldiers who were to carry out the ceremony the next day, refreshing our basic drill, learning the rifle drill and wearing, for the first time, the bearskins for which we had been fitted. I had not done rifle drill in a long while. In fact the last time I'd been on parade with a rifle was when I was an officer cadet back in the 1970s. So I had a steep learning curve but managed to pick up enough to survive that afternoon.

We were in a platoon of twenty young soldiers (the average age must have been about nineteen) and they were the cliché of a platoon. There was the loudmouthed one; there was the guy who was always cracking jokes; there was the silent one who'd say something once in a while, but everyone listened when he did; and there was the one who everybody picked on, but who gave back as good as she got. We spent the whole afternoon with them and they were excellent. After our first hour or so, they got used to the idea of having the CDS in their ranks, started to relax a little bit and helped me with my rusty drill. We went through the whole parade routine time and time again, and they spent the afternoon bringing me and Gilbert (but mostly me) along.

The next morning, we showed up at 7 a.m. at Carleton, put on the scarlet tunic, bearskin and boots, and underwent inspection by the sergeant major. We got on the bus with the rest of the Guard, drove to Cartier Square Drill Hall, marched in, laid our weapons down, went for a last break and came to attention. The officer in charge told us all, "Okay, let's have a good one out there today," and off we went.

When we marched out of the drill hall, I swear a thrill went down my spine. There we were, part of the Ceremonial Guard, marching with the band playing and hundreds if not thousands of people standing around taking pictures and applauding. It felt great to be dressed up, looking sharp and representing the Canadian Forces. We marched up Elgin Street through the people lined up along the way, including Joyce, our daughter-in-law, Caroline, our grandson, Jack, and my cousin Jill, who were standing on a corner waving at me. Of course I couldn't look at them. We marched onto Parliament Hill, with the first guardsman's foot striking there as the clock started chiming 1000 hours, and performed the Changing of the Guard. We were part of the Old Guard (I don't know if that was a shot at me because of my age, but they do less drill once on Parliament Hill) and also in the rear rank—probably good things considering my talents. It was a bright, hot day, about 33 degrees Celsius, and I was wearing a thick scarlet tunic and the tall, heavy bearskin hat but still feeling pretty good. Then I noticed the guy in front of me. A steady stream of perspiration was rolling down from his bearskin, which comes in to a little tail in the back. I realized that everybody was sweating like that, including me. You lose about five pounds of liquids in that two-hour parade in the sun. But it was absolutely magnificent to be a part of it, and afterwards even Danny Gilbert was grinning from ear to ear and said it made him feel seventeen again.

Of course, the fact that we had been guardsmen for a day got some media attention, which was all good. That Changing of the Guard ceremony is one of the top tourist attractions in Canada, yet the thousands of visitors who watch it—and most Canadians, I suspect—are oblivious to the fact that those young men and women putting on that magnificent show are all soldiers, army reservists, working there for the summer. They are fully qualified infantry soldiers who serve across Canada and in many cases on missions around the world. I thought that anything that reminded people that these were their soldiers was a good thing.

While doing my job, particularly while communicating to each and every man and woman in uniform our vision and plans to implement it, I got the chance to visit a lot of different units and see the various specialties across the army, navy and air force, a chance to really see what each did for the Canadian Forces. I believe in direct communications, which can perhaps be augmented by other methods but not replaced by them, and that meant talking to people directly. Easy to say but difficult to do, because in three and a half years I spoke to over 70,000 of the 89,000 men and women in the Canadian Forces and to thousands of their families as well. I talked to them in Taliban country, in aircraft cockpits, on ships at sea and in every garrison and station around the world that I could get to. I spent time with search-and-rescue technicians, fighter pilots and navy divers to witness their incredible skills and professionalism and appreciate what great work they were doing.

One of my first visits was to Joint Task Force 2 (JTF 2), our special forces unit based near Ottawa, no strangers to me after many operations. JTF 2 troopers are the Olympic athletes of soldiering, our version of gold medallists, taking on the most difficult missions and tasks with a level of skill and professionalism that has earned the respect of special forces units around the world. Like the U.S. Delta Force or the British Special Air Service (SAS), they get the most dangerous and demanding of missions, from hostage rescues to acting as bodyguards for VIPs (like me!) to operating for long periods of time on their own in enemy territory. For my visit, JTF 2 put on what their guys called the granddaddy of all demonstrations. At one point I ended up in a small inflatable boat running at about 50 knots an hour around Lake Ontario, getting a chance to do some cruising with a dozen of JTF 2's "operators," as the members of this immensely capable unit call themselves.

In that one-day demo, we went from Ottawa to Kingston to Petawawa to Carleton Place, and then to somewhere in between, where I was "volunteered" to be a hostage in one of their training exercises. Two big, burly soldiers, playing the bad guys, grabbed me, hustled me off and sat me down in the middle of a dark room. They warned me to sit very still. A few seconds later there was a tremendous series of bangs and flashes (which were the stun grenades the assaulters threw into the room before they charged) and a lot of gunfire. They turned the lights on, and the two guys who'd grabbed me were gone; in their place were two target dummies on either side of me.

I asked one of the operators, "Were you training with blank ammunition?"

He just grinned and showed me the two neatly grouped bullet holes in each of the targets' heads. "All our training is with live ammo, sir."

It was a long, tiring day, but an exciting one that helped me focus even more on building special forces capabilities, based on these outstanding soldiers. It was a rare chance to see those who are truly the standard setters and what they can do when they're physically and mentally well prepared, superbly trained and equipped and are under great leadership. When they are freed from the obstacles and restrictions that you find in most organizations, they can accomplish miracles. JTF 2 has been doing that, from the air, on the land, and either on the sea or beneath it, for nearly two decades. The special forces have developed their skills and abilities to a level that is almost difficult to believe until you see them in action, and it was great to see it all coming together.

I also got the chance to visit with people from a different kind of special forces unit, and a uniquely Canadian one at that. They are the Canadian Rangers. One of them was Sergeant Allen Pogotak, an incredible northern soldier from an organization whose numbers rarely get to 4,500 yet whose footprint stretches across the nation from the northern part of Vancouver Island to Newfoundland. The Rangers are all part-time soldiers, most of them Inuit or First Nations, who, for a pittance in pay, act as Canada's eyes and ears across the desolate North. They are famous for their survival and tracking skills, and they also act as training experts and guides when our southern (okay, relatively southern) soldiers deploy for training or operations in the Arctic. In 2007, Allen guided a platoon of thirty soldiers on the longest sovereignty patrol in Canadian history, a 5,000-kilometre trip on Ski-Doos and sleds across vast stretches of ice and snow to place the Canadian flag on the northern tip of Ellesmere Island, Canada's most northerly point of land. That patrol overcame engine breakdowns, overturned sleds and lost supplies, frostbite and other injuries, all in 75-kilometre-an-hour winds and ambient temperatures of minus 42 (it doesn't matter if it's Celsius or Fahrenheit—that's cold). One night, when the patrol had stopped on a windswept stretch of sea ice, a polar bear invaded their small campsite looking for food, which to a polar bear usually includes people. Allen approached that enormous killer of the North and talked to it in Inuktitut until he somehow convinced the bear to look for a meal elsewhere.

I asked him how he managed to do that, and Allen explained that he had talked to it in what he called "a whisper of a shout" and the bear left because, well, Allen knew what to say to get him to leave. "We know the North, sir, this is our home," he told me. "We know these things because they save our lives. For instance, if you are ever in the North, sir, and find yourself in such unfortunate circumstances as to be chased by a polar bear, remember to break to your left, not your right. A polar bear cannot turn to its left as fast as it can to its right. So if you break to your left, sir, you will live four seconds longer than if you break to your right."

Allen grinned at me and I realized he had completely sucked me in. I had been so enthralled listening to the remarkable insight of this quiet, dignified Canadian Ranger that I didn't figure out that he was pulling my leg until it was too late. I gave Allen a well-deserved commendation and never forgot his advice about polar bears.

We needed and wanted to showcase these great servicemen and servicewomen, like Sergeant Allen Pogotak, so that Canadians could see what incredible people were serving them. I realized early on that celebrities could play an important part in bringing attention to them—sailors, soldiers, airmen, airwomen and their families—and, in short, help us implement our "Recruit the Nation" strategy. Celebrities were a way to reach audiences we could never hope to influence, no matter how many recruiting commercials we aired. All we had to do was introduce them to our people and let the celebrities do the rest. There was no doubt a good story would follow, because our people were so impressive.

I started inviting prominent people to join me on my regular visits to Canadian Forces bases and missions, so that they could see our troops doing what they did so well and make up their own minds about how wonderful those men and women in uniform are. This included having groups of Canadian celebrities visit our sailors in the Persian Gulf, air crews who ran one invisible mission after another there, and our troops in Afghanistan. We flew to the Persian Gulf, where our supply base for the Afghan mission was located, in the fall of 2005 with CBC TV personality (and fine Newfoundlander) Rick Mercer, Hockey Hall of Famer Guy Lafleur, Olympic gold medallists Catriona Le May Doan and Daniel Igali and several others in tow.

Catriona Le May Doan was incredible during that visit; she's such an amazing lady and represents our country so well. She's also incredibly articulate and resonates with audiences.

She's absolutely beautiful to start with and was like a beacon when she went into Afghanistan, drawing the soldiers' attention like bees to honey. Whenever Catriona had to put on a helmet or bulletproof vest or carry her bags more than a few feet, she had at least a dozen soldiers there to help her in a matter of seconds. I might have been Chief of the Defence Staff, and therefore their boss, but I was left to fend for myself. When she returned to Canada, I happened to hear her on the radio a couple of times talking about the visit to Afghanistan. She was so eloquent and complimentary to the soldiers that it certainly far surpassed anything I could have said. Guy Lafleur, who played for five Stanley Cup–winning teams, must have played a hundred games of ball hockey with the soldiers; all of them wanted to be able to say they'd played on his wing or had stopped one of his shots. Daniel Igali, the Olympic gold-medal wrestler, put on a little demonstration. One of our special forces troopers, an enormous, strong and agile man who had taken lots of unarmed combat training, challenged him to a friendly wrestling match. Daniel pinned this big, strong guy three times in less than five minutes, which just goes to show you the difference between top Olympic athletes and us mere mortals.

On our last day in Afghanistan, we gathered about 700 troops together just before our departure to talk to them together. After I had a chance to speak, I asked everyone who had come along on the visit to say a few words. Daniel Igali spoke last and talked about how proud he felt when he won the gold medal, representing Canada, his adopted homeland (he was born in Nigeria), but said that pride was, in his eyes, insignificant compared to what he felt for all the men and women in uniform wearing the

Canadian flag on their left shoulder and serving their country. After he gave that speech someone said there must have been a dust storm, because everybody seemed to have a little something caught in their eye, causing them to water up! It was one of those times and places when it was so great to be Canadian.

Guys like Rick Mercer, of course, could reach an entirely different set of Canadians. During that visit to Kabul, Rick was like a kid in a candy store. He talked to almost every soldier in Camp Julien, our main base in Kabul, and had a great time. Rick is a great talker, as I found out for myself on our trip home. By the time we got on the plane to fly back I was exhausted, having been on the go for almost three weeks, working flat out, and I decided to go up to the flight deck of the C-130 that was flying us back to Camp Mirage, in the Persian Gulf, for the next leg of the trip back to Canada. I knew that there was a fold-out bunk behind the pilots in the cockpit, and I needed some rest. So as soon as we took off, cleared any potential surface-to-air missile threat and were able to get our seatbelts undone and our flak vests and helmets off, I climbed up onto the bunk and settled in for a nap. It's a four-hour flight from Kabul to Camp Mirage, so I was counting on a good three and a half hours' sleep. I got into the bunk, squirmed around to get comfortable and, when I turned to face the front, there was Rick Mercer's face a few inches from mine. He talked for the entire four-hour flight and, needless to say, I didn't get any sleep!

What Rick talked about was the opportunity to showcase some of the incredible people that he had met in Afghanistan, not only to get a great segment for his television show, the *Rick Mercer Report*, but also for Canada's benefit. That's how we got the idea of going skydiving together.

About a week after our flight, Rick and I met in Canadian Forces Base Trenton, Ontario, at the Canadian Forces Advanced Land Warfare School, where military parachuting is taught. We were given ground instruction on what to do, with Rick's crew filming everything, and then we hopped into a small plane. It was nip or tuck whether we would be able to jump that day, because while we were ready to make the leap, there was cloud cover underneath so we couldn't see the ground, and obviously you want to see the ground when you're jumping from high altitude.

We were flying at 10,500 feet, in a circle, with the ramp open, for a while and Rick looking down nervously the entire time. Eventually we got the signal to go, and off the ramp we tumbled, head over heels. We were doing a tandem jump, with each of us strapped to one of the school's parachute instructors who pulled the rip cord and controlled the parachute once it opened. We were in free fall for 5,000 feet, and another 5,000 or so under the canopy of the parachute. Rick Mercer talked for all 10,000 feet. It was a very popular segment of his show, but for us it was a priceless chance to showcase the amazing skill of those instructors at the school: their fitness level, the teamwork involved and the kind of exciting challenges they faced every day. Millions of Canadians saw the episode and his coverage of the Afghan visit with the other celebrities. After that episode aired on the *Rick Mercer Report*, our recruiting numbers jumped again.

From Mercer's point of view, the footage proved a great service to his country but also made for great TV, and there's nothing wrong with combining both. NHL players like Guy Lafleur, "Tiger" Williams and Bob Probert reached audiences that we couldn't even begin to get to ourselves, and they reached them with powerful stories about our sons and daughters serving so far away.

The only Canadian who appeared to disagree was Gord O'Connor, the defence critic for the opposition, running for a seat in what all knew was an imminent election. O'Connor made some comments to the media that he considered the trip inappropriate and that civilians should not be in a combat zone. Rick Mercer immediately savaged him in his blog. It was perhaps a harbinger of things to come.

We built on that initial success by making a Christmas visit to Afghanistan in 2006, when I brought Rick back as well as comedian Mary Walsh; Damhnait Doyle, a singer out of Newfoundland; Max Keeping from CJOH TV in Ottawa; the band Jonas out of Montreal; and several other dignitaries. We were accompanied by John Baird, the Minister of the Treasury Board; Laurie Hawn, the Parliamentary Secretary for Defence; and House Leader Jay Hill. Most of the soldiers in Afghanistan at that time were based in Petawawa, just up the road from Ottawa, so they all knew Max. We flew into Camp Mirage in the Persian Gulf on December 22 and jumped, by helicopter, to our frigate HMCS *Ottawa,* which was in the Persian Gulf on deployment. We spent Christmas Eve on the *Ottawa,* cruising those calm, warm and sometimes dangerous waters. I visited every part of the ship, shook the hand of every sailor, soldier (there were even a few of them on board), airman and airwoman (they ran the flight detachment for the Sea King helicopter), and smoked cigars all night as we socialized.

On Christmas Eve morning, the ship's company mustered on the flight deck at the aft end of the ship (I was already into nautical terms after only eighteen hours on board), other than those who were absolutely required to run onboard systems. First, I took the microphone, addressing the group, promoting some individuals, recognizing others with a Chief of the Defence Staff coin (I always carried a few coins I had specially made to recognize our soldiers for their efforts) and telling them all how proud I was to be their Chief and how much all Canadians appreciated them. Each of the others also spoke. Max Keeping was a major hit. I had forgotten that each of our ships' companies selected a major charity to support, based in the city for which the ship was a namesake. The ship's company of HMCS *Ottawa* had selected the Children's Hospital of Eastern Ontario (CHEO) as their charity and had raised significant dollars to support it. I was able to introduce them to Max, and used his nickname, "Mr. CHEO," after all of his work to support the hospital, and the connection was made. The last person I asked to say a few words was Damhnait Doyle. Damhnait turned to me and said, "You know, General, I don't know if this is appropriate or not, but do you think it would be all right for me to sing 'O Canada'?"

"Yes," I said, "I couldn't think of anything more appropriate."

It can get hot and humid in the Persian Gulf. That day it was about 27 degrees Celsius, with calm water, and the sun was burning. More than 200 Canadians, 10,000 kilometres from family and home, stood there on Christmas Eve, listening to and joining in her beautiful rendition of "O Canada." There wasn't a dry eye.

After that everybody wanted their picture taken. All the Newfoundlanders on the ship got together (57 out of a crew of 245)
with a Toronto Maple Leafs shirt in front and had their picture
taken with me, Rick Mercer, Damhnait Doyle and Mary Walsh.

From there we went into Afghanistan. After landing and
attending a small reception on Christmas Eve afternoon with a
lot of the staff on Kandahar Airfield, I headed out to our forward
operating bases (FOBs), in Taliban country, to be with those
carrying the weight of direct combat. Only a limited number of
people could come because of the space on the helicopter, but
we brought Rick Mercer, Jay Hill, Laurie Hawn and John Baird
and visited every subunit and soldier, including a few Americans, that we could find. I spoke to about ten different groups in
the next twenty-four hours out at FOB Wilson, Sperwan Ghar,
Ma'sum Ghar and the provincial reconstruction team camp in
the centre of Kandahar City. Early on Christmas Day we wound
up at a forward base called Strong Point West, serving Christmas
dinner to a company of Patricias, as well as some gunners, a few
engineers and several crews of reconnaissance vehicles from my
old regiment, the Royal Canadian Dragoons.

These men and women had just returned from some intense
firefights with the Taliban, and for them this was a particularly
welcome change of pace. As they came back into the ruined
compound on Christmas morning and took their helmets off,
their hair was standing straight up because of all the dust and
sweat in it. One of the youngest soldiers in that group had hair
that was just all over the place, like a punk rocker, so I licked my
hand and smoothed it down for him, which got a good laugh
from his friends.

The troops really appreciated us being there. People like Rick Mercer, who served gravy over the Christmas dinner that morning at Strong Point West—literally out on the very front lines of the fight—gave those young soldiers a direct connection to Canada that was priceless. When you are 12,000 kilometres from home on a dirty, dangerous, dusty trail, and someone is shooting at you, you can be forgiven for thinking you are all alone. The presence of people like Rick and the other celebrities in that lonely firebase put the lie to that and gave the soldiers a visceral connection to Canada, Canadians and, somewhat, their families. The visit was fun, but more importantly, I thought, incredibly worthwhile, because it also helped Canadians get a perspective on the Canadian Forces that otherwise they never would have gotten.

The last story from that visit reflected my belief that sometimes you just have to do things and hope they come out right. The week prior to this visit I had been in Petawawa, at the request of Peter Mansbridge, to participate in a series *The National* was doing on CF operations in Afghanistan. I had met with six of our recent widows for coffee, accompanied them to the drill hall where the show was being aired and, after participating, met with many of the two-hundred-plus family members attending. One young lady spoke to me and said her husband was deployed in FOB Wilson. I said I would see him on Christmas Day, and asked if there was a message she wanted me to give him. Melissa Leblanc said, "Tell him I love and miss him, and to stay safe until we get him home." I said, "We can do better than that," and pointed at my cheek. She reached up and kissed me. When we arrived in FOB Wilson on Christmas Eve, after meeting and speaking to about 350 soldiers, the last one in line was Master Corporal

Jeremy Leblanc. I said, "Is your wife Melissa?" When he replied in the affirmative, I said, "Look that way," and kissed him on the cheek. It got a rousing laugh from the others, but unbeknownst to me, someone—I believe Christie Blatchford of the *Globe and Mail*—had taken a photo. I did not mention the story again, but about two months before my retirement, Jeremy Leblanc put the story on the Internet and the guy who manufactured my Commander's coins sent me a plaque with the photo and the story engraved. Jeremy's closing line in the story was that my "moustache tickled!" Sometimes you just have to go with the flow and hope it turns out right.

On that Christmas Day I was ecstatic that we had brought Canada to our troops.

Another reason for our outward-looking approach to Canadians was to give some long-overdue recognition to the troops, something that we had continued to not do well. In September 2005 I was invited to give the Dick and Ruth Bell Lecture to about three hundred people at Carleton University. During the question period following my presentation, one young woman, among a few protestors, stood and gave a long, shrill speech masquerading as a question. She called me a warmonger and said I was making the Canadian Forces part of the U.S. military and ended by asking, "Will you resign?"

Well, I thought she'd wasted enough of everyone's time, so I kept my answer short. "No," I said and then took another question.

In the audience, however, which filled every seat in the auditorium, there were also young men and women in their uniforms, all of them students in various programs at Carleton, all proud to be in the CF and proud to wear their uniform. They also spoke up during my speech, pointing out the many positive things the Canadian Forces were doing in Afghanistan and elsewhere around the world. It turned out to be an incredibly enjoyable evening, despite the ignorance of two or three. The great-looking kids, those men and women in uniform, stood out and had an extremely positive impact that more than balanced the negative, and from then on I started having one or two with me, from each branch of the Canadian Forces, whenever I appeared somewhere. It was a realization, yet again, that the best marketing for the CF was the young men and women who made us what we were.

The CDS gets invited to speak at a lot of events, and I'd certainly done my share of talking the first few months in the job. But I noticed that it's all well and good for General Hillier to say something and if I speak very well, maybe it can have impact. However, if General Hillier gives a speech and at the same time shows some pictures, primarily of men and women in the Canadian Forces, it fires up people's imaginations in a way more powerful than words alone. Then it was even better to complement both those things by having two or three of those young heroes, out of the thousands I was speaking about, on hand, to stand up and represent that modern-day, average, run-of-the-mill, ordinary Canadian man and woman who has accomplished extraordinary things because of dedication and sacrifice in the service of the country. That proved an enormous hit.

After the first time I did it, somebody in the audience came up after my speech and told me, "You just don't know how powerful that is." I really didn't, but after that conversation I sure hoisted it aboard and started bringing along at least a couple of our young people in uniform and introducing them to the audience. It was so great for getting our message out and giving those young heroes a little public recognition.

We were trying, at the same time, to both revive and revolutionize our system of medals and decorations in the Canadian Forces, which had become so out of date as to be almost irrelevant. So having people stand up, be thanked and be recognized, even informally, was a way of making up for the shortcomings of the formal system. We were able to do it in a timely fashion—we could bring in some kid right off a ship, where she had served with distinction in the Persian Gulf or in the North Atlantic, and stand her up and tell everyone what a great young woman she was and what incredible things she had done for our country. Every time I did that people would give them a standing ovation, and you could almost see those young men and women grow another two feet.

We had to do something to recognize the great work our people were doing, because the way we awarded medals, decorations and commendations had become the epitome of governmental bureaucracy. Our recognition system was really failing. If, when I was in Petawawa, I was presenting a Canadian Forces subunit commendation to a company in my brigade almost five years after the action to earn this commendation, then we had failed. I wanted to shorten the time it took to hand out medals and awards by taking the process out of the hands of committees and have commanders sign off the awards instead, which would have really cut the time for these things to a matter of days or weeks. The way it was working, it took six months after units came back from operations to get the recommendations for medals into the system, another six months for everyone to get their act together, consider the recommendations and formally write them up, and six months to a year or more to go through the process of deciding whether or not it was deserved. It was ridiculous.

Try as we would to change that system, however, we often found our hands tied by the process around Ottawa. It was really frustrating, but we took to driving through it as hard as we could, trying to streamline a process that was ludicrously complicated at the same time as we were trying to find creative ways to do end runs around it. I handed out a lot of Chief of the Defence Staff commendations and Canadian Forces medallions, both of which were within my power—and only my power—to award as I saw fit.

Everyone inside the Canadian Forces supported this initiative. We cut a bunch of the red tape and focused on what we needed to do and how quickly we needed it done. Take Sergeant Pat Tower, who won the Star of Military Valour for his incredible heroism during the fighting in the Panjwayi on August 3, 2006, when he charged across 100 metres of open ground through Taliban machine-gun fire. It was ideal to announce his award quickly so that he'd still be among the battle buddies he accomplished such great deeds with. That's the thing that meant the most to Pat Tower: being recognized in front of his comrades. It was important that he be recommended for a medal and that we could announce that medal before his unit left the theatre of operations. We wouldn't need the actual medal to be pinned on him then—the hardware is almost irrelevant to these guys. What's important is that they're recognized at an appropriate time and in front of the people who mean the most to them.

That's what we were trying to move toward, but it was extremely difficult to do in Ottawa, a town that thrives on process. The roadblock was the government's Awards and Honours Committee, which has representation from a number of federal departments and ministries and which must approve all medals for bravery. Any change to that process must also be approved by that committee, and it is deeply resistant to change, particularly change that would essentially put it out of a job. Even with all of our pushing, we still had people waiting for medals years after the missions were over because the committee had to weigh in and everything had to be prepared in a certain manner. We made many improvements. In most cases, thanks to Major-General Walt Semianiw, our head of military personnel, and his key man, André Levesque, the head of honours and recognition, we managed to trim the waiting period dramatically, but we never did resolve all the problems with that system.

Whenever we did hand out those awards, we made sure it was done right. We brought all the recipients to Ottawa, with their families, and had the Governor General present the awards in a ceremony at Rideau Hall. In one case, we had to move the whole ceremony to the Château Laurier hotel, and another time to the Museum of Civilization, because we expected such a big crowd.

Michaëlle Jean, who succeeded Adrienne Clarkson as Governor General early in my time as CDS, was very interested in the military and often asked my advice about how she could exercise her role as Commander-in-Chief of the Canadian Forces.

I said, "You know, recognition is so important; we don't have it right, and one of the things we are looking at is a ball, a gala ball, to have heroes with their family members attend as part of that recognition."

She was most enthused about it and said, "Let's do it! Let's do it at Rideau Hall."

The Commander-in-Chief's Ball became a new tradition. At that first gala, we brought 110 heroes to Rideau Hall for an outdoor reception, with everyone in formal dress. Soldiers, sailors, airmen and airwomen from the rank of private to general attended, along with their wives, husbands, partners or any other family member that they wished to bring. We brought in the Canadian Forces band, some of the singers from other bands across the CF, some celebrities from the NHL, entertainers like Rick Mercer, singer Lori Anna Reid, the band Jonas, and business and community leaders.

I had been trying to get the Canadian Forces bands, but particularly the CF Central Band stationed in Ottawa, to break out of their cocoon of only playing marching music for military parades and do something a little different, because I knew what incredibly talented musicians and performers they were. Every time I was at some event with them I told them, "I know you can play military music, I hear it all the time. What I want to see are some of those incredible talents that you have in all these other areas. I want to hear some Johnny Cash." I really like Johnny Cash.

The musicians all told me that they had always been told they weren't allowed to do anything like that. "Well, that's done with now," I said. "I want to see your talents showcased every place we can find, outside of just the military. Yes, the military music's important because the pomp and pageantry brings dignity to our ceremonies. But I want you to do more."

Johnny Cash became a bit of a running joke between me and the band. At the Commander-in-Chief's Ball, Sergeant Mike Emberson sang "Ring of Fire," with the entire band playing backup. He did a magnificent job, and they did it because they all knew how much I loved Johnny Cash.

The stars of the evening were the thirty soldiers, sailors, airmen and airwomen, all of whom had won the Medal of Military Bravery, Star of Courage, the Star of Military Valour or a Mention in Dispatches. It was a great evening for them and for their spouses or families. One sergeant's wife said to me, "This is like a Cinderella evening. I only found out about this three weeks ago, and three weeks was just about enough time for me to get a new dress and get my hair done, get my nails done. I wanted to be ready for tonight."

One of the supporters we'd invited was Paolo Aquilini, one of the brothers who owns the Vancouver Canucks. Paolo had been with us on the trip to Afghanistan in the spring. He came up to Joyce and me at the reception and asked us to be his guests, with two tickets for the playoff game, at Scotiabank Place the following night, between the Ottawa Senators and the Anaheim Ducks.

I said, "Paolo, I'd love to go, but we've got a young kid here that this would probably mean the world to." Private Jess Larochelle, from 1st Battalion, Royal Canadian Regiment, in Petawawa, had won the Star of Military Valour—the second highest medal for bravery in Canada, second only to the Victoria Cross—for defending his observation point during a Taliban attack that had left him badly wounded, two of his buddies killed and three more wounded. He was an incredible young man, and Paolo was impressed with the story. Jess had brought his girlfriend, a lovely young lady, and they were wandering around Rideau Hall with their eyes the size of saucers. I called him over and said, "Come on over here, young man—someone wants to meet you."

Paolo gave him the tickets and Jess was profusely thankful. Afterwards he slid up to me and said, "Sir, I've never been to an NHL game before, so I don't know where these seats are. Do you think they're okay?"

I laughed and said, "Well, I think you'll find they're decent seats."

I ran into Jess about a week later. He said that, yes, they were good seats: right behind the Ottawa Senators bench. "Sir, I couldn't see the play on the ice very well," he said. "This guy on the Senators bench, wearing number 11, kept standing up and blocking my vision."

That gala ball was not only one of the best things we did, it was also one of the most enjoyable. We had a great evening and did not shut down until two in the morning, by which time I think Her Excellency had long since gone to bed.

CHAPTER 19

DEFENSIVE MANOEUVRES

By the time the federal election was called at the end of November 2005, the Canadian mission in Afghanistan had largely shifted from the capital to the south, where work by our provincial reconstruction team had already commenced. We had cleared our people and equipment out of Camp Julien in Kabul and, with a massive logistics and security effort, moved it to Kandahar Airfield, the main coalition base in the south. The PRT was at its own much smaller base camp in Kandahar City, and we were well into the process of getting the 1st Battalion PPCLI battle group out the door and on their way to Afghanistan. All through the eight-week election campaign we were building our infrastructure in Kandahar and training and deploying the battle group and the brigade headquarters, which would run all coalition operations in the south. Back in Canada, we were finishing the reorganization of the Canadian Forces command structure. We had disassembled the organization of the Deputy Chief of the Defence Staff, which under the old system had been responsible for all our troops overseas, and built the new Canada Command and Canadian Expeditionary Force Command. Those two organizations were still only small teams and we hadn't formally stood them up, but they were already taking charge of operations and were growing exponentially in scope.

So the Canadian Forces had a lot going on in the middle of the election campaign. It was busy, to say the least, and I spent my days trying to keep everything on an even keel and the military out of the news as much as possible while the campaign ran its course. When the RCMP scandal blew up in the middle of the campaign, it came as a bit of a relief in NDHQ, because we were happy to have some of the media attention focused on someone else during a time when dumb things can occur.

Then, on January 15, a suicide car bomber drove into a Canadian convoy near the provincial reconstruction team camp in Kandahar and blew himself up, killing Canadian diplomat Glyn Berry and critically wounding three soldiers. Thankfully, the incident didn't become an issue in the campaign—we had feared that casualties might become a point of discussion during the election—but it did have a significant effect on our operations on the ground in southern Afghanistan. Berry was the first Canadian diplomat ever to be killed in the line of duty, and his death caused near panic in the Department of Foreign Affairs and CIDA. Both departments essentially disappeared from Kandahar after that and stayed away for much of the critical period that followed. Berry was, like former Canadian ambassador to Afghanistan Chris Alexander, that rare diplomat who was committed to the mission, active and interested in results rather than protocol and process. After his death, Foreign Affairs scaled down its participation in the provincial reconstruction team and we went from having an active and engaged senior diplomat in the PRT to having just one person under orders not to leave the safety of the PRT camp under any circumstances. That made Foreign Affairs pretty much completely ineffectual at doing their jobs and set our operation in Kandahar back a minimum of two years. Two of the three elements of the government's so-called 3-D approach—defence, diplomacy and development—were now largely out of the picture.

The 3-D approach, or what I preferred to call a Team Canada mission, was a realization that rebuilding failed or failing states was not a security, governance or economic problem; it was all three, and had to be approached with that in mind. Security operations without building a government that could continue to build sta-bility were useless. Equally, unless jobs were available and people could feed their families, no amount of security operations or gov-ernment works could stop men from accepting a few dollars to pick up a weapon and shoot at somebody. Our theory was that we had to help build on all three concurrently to have any lasting or real effect. Despite the countless meetings in Ottawa, we had not made much progress. The attack on January 15 and Glyn Berry's death now made practical co-operative work impossible.

We had meeting after meeting with the Privy Council Office (PCO), the Department of Foreign Affairs and CIDA, telling them it was pointless for the military to be doing our mission unless they were holding up their end by helping to rebuild Afghan society. We worked on every single level throughout the Government of Canada, but Ottawa was so casualty averse that our efforts were to no avail.

We were all worried about casualties and worked hard every day to minimize them, but the fact was that having the few civilians in the PRT confined to the reconstruction team's camp meant 3-D was a farce and we were on our own. That meant that our soldiers had to do all the necessary tasks outside the wire, beyond the safety of the base camps, whether it was training Afghan police in the districts, getting small aid projects going, rebuilding a road or working with the tribal chiefs to build effective local government. Unfortunately, it took three years to get CIDA and Foreign Affairs back to full participation in the mission, and the effects of that gap are still felt. Berry's death was a wake-up call to Foreign Affairs and CIDA that they were working in a different environment than the embassies and relatively peaceful countries of the past, and their response, sadly, was to stay in the base camp. There were good people on the ground working for both departments, people who wanted to get out and do their jobs and who were equally frustrated as we were, but they were all told by their bosses back in Ottawa that they had to remain in base camp.

Berry's death was tragic, on many levels, but the attack itself could have been much worse. When the driver of the car accelerated toward the convoy, Master Corporal Paul Franklin, the driver of the G-Wagen carrying him, saw a flash of motion out of the corner of his eye and swerved at the last second, increasing the vehicle's distance from the explosion to two or three metres. The car bomb was a big one, and if Paul hadn't responded as quickly as he did, everybody in that vehicle would probably have been killed—if the suicide bomber had detonated the bomb another metre closer, the blast would have destroyed that vehicle completely. As it was, the three soldiers inside, William Salikin, Jeff Bailey and Paul himself, were very badly wounded and their lives have been changed forever by their injuries.

Our operations in Afghanistan were heating up as the election ran its course and while we were continuing to transform the Canadian Forces. We were not commenting on or involved in the campaign, obviously, but we paid close attention to the defence policies of the different parties. From my perspective, it seemed that one of the few things—perhaps the only thing— that the Reform Party, the old Progressive Conservatives, and the new Conservative Party agreed on completely was the need to increase funding and support for the Canadian Forces. When we had published the Defence Policy Statement in 2005, the Conservative opposition at the time said that most of the ideas in the statement were good ones but claimed that this was only because the Liberals had stolen most of those ideas from them, the opposition. So it seemed that going into the election, the two leading parties generally agreed with the direction we were taking the Canadian Forces.

The Conservatives issued their defence platform fairly early in the campaign. The CF and the Department of National Defence looked at it and estimated that the plan was going to cost somewhere between $10 and $20 billion more to implement than we had in the budget, even with the increases made by the Liberal government. We felt that there was no way we would get that money from any government. The Conservative plan had been costed, however, at somewhere around $6 or $7 billion. Many of the parts of their defence policy were absolutely in line with what we believed, although there were questions about other initiatives;

but what we weren't sure about was the money: how much all of it would cost and whether or not that much additional money would be coming out of the new, minority government that emerged after the January 23 election.

In early February, just after the Conservative victory, Deputy Minister Ward Elcock and I were invited to Stephen Harper's office—he was still in the Opposition Leader's office, as he was prime minister–elect until his new government was sworn in—and with Derek Burney, Chief of Staff for Harper's transition team, and the Prime Minister–elect, we discussed what was happening with the Canadian Forces. Most of the time we talked about the Afghan mission. We pulled up a bunch of chairs around a coffee table, and I laid out three large-scale maps of Afghanistan and walked Harper through what was happening on the ground, where our troops were, their job and the challenges and risks.

Mostly it was Harper and I talking while Elcock and Burney offered the occasional comment. Though Harper didn't have a lot of questions, he got right to the point in those he did have. We talked through our mission in Kandahar, where ISAF was located, where the American and other coalition troops were going to be, and what our goals were. I walked him through it all in great detail, right down to the geography of Kandahar Airfield, the location of the provincial reconstruction team camp, the main centres of population in Kandahar province and where the trouble spots were. He was also interested in the border with Pakistan, how that played into our mission, and in the threat from the Taliban. We were still defining that threat, but I made it clear to him that this was not going to be an easy mission; it was going to be tough.

I had met Harper only once or twice before and didn't really know the man, but we had a pretty free and frank exchange that morning—a good conversation. Nobody from the Privy Council Office was there, nobody from the bureaucracy taking copious notes, which I thought was a pretty good approach to take. He was a very quick study: he brought up some of my points months later, asking me to follow up on what had occurred. He was quick to challenge, which I welcomed: he was my boss after all, the Prime Minister–designate of Canada, and had not only the right but the responsibility to challenge his Chief of the Defence Staff. Harper indicated clearly, right from the start, that he was going to be engaged in the Afghan mission, and the fact that our first meeting lasted an hour and a half was indicative of his involvement. He grasped the military situation quickly and had obviously been following the mission, though he didn't have as many details as I was now giving him. It quickly became apparent to me that he supported the mission and what Canada was doing in Afghanistan.

At the end of discussion, I said to him, "I realize that you're just coming into office as Prime Minister and we have a change in government. We are now in combat operations, with young men and women dying, so the Prime Minister of Canada needs to have complete confidence in his Chief of the Defence Staff. As you know, I was selected by Mr. Martin, and if you want me to continue I'd be delighted, but if you don't I'm prepared to step aside and let you select your own Chief. You have to have a CDS who you have confidence in."

That was the first and only time I ever offered Prime Minister Harper, or anyone else in his government, my resignation. Although there was a lot of speculation, in media and government circles and even within the Department of National Defence (including from several people who should have known better), that I regularly threatened to resign to get my way, quite the opposite was true. Threatening to quit might have worked once, but the government would have lost patience with this pretty quickly—no country can be run on such a fickle basis. If I had threatened to resign as many times as some people said I had, my term as Chief would have been

pretty short indeed.

I was fully prepared to voluntarily step aside if he wanted to pick his own Chief of the Defence Staff, and I wanted to offer him that option right away. I felt it was that important that the Prime Minister have confidence in his senior military officer and have his own team running the show.

He immediately said, "Oh no, no. We'll see how things pan out, but I want you to continue as Chief."

About a week after that meeting, the new government named its first Cabinet and I went to Rideau Hall for the swearing-in ceremony, at least in part to find out who would be the new Minister of Defence. As I sat in the reception room, waiting for the ceremony to begin, I turned around and saw Gord O'Connor. I thought to myself, "Well, obviously he's going to be a minister, and he's probably going to become the Minister of Defence." I was soon proven correct.

The rest of my staff had found out almost an hour earlier on their BlackBerrys back in NDHQ (I had turned off my BlackBerry while I was at Rideau Hall). O'Connor's appointment caught me and most of the CF and DND command team by surprise. We had had hints from people on Parliament Hill who were pretty closely tied to the process of naming that first

Conservative Party Cabinet that Gord wasn't going to get the defence portfolio. Historically, opposition defence critics rarely end up getting appointed as Defence Minister when their party forms government, so most insiders were predicting that he would not become defence minister.

When Ward and I met with O'Connor after he was sworn in, he told us the Prime Minister had said to him, "You designed the defence policy plank of our party, and now you've got to implement it."

Despite all the rumours around Ottawa about how much we hated each other, Gord and I got along and worked well together, most of the time. I had kept in touch with him after he retired from the Canadian Forces and we would go for coffee occasionally. While he was opposition defence critic, I would meet with him periodically to brief him on events (with Bill Graham's full knowledge and approval). In most cases, we were relaxed and open with each other whenever we met. As I said to him, just before he left the department, "You know, Minister, you and I agree on far more than we have money to do." He agreed with that.

I met with him the day after the swearing in, along with Ward and a few other key officials, and started briefing him; I wanted him to be up to speed as quickly as possible. As a former general, Gord obviously knew the basics about the Canadian Forces, which was good, because we've had ministers in the past who didn't know a corporal from a colonel. He'd been away from the military for twelve years, however, and we needed to bring him up to date on the latest issues and some of the threats. And while he had a great understanding of the ABCs of defence and the Canadian Forces in particular, that understanding led him to want to sometimes meddle in the day-to-day detail in the first few months, which caused some minor friction between us.

Gord constantly reached out for information from generals or colonels in the army, navy or the air force, or would go directly to a colonel running a base with a question. It seemed to me that he was asking the advice of the lower ranks of the Canadian Forces in order to get the answer he wanted, not the answer I would necessarily have given him as head of the Canadian Forces. He preferred to hear advice that he liked, that was in line with his own views. Then he'd launch an initiative based on that advice, and my senior commanders and I would have to fight time-consuming, and ultimately unnecessary, rearguard battles to convince him that his ideas were not necessarily good ones, or, even if they were, weren't workable.

Part of the problem was that Gord did not really trust the system we had, and seemed to have little respect for most general or flag officers, perhaps because of his experiences in the Canadian Forces during the early 1990s and the Somalia affair. We didn't have much credibility in his eyes. He appeared to put much more value on anything people at the rank of colonel or below told him and little in the words of anyone who was a general or admiral.

I had to remind him that it was my job to give him advice on behalf of the entire Canadian Forces. I said, "Look, you can be Minister of Defence and CDS, or I can be CDS, but we both can't be CDS. We've got to clarify some issues here. My job is to offer you advice and, as you told me, you don't have to accept it—I understand that. But if you don't accept my advice on the bigger issues, then we have a problem, and some decisions to make."

While we agreed that Gord O'Connor would drive the political end of the Ministry and I would provide advice and guidance from a Canadian Forces–wide perspective, it did not always work that way.

We had other disagreements as well, including one over the changes to the command structure formalized in the period between the election campaign and the new government's taking power. We had held ceremonies standing up the new Canada Command and Canadian Expeditionary Force Command in early February, just a few days before the first Conservative Cabinet was sworn in. Gord seemed to take it personally that I had not waited on his approval before formally standing up these new commands. At one meeting, he accused me of taking advantage of the brief window between the defeat of the previous Liberal government and the new government taking power to push through these changes and undercut any policies they might have wanted to bring in.

I told him pretty bluntly that that was bullshit—these changes had been approved by the previous Liberal government and the ceremonies had just put the final, formal touch on it all, publicly announcing what had already been done. I said, "Look, we were just formally announcing something that had already occurred, and since we are already on operations, we couldn't wait—we had to go ahead."

Ward Elcock backed me, but Gord and I still had what the troops call "an energetic conversation" over that issue. In hindsight, I think I made a mistake in announcing the new commands publicly—we should've just gone ahead and done it, and the new government and the media probably wouldn't have even noticed.

Instead, Gord got fired up about it, I came back just as hard and that resulted in an angry meeting in the Minister's office.

Those were not showstoppers, however, and we worked through them. The initial major source of friction, more important than all the others combined, was over the Conservative plan, drawn from their campaign platform on defence, to buy strategic lift transport planes. Gord came into the department determined to make things happen and one of his first priorities was the purchase of strategic airlift: big transport jets, C-17 Globemasters, which are designed to carry large loads over long distances. He felt that was absolutely the right thing to do and insisted that the department begin moving immediately to purchase the planes.

I said, "Well, that's great, but first of all, we don't have the money, and secondly, we need tactical airlift, too."

I told him that taking the money we were going to spend on a replacement for the Hercules tactical transport aircraft and diverting it to buy new long-range strategic transport aircraft just wouldn't work. It would fundamentally cripple our ability to conduct operations. This was where Gord's out-of-date understanding of the CF became a real challenge. In his view, we were using the C-130 Hercules (a short-range tactical airlift plane) to fly from Trenton, Ontario, into Afghanistan when we should have been using strategic airlift for that job—big long-range jets like the C-17. If we bought enough of those Globemaster strategic airlift planes, then we could get rid of most of the tactical airlift Hercules and use the money saved for other projects. But the Canadian Forces needed those tactical transport planes because they were the only aircraft that could fly everything from soldiers to humanitarian aid into remote, often crude airstrips, potentially under enemy ground fire, which was always a threat when flying into Afghanistan. Our existing fleet of Hercules transports was nearly forty years old and we needed to replace them, probably with the newest model—the C-130J Hercules.

So while Gord was pushing hard for strategic airlift, we were pushing back just as hard to buy new tactical planes. I was all for buying new strategic airlift, but not if the cost was so high we would not be able to replace those old Hercules. We still had to have the tactical airlift, even if we bought the big strategic planes. The Canadian Forces had been renting big Antonov transport planes from a Ukrainian-based company for those long-range cargo-hauling trips around the world, which was not ideal, but as I told Gord, "We can always rent strategic airlift. Even in the worst-case scenario you can still get them. You can't rent tactical airlift. You can't rent commercial planes to fly into a place where there might well be missiles or other things fired at them." In fact, we knew that in Ottawa the decision process in government was so slow that we would almost always have rented aircraft waiting to load before the government had made a decision to commit us anywhere. Our response as a country to the tsunami in Sri Lanka and the earthquake in Pakistan had proven that.

We had heated discussions on this issue. At one point Gord called me to task in front of the Defence Management Committee—which I was on, along with the Vice Chief of the Defence Staff, the army, navy and air force commanders, the Deputy Minister, and one or two assistant deputy ministers—saying he was not satisfied with the negative response he was getting on this strategic airlift question. So we worked on a compromise. I eventually went to Gord and said, "We can support you on strategic airlift. With the money that's coming in we can get four C-17s and sixteen C-130Js, which will satisfy both you and me that we are getting what the CF needs."

He agreed, and we worked really hard to get both launched. Gord proved very effective early on at pushing programs through Cabinet and got approval to purchase the C-17s and tactical aircraft C-130Js, along with new transport helicopters and trucks for the army. That C-17 purchase was probably the fastest acquisition program in the history of the CF. We got Cabinet approval, negotiated and signed the contracts and had the first one delivered in August 2007, less than eight months after we had signed the final contract.

Two days after that first aircraft was delivered to Canadian Forces Base Trenton, it flew its very first operational mission, delivering humanitarian aid to Kingston, Jamaica, to help them deal with the aftermath of Hurricane Dean. Two days after that it was flying its first mission to Afghanistan to deliver much-needed ammunition for the fight in Kandahar. By March 2008, the other three aircraft were in service. Gord deserved full credit for pushing the whole process through so quickly. Public Works Canada raised its usual bureaucratic objections and obstacles, but he brushed them aside and made the best deal possible. These big, long-range transport planes revolutionized the capabilities of the Canadian Forces, and at the same time we launched the process of getting new tactical transport aircraft, which, once the contract was signed and we knew when the aircraft were coming, allowed us to use our current, aging C-130s much more effectively.

Gord had been brought into the defence portfolio to deliver on the Conservative platform, and he wanted to complete the agenda in eighteen months. While that launched us on many projects in a very energetic way, I had reservations about whether or not many of the targets set in the platform were possible, much less desirable.

The Canadian Forces did its best to implement the changes Gord wanted, but in the end we had neither the money nor the people to do it all. The $15 billion to $20 billion Conservative platform would supposedly cost only $5 billion a year. Then, when the new government took power and installed its Defence Minister, instead of $5 billion a year, he got a total of $5 billion over five years. Gord had envisioned getting a defence budget increase of $1 billion in each of five years, adding it to his baseline budget each year so that at the end of five years he would have had $15 billion to spend during that five-year period. What he got was a total of $5 billion spread out over those five years, and he was still trying to implement the entire $15 billion program. That plan called for increasing the number of personnel in the Canadian Forces to 75,000, buying all these new transport aircraft and starting up new and expensive programs across the Arctic, including new Arctic patrol ships to the North. The difference in cost meant that the new money could pay for the desired increase in personnel up to 75,000, but nothing else.

The platform also called for new army reserve battalions to be created across the country, viewed by some as replacing the existing reserve structure. The Canadian Forces would base large numbers of soldiers to augment those already in places like Comox, B.C., or Bagotville, Quebec, or Goose Bay, Newfoundland, where we had few facilities to house them, and, militarily, no need for them. If this policy had been implemented, we would have had so many people committed to bases that we would have essentially been left with none to deploy. In short, we would have 75,000 soldiers, sailors and airmen or airwomen all bravely defending the country from dozens of bases inside Canada. Our last line of defence would have been our first line of defence.

Ron Buck, Vice Chief of the Defence Staff, and the army, navy and air force commanders were all trying to sort through this to achieve, at the front end of the government's mandate, the two or three things in the Conservative platform that we all felt could be accomplished within the budget available. After a few weeks of back and forth on these and other issues between Gord and me, I went to his office one day and said, "Minister, there's already a bunch of gossip about bad blood between you and me. Look, you and I agree on far more things than we have money to spend right now, so let's focus on what we can achieve together and turn around this perception that we're always at each other's throats."

We both agreed to do this. Every once in a while he'd call up and say, "Hey, do you have a few minutes to come in and chat, Chief?" and we would sit in his office and talk out whatever issues had come up. When we sat and talked through the challenges in a more relaxed way, we worked much better together.

As all of this was going on, we were vigorously marketing the Canadian Forces to the public. One of the Conservatives' objectives was to grow the military at a scale that was even more ambitious than the Liberals' plans. We needed new recruits in large numbers. I reached out a lot through public appearances and the media because the Canadian Forces had to connect with Canadians, and our own people in uniform, and tell them about our transformation and our missions, particularly the one in Afghanistan. If we could not recruit—one of many goals in the "Recruit the Nation" strategy—we could not implement any policy, no matter how much money we had.

On March 3, 2006, I went to Toronto to attend editorial board meetings with the *Globe and Mail* and the *Toronto Star* and to take part in several television interviews. I returned to Ottawa very early the next morning and was interviewed by Craig Oliver on CTV's *Question Period*. The next workday, on Monday, nearly every paper in the country had a photo of Rick Hillier because of the editorial board meetings and interviews, and while that coverage was extremely complimentary to the Canadian Forces, it made people on Parliament Hill uncomfortable. O'Connor called me into his office that morning. After we had talked through some routine business with our staff present, he asked to speak to me alone. When the door was closed behind the others, Gord turned and said, "We want to see less of you."

"What do you mean?" I replied.

"Well, there are some people who think you're out there too much and they think we should be seeing less of you."

"Which part specifically are they talking about? Which interviews or stories didn't they like?"

"Well, there's no part specifically—they just want to see less of you in the news."

Gord was very relaxed, not confrontational at all. While he was never specific about who had been complaining about my profile, there was no doubt in my mind that this "request" was coming from the Prime Minister's Office staffers and that Gord was acting as the front man, loyal soldier that he was.

"I understand what you're saying, Minister," I told him. "But I have to tell you: I can't work that way. We are trying to connect with the public; I'm trying to make sure that we implement the policies that you've given us. I simply can't work any other way. I have to be able to talk to Canadians and tell them what their sons and daughters are doing for them."

We left it at that. I walked out of his office with no intention of changing the way I was doing things. If he had ordered me to stop doing interviews or media appearances, I would have had to consider my options. I was never again asked to keep a lower profile, but I believe it became a constant sticking point with the Prime Minister's staff whenever I was in the media. The Prime Minister's Office or Privy Council Office would say, "Why are you giving that speech?" or "Why are you going to the Press Gallery dinner?" or "Why are you doing that interview?"

I would say, "Because it's the right thing to do." I just got on with doing what I felt had to be done. And I presume they continued to be unhappy with me doing it.

The staffers wanted me to change the way I was doing the job of Chief of the Defence Staff and I was determined not to let that happen. This wasn't making policy or commenting on government policy—that was not my role and wouldn't have been appropriate. I was articulating what the Canadian Forces were doing to carry out that government policy, and trying to get our people to act on that policy. The people in PMO just couldn't understand the importance of connecting the Canadian public to their military, or cared not at all about it. The connecting-

Canada's hockey teams supported us, even if they didn't always win themselves. At the Toronto Maple Leafs Canadian Forces Appreciation Game at the Air Canada Centre, February 3, 2008.

Supporting our wounded. Paul Franklin, told he'd never walk again, walked onto the ice with his son Simon at Scotiabank Place to drop the puck for the Sens-Leafs game. Captains Daniel Alfredsson and Mats Sundin take the face-off. The Sens' support to our troops and families has been great!

With Peter MacKay (to my left), Warrant Officer John Barrett, and Lieutenant Chris Hillier. I still have the chance to contribute after retirement—Gowlings, the law firm I now do some work for, gave me their box at Scotiabank Place to host soldiers and their families during the Ottawa Senators CF Appreciation Game, November 3, 2008. Notice that I'm now saving money on haircuts!

Lisa Miller and Karen Boire organized the Rally in Red on Parliament Hill, September 2006. They wanted a photo and, at the last second, turned and kissed me. It's now a happy tradition.

But if you receive, you must give. Delivering a kiss to Master Corporal Jeremy Leblanc from his wife, Melissa, on Christmas Eve, 2006, in Forward Operating Base Wilson.

Recognition of heroes, October 23, 2006. Right to left: Sergeant Pat Tower (in scarlet), Star of Military Valour; Sergeant Mike Denine, Medal of Military Valour (MMV); Master Corporal Collin Fitzgerald, MMV; Corporal Jason Lamont, MMV. These commendations took a mere sixty days to finalize.

In April of 2007, I announced the launch of the Military Families Fund, which supports the families of our troops—who serve Canada in their own way. Some of the family members attending broke into tears.

Jackie Girouard, who lost her husband Bobby in Afghanistan in November 2006, graduates from Basic Recruit Training on May 22, 2008, watched proudly by her son Mike, now a grad of RMC, while her other son Bobby was deployed to Kandahar. Jackie is my personal hero.

Those who come out to line the fence at CFB Trenton to support the families receiving the bodies of their loved ones are a powerful presence. The flag by my hand bears the name of every soldier lost in Afghanistan.

Inspecting troopers of the Royal Canadian Dragoons and soldiers of the Royal Canadian Regiment on Parliament Hill, June 2008, in celebration of their 125th anniversary as Canada's senior regiments.

Highway of Heroes: the name of the road from Trenton to Toronto, travelled by our fallen soldiers upon their return to Canada, needs no explanation.

The support of thousands doesn't make the families' grief any less, but the show of appreciation does keep it from being worse.

Catriona Le May Doan's willingness to travel to Afghanistan and show her appreciation for what Canada's sons and daughters are doing there was powerful. Every time she went to pick up her flack vest, or in this case put on an explosive ordinance disposal protective suit, half a dozen men jumped to help her. I, their boss, was left to fend for myself.

I had a special relationship with the Dutch. They recognized me twice—once for my work in Bosnia in 2001, and also on my departure as CDS. Here, in June 2008, the Dutch Ambassador to Canada, Karel de Beer (far left), awarded me the Commander in the Order of Orange-Nassau on behalf of Her Majesty, Queen Beatrix of the Netherlands, in the presence of Prince Floris and Princess Aimée (right), and my wife, Joyce.

Special guests recognized at the Change of Command Parade, July 2, 2008. Those special heroes, like Master Corporal Jody Mitic, Sergeant Alannah Gilmore and many others, made the inspection during the parade an emotional event. They inspired me, as their CDS, to do what I did.

Departing the soapbox for the last time, I warned the "Field Marshall Wannabes," those in the Civil Service who wanted to control and command the CF, that they had no responsibility or qualifications for that job.

One last rank ride, and a chance to salute those who I respected so much, in the final seconds of my time in uniform. I was surprised by my relatively unemotional approach to the departure, except when I passed one young NCO who was saluting me and crying at the same time.

One Hillier departs, another serves. Odds are high that Jack, our first grandson, will also serve Canada in uniform. He salutes with his left hand.

Nothing more precious than hearing grandson Jack, four, sing out "Poppy," or getting a smile from Matthew, eight months.

with-Canadians campaign had fired up the public in a huge way and maybe this thing could have been ridden, instead of constrained, but that didn't happen.

If we had had a less vitriolic Parliament and political context, we might have been able to combine the best of the Conservative and Liberal visions for defence. The Conservative approach had gone straight into the details. The Liberals had started with a vision, articulated in the Defence Policy Statement, including the strategy to implement it, but without the detailed plan. We were working on that when the election was called and they were suddenly out of office. The Conservatives had planned the tactical policies—the details of which equipment to buy and where to base our soldiers, for example—but refused to accept the Defence Policy Statement, which really said how it all would work together to achieve more for Canada. So it was a bit of a tough spot. We were implementing pieces without really seeing the big picture. Some of the government's ideas were very good indeed, but we still needed the overarching pieces because not all of the ideas were realistic and a good chunk weren't affordable. I had, at this point, worked for two different defence ministers and two prime ministers, and we still had to come up with a coherent strategic plan, all while we were at war (even though we weren't really calling it that). Continuity of approach is important, particularly when your people are fighting and dying in a foreign land. It was only in the last six months of my appointment that the vision, with the strategy and details in it, started to emerge. Much of the credit for that is due to Peter MacKay, Defence Minister as of August 2007.

After Gord and I had cleared the air over the tactical versus strategic airlift, we launched into major procurement programs and succeeded in getting them through the budget system, which consumes Ottawa. When we agreed to buy four of the big C-17 transport planes and sixteen of the new C-130 tactical aircraft, we were working off the same page and we were unbeatable, for a short time anyway. We again launched into what we called the "Big Four" acquisitions, which was modified to become the "Big Five" with strategic airlift (C-17 Globemaster planes): sixteen of the new C-103J Hercules tactical transport aircraft, a heavy- to medium-lift helicopter, a new fleet of heavy trucks, four C-17 Globemaster transport planes, and ships to resupply the fleet at sea. We worked in unison to get these pieces of equipment, and in the spring of 2006 we got the programs through Cabinet, over the obstacles in the bureaucracy, and actually began signing contracts and making purchases.

We sat down, looked at the Canadian Forces equipment needs and said, "Look, how much can we push through at one point in time? How much can the Government of Canada bite into, chew up and digest, as one meal?" and also asked what were the absolute "must have" pieces of equipment. Not much had changed in the "need" category and, for once, Gord, Elcock and I came together as one force to get them approved.

The army needed new transport trucks urgently. New trucks don't sound very sexy as a defence issue, but they are the backbone of the supply chain that keeps the fighting troops going. We needed a lot of them, and we needed them quickly, because those we had were nearly twenty-five years old, hard-used, rusting and increasingly expensive to maintain. We needed helicopters because the battle groups in Afghanistan needed a way to get around a battlefield that was becoming more dangerous by the day, and helicopters were the only real option to move troops and equipment with low risk. Helicopters help save lives, deliver humanitarian support, lift a piece of artillery from place to place or evacuate people during a natural or humanitarian disaster. They can manoeuvre at night, with surprise, without being held hostage to ambushes or roadside bombs. The CF had to have helicopters, and we pushed hard for them. It was clear that the air force's C-130 Hercules fleet was dying of old age and long flying hours even more rapidly than previously thought, and obviously the C-17 strategic airlift planes were a key part of the Conservative Party's platform and so clearly they were going to be one of the five.

Lastly, the navy needed desperately to replace its tankers, the ships that refuel and resupply the rest of the fleet. They should have been replaced in the 1990s, but because of funding cuts the existing ships had been patched together and kept afloat, and were literally rusting out. We had to move quickly to implement the Joint Support Ship Project to replace them because the construction of ships takes years and we were not yet started. The need, leading to the plan, was for at least three innovative new vessels that could carry fuel and supplies for the fleet, and several shipboard helicopters for air support that included space that could carry heavy equipment for the army or selected combat or support units.

The Mobile Gun System (MGS) also came up for discussion. We both knew that the soldiers on the ground needed to put lots of firepower on targets right in front of them, the sort of mission that a tank would usually handle, while being well protected from return fire. Our Leopard tanks, filling that role, were old, their armour was wearing thin and, to me, the MGS looked like a good way of replacing that capability; in effect we would be putting a big howitzer on a relatively light vehicle and getting the same effect as a tank for a fraction of the weight and cost. Lieutenant-General Marc Caron, who had taken command of the army from me, saw some challenges and approached me. He said, "Are you wedded to the Mobile Gun System?"

I said, "Marc, absolutely not. I'm not wedded to anything."

We had thought that the MGS could deliver an effect nearly identical to a tank if the technology of mounting the cannon on a relatively light vehicle could be made to work. It turned out that it couldn't; we would have had a lightly armoured, wheeled (as opposed to tracked) vehicle with limited mobility, limited armour protection and limited accuracy with its gun. We reassessed and Gord asked me if I would support acquiring Leopard 2 tanks that had become available after downsizing by various military forces in Europe. The Leopard 2 was a modern tank, the most capable in the world, and I assured Gord we thought alike on this, as the MGS could not meet our need and we needed the capability. We got a superb deal: Germany loaned us twenty tanks for immediate use in Afghanistan and paid to modify them to be more resistant to land mines, while the Dutch agreed to sell us another eighty Leopard 2s, plus twenty of the other variants of the tank (engineering tanks and tank recovery vehicles, for example). We were continuing to give our soldiers in the field the equipment they needed.

We knew that these weren't the only critical equipment

needs of the Canadian Forces. In our assessment, however, it was as much as we could get through Cabinet and the bureaucracy right away and, indeed, as much as we could handle in implementation. We went after what we thought we could get in one fell swoop, which we knew was only part of what we needed, but the rest of the stuff would follow in behind the Big Five.

Gord, Ward and I worked well as a team, briefing every single government department in town on these five projects. We worked and met with every bureaucrat in Ottawa. Anybody who had to walk close to an office that had anything to do with one of those projects, we met with them. Ward and I, often accompanied by Vice-Admiral Ron Buck, the Vice Chief of the Defence Staff—an outstanding officer and a real help in pushing this process through—would go in and sit down, and Ron would brief them on the details of the procurement. I'd tell war stories about the time I was trying to fly into Afghanistan with Rick Mercer and all these other celebrities and the first two C-130s we boarded broke down before we finally got one that could take off, and I'd say, "Look, this is why we need this." And it worked.

We had been to Cabinet two or three times during this process and were led to believe that we might not get all five projects through at the same time. The bureaucratic steps were enormous. We would be told that we had to go to this subcommittee of Cabinet. When we went to that subcommittee, they said we'd have to go back to this other subcommittee. Eventually we presented it before the full Cabinet, after having gone through every subcommittee in Cabinet, regardless of its role. The Big Five got the support of all of them (not surprisingly, since many had almost exactly the same members), though this greatly surprised many of the key ministers around the table who had told us that we wouldn't be able to get our plan through.

Implementing those projects sometimes proved more difficult than going through those subcommittees. We were able to buy the C-17 Globemasters right away because the aircraft were available. The contract was signed for the new C-130J Hercules planes in fairly short order and the wait is relatively short for the actual aircraft to be delivered. The heavy-lift helicopters were more of a problem and, in 2008, we were still sorting out the contract to buy them, although we managed to get some Chinooks, bought as an urgent requirement, operating in Afghanistan by December 2008. The Leopard 2 tanks were delivered in 2008 and the new trucks, at least those for use in Canada, are coming into service.

The equipment was a sign to our soldiers, sailors, and airmen and airwomen that the government's defence policy wasn't just words on a page; it wasn't just about reorganizing the structure of the Canadian Forces; it wasn't just about trying to improve leadership. This was about a serious commitment to re-equipping our military with the tools they needed. That sent a wake-up call right around the country, certainly to the forces and even to NATO and our other friends and allies around the world: Canada was serious about defence.

CHAPTER 20

MAKING CANADA SMALL

Although we now had approval for the major purchases—an almost unprecedented success in defence or any other procurement program within Canada—we had also garnered more than our share of enemies throughout the Ottawa bureaucracy and triggered an increasing resistance to our plans. Many other departments were unprepared for our quick move on major programs following the installation of a new government because they were still trying to bring their own plans together. Senior bureaucrats became resentful and even jealous of our success. We were moving as quickly as we could to get the equipment that we all believed was fundamentally important, while their own programs were stalled because they weren't as capable of making things happen. The deputy ministers and assistant deputy ministers of other departments saw the money flowing into the Department of National Defence and realized that meant less for them and their pet projects. Sadly, the result was a slowly building resistance to our other spending priorities, with everything from insidious delays to active opposition from many senior civil servants being the result. I had been warned early on, and many times after, that this would occur.

That early success haunted us when we brought forward what we needed for our front-line soldiers in Afghanistan. When we tried to get an urgent operational requirement implemented, such as additional armour for our tanks—which had particularly worn and thin belly armour—we were faced with bureaucratic processes that reduced progress to a snail's pace, and the tanks weren't upgraded for months. The project was broken into pieces, few treated urgently, and the result was a much longer window of vulnerability for their crews than necessary.

We needed to make a host of smaller equipment purchases that were urgently needed in Afghanistan, in addition to the big ones like the tank armour—from the new M777 howitzers to the RG-31 Nyala mine-resistant vehicles. These weapon systems were a godsend for the intense fight in Kandahar province. During one of my visits to Afghanistan, a sergeant from the Royal Canadian Regiment said to me one day, "Sir, that Nyala, it's a pig, you know? Doesn't have good cross-country mobility, it's underpowered and it breaks down all the time."

I said, "Sergeant, I know what you mean, only it does one thing pretty well."

He said, "What's that, sir?"

I said, "Well, it saves lives."

The sergeant chuckled. "You're right, sir; you're right. I guess we'll take them."

We had more than sixty shipped directly from the South African manufacturer into Afghanistan.

Hundreds of other, smaller purchases were equally vital. We had to buy more of the latest generation of night-vision goggles that gave our soldiers enormous advantage in taking on the Taliban fighters during darkness; satellite radios to communicate over the vast distances or to contact the ground-attack and other aircraft that were flying in support of our ground troops; additional desert-pattern combat uniforms because the wear and tear on our existing ones was brutal; and additional ammunition.

That we needed additional ammo was truly a surprise to us, and it became a big issue, as we were getting into lengthy firefights more frequently. At one point during Operation Medusa in September and October 2006, the 1st Battalion, Royal Canadian Regiment, under Lieutenant-Colonel Omer Lavoie, was at the point of the spear for the major offensive against the Taliban in Afghanistan. The fight was so intense that we ran perilously close to being out of 155 mm artillery and some other types of ammunition. Those guns, which we were fortunate to have purchased earlier that year, were at times firing more than 200 rounds each per day. Lavoie said they were his key weapon system.

In the direct firefights, ammo expenditure was also far greater than anticipated. One troop of four fighting vehicles, the LAV III, with its 25 mm cannon, fired, over five days, nearly 16,000 of those 25 mm rounds. We were not well prepared for this usage and had to look for extra ammunition from several different countries until we could produce sufficient supplies of those rounds ourselves. All this ancillary kit was unimaginably important to the troops on the ground, and we put our weight and efforts behind the dozens of these urgent operational requirements from late 2005 until early 2007.

My concerns over the culture at the senior levels in the public service peaked during one meeting with several very senior officials at the Privy Council Office. One of them, having been informed that a minister was going to see the Prime Minister directly in order to clarify his specific responsibilities and to seek direction to move a program despite bureaucratic resistance to it, screeched, "He doesn't have the authority!" I actually settled back in my seat, in some shock, and thought, "Wow." If unelected officials think that they have more authority than an elected member of Parliament, and a Cabinet minister to boot, then we are in need of a revolution in the senior levels of the public service. This mentality is doing our country a great disservice.

It is impossible to overestimate the amount of jealousy that developed in other government departments or the lengths that some senior bureaucrats would go to in order to sabotage a rival. I often saw sticks stuck in the spokes of the wheels of many of our programs. Defence had hundreds, even thousands of projects on the go, and we could not make each one of them a top priority, so some programs were slowed to a crawl and others were stopped cold by bureaucratic delays, petty infighting and sometimes the incompetence of those who were responsible for moving those projects through. The reality was, we in the Canadian Forces and the Department of National Defence were at war but the rest of government was not, and sometimes our war felt like it was in Ottawa, not Kandahar.

This wrangling over defence budgets and moving programs through the convoluted purchasing approval system led me to believe that Canada needed to revolutionize the way we structure bureaucratic support to our elected leaders. I think it will really require an overhaul of the civil service's very senior leadership, its structure and, particularly, its culture. A friend of mine, who often functioned as a sounding board, said that our bureaucracy makes Canada small. Instead of providing incisive leadership and focused support to our elected leaders to help our country be the influential and powerful G8 nation that it could be, we often find the opposite. Canada could have a real impact on the international stage, throwing the kind of diplomatic, military and development weight that befits our nation, but for the small-mindedness of some of the most senior civil servants, who only care about power in Ottawa.

The federal public service comprises several hundred thousand people working in offices and facilities across Canada. The vast majority—and I repeat that, the vast majority—of those men and women are incredibly skilled, focused on trying to do the best job they can and just as frustrated as I am by a culture that counts process as product, rewards risk aversion not risk management, mistakes management for leadership and is driven by careerism. The risk-aversion culture means everybody can say no but few can say yes. There are always more questions that can be asked, more inane options to have analyzed, more committees to review and comment and, always, a reason to say no, not now.

You can imagine the frustrations of those who work within this culture where process is everything and output is considered downright dangerous; where days, weeks, months and even years are spent trying to articulate policy positions on which to base decisions, when that policy is already in practice. Writing and preparation of reports becomes the work of half of a department in a culture like this, so that 50 per cent of the remaining half can read them. The result is delay. Actually doing something is sometimes negative, because any action might put you or your department at risk if the initiative does not succeed. All of this makes Canada ineffective, and smaller, on the world stage—a country that lacks innovation, a nation that follows when it could be leading and a country where Ottawa becomes a closed circuit, with new ideas or thought processes seen as dangerous.

I saw time and again the Government of Canada, elected by the people of Canada, having its hands tied by the bureaucratic process that has built up over time. Ministers trying to implement their mandate would be worn into submission by the brutal slowness. Whether it was for major purchases of equipment—urgent operational requirements for a place like Afghanistan—getting a pragmatic approach to industrial regional benefits from the acquisitions or dealing with international trade and arms regulations, process was everything.

Our public service is a place where people change jobs at the senior level so frequently, and across such a wide spectrum, that they quickly become jacks of all trades and almost never masters of one. Senior civil servants move from Foreign Affairs to Public Works to Justice to National Defence in the span of a few short years, usually not staying in any one department long enough to develop any deep expertise on the issues facing Canada. It doesn't work that way in other countries. While working with our allies—the Netherlands, United Kingdom, France, the United States—I saw civil servants specialize, developing awesome and deep expertise in areas such as national security or international relations.

In Canada our approach leads to a focus on management, not leadership. Those at the most senior levels know that their present appointment will only last two or three years and all they have to worry about is keeping everything running without irritation. Results become somebody else's problem, as those senior bureaucrats will have moved on by the time the results are evident. Think of a torpedo in the water, speeding along toward an enemy ship. Senior managers ride along on it for a little while, spend a lot of time talking about it or making up PowerPoint presentations about it, and maybe rubbing the sides a bit to make it ride more smoothly. They start a program to find a new, more fitting name for the torpedo, twin it with an appropriate city around Canada, talk about the jobs it would bring, organize teams and committees to paint it in eye-catching colours, celebrate its multiple anniversaries and focus on it for charitable events. Never would we worry whether or not the torpedo is on course. Never would we see whether or not it hits the ship. Never, ever, do we work to change the course or depth setting of that torpedo. Managers in government have careers built on transactions from that torpedo.

That sort of management process squeezes the life out of good ideas by extending them almost indefinitely, through excruciating analysis. Any energy, imagination, innovation or originality disappears, so that by the time a program actually gets to start—if it has survived long enough—it no longer resembles the original idea, fails to accomplish what it was supposed to and now costs one hundred times more than initially predicted.

The "big idea" in Canada is doomed from the start. Meanwhile, another entirely new bureaucracy will have grown up around it.

The good leaders at the senior level in the Public Service stand out—and make no mistake, there are lots of examples. Ward Elcock, who was Deputy Minister of National Defence, is a good example of the best kind of civil servant that this country can produce. Ward had a strategic view of how he, as a civil servant, was going to help his Minister and the Government of Canada achieve their goals. He understood international politics, domestic security and our continental relationship with the United States. Most importantly, he understood the necessity of getting things done. Ward knew that endless process and policy are not the product and that being part of a team that works allows us all to make Canada stronger. He drove through bureaucratic barriers and got the C-17 and the tank purchase completed. Through his work, those C-17 transports were bought and paid for before the bureaucracy really understood what had happened and, as a result, we now have a worldwide military transport capability that serves Canada admirably and would have been cheap at any price, but we paid a particularly cheap price.

Wayne Wouters, Deputy Minister at the Treasury Board, is another. He is a crusty, experienced leader who does not suffer fools gladly and has seen and done it all. Wayne got results, and this was particularly appreciated when he stickhandled a pay increase through for our soldiers. It was important that we do this as a way to illustrate to our troops that our country supports them, but many were against it. The public service unions were all negotiating future contracts, and worrywarts were concerned that those increases for CF men and women would complicate the negotiation process. Wayne understood its importance to us and quickly made it happen.

Others at this level were not nearly as competent or dedicated, yet they could all affect what DND and the Canadian Forces could do to serve Canada. Many found ways to insert themselves into the procurement process so they could both protect their turf and ensure they were visible in Ottawa. The result was that progress slowed sometimes to the point where critical equipment could not be bought in a timely fashion and delivered to Afghanistan where the troops fighting the Taliban desperately needed it. We waited weeks, months and then more months for basic commodities, all of which had to go through the bureaucratic approvals system five or six times. Even a relatively simple transaction like leasing transport helicopters to fill the gap in Kandahar until the new Chinook transport helicopters were delivered took forever.

We started the process of leasing those choppers in January 2008. I wanted the lease signed and the helicopters in theatre three weeks later. Instead, it took eight months to finally get a helicopter flying in southern Afghanistan. It was incredible to me that a nation as large and rich as Canada took that long just to arrange something so straightforward and relatively inexpensive, compared to some of the big-dollar purchases that a government makes. It's even more incredible that such timelines and delay are deemed acceptable when they are potentially putting our soldiers' lives in danger. The upgrade of the already purchased Leopard 2 tanks, after almost three years, still is not in implementation.

Representatives for competing companies combined with the opposition in Parliament to too-often exacerbate the problem posed by bureaucracy. One of the objections raised to these necessary purchases was we were going "sole-source"—we wanted to buy a specific piece of equipment from a company without the full, very time-consuming bidding process because we knew that one company made exactly what we needed. These types of acquisitions have always been part of the normal government buying system, using advance notification of contracts that are to be awarded. To use the C-17 Globemaster transport jets as an example, the Department of National Defence would send out a notice to industry saying that we were going to buy that plane unless somebody demonstrated to us that they had an aircraft that could also meet all of our requirements and therefore compete with it. They would have thirty days (or whatever time limit is set) to tell us that.

Once the opposition got word that a contract would be sole-sourced, they would make it sound as if we had committed a criminal act. They were often egged on by competing companies, who, regardless of the circumstances, believed they had lost an opportunity to make a sale and adopted a scorched-earth policy. In other words, if their company couldn't win the contract, they would try to make sure that no one would, and be willing to see the entire procurement program fail and the Canadian Forces do without that badly needed equipment. Most of what the opposition would say was inaccurate (often wildly so), but it would make headlines and create pressure within the civil service to review the situation one more time. Unfortunately, men and women in uniform lived with the consequences. So many important acquisitions were stalled by bureaucratic paralysis that I would often wake up in the middle of the night trying to figure out how we could do better.

The struggle for appropriate control over expenditures competes always with the need to actually deliver something. In Ottawa, those controls now make it almost impossible to deliver and lead to frustrated end runs to accomplish that which the bureaucracy was established to do in the first place. The inability to do more makes Canada small.

For years, I saw first-hand the sensitivities involved in supporting the CF equipment programs, but one incident stands out in my mind. I spoke each year to the Canadian Defence Associations conference, in late February, in Ottawa. Each time I selected a theme. In 2005, it was "We are changing"; in 2006, "We are changing and commencing what will be tough operations in Kandahar"; and in 2007, it was "Decade of darkness." Over the previous two years, the impact of the lack of support to the CF (which had been going on for some time) had started to become clear to us. It was going to take years, if not decades, to rebuild. So that became my theme. I described the confluence of the perfect storm of budget cuts, increasing operations, fewer people, the Somalia scandal, and so on, and called it a "decade of darkness." Everyone in the audience listened in rapt silence, understanding perfectly the challenge we now faced. Everyone except Denis Coderre, that is, who was the opposition defence critic. He immediately went to the attending press and accused me of attacking the Liberals. Since I had not focused my speech that way, and never mentioned the Liberals, I thought his approach was dumber than dirt. Coderre, by his actions, in a time of massive support for the CF, had identified his party as the culprit in the near-death experience of the Canadian Forces. That wasn't what I had said and it was not exclusively their fault. Dumber than dirt!

The Canadian Forces have always been an anomaly within the Government of Canada in that we're employees of the government but we're not part of the Public Service of Canada. My view was simple. As Chief of the Defence Staff, I worked for the Minister of National Defence and the Prime Minister, who both answer to Parliament, and took my orders from them, orders that often put soldiers,' sailors,' airmen's and airwomen's lives at risk. Lives were at stake. I took orders directly from elected officials only, not from appointed bureaucrats who had no expertise in national security, multinational operations or command or, most importantly, responsibility for the actions that might cost lives.

As the mission in Afghanistan began heating up in 2007, various folks around Ottawa became very focused on our actions there and wanted command of Canadian Forces units on the ground to fall under civilian jurisdiction. These field marshal wannabes wanted to have a say in every single tactical mission in Kandahar province by having the ambassador in Kabul or another representative actually take command of our troops. These civilians' time on the diplomatic cocktail circuit undoubtedly had prepared them well for those challenges, but the mere fact that they proposed it indicated a superficial understanding of what was at stake. I essentially told them to get lost. I was responsible for the lives and limbs of young Canadian men and women and was accountable to their families, the Minister of Defence and the Prime Minister. The civil service had no say in the matter.

The squabble over our Strategic Advisory Team in Afghanistan provides perhaps the best example of the kind of bureaucratic interference our troops often faced. I got the initial idea for the SAT during my time in the Balkans when we wrestled with how to help the local citizens build a government almost from nothing. There was no "government in a box" ready to be delivered to them, as Lieutenant-Colonel Ian Hope once told me, and no country had a deployable unit that could help countries like Bosnia or Afghanistan build support structures for the leaders of these nascent democracies. As Commander of ISAF in Kabul in 2004, I took a strategic planning team of about fifteen to twenty officers and involved them in helping the Afghan ministers draft a vision for rebuilding Afghanistan, the strategy to implement it and the detailed plans to make it successful. Various representatives in Kabul, including the European Union Special Representative and Chris Alexander, the Canadian ambassador, were enthralled with the approach and ensured it got on the desks of Afghan Cabinet ministers, particularly the Minister of Finance, Ashraf Ghani, and President Karzai. Karzai and Ghani realized that the new Afghan government lacked the expertise to carry out their plan, so Mr. Karzai said to me, "I need help. Can you provide us help to carry it out?"

I said that we could, but that we needed to bring all the international players on board, including the coalition forces, the International Monetary Fund and the World Bank. Two nights later, Minister Ghani hosted an event in his house for about twenty representatives from all the key international organizations in Afghanistan and asked me to outline this approach for them. Ghani started the evening off by saying that Afghanistan's greatest enemy was the incoherence and slow pace of the process of rebuilding the country (in hindsight, prescient words as we face the results of that slow and inefficient process now) and that the SAT could be the solution. Ghani handed off to me and I unfolded a bedsheet-sized paper diagram, laid it on the living-room floor, knelt at one end and gathered the others around. With a laser pointer, I walked them through our straightforward approach of the vision and strategy the Afghans wanted, how we could commence and improve implementation, who would have responsibility for doing what and what we could achieve. The presentation made a powerful point about the challenges of the rebuilding process, and a significant number of those international players bought into the SAT concept immediately. When I left as the NATO commander in Afghanistan, however, that team went with me and was not replaced.

I went back to Afghanistan for a visit in spring 2005, soon after becoming CDS. When I met President Karzai, he asked me, "What happened to all those officers who were helping us? They were worth their weight in gold, because they were helping us sort ourselves out to do our jobs. We trusted them because they were not working to any agenda except helping Afghans."

I explained that NATO was too focused on other things to get involved, but added, "If that team really was valuable, I've got some young officers I can put together and they can come in and work with you."

Chris Alexander was completely supportive of this idea, as was Peter Harder, the Deputy Minister of Foreign Affairs, so we created (or recreated) the SAT and began rotating officers in for a year at a time. The advisory team, under Colonel Mike Capstick, went to work helping the Afghan government develop an effective way to develop and use proper budgets, administer their departments and do all the small but vital things that keep governments running properly while delivering effectively what the population needed. This became known as the Afghan Development Strategy. The team worked to help the government of Afghanistan do the work of government—not making policy for them, but helping them get their ministries and departments running effectively. It was praised from all quarters. Every time I went to Kabul or to NATO meetings, I heard unending compliments for the SAT, especially from the deputy ministers or ministers in the Afghan government who said that it was one of the few programs that actually worked to help their government sort out its affairs. The North Atlantic Council, the governing body of NATO, went to Afghanistan. Its members said afterwards that they believed that our SAT was the only innovative thing they'd seen on this mission.

Following the Manley Report in 2008, the Department of Foreign Affairs and the Privy Council Office changed their mind about the SAT. Suddenly it was all about control, and they began to express concerns that the team was military, not civilian. Bureaucrats in Ottawa began grumbling about how the Canadian Forces were doing things in Afghanistan that were not our responsibility. Their daily cry was that we were overstepping our boundaries. Sadly, while they were, in Ottawa, talking about doing things, we were actually doing them on the ground in Kandahar. But because the SAT wasn't working for the civil service, it obviously wasn't working in Canada's best interests and pressure to get rid of the team increased. To abandon it entirely would have been too obvious a move, so—as cover—wanting to "civilianize" it became the item of discussion. So finally I said, "Okay, no problem. We have no dog in this fight. We will hand it over to you as soon as you've got a team to replace them."

Those who helped get rid of the SAT soon realized they had a problem: they didn't have the people willing to go into Afghanistan; they didn't have the organizational wherewithal to put them on the ground and support them there; and they certainly didn't have the trained strategic planners we had in the CF—in short, they just couldn't do the work. In the summer of 2008 we finally pulled the SAT out of Kabul, but it was never fully or effectively replaced. This great Canadian initiative, complimented and praised by Afghans and the international community alike, is now history.

The Government of Canada is going to have to take a hard look at the culture of our bureaucracy. If Canada is going to remain a significant player on the world stage, we have to change the way we support elected leaders to implement their programs. We have to do more to develop leadership in its ranks and change the culture to one of product over process and effect over policy. A government that wins a majority might even consider installing its own leaders at the very top levels of the bureaucracy so that they can have some confidence that their agenda will actually be implemented. The government does that now with the Chief of the Defence Staff, which is why I offered my resignation to Stephen Harper while he was still the Prime Minister–elect.

Gord O'Connor said something to me in his office one day early in his tenure as Defence Minister, a suggestion that I immediately dismissed, which I now regret. He said, "Chief, if you want to go down the road of separating the CF from the department, breaking clean of the public service, I'm okay with that."

Working on the premise that Ward Elcock would be around forever to make things happen, I said, "No, Minister, I don't believe that is necessary. A good partnership is the best way to continue." In hindsight, separating the Canadian Forces completely from the government bureaucracy in Ottawa may be the only way to ensure it remains effective.

John Ibbitson, in his new book *Open and Shut,* describes the closed system in the bureaucracy in Ottawa and how it inhibits getting things done. He is right, and it must change. How and when is the only question.

Chapter 21

HIGHWAY OF HEROES

If anybody had told me that we were going to go into intense combat operations, sustain total casualties of over 100 soldiers killed and about 400 wounded, and suffer all these losses within three years and that Canadians would still support the mission, I would not have believed them. It is particularly remarkable that support for the Afghanistan mission has remained so strong when nobody has really told the public the rationale behind the mission, what is happening on the ground, some of the really positive advances that have been made or the full context of our operations there. The majority of Canadians understand that we are a G8 nation and that that means we have responsibilities around the world, a world in which the strategic context has changed so dramatically. The Cold War is over and with it the ability to do much in the way of peacekeeping. We are facing an enemy I have often compared to a ball of snakes: slippery, poisonous and difficult to grasp. Our policy of deterrence, which kept a lid on things for so many years during the Cold War, is now irrelevant. There's a lot more fighting to be done. If Canada is not going to be one of those countries willing to do that fighting, then who will?

Most Canadians understand that our actions as a country have got to match our words. Actions speak loudly and articulate our values far more clearly than speeches at the United Nations. You cannot see values, but you can see actions, and that is what truly matters. When we are pushing hard at the United Nations for the responsibility to protect others to become international policy, well, words are easy but actions are more difficult. Many people, including me, seriously misjudged Canadians' ability to accept the consequences of undertaking such a dangerous and costly business as the counter-insurgency fight in southern Afghanistan. We especially misjudged the public's willingness to wrap their arms around those who have paid the price of that fight in a way that we've not seen in this country since the Second World War. That is the most positive part of Canada's reaction to the Afghan mission, and it has carried all of us in the Canadian Forces through those tough times when we lost our fellow soldiers. The Canadian public reacted to the deaths of their soldiers in combat in a way none of us, in our wildest dreams, ever expected.

It was probably such a surprise to us because for so many years our political landscape had been dominated by a select group in Canadian society, self-proclaimed opinion leaders who I prefer to think of as snake-oil salesmen, who had been allowed to create the impression that Canadians were very sensitive, would advocate only "soft power" and would support their military only in the role of peacekeepers. To the contrary, Canadians, in enormous numbers, understood the sheer lunacy of "soft power" and that really, in life, there is just power, soft or hard, and that the levers of influence always work both ways. Focusing on only one as a national strategy is akin to getting in the boxing ring with only one arm—you will lose every time to the two-armed opponent. Canadians had been talked into soft power, but it diminished this country's credibility and effectiveness terribly.

The vast majority of Canadians I spoke to simply wanted more information on the Afghanistan mission—they were starved for information on why we were there, what our national interests were, what activities our troops were involved in and what else we were doing on the ground to support those activities. In particular, they wanted to ask what progress we were making, did we have the right strategy, were other countries doing enough and was there a light at the end of the tunnel. I gave a lot of speeches and public presentations on the mission, outlining the kinds of thoughts I share here. At the start of every talk I always asked for a show of hands to see who supported the mission and who was against it. At almost every speech I gave, the audience would start out at about 50–50 in their support for our presence in Afghanistan. By the time I wrapped, that support would be at 75 to 80 per cent or higher in favour. It's not that I'm a particularly brilliant debater, but when I gave Canadians information on the mission, they came to see what it was all about. At the end of almost every presentation, people would line up to tell me, "General, every Canadian needs to hear this." The communication strategy for explaining the Afghan mission to Canadians was, sadly, almost invisible to the ordinary Canadian, and what they saw—or, more accurately, did not see—in the media was of no greater help.

By the late summer of 2006 it was becoming obvious that the Canadian Forces were engaged in major combat in southern Afghanistan, fighting that was even more intense than we'd expected. Our first battle group on the ground, 2nd Battalion, Princess Patricia's Canadian Light Infantry, under Lieutenant-Colonel Ian Hope, was engaged in major firefights both in Kandahar and in Helmand province, and we had lost soldiers during that first six months. Our first fatality in Kandahar, as mentioned earlier, was a diplomat, Glyn Berry, and his unfortunate death in a suicide bombing led to Foreign Affairs and CIDA effectively constraining their contribution during the most crucial portion of the mission—the move from a U.S.-led coalition to a NATO-commanded operation. We suffered other deaths over the next few months. One particularly bad day was in April 2006, when we lost four soldiers to one roadside bombing: Corporal Matt Dinning, Bombardier Myles Mansell, Corporal Randy Payne and Lieutenant Bill Turner. The fighting was clearly intensifying; the Taliban were obviously surging into the area and increasingly taking on our soldiers head to head.

Gord O'Connor and I spoke by phone just after getting the news about our four casualties and felt that we had to speak publicly to the loss of those four good men. Early that Saturday morning we presented ourselves at NDHQ and spoke to Canadians through about a dozen journalists. We both knew this was a critical time and that how Canadians responded would dictate, largely, the future of what we did as a nation. The questions were predictable—about the future of the Afghan mission, whether we could afford more casualties, if the vehicles and equipment were good enough, and whether or not we were "winning"—and both of us worked to commemorate the four soldiers we'd lost, figuratively wrapping our arms around their families, talking to overall preparation for the mission and, most importantly, staying the course.

In September 2006, I went to Meech Lake to brief Prime Minister Harper and his Cabinet on the mission and present some of the measures we thought were necessary to deal with the increased threat we had been encountering all spring and summer, but particularly the threat that became obvious at the front end of Operation Medusa over the Labour Day weekend. We had been giving Prime Minister Harper and key Cabinet ministers daily reports and almost daily briefings on the situation in Afghanistan as it evolved—what operations were coming up, what they involved and what we saw as the risk levels—so they would be prepared appropriately. Prior to the Labour Day weekend, I had briefed the PM in his Langevin block office. I told Harper that the context of the mission had changed, that the Taliban were stronger than we had anticipated, surging into the area and trying to build a base within striking distance of Kandahar City.

The Taliban were trying to take advantage of the handover of command from the American mission—Operation Enduring Freedom—to NATO. Their ultimate goal in the south was to attack and take Kandahar City or at least psychologically isolate it from the rest of the country and, by doing so, discredit NATO forces early. We needed to respond and focus our mission on the evolving and growing threat while remaining true to our original objectives and approach. Canadian Brigadier-General David Fraser was our commander on the ground, and NATO's as well.

433

David had been our commander in Kandahar since early in 2006. He had done a thorough analysis of the situation and was under constant pressure from British Lieutenant-General David Richards, his overall commander in Kabul, to quickly and robustly counter this first major challenge to NATO. In the first days of September 2006, he launched Operation Medusa, a major offensive into the Panjwayi and Zhari districts just out-side Kandahar City, to knock the Taliban back on their heels. We knew it was going to be a major operation, so I went to brief the Prime Minister in person and walked him through what we were going to do. I compared the operation to a boa constric-tor wrapping around its prey: we were going to squeeze and squeeze and squeeze the Taliban into smaller and smaller areas, using the Canadian, British and American troops under David's command. Prime Minister Harper was very engaged, focused, and the discussion went well. He quickly grasped the concepts that I was laying out for him and the thrust of the operations I had sketched out on my maps of Kandahar. This was certainly a defining moment, when we switched from what were really peace-enforcement operations involving some combat to actual full-out combat.

The Taliban were challenging NATO, confronting our forces directly, the first time they had been able to do that since 2001. They were trying to take and hold a piece of ground and eventu-ally extend a stranglehold around Kandahar City. Afghan Cabi-net ministers told me later that if Kandahar had been perceived as being under siege or surrounded by the Taliban—let alone falling to them—the Karzai government would have fallen and all the progress in helping Afghans run their country under a basic democracy would have come to a crashing halt. By taking on the Taliban in the Panjwayi District of Kandahar and bloodying their nose, Operation Medusa saved the fragile government of Afghanistan and allowed it to continue to make progress.

At the end of the briefing, the Prime Minister asked me what the worst-case scenario might be. I responded, "Well, it's not the worst, but certainly a bad scenario would be to get a bloody nose right at the start and have to deal with the impact of that back here, as well as losing some of our great soldiers, while we still have to continue the operation. The stress in Afghanistan, and here, would be enormous."

I knew that taking casualties early in the operation could hurt us and set back Medusa, particularly in the political arena back here in Canada, so I assured Harper that we were doing everything to prevent that. Dave Fraser had been planning on taking a mid-deployment leave in Canada in late August, spending a day with Ward Elcock and me to brief the Prime Minister, another day to oversee the homecoming of the Princess Patricia's battle group to Edmonton and yet another day to formally leave his old job, commanding our brigade in Edmonton. I attended those events, and Dave and I, along with the commander of the western area, Brigadier-General Tim Grant and the Chief of Staff of Army Operations, Brigadier-General Guy Thibault, decided to take the opportunity to get in a round of golf at an Edmonton course. Dave and I rode in one cart, Tim and Guy in another. At the first tee, we received a call from Lieutenant-General Mike Gauthier, responsible for international operations and just en route to the Persian Gulf from visiting Kandahar. Dave and I spent the next two hours on the phone with him, talking about the situation in southern Afghanistan, the mission and the threat from the Taliban, taking turns hitting the ball and talking to Mike. At the end of the ninth hole all three of us agreed that Dave had to return to Afghanistan immediately. Events were moving so rapidly and much too violently for him to be away from his command, even if he did desperately need a break with his family after six months away.

Dave phoned his wife, Poppy, and told her he had to return to Afghanistan. She said she would come and pick him up. I drove the cart to the clubhouse, made arrangements with my aide to get Dave's transport sorted out to take him the fastest route back to Kandahar that night and dropped Dave to meet Poppy. I drove his clubs over to their van, waited while they walked over and then told Dave I would see him at six that night to get him off on the first leg on his flight back. Poppy was in shock. She had not known that her husband would only have a few hours to spend with her and that the family vacation to Banff would have to be put on hold. As tears welled up in her eyes, I played the coward, told Dave he was on his own and ran away. He has not let me forget that.

Dave was back in theatre within thirty-six hours and deployed directly into the field, in Panjwayi District, where operations were intensifying. I spent a lot of time in teleconferences with Gauthier and others going through all that was happening in Afghanistan and, on the Labour Day weekend, Operation Medusa was launched. Almost immediately we heard that the worst-case scenario had already happened. We lost four of our soldiers from the Royal Canadian Regiment: Private William Cushley, Sergeant Shane Stachnik, Warrant Officer Richard Nolan and Warrant Officer Frank Mellish were killed in the first attacks on the Saturday in intense firefights with the Taliban around the White School, a Taliban stronghold on the north bank of the Arghandab River, west of Kandahar City. Obviously, that was a tough time, and it meant we had a lot of work to do in Afghanistan, recovering from our losses and pushing ahead with the operation. We had, unfortunately, a lot to do in Canada as well, with the CF and army chain of command all involved in tracking down families spread across the country on holidays and breaking that most heartbreaking news to them. We assigned assisting officers and stood up the teams that would support the families of those fallen soldiers for the immediate future.

Before we finished our last discussions on the casualties, after a sleepless night, I said to Mike, "Hopefully, we won't need to talk to each other much for the next two or three days." I went home and had dinner. At about seven o'clock that night Mike called and said, "Sir, we've got a bad one."

A U.S. Air Force A-10 ground-attack plane had fired on one of our companies with its 30 mm cannon after the pilot mistakenly focused on them, rather than on the enemy position less than two kilometres away. Private Mark Graham, a soldier with Charles Company of 1st Battalion, Royal Canadian Regiment, and a former Olympic-class sprinter, was killed, and more than forty soldiers were wounded, some terribly. The first reports to me, however, indicated that we had anywhere up to twenty-five dead. I thought, "Oh my God, this is really going to be a blow to Canada."

Experience on operations, however, had taught me that first reports are always wrong, especially in the middle of an intense fight like the Royal Canadian Regiment was in, and that second reports are also wrong. The third report is usually wrong too: it's only after that that you start to get accurate information and useful details. Still, I was prepared after that first report for a much greater tragedy than had occurred.

The pilot of that A-10 had been attacking a Taliban position in front of our troops at dawn. He had tipped up his night-vision goggles, because in the pre-dawn light they were unhelpful, and mistakenly took the Canadian position for that of the Taliban as he swung into the attack from more than five kilometres away. The combination of the change from night vision to naked eye, the dim early morning light and the closeness of the Canadians to the Taliban strong point deceived the pilot for just long enough to cause a tragedy. He fired a one-second burst from his 30 mm chain gun into our troops by mistake. The difference between the Canadian position and the Taliban position—they were holed up in, and near, an old schoolhouse—in that pilot's gunsight was only a couple of millimetres. The Royals had been burning their morning garbage before setting out for the day, and that small fire was all it took to create a split second of confusion in the pilot's mind. He realized very quickly that he was hitting the wrong target and pulled up, but unfortunately it was too late.

That American pilot beat himself up pretty badly over it. He was a very religious man and was devastated. As his commander in Europe told me later, "There's nothing the U.S. Air Force could do to him that would be nearly as bad as what he's doing to himself over this." There was no repeat here of the arrogance that all of us in Canada perceived in Major Harry Schmidt, the pilot involved in our casualties from the friendly-fire incident in 2002. Nonetheless, it was a traumatic time for the Canadian Forces to lose so many soldiers over that one painful weekend. The families who now faced the worst days of their lives were on my mind constantly. I went to brief the Prime Minister on the Tuesday and brought him some video to demonstrate what the pilot in that A-10 would have seen and explained that it happened just at dawn, when he'd switched from night- to day-vision systems. It was simply pilot error: he just got oriented to the wrong target.

On September 4, Mike Gauthier and I went golfing together early in the morning at the military course near Ottawa airport. We ripped through eighteen holes at speed, smoked about twenty cigars each and rehashed the entire operation as we walked the greens and fairways. We talked over how our soldiers and commanders had performed—not the tactical business of how the battle was fought (that was David Fraser's business), but how our chain of command had worked at the top and bottom ends and what more we needed to do to help David. One of the things we realized was that we needed to speed up our ammunition supply chain because we were using up ammunition at a tremendous rate. We had to put together an operational support committee to go out and chase down more. We bought 25 mm rounds from the Americans, Australians and New Zealanders and got 155 mm howitzer rounds from the British and Americans; we were getting our ammunition wherever we could find it. Dan Ross, the Assistant Deputy Minister of Materiel in DND, and Major-General Daniel Benjamin, who ran our Operational Support Command, were instrumental in working this out and supplying the battle that was raging overseas.

We also came to the conclusion that we needed more on the ground to win this fight. We were not looking to win by a hockey score of 3–2: we wanted to win 100–0 and had to upgrade our equipment and personnel to achieve that. We needed more than just the Infantry in this kind of counter-insurgency fight; we needed much heavier equipment and firepower. That's when we came to the realization that we needed tanks, along with another Infantry company on the ground in addition to the three-company battle group we'd sent in under Ian Hope for the first rotation. Lieutenant-Colonel Omer Lavoie, commanding the 1st Battalion from the Royal Canadian Regiment in Petawawa, had the same size force in the second tour and was now engaged heavily in the Panjwayi District. He, Dave Fraser and the army commander, Andy Leslie, all saw the need for the reinforcements similar to what we had discussed. In short, we needed more troops, more guns and—a shock for Canada after years of peacekeeping—tanks.

The Prime Minister was at his best during Operation Medusa and in the month that followed. He was shaken by the casualties, as were we all, but determined to carry on. He was solid in his support for the operations and determined that this was what we had to do. Like all of us, he had known that we were going to pay a high cost, but he was solidly behind what we were trying to accomplish in the mission.

We had to go back to Cabinet after that first long weekend of Operation Medusa and present a list of urgent operational requirements for the mission, including deployment of a squadron of Leopard 1 tanks to the theatre; an additional company of infantry both to protect the provincial reconstruction team and to free up the company now doing that for mobile operations; extra combat engineers; more of the new M777 howitzers;

and more of the unmanned aerial vehicles, which we had to buy in Europe. The support we got from Cabinet was outstanding, particularly from the Prime Minister, Senator Marjory LeBreton and Peter MacKay, who was the Minister of Foreign Affairs at the time. Gord O'Connor was also at his best in that meeting: he understood the background, knew the details and answered every question that came up completely and with the appropriate touch. It really was enjoyable to watch. While Privy Council Office focused on how many options could dance on the head of one briefing note, we walked out of that meeting with the government's support, approval for everything we'd sought and what the soldiers truly needed.

At the end, the Prime Minister asked me, "Is this the end of it? Will we need more troops, more equipment sometime down the road?"

"Well, we think we have the end of it now," I told him. "But this is an active operation, and if the context changes we will need to change to ensure we have the right things on the ground to do the job."

We had always known that as we shifted to our mission into southern Afghanistan we were going to face greater risks. The Taliban were still active in Kandahar province, and the American battalion that we were replacing had had constant engagements with them. Bill Graham and I had both made concerted efforts to make sure that message was clear to Canadians. Canadians actually did get that message. Families who had lost their loved ones have told me in Trenton, as we all waited for the body of that loved one to come off the plane, "Thank you for being so honest and so clear. Our boy knew what he was getting into and absolutely still wanted to go on the mission."

What would I say in hindsight? I'd say that we are soldiers. This is our profession: the management of violence on the behalf of a legally elected government, in pursuit of legal missions around the world to help others. We know that when we go into missions like Afghanistan we may take casualties, and that is the risk of our profession. It's what differentiates the profession of arms from any other; we face unlimited liability from the moment we sign on the dotted line. We are trained and prepared to do the job. The young men and women who were going into a mission in Afghanistan to do their job understood the risks. They wanted to go, they believed in the mission, they felt they were very ready and they accepted that risk.

Knowing all of that made it not one bit easier when I got those phone calls in the middle of the night saying that we'd lost another soldier or soldiers. I always say that nobody phones at three in the morning to tell me that I've won the lottery. When that phone rang, I knew what it meant. Because of the time zone difference between Afghanistan and Canada (roughly nine hours), inevitably whenever there were casualties it was the middle of the night by the time I got the news. Those calls would come anywhere from midnight to four in the morning, saying that there had been an attack, an IED (Improvised Explosive Device) strike, a suicide-bomber detonation, a firefight or an ambush and that we had taken some casualties. The calls always came from Mike Gauthier, who would sometimes phone me directly as soon as he had gotten word, or Colonel Peter Atkinson, my special assistant, and later, his replacement, Colonel Perry Matte.

After only a few of those calls, which always seemed to come in bunches, I got to a point where when the phone would ring, I'd sit up in bed and turn my light on. I had my phone set to five rings before it would go to the answering machine. By ring number five I'd pick it up, knowing what was coming, and by then I was fully awake. Joyce dreaded these calls even more than I did. I'd answer the phone by saying, "Okay, how bad is it?"

I thought about the families first. As I sat there on the edge of my bed, I knew that those families did not yet know they were going to have the worst day of their lives. It was always emotional and I could never sleep after.

We always tried to notify the families in person, never by phone. Teams at every base from which soldiers had deployed— one of the commanders at the home unit, somebody who knew the individual and one of the padres—were ready so that when we lost soldiers, they could do their work appropriately. One of the widows from Petawawa told me that as soon as she looked out the window and saw the cars stopping at her house, with people in uniform getting out, she knew right away that something bad had happened to her husband, but she wouldn't answer the door. She felt that as long as she didn't, it wasn't real. She knew, however, in her heart of hearts, that her husband was gone. I'm not sure I could ever break that terrible news to anyone, but our people did it and did it with tremendous compassion and concern, because that was what they had to do to look after the families.

Early in the mission, I would try to speak to the families of our fallen soldiers as soon as possible, when they were ready. We would phone the mom, dad or wife of the soldier we had lost, always synchronized with the lineup of others who also wanted to phone to give them their condolences, from the Governor General and the Prime Minister right down to their local member of Parliament or mayor. One of the first things we did was shield those families as much as possible from everybody else, so we always dealt with the assisting officer, who from the very first notification was with the families day and night and knew their state of mind and willingness to take such a call. Knowing that I was going to meet that family at Trenton when their loved one's body came home, I stopped making those calls. I found it very difficult and impersonal to engage a family—moms and dads, wives, brothers and sisters that I had never met—over the phone after their loved one had just died serving Canada, under my command. It was very hard to have a conversation in those circumstances, and I sometimes finished it asking myself, "Did I really help there? Did I help them get through their loss by that phone call?" I could not answer yes all the time, so I made the decision to stop phoning.

However, we remained determined to do everything we could to look after those families. We made a commitment when the first casualties began returning home from Afghanistan that when we lost soldiers, our first priority, our first focal point, was not to worry about how this looked in the media or how it was going to play out politically. Our first priority was to look after the bodies of those soldiers and ensure that they were recovered, treated with dignity and received all the appreciation, honour and respect that they had earned. Secondly, we were going to look after those fallen soldiers' comrades—their battle buddies—because they were under stress, particularly when we had multiple casualties from one platoon or section.

Not to minimize the impact of any death, but when you lose six soldiers from one small, tightly knit group in a single day—as happened twice—the impact of that loss can be shattering to the survivors in that group. Thirdly, we were going to look after the families in the best way that we could, and help them through what we knew were going to be terrible days, the worst of their lives. Lastly, we were determined to make sure that the sacrifice would be remembered, never forgotten, by Canadians. Nothing we did was going to make things better for the families, but if we didn't do all of the appropriate things, and do them all very, very well, then we sure could make it worse. If those families, once they got the news that their boy, or their husband, or their dad, or their brother, or their daughter or wife or mom had been lost, thought that that sacrifice had not been noticed, was not appreciated, was in vain, was simply a waste and would not be remembered, then their grief would be much worse. We dedicated ourselves to ensuring that would never be the case.

I made a commitment from the start that if we took casualties, it would not only be those of us in uniform grieving: all Canadians had to participate and experience that loss in some fashion. We had learned some lessons during the Bosnian campaign and other missions. When the bodies of soldiers came home from those missions, it really seemed as if the only people who noticed were those in uniform, and often not many of them. For a long time there was a very clear feeling in the Canadian Forces that no one noticed the loss of life, the soldiers' sacrifice, let alone that it was appreciated or marked with respect by Canadians. That hurt the soldiers badly, an emotional impact that cannot be overstated. We vowed that we were not going to let that happen again. If we were going to take casualties and we were going to grieve, our nation was going to grieve with us. If Canada as a nation was to continue to ask young men and women to go out and put their lives in jeopardy on its behalf, then it owed us that recognition.

Starting with the friendly-fire deaths in 2002, whenever we lost a soldier we were determined to bid them farewell publicly. We would give them appropriate memorial services in Kandahar, fly them into Canadian Forces Base Trenton with the families present, and if those families wanted either the media or large numbers of people there, that's what would happen. We didn't ask journalists to cover those ramp ceremonies—we were just determined to make it a public event, along with the military funerals and memorial services, all within the view of Canadians.

Our new policy faced a few hiccups, particularly when we had pressure from PMO staffers suggesting that this was perhaps not the way it should be done, that we should keep the aircraft with the soldiers' remains out of sight or we should do it late in the evening or early in the morning. This was a line in the sand for me, and to his credit, Gord O'Connor supported me completely. We were of one mind that we had to offer the families that visible support. That led to some sharp conversations late one Friday night in May 2006.

Gord and I were at Royal Military College in Kingston attending the graduation ceremonies and knew we had another casualty returning home from Kandahar: Captain Nichola Goddard, a forward observer with the Artillery, our first female soldier killed in combat. She had been killed in a firefight in the Panjwayi. Gord and I were called into a back room in one of the buildings at RMC to talk to several members of PMO who were on the line telling us they wanted a change in what was going to happen with the repatriation of her body, and any others after that. The PMO said, "Look, don't bring the Airbus in, or if you bring the plane in, turn it away from the cameras so that people can't see the bodies coming off or do it after dark or do it down behind the hangars or just bar everybody from it." They clearly didn't want that picture of the flag-draped coffin on the news. I turned to Gord and said, "Minister, we ain't going to do that. It's as simple as that."

Gord, God bless him, told the PMO, "We're supporting the families here, and the families want Canadians to see this because they need to know that all Canadians are grieving too." Our view was that if the family didn't want to talk to the media or didn't want the media present, then they could make that decision. The family was our first priority, so we did exactly what they wanted, not what we might have preferred. The vast majority of families who unfortunately had to go to Trenton have all said yes to media presence.

We had set our mind to supporting the families, and to doing so much more effectively than we had ever done in the past. The entire command group of the Canadian Forces would go to Trenton to try to help those families through their loss, try to inspire them to keep going and get through life a day at a time. In the end, these families proved incredible: we left Trenton inspired by them, by their courage and their dignity. Everybody cried at Trenton. But everybody laughed, too. The families would tell stories about their son—or in the case of Nichola Goddard, about their daughter—about their husband or about their father. They would tell funny stories that would cause us to laugh and shake our heads, or make our

447

hearts swell with pride. Lincoln Dinning and his wife, Laura, talked about the rebel with a cause who had been their son, Matthew, and how he had found his niche in life. Laura Greenslade filled us with stories of her boy, David, that made us all feel he was our boy. Lieutenant-Colonel (Retired) Peter Dawe, an old friend, and his two sons, also army officers, talked with such pride about their son and brother, Captain Matt Dawe, killed with five others from his platoon on July 4, 2007, that we felt that pride also.

None of those ceremonies in Trenton was easy, but some were harder than others. This was particularly true when we had small children in attendance with the widow. Those were the ones all of us absolutely dreaded.

I did not get to meet all the families, but I did meet the vast majority of them, and in fact ended up developing a lasting link with many. Joyce and I marvelled at the way those families could soldier on, continuing to contribute to their communities, remembering, grieving and still living. Jackie Girouard, whose husband Bobby, the Regimental Sergeant Major of the Royal Canadian Regiment battle group, was killed by a roadside bomb in November 2006, has become a good friend. Jackie continues to inspire us as she, her two sons and her son-in-law all serve Canada in the Canadian Forces. I inspected her graduating platoon when she graduated from the recruit school in Saint-Jean on May 22, 2008.

Charmaine Tedford, whose husband Sergeant Darcy Tedford died in 2006, is an incredible, beautiful lady who showed such dignity, strength and courage after she lost her husband and her children lost their father. Charmaine has the heart of a lion and carries on with such courage. Lincoln Dinning and his wife, Laura, lost their son, Matthew, when a roadside bomb destroyed his G-Wagen vehicle in April 2006, killing him and the three others on board. Their other boy had applied to join the Canadian Forces and wanted to be a military policeman, like his big brother. There was some bureaucratic holdup in the recruiting system, but, at Lincoln's request, we fixed it so this young man could also enrol. They lost their oldest boy in April, and six months later their second son graduated from training. He started serving in Kandahar in 2009.

Then there were the Dallaires, an unbelievably strong family living in Calgary. Their son Kevin was killed in a firefight in the Panjwayi District on August 3, 2006. Kevin's father, Gaetan, is also someone who gives—he has donated blood and plasma something like 175 times. I got to know him and his wife, Diane, well and brought them to Rideau Hall, along with Jackie Girouard, for the Commander-in-Chief's Heroes' Ball in June 2007. The Dallaires had heard that I was a Toronto Maple Leafs fan and, just before I retired, a package showed up at our house. I opened it and found a framed picture of the Leafs scoring a goal. The guy who scored the goal has his back to the camera while he celebrates with Mats Sundin and Bryan McCabe. Gaetan and Diane had taken it to a photo shop and had them insert the name "Hillier" on the back of the sweater. It's absolutely hokey, but Gaetan and Diane Dallaire gave it to me, and that made it priceless. That picture hangs over my bar in a place of pride.

Some of the parents, like Maureen Eykelenboom, whose son Andrew (or Boomer, as he was known), a medic, was killed in 2006 by an IED, became an ongoing inspiration. She is such a bundle of energy and a great lady. When I first met Maureen on that terrible day in Trenton, she said, "General, we're not going to let my boy sacrificing his life be forgotten."

"Maureen, you're absolutely right," I said.

She said, "I'm going to establish a legacy on his behalf. We're going to do something. I don't know what yet, but we're going to do something. Can I count on you?"

I said, "Yes, you sure can."

Then she said, "Do you know that my maiden name was Hillier?"

"Well, that explains why I'm so cowed," I said. "I've been bossed around by Hillier women all my life. My mother, five sisters, my wife and now our daughter-in-law. Maureen, why should you be any different?"

In September 2007 I went to Comox, B.C., and participated in a fundraiser for the Boomer Legacy, a fund that Maureen has established. She has raised a significant amount of money and made major contributions to people in southern Afghanistan through our provincial reconstruction team to make life better for those who have so little. Maureen represents the families as one of the directors on the board of the Military Families Fund, established in April 2007.

Joyce and I got pulled into those family circles, each incredibly strong, different and so enjoyable, and built friendships with them from day one of their terrible tragedy. Every one of them touched us.

The wounded soldiers who came home were just as inspiring. The suicide bomber who killed diplomat Glyn Berry early in 2006 also left three of our soldiers badly wounded—Jeff Bailey,

Will Salikin and Paul Franklin. I went to Edmonton to welcome them back to Canada and meet their families. Our doctors and nurses had taken good care of them, setting up a mobile hospital for each on that Airbus. Their families had flown to Germany as soon as they possibly could to meet up with them and so were also on the Airbus. I had a chance to meet the Bailey family, Will Salikin's mom and Audra Franklin and her young boy Simon before I even went to see the three guys. Since their boys were being prepared to move to the hospital immediately and I didn't want to get in the way, I pinned their Afghan medals on the families. Paul Franklin had two medals, so I pinned one on Audra and one on Simon in another of those memorable and emotional moments that stay with you for life.

Bailey and Salikin were unconscious, but Paul Franklin was the same effervescent, energized guy as ever, even lying on that stretcher after having just lost one of his legs and being told he should have the other one also removed (he lost it a few days later). Paul is one of those phenomenal people who positively affects everything around him. Because of his work, his energy and his focus, he has helped revolutionize the way the wounded are cared for in the Canadian Forces and how the military and the public perceive and appreciate them. Paul has no reverse gear: he just moves forward.

Master Corporal Jody Mitic, a sniper who lost both of his feet after stepping on an anti-personnel mine, is also like that. Two years after he sustained his injuries, he managed to run a five-kilometre course in thirty-eight minutes on his artificial legs. Those two soldiers became the inspiration for all of us. If they can do all these things, we can too, easily and without complaint.

The one thing all of our wounded soldiers had in common was that not one of them wanted to leave the Canadian Forces. The first thing each of them said to me—and I saw almost all of them—was "As soon as I get better, I want to go back to Afghanistan." I went to see one young platoon commander from the Van Doos, Lieutenant Simon Mailloux, who had lost his right leg below the knee. His first question for me was "Is there a place for me in the Canadian Forces? I'm a soldier and I want to be in the army."

I told him, "Yes, there's always a place for an awesome leader like you, always."

"Good. As soon as I get better, I want to get back into Afghanistan, because that's the mission and I didn't complete my mission. I need to go back to complete it."

Every one of them was exactly the same. That's when I knew that we weren't going to release any of those wounded kids from the Canadian Forces. Previously, if a member of the Canadian Forces couldn't pass the physical fitness test, they were released from the military. I thought we just couldn't force these great people out the door. Unless they asked to be released, even if they were severely wounded and didn't meet all the fitness standards, we were going to find a way to keep them.

Those repatriation ceremonies were still the toughest times to be Chief of the Defence Staff, and I wouldn't have wished them on anybody. But they gave Canadians, from coast to coast to coast, the chance to grieve along with those of us in uniform, because every young man and women over there is the face of Canada, representing all Canadians. The response by ordinary Canadians, unscripted, reassured our soldiers and their families that they were not alone. While we weren't perfect in all that we did, we set a standard in care for the families of our fallen and for our wounded soldiers that the United States military and the British and Australian armed forces are all looking at in order to meet their responsibilities as well.

One of the things that always struck me was the support that all those families got at CFB Trenton itself. The men and women there, both civilians and uniformed, were fantastic. The organization at Trenton to look after families as they arrived was superb, and we saw all types of families—families that were very tight, cohesive and stable, and others that were much less so. Those hundreds of people at Trenton were dedicated to doing everything possible, professionally and with the utmost compassion, to make the ceremonies go off without a hitch: the commissionaires who let people into the building where we went to wait for the plane to land; the crews that ran the elevator that brought the coffins from the aircraft; the landing crew and the ground crew that got the airplane in position; medical personnel who looked after so many overcome by the tragedy; the military police who escorted the bodies to Toronto; and all of the others, who were mostly invisible but who were essential to making everything go right.

It was inspiring watching people in Trenton standing at the repatriation ceremonies. Hundreds of them would turn out every time, in their dress uniforms, to pay their respects when a body came off the aircraft. They came out despite the fact that they didn't know that soldier and had no connection to the family beyond the fact that they were also soldiers and they were part of the same service. (I use the word "soldier" in the most generic fashion—"soldier" here equals soldier, sailor, airman and airwoman, since most of those at Trenton were wearing air force blue.) None of them had to be there; they hadn't been ordered to show up, yet hundreds did every time. Cold, wet or sizzling hot, it didn't matter—they were there.

Crowds of ordinary men, women and children would come to these repatriations as well. As the coffins came down from the Airbus and were carried to the hearse, I could see, every time, a crowd of people lined up along the chain fence that separated the air base from the main road in Trenton. It didn't matter what the weather was, there would be quite literally hundreds out by that fence, waving Canadian flags, showing their support for the families and grieving with them. I went out and walked along the fence a couple of times to talk with some and thank them for their support. There was one lady who said she had come out for the repatriation of the four soldiers killed at Tarnak Farm in 2002 and felt she just could not stop coming; she had to pay her respects. She had this little Canadian flag in her hand, about twelve inches by eight, and on it was the name of every single soldier whose body had come home.

One time a group of leather-clad, bearded men on motorcycles, accompanied by some women, rolled up to the fence, and I said, "Who the hell is that?" It turned out these were all former serving members of the Canadian Forces who had formed a club called the Canadian Army Veterans Motorcycle Units. Every time there was a repatriation, twenty-five or more would ride down from Ottawa, Barrie, Kingston or Toronto.

When the hearse carrying the coffin would start west down Highway 401 toward Toronto, it wouldn't get far before seeing the first incredible displays of public support. All along that 150-kilometre stretch of highway, on all fifty of the overpasses, thousands of Canadians would wave flags, salute or just take off their caps and stand silently as the convoy with the hearse passed below. One day, as I was flying by helicopter to Toronto after receiving a body in Trenton, we flew over that highway and I could see them all stretched out below me: little children, older folks, younger people, paramedics, firemen and policemen with their vehicles, many with Canadian flags, saluting, waving or just standing there. It may not have helped the families—it didn't change the fact that they had lost their loved one—but the inspiration, I think, that came from ordinary Canadians going out that way to show their respect and appreciation helped carry all of us through those difficult days. When Dalton McGuinty, the Ontario Premier, renamed that section of highway the "Highway of Heroes," he became a hero himself, to those of us in uniform and to our families. The actions of ordinary Canadians allowed us to continue in our service with confidence that the country was behind us.

CHAPTER 22

FINAL DAYS

On February 6, 2007, I woke to a front-page headline in the *Globe and Mail* that brought me back to the bad old days of Somalia: "Military investigates claim Canadians abused detainees."

I wasn't surprised about the media coverage or the screaming headline. We had been concerned about the policy on detainees in Afghanistan from the moment we sent our very first battle group on the ground in 2002, and the issue had been bubbling away on the back burner in Ottawa for months. Over the first four years of operations in Afghanistan, there had essentially been no Canadian policy on handling of the prisoners we took in operations against the Taliban. In that regard, we were no different from any other NATO nation, none of which had a policy on detainees either. The minuscule number encountered meant we could operate that way, and we knew that there would never be a perfect solution to handling them anyway. The headline would not change things from the CF perspective, except for the fact that the bureaucracy and elected representatives' focus and energy in Ottawa are driven almost exclusively by headlines, and we knew the story would cause significant work and angst.

Things had changed after spring 2006, however, when we moved south to Kandahar and our soldiers would often take prisoners after firefights with the Taliban or in other operations around Kandahar City that uncovered caches of weapons, explosives or suicide bomber vests. We wanted to ensure that those we did detain were being appropriately handled and that we were doing absolutely the right thing with them. Initially, the only option was to hand over everyone captured to the Americans, because we were part of the Coalition Forces. We were helping set conditions for NATO to expand across the entire country, but since that expansion had not yet happened, handing detainees to the Americans was logical. As the mission progressed and ISAF began planning to assume responsibility for the southern provinces and the mission there, the issue needed to be revisited.

After the analysis, the decision was made, within a multi-department context, that the right thing to do was transfer prisoners to the Afghans and let the Afghan judicial system, fledgling though it may have been, handle them. After all, Afghanistan is a sovereign country and, almost without exception, it was Afghans that we were detaining.

The Canadian Forces, with Foreign Affairs, were concerned about how the Afghans would treat those prisoners, just as there are concerns with any developing nation, and so in late 2005 we began discussing how we would handle them—the Taliban and suspected Taliban grabbed during operations. Foreign Affairs took the lead and drew up a memorandum of agreement with the

Afghan government. David Sproule, our ambassador in Kabul, was at the forefront of developing this agreement. Bill Graham, Ward Elcock and I were of absolutely one mind that an agreement with the government of Afghanistan was the way to go.

In December 2005 the agreement was finalized, needing only the signatures from Canada and Afghanistan to bring it into force. I happened to be visiting our troops in Kandahar and was asked if I would consider signing the document for Canada during the couple of days I planned on spending in Kabul. General Abdul Rahim Wardak, the former Chief of the Defence Staff who was now the Afghan Defence Minister, was going to sign on behalf of the government of Afghanistan and had requested that I sign it with him. Wardak and I had become close during my time as ISAF commander, when he was CDS for Afghanistan. He knew and trusted me. Foreign Affairs had no problems with this, so during my trip to Kabul, David Sproule accompanied me to visit Minister Wardak and, with Sproule orchestrating the shuffling of the various copies with signature blocks marked by yellow stickies, we signed the agreement, bringing it into force.

In the summer of 2006, when operations in the south really started to pick up and our soldiers were involved in an increasing number of firefights with the Taliban, we started to take more prisoners. We thought we had a good process in place, although obviously it was not perfect. Eventually—no surprise—people back in Canada started squawking about the issue. Opposition politicians and several specific individuals were trying to spin the story for their own purposes, and the result was that screaming newspaper headline insinuating that Canadian soldiers were abusing detainees. The allegations were that our soldiers had roughed up two suspects who had been found with the components of roadside bombs (one of them had explosive residue on his hands). The stories on these alleged incidents of abuse didn't mention, until near the end, long after people had stopped reading, that the cuts and bruises resulted from struggles with Canadian soldiers while they were being taken prisoner.

This was yellow journalism: innuendo, implication and assumption without basis in fact. The Canadian Forces handled the detainees correctly and professionally. We were capturing these guys red-handed, in many cases in the middle of firefights or attacks on Canadians, and many were found with gunpowder or explosive residue on their bodies. Sometimes those detainees were taken in the middle of violent actions where our own soldiers had been killed or wounded, and it spoke to the incredible professionalism and values of our young men and women that they were taken alive at all. In one case, a section of ten Canadian soldiers was fighting through a compound to clear the Taliban fighters out and finally isolated the last one on the roof of a mud building. He was too close to our soldiers for them to call in an air strike or artillery fire, and he had sufficient cover on the roof that he could not be shot and grenades could not kill or dislodge him. He continued to fight until he ran out of ammunition and then surrendered only after having wounded several Canadians. He was taken prisoner, and the fact that he was not killed during the hot emotions of that violent firefight validated the discipline, professionalism and values of our soldiers and their leaders. It takes that incredible discipline and professionalism, when you've been in a firefight in which your buddies have been killed or wounded around you, where you have been shot at yourself and are both scared and energized, to maintain your cool and do the right thing. That our soldiers handled the situation correctly was an enormous compliment to them and to the excellent leadership in place. We had all learned our lessons from Somalia.

We investigated these allegations of abuse and found nothing. The proof in the pudding was that even the Afghans we were detaining told investigators that the Canadian soldiers had treated them well. That made me prouder than ever of the young men and women I was leading, and more determined than ever to call the witch hunt that was happening in Canada what it was: bullshit. Not only was there no fire here, there was no smoke. Despite the unseemly innuendo, implications and downright gossip, in the end everyone who's looked into it has concluded that, in fact, nothing happened.

That didn't stop the issue from continuing for months and becoming a massive kerfuffle. The frustrating thing for me was that despite the fact that even the Afghans we were detaining had nothing but good things to say about Canadian soldiers, back in Canada several individuals continued to beat on this drum in an attempt to raise their media profile. None of them had any details or facts about what was actually happening on the ground in Kandahar and, in our view, they cared not a whit about that.

This suggestion that Canadian soldiers were not abiding by the laws of war coincided with complaints that the Afghans were abusing some of those handed to them. Their judicial and prison systems were still somewhat nascent, and there was always some risk that abuse could occur. That, unfortunately, is not abnormal in failed states and occurs even in solid countries like Canada. After indications that some abuse might have occurred, the CF felt it was a necessity to have Canadian officials make regular, unannounced visits to Afghan prisons to ensure the people we transferred were being treated humanely. The first visit noted details that caused us some concern and, in the view of the commander, Brigadier-General Guy Laroche, meant that we had to have those visits continue and other measures in place. Guy, who had my complete support, felt a variety of steps would allow him, hand over his heart, to say that he had confidence we were meeting not only the letter but also the spirit of international law.

We wanted to have a lot of those visits, but it took an awfully long time to get them organized and in place. Meanwhile, we continued to take detainees but, with concerns triggered by the first visit, we lost confidence that basic, responsible measures were in place to ensure the humane treatment of prisoners and protect the Canadians who had transferred them. Guy Laroche decided to stop the transfers until those measures were in place, and the chain of command, up to and including me, backed him. Foreign Affairs, CIDA, Corrections Canada and the RCMP had some work to do.

As this issue continued to percolate, the Canadian Forces were accused of refusing to release any information about those captured, including how many there were, who they were or what had happened to them. The implication was that we were somehow hiding something. I was an early and continuous proponent of openness and transparency in the Canadian Forces and had been very much in favour of the media-embedding program and the commitment to give reporters, and therefore Canadians, as much access to our operations in Afghanistan as security of our own men and women would permit. Operational security and the safety of our soldiers, however, had to take precedence.

I was not willing to jeopardize any of our soldiers by releasing information about the numbers and locations of Taliban fighters or foreign terrorists taken in our area of Afghanistan. We were aware, very early in our mission, that the Taliban were putting an enormous effort into trying to determine what had happened to their fighters and commanders. All they knew was that some of them—indeed, in many cases when they went up against Canadian soldiers, most of them—didn't come back from ambushes or firefights. They didn't know who had been killed, who was in jail or who had been released, perhaps as turncoats or double agents feeding information back to us. In many cases, we would capture a Taliban insurgent and hand him to the Afghan police or intelligence services, and he would tell them everything he knew. Then they would release him and he would return to the Taliban and continue to feed information to the Afghan authorities. The Taliban leaders didn't know for certain who we had captured, who had fled the area and gone into hiding for a while and who had told us everything he knew.

One of their fighters would show up after being missing for a couple of weeks and the Taliban commanders would debate if he was still one of them or if he was a traitor. They were forced to put a huge amount of effort into trying to figure that out and in some cases are believed to have executed their own people because of their suspicions (the Pakistanis tell numerous stories of the bodies of suspected traitors found on the roads near the Pakistani-Afghan border). Sometimes we could not get anything out of prisoners and couldn't prove them guilty (the Afghans did have a judicial process that had to be observed) and so we released them. Those people would still be under suspicion when they went home.

The more effort the Taliban put into determining what had happened, the less time and energy they had to plan and carry out attacks against us. That was an important edge and a fundamental reason not to talk at all about detainees.

Even something as simple as the exact number of detainees taken could have helped the Taliban. We were capturing insurgents and suspected insurgents in a very small area: most in the Panjwayi and Zhari districts, about the size of the city—not the region, but the city—of Ottawa. Releasing how many were taken would have given valuable information to the Taliban by telling them how many of their fighters had been taken prisoner as opposed to having been killed or having deserted. A lot of the people back in Canada who were after those numbers and other information about detainees really didn't give a damn about the safety of our soldiers. They were just interested in promoting their own agendas.

Some of the solutions the opposition critics and the many so-called analysts or "military experts" offered were ludicrous. Some even suggested that we bring these detainees back to Canada and hold them in jails here. That just blew me away. How could we remove prisoners from a sovereign country where we're operating with their agreement and as part of a NATO mission? Under whose laws would those prisoners be transferred? The effect on Afghanistan would have been disastrous. As I reminded Canadians, how would they feel if Afghans came into our country, started detaining Canadians and shipped them back to Afghanistan without so much as asking our permission?

There was particular disappointment on my part with the way our opposition parties and Parliament worked on the issue. I was not surprised, just disappointed, and when speaking at the Garrison Ball in Toronto in February 2008, tried to hold them accountable. "Why," I asked, "as every politician evinces concern and support for our troops, was the majority of questions during Question Period about detainees? In the previous session of Parliament, approximately 150 questions concerning defence were posed. Less than half a dozen had been about getting troops the equipment they needed, the dollars necessary or anything positive. Over fifty of those questions, however, concerned detainees. If the weight of questioning reflects what you think is important, why aren't there many more questions on how the troops can be better prepared, protected and supported?" Opposition members, some of whom were in attendance, were quick to take offence and say that the questions on detainees were also to protect our soldiers, from potential conflict with Canadian or international law. I believed them, but, sadly, I was the only one in 89,000 men and women in uniform to do so!

The treatment of detainees continued to bubble as an issue in Canada until the release of the Manley Report on the mission in Afghanistan in January 2008, which happened to come out just following the commencement of continual Foreign Affairs visits to the prison where most of those we detained were taken. These visits, along with improvements in prison infrastructure and Afghan police training, were necessary for us to recommence the transfers. Guy Laroche was clear on this and resisted many nuanced types of pressure to restart before the changes were made. I, yet again, got shrieked at during PCO meetings as I backed him.

The Government of Canada was well aware of our decision, and Foreign Affairs, with CIDA, the RCMP and Correctional Service Canada, were mandated to help the Afghans improve. Thus, for weeks while those improvements were happening, we held those captured in an interim facility on Kandahar Airfield. Fortunately, the pause coincided with a lull in operations and hence a reduction in the numbers of prisoners.

In the middle of this, I took a short vacation to the Dominican Republic in late January 2008. I had already interrupted my break twice to fly back to Ottawa for Cabinet meetings on Afghanistan (the release of the Manley Report) and a defence strategy (the Strahl Committee meetings). I got back to the resort where Joyce and I were staying late at night after the second trip, tired from the travel. I was having a few drinks with friends when my BlackBerry buzzed with a message from my staff in Ottawa about a statement out of the Prime Minister's Office on detainees. The spokeswoman for the Prime Minister, Sandra Buckler, had told the media that the Canadian Forces—me specifically—had not informed the Prime Minister that we had stopped the transfer of detainees from Canadian to Afghan custody. The previous fall, we had told Foreign Affairs, CIDA and the rest of the government that unless inspectors visited Afghan jails continually and built confidence that those detained by us were still being treated humanely, we were not going to transfer any more.

We had made sure everyone knew that we were stopping those transfers—it was a sensitive issue, after all, in the newspapers almost every day. So there I was, on this beautiful beach in the Dominican Republic, working on my second rum and Coke, being blamed for something that simply wasn't true. I shut off my BlackBerry and had a third drink.

When I got back to Canada a few days later and reporters asked me about that evening and what they perceived to be conflict between Harper and me, I told them, "I was on my third rum and Coke and didn't give a damn." They all interpreted that to mean I called up the staffers in the PMO and shouted at them, but in fact nothing could have been further from the truth. I just didn't give a damn about wasting time to address what I considered another of the issues that were characteristic of Ottawa, with its vitriol. I certainly didn't care enough to call Ottawa in the middle of the first real vacation Joyce and I had taken in a long time and, lastly, as Chief of the Defence Staff, if I had been going to phone anyone, it would have been the Prime Minister, not his staffers. The upside of my response was that I have a constant supply of rum and Cokes sent to me whenever I'm in restaurants or pubs!

Gord O'Connor was a casualty of the entire detainee uproar. It's hard to say when we realized he was leaving as Minister of National Defence, but Gord had been taking a beating in the media and in the House of Commons because of his supposed mishandling of the job. Personally, I thought he had accomplished some wonderful things as Defence Minister. Sure, he and I had some challenges over a few issues, but rare is the relationship that does not. In fact it is normal, and Gord had done much during his time as Minister: he had delivered, with the C-17 acquisition alone being more than any combination of ministers since 1989 had brought. The criticism over the detainees crescendoed in the spring and early summer of 2007, and obviously a Cabinet shake-up was in the offing. There had been a lot of noise in the media about the two of us feuding, so in late June I, again, said, "Minister, how can we put this speculation about you and I being at loggerheads to bed? We agree on far more than we have money to do. We're on the same side on the key, major issues."

He agreed. "I'll do what I can."

But in a little over a month, in August 2007, I was in Rideau Hall for the swearing-in of a new Cabinet. Gord came over to me before the ceremony, shook my hand and told me he was leaving as Minister to be out of the limelight for a little while. A few minutes later I found out who the new Minister was, when Peter MacKay walked over and told me he'd be taking on the role.

At the ceremony, I was sitting in the front row on the right side, about two metres away from a bank of cameras, all pointing in my general direction as they tried to capture the attendees and arrivals. I sat next to Monte Solberg, the Conservative MP from Medicine Hat, and his wife, chatting with them, waiting for Her Excellency the Governor General to arrive and start the ceremony. Hearing a rustling in the crowd, I turned around to see who could have caused that stir and, as I looked over my left shoulder, I saw Julie Couillard, Maxime Bernier's date. She was wearing the low-cut dress that the Ottawa media buzzed about after the ceremony, and all I could see was boobs. I immediately realized that those media cameras were in a direct line from them to me to that cleavage, and unless I wanted my picture slapped on the front page of the *Globe and Mail* staring at Ms. Couillard's chest, I had better keep my eyes to the front. So I whipped my head around double-quick time and kept it facing forward, despite the view behind me. That was my first and only sight of the dress that caused so much ink to be wasted in our newspapers.

Almost as much ink was wasted on speculation that I had been responsible for Gord O'Connor's being forced out of the defence portfolio and whether or not I would get along with the new Minister. Peter MacKay was a pleasure to work for and with, right from his first day as Minister. Peter is a leader, as his actions show. I had had a very good relationship with him when he was Minister of Foreign Affairs. He was very supportive of the Canadian Forces and the mission in Afghanistan and had made a positive impression on me at Cabinet meetings. When he became Minister of National Defence, he didn't pretend he knew it all—he got his briefings, dug into the issues and got into the details of the job and a few months after he took over the portfolio I ended up travelling with him to Afghanistan and the Persian Gulf. He had an excellent rapport with servicemen and servicewomen and very quickly developed a good feel for the job. We made a real effort to be seen together and to demonstrate that we spoke with one voice, a key part of our relationship. We had very similar views on how to rebuild the Canadian Forces, and he sought advice on what was needed and how to move things along as quickly as possible.

Unfortunately, we found out soon after the change of ministers that Ward Elcock would be leaving as Deputy Minister of Defence to go to a job in Privy Council. Ward had been an incredibly important part of the transformation of the Canadian Forces and a stalwart as Deputy Minister, the best in the history of the department. He would be sorely missed, and I felt like I was losing my right arm. Ward was later appointed Chief Coordinator for Security for the 2010 Vancouver Olympics, bringing some desperately needed leadership to that challenge.

Peter and I worked together seamlessly. He's a strong leader, with a core of steel, but at the same time he doesn't pretend to know everything. We had a very similar point of view on most issues—not completely of one mind, which isn't healthy in any case, and we certainly had different views on some issues, but he realized that he had to carry the political weight, and he relied on me for military advice. Our relationship worked exceedingly well. When I made my decision to step down, early in 2008, I told him that one of my regrets was leaving while he was still Defence Minister.

Soon after Peter became Minister, the Manley Panel was put together and began analyzing the mission in Afghanistan to help the government lay out its future strategy. At the same time an ad hoc committee, chaired by Chuck Strahl, was formed to develop a detailed strategy and plan for the nation's defence, so we had a lot to keep us busy. The fall and winter of 2007 seemed like one constant work cycle followed by a constant briefing cycle. We must have spent fifty hours preparing, briefing and discussing issues with the Strahl Committee.

The Manley Panel did its job well. The first day they assembled in Ottawa, in late October 2007, I was asked to sit with them at dinner to discuss the mission. I drew three triangles on a flip chart, flowing from one to the other and then to the third, with each designed to show the stages of the mission as I perceived them, moving from a focus on security, supported by efforts on development and governance (with a rating of "weak" in those areas), to a focus on development and, finally, to a focus on governance as we progressed. There was much discussion, but clearly the talk, and the simple sketch, resonated well. Their report reflected much of what I believed was right about the mission, but also, in a larger sense, about how Canada should work internationally.

Peter was a key player in the development of the defence strategy, its focus and the detailed plan to implement it. It was under his guiding hand that we developed and eventually released the government's Defence Policy Statement. That overarching strategy had been missing from the Conservatives' defence policy when they were first elected, and he guided it through Cabinet and the political process. But the real worker was Walt Natynczyk. Walt, the Vice Chief of the Defence Staff, had, with a small team, built an impressive picture of the threats as we saw them, the capabilities (mixture of troops, equipment, training and leadership) required to counter those threats, the cost of those capabilities and priorities that we believed were necessary to follow to be successful. In short, we laid it all out for the Cabinet committee and, in hours of discussion and questions, helped the members understand what had to be done and the consequences of determining to do that.

Walt's confident command of both strategic issues and tactical detail, his ability to communicate, his forthrightness and his people-friendly personality were obvious to all and instilled confidence in the ministers that this really was a complete and transparent approach. The team was working well, and in the hours we spent in that Cabinet room, I saw, as Churchill put it, the "beginning of the end" of my tenure as Chief of the Defence

Staff. It was obvious that Walt was gaining credibility every single day and would make an extremely competent successor. He had come into his own and I began to think that I would be completely comfortable stepping down. I had been thinking about my exit, specifically when and under what circumstances, from the day I took the job. Seeing Walt work so masterfully with Cabinet ministers and members of Parliament made me think that the future of the Canadian Forces would be in good hands. It put some finality to what I'd been trying to achieve in transforming the CF. It was all coming together.

One of the issues that again came to the forefront as a result of the Manley Panel's look at the Afghan mission was the whole question of NATO's command of the operation and the fact that many of the member nations were just not pulling their weight. It had become increasingly clear to me that NATO was set up to do almost anything but run an operation like that in Afghanistan. Like the United Nations and so many of our own government institutions, NATO was shaped and structured for, and by, the Cold War. The alliance's military chain of command was certainly set up to fight the Cold War: its command and control structure was designed to make long-term strategic military decisions in Central Europe, as opposed to running a short-term operation elsewhere. NATO is based on consensus, with all the members of the alliance agreeing on every single little issue. That kind of consensus is simply not possible when you're trying to win an up-close-and-personal battle like the one in Afghanistan.

With the collapse of the Soviet Union and the elimination of the threat that prompted NATO members to pull together as one, the alliance became badly split between the European Union members—France, Germany and Belgium, and to a certain extent Spain and Italy—and the Americans, who the European countries (with the exception of Britain) believed were dictating NATO strategy with superficial consideration of Europe's overall interests in the post–Cold War world. That split was exacerbated by the U.S. approach after the World Trade Center attack, when the "Coalition of the Willing" strategy combined with an "if you are not with us you are against us" attitude to alienate many countries and possibly cause the strategic opportunity of a century to be missed.

473

The enormous military headquarters and bureaucracy that grew within NATO aggravated that split, making it a wonder that any decisions got made at all. There was no appetite for reform, however, and European nations seemed more concerned about keeping headquarters alive and well in their own countries than about being organized to run operations effectively. Throw a real live shooting war into that mix, 8,000 kilometres away from the alliance's centre of gravity, and you have a massive challenge. That challenge has very real implications for thousands of young men and women fighting and dying on the ground in Afghanistan.

NATO never really wanted to get into Afghanistan—it backed into it, largely against the will of many members, though all did acquiesce. The first tentative step was taking over the ISAF mission in and around Kabul. That force, a purely European mission, had to change to reflect the international effort. This coincided with both Germany's and Canada's desire to do more in Afghanistan, but not under American command. It wasn't going to be a UN mission—the UN had made it clear that it was not interested in running any military force in Afghanistan—so that left NATO. Under immense pressure from Germany, Canada and the U.S. (which was after NATO to do more in the War on Terror), the alliance agreed to take over ISAF, with its twenty-six member nations signing the agreement to do so with a cohesion that was, at best, shaky.

When the NATO members agreed in 2003 to expand that ISAF mission into other parts of Afghanistan outside Kabul, they decided to do it by sending provincial reconstruction teams rather than military forces to conduct security and counter-insurgency operations. That compounded the mission's challenge because it allowed the majority of NATO's members to avoid playing the direct combat role where it was most needed, fighting the Taliban insurgency in the south. NATO made another decision during the expansion, one that was a massive error: to allow each nation to select its own specific geographical area of operations. That let each country set up its own little fiefdom, all of them scattered across the country, and destroyed any flexibility for the use of forces. None of those countries would move out of their area. The Germans, for example, would tell NATO they'd love to help out in the south, but that they couldn't leave behind all of the progress they'd made in the north because they felt it would fall to pieces. It wasn't just Germany—unfortunately, every other country not in the south is exactly the same way.

Since many of the member countries had only reluctantly said yes to the mission, its expansion across the country and into the southern provinces, they were even more reluctant to provide sufficient forces, put them where they were needed most or remove caveats from their deployment that prevented them from being used to fight. Caveats weren't new or, in the past, confined to the European countries. Canada had had similar constraints on its battle groups in Bosnia and during the early stages of the mission in Kandahar and Kabul; but when we went south in 2006, that changed. We went into operations as one of the few countries without caveats. Unfortunately, it didn't change for most others. So yes, the Dutch were with us in southern Afghanistan, the Danes were there, along with the British, the Romanians and the Americans, but that was pretty much it. Australia, a non-NATO country, was there also, but the rest of the NATO countries stayed away. Promises of *in extremis* assistance were a placebo to take some sting away from the constant "no" that always came following requests to send troops to the south, and meant nothing. After a while, even those countries offering the *in extremis* help were embarrassed to say the words, since we all knew it was a worthless commitment.

With the Taliban resurgence, we didn't have the troops on the ground to do the job the way it had to be done. Canada was in the middle of a life-and-death firefight in the south, and few in the alliance were willing to step up and help. We were essentially in it by ourselves, with Americans and British troops, and that made me angry.

NATO's Military Committee, which makes strategic military decisions in the alliance—again, by consensus—meets three times a year, and I attended most of those meetings. They were incredibly frustrating. The generals and admirals, surrounded by their staffs, would hold endless discussions on exactly the same issues every meeting, without much change. It was circular:

nothing spun out. Neither the NATO Secretary-General nor the North Atlantic Council received clear, tough, pragmatic military advice from these meetings; we were often wasting our time. At one of the meetings, right after the fighting in the Panjwayi during Operation Medusa, I said to my peers, "Canada feels like we've been abandoned by our allies in the Kandahar province fight."

The response was interesting. Many looked at the table, a few said they had been constrained by their governments, several pledged to renew efforts to commit to the south, but for the most part nothing much changed. The exception, by its striking loneliness, was the U.S. Chairman of the Joint Chiefs of Staff, General Peter Pace, who immediately spoke up and said, "The United States of America will never see our friend and ally, Canada, on its own." Resources, in every form, started flowing from the Americans the next day.

I lost my temper a little at that meeting and said to the Military Committee, "We don't want help for us. That is not what we are asking. What we want is NATO to be successful in its mission. Right now, in Kandahar province—which President Karzai, by the way, described as the centre of gravity for his country—you've got this massive Taliban threat, and it's going to have to be dealt with. We're doing that by ourselves, because the battalion that NATO had said was necessary to go with us in Kandahar is not there; neither are numerous other forces, helicopters or UAVs. So don't be talking about coming to help Canada. Talk about giving the ISAF Commander the necessary forces and flexibility so he can handle this for NATO and for Afghanistan. In short, let's set conditions for success for the mission that every country here accepted. It's not about helping Canada; it's about doing the job we, as NATO, signed up to do." Unfortunately, the lack of will to prosecute this mission, reflecting the reluctant acceptance of it initially, meant that nothing of significance happened.

Canada was actually helping NATO do what it had signed up to do, and those countries who refused to send their troops into southern Afghanistan or restricted how they could be used needed to follow our lead. The NATO Secretary-General went around to the members of the alliance constantly, to beg two more helicopters or five hundred more troops or something else for Afghanistan, in an alliance that has millions of soldiers and thousands of helicopters. It was embarrassing.

NATO had yet to articulate a clear strategy for what it was doing in Afghanistan. It failed to operate as one cohesive block in dealing with Pakistan, greatly diminishing its ability to affect what happens in that country—which, by the way, affects every-thing in Afghanistan. In short, Afghanistan has revealed that NATO has reached the stage where it is a corpse, decomposing, and somebody's going to have to perform a Frankenstein-like life-giving act by breathing some lifesaving air through those rotten lips into those putrescent lungs, or the alliance will be done. Any major setback in Afghanistan will see it off to the cleaners, and unless the alliance can snatch victory out of feeble efforts, it's not going to be long in existence in its present form. As Dr. Barney Rubin, an internationally renowned expert on Afghanistan, said, "NATO is condemned to success in Afghanistan. Anything else will be the end of the alliance."

CHAPTER 23

TIME TO GO

April 15, 2008, the day I announced I was stepping down as Chief of the Defence Staff, turned out to be a long day. Over the previous weeks and months I had been calculating the right time to depart. I wanted to leave with the organization on a high, with conditions set for my successor to continue to drive the changes we had begun.

My plans to depart had looked like they might be waylaid at one point in the previous months. I had met with Prime Minister Harper in December 2007 and, in the course of our meeting, had discussed the term of my time as CDS—how long my role would continue and when I might go. He articulated his desire that I look past the short term. My focus had been on determining what would be our next big challenges, which I thought would happen between the summer of 2008 until at least spring, possibly summer, of 2011. My belief was that during this period we required one single hand on the leadership tiller to steer the program of change and to see us through the 2010 Olympics in Vancouver, the G8 Meeting in Canada in June 2010 and completion of the next stage of the commitment in Afghanistan. So the time frames were, in my view, neatly laid out from when I had assumed the appointment in February 2005 with a mandate to effect change in the CF until the summer of 2008, followed by a second period until the summer of 2011 and then a third significant period that started after that summer.

So if I were to stay, it would mean a very long extension of my term indeed. The truth is, I didn't have the appetite to stay on another three years. The work was intense and fatiguing, and despite the exhilaration of helping bring the CF and its incredible men and women back into their rightful place in Canadian society, I was ready to go. My wife and I were consumed by the demands of my being CDS.

Joyce and I discussed it many times, but ultimately she left the decision to me. Always the great and supportive wife and partner, she said she would support me no matter what I decided. The speculation about my departure by those with a desperate urge for the spotlight continued, but it had abated somewhat over the previous couple of months. I decided that the conditions were as good as they would get. I didn't want another three years. The time had come for me to go, and to go right away.

Having the right successor in place was my first, and overwhelming, consideration. I knew various hands would be in the pot, trying to pick someone who would fit many perceived needs: a CDS who could be controlled by government; someone who would be subservient to the public bureaucracy, much like a civil servant; someone who would do only what they were told.

I needn't have worried about the candidates, however, given the leaders available to be considered as the next CDS. Walt Natynczyk was first among equals in my opinion, but others were also more than capable of doing the job, with operational experience, command time and a great understanding of the challenges in Ottawa. Above all, however, they were strong leaders, with solid management capabilities. The "gene pool" was deep, and no matter who was selected, I believed we would have the right leader: Angus Watt, who was running the air force so efficiently; Mike Gauthier, who understood Afghanistan completely; Dean McFadden, a recently promoted naval officer whose leadership impressed all; Andy Leslie, the army commander and operationally experienced soldier. Any one of them, or several others, would have been right.

I still had some things left to do before handing over to whoever was selected. I wanted to ensure that the long-range unmanned aerial vehicle we so urgently needed in Afghanistan was brought into service quickly; I wanted to help finalize and release the Defence Strategy to prepare the groundwork for which equipment needed to be acquired next and what further changes needed to be made in the military; and, lastly, I wanted to articulate how the CF would handle the transition. I was not forgetting that we were still intensively recruiting and training all across Canada, running operations in our country and the continent, operating in a dozen nations around the world and fighting a war in Afghanistan. There was no time to relax and put my feet up, even if my usual energy and impatience would let me do that. Our men and women in uniform and their families still needed leadership.

My team of confidants, including my senior commanders plus Walt Natynczyk, Tom Ring, George Petrolekas, Serge Labbé and others, advised that the eyes of the country would be upon us and a change of command between me and my successor would be the ultimate opportunity for a "Connect to Canadians" event in 2008. My wish had been to announce my retirement at about eleven in the morning and then to exit NDHQ, handing off to the Vice Chief of the Defence Staff at noon. I would stay on leave until my successor had been selected and then return only for a brief handover. I didn't find lengthy transitions, emotional farewells and the prospect of being a "lame duck" CDS very appealing; the very idea made me uncomfortable. I quickly discovered, however, that it would not be possible to leave exactly the way I wanted, and I'd have to compromise. My advisers said that I should use the opportunity to showcase the CF. We would get huge TV and radio coverage, live and recorded, across the country, as well as print media for days and weeks. That coverage would be worth hundreds of thousands of dollars, possibly millions, and would help connect the CF to Canadians and boost recruiting more effectively than anything else we could do.

That was the future as I worked through April 15. I had made an appointment to see the Prime Minister to tell him directly. I had told Peter MacKay of my intentions. I was prepared to participate in a hastily called media scrum when the news broke and had not much else to concern me through the day, except an invitation that night to attend CTV's fiftieth-anniversary party in Ottawa. Knowing Ottawa and the political machinery as I did, however, I expected the news to be leaked before I even went to see the PM. It's the way the city works. So I decided to take the initiative and leaked the news myself, the night before.

Don Martin, from the Parliamentary Press Gallery, had indicated through contacts that he was aware of retirement discussions. I suggested we meet for a beer at D'Arcy McGee's on Sparks Street in Ottawa on the night of April 14 and, at about 7 p.m., we did. Over a beer with Don, I told him exactly what I was doing, when, and what had led me to it and then asked him to play it in the morning as soon as rumours started to build. He was in shock. He did as I suggested, however, and the next day when breathless reporters quoted breaking news and Julie Van Dusen "ambushed" me at the entrance to NDHQ, I smiled a little, knowing where it had all started. For once, the tables had been turned!

Following an invigorating daily run around the Ottawa River bridges, I met the PM in the middle of the afternoon for a friendly discussion. I then returned to NDHQ to participate in the ensuing media scrum. One of the first questions was from a female reporter who I immediately recognized. She and a man had been walking down Sparks Street when I had jogged through, and she had recognized me. She turned in my direction, in her high heels and tight skirt, clutching her purse, trying to pull out her recording device, asking questions and trying to keep up with me. She was a sight indeed, and I joked with her about it. After several other interviews, I went to the CTV reception at Milestones, met quite literally hundreds of people, including several Liberal members of Parliament who asked me to consider running for their party. I arrived home after 10 p.m. that night. Joyce and I sat down, opened a bottle of champagne and toasted the next stage of our life.

The first issue I wanted to finalize before leaving was a reassessment of Colonel Serge Labbé's performance and whether or not his promotion to general was merited. Serge had been a colonel for more than seventeen years, and had paid a huge price when he, as the commander, and the professional he is, accepted responsibility for the Somalia debacle. Serge had continued to soldier with professionalism second to none. I had received several letters from high-ranking individuals in NATO who had worked with Serge and recommended his immediate promotion based on what they had seen of his immense capabilities.

Serge had been very high profile and had a huge amount of credibility among those who had served with him. Four of the units under his command in Somalia performed admirably. A few of those in the fifth unit, the Airborne Regiment, imploded and lost any discipline they had, at the same time as the regiment itself lost responsibility and accountability in its chain of command. The results were disastrous, particularly the death by torture of Shidane Arone. Something had happened inside that unit over many years, leading to a loss in discipline, cohesion and morale, as the Board of Inquiry went on to show.

Nonetheless, Serge accepted responsibility. He was the commander. It was on his watch, and despite the fact the other four units had done marvellous work and that the conditions for that disaster were set long before he or the regiment arrived in Somalia, Serge accepted responsibility. He did not try to duck or deflect it.

His announced promotion to brigadier-general was cancelled. His file had been contaminated by the events in Somalia, but Serge went on to serve, as a colonel, in six or seven different postings. He served on four different missions, including Cooperative Endeavour exercises—NATO exercises designed to build relationships with NATO wannabes who wanted to both stop fighting each other and acquire a Western mindset. Serge served in Turkey with the NATO Corps headquarters and in Joint Forces Command in Brunssum, Netherlands. He served in Brussels, at NATO headquarters. Wherever he went, Serge got nothing but compliments and strong performance evaluations. He received letters of support from the Chairman of the Military Committee—a German four-star general and the senior ranking NATO officer—who said we should promote him right away.

When I was preparing to command ISAF in October 2003, bringing together that multinational team, Serge came to my direct attention. I had one officer with me, Colonel Bill Brough, and the challenges we faced were immense. Serge had already given as much thought to the challenges as I had and he laid out a whole variety of options to assist us in our preparations. His plans dovetailed beautifully with my own thought process and vision. Serge then single-handedly brought that JFC headquarters and the contributing nations in line to provide the right people at the right time so we could conduct key leader training, complete a reconnaissance in Afghanistan, train our headquarters team in Germany and then conduct the mission rehearsal exercise. Serge did incredible work that would have caused the vast majority of officers who were superior in rank to him to cower. The Europeans, and I, were impressed.

Serge continued that magnificent work as my assistant chief of staff in Kabul. We deployed into Afghanistan and he became the mainstay at the headquarters. In early April 2004, we brought in the French officer who was going to replace me, Lieutenant-General Jean-Louis Py. After welcoming him and his team for their preparations, I said to him, "You know, Jean-Louis, one of the criteria for us declaring our mission a success, once we're finished, is having you set up for success when you take over, and so here's what I would suggest to you. We'd like to have you here for a minimum of four recces, the first one to be focused on the strategic picture, the second one on visiting various places to get a feel for the country, the third concentrating on the tactical level and the last preparing you for the upcoming elections." So Jean-Louis and his team ran the first reconnaissance, staying for four and a half days. The night before he was to leave, he and I wound up our discussions with a glass of wine.

I said, "Jean-Louis, it's been a good week from my perspective. What else can we do for you?"

He said, "Rick, it's been outstanding, and there's only one thing that you could do for me now that would improve what you have done so far."

I said, "What's that?"

He said, "Leave me Serge Labbé. If I had Labbé, I'd be confident that my headquarters would be ready to do this job in a moment, just as yours is now."

I commissioned the Director General of Military Careers to convene a special career merit board, something we did frequently when an anomaly was noticed, and compare Serge's file to others of his seniority. Roger MacIsaac did it quickly, selecting appropriate members, providing files of a disparate group of Serge's peers; and when the process was complete, he confirmed that the merit board believed that Serge should have been a general long ago.

When I met with Peter MacKay out at the Ottawa Airport in June 2008, along with several of his advisers and my successor, Walt Natynczyk, I explained the situation and recommended that Labbé be immediately promoted to brigadier-general, with seniority dating back to 2000. MacKay agreed and approved the promotion then and there. Again, I thought this was a reflection of his ability to quickly grasp issues and do what was right, and certainly a demonstration of his decisiveness.

I'm proud of what happened because it was right. Serge Labbé is a leader and, like all of us who have been or are leaders now, cannot guarantee everything going right all the time. I always felt (one of my little axioms, if you will) that I gave good leadership about 80 per cent of the time but my intentions were always honourable. I always wanted to give and tried to give my best, but, hey, I fell short just like everybody in life does occasionally. But because my intentions were honourable and understood by those who worked for me, when I fell short they carried me. I think that's what happens in most cases. Serge and his wife, Hope, attended the pre-parade reception on July 2. I asked Hope to help in the promotion. She put one brigadier-general's epaulet on Serge's shirt and I did the other. Since we had kept it a surprise, he had no tunic available and so attended the ceremony after with a general officer's rank on his shirt and colonel's rank on his jacket.

Admiral Mike Mullen, the chairman of the U.S. Joint Chiefs of Staff, phoned just a couple of days after I had made the announcement on April 15 that I was retiring. He said, "Rick, I'm looking at the very chair you were sitting in just weeks ago, when you said that the Prime Minister had offered you the opportunity to stay, and now you're going?"

I said, "Yes, Mike. I also said that I was considering all of my options, and I really wasn't enthusiastic about staying for that length of time." Anyhow, we were laughing about that, and he said, "Look, I just want to say, I was in Canada, one of the very few times I've been there, in 2003, with Secretary of Defense Rumsfeld. When we left Canada, we were talking amongst ourselves and the essence of our comments was that we had written off Canada as a serious player, a serious contributor, to anything that was going to happen around the world. We had written you off. Now you guys are at the forefront of everything positive. You're setting the example for countries in Europe to follow, for other Western countries, for any country around the world to follow, and you guys are doing it. It's absolutely incredible." Coming from the senior military officer in the United States, our most important relationship by far, that was an almost unbelievable statement, and showed recognition and appreciation for the impact Canada was making around the world. Obviously, part of our plan was to raise Canada's profile, and with that heightened profile, credibility. Mike's comment validated everything we had being trying to achieve.

I then went to NORAD, in Colorado Springs, in early May to participate in the fiftieth-anniversary celebrations for that very successful alliance, built to protect North America from air attack. At the anniversary dinner, Bob Gates, who I had worked with many times since his return as the U.S. Secretary of Defense—he was a distinct and pleasurable change from Rumsfeld—came up to me and said, "Rick, I just want to tell you that we're going to miss you. Sure do appreciate what you've done and the way you've been a part of a change that was desperately needed. We're going to miss you." It was heartwarming to hear the Secretary of Defense say that because I took it as a compliment to those thousands in uniform and those who supported them, in our country.

I still had to finish a number of items other than the personnel issues and NORAD'S fiftieth-anniversary celebrations. I left Colorado Springs and flew directly to Europe to attend the spring meeting of the NATO Military Committee. It was even more intriguing to sit around the table at that meeting now that I was departing and, in my last meeting, to observe the immense respect Canada's opinions and actions received. This was a far cry from my first meeting, when we were part of a nameless mass of "others" in the alliance, deferring to the several bigger nations. As I talked about what we were doing on NATO missions, the challenges and the fact that we were now bringing in big helicopters to Afghanistan, adding escort gunships, deploying the longest endurance UAV in the world and a host of other initiatives, all supporting the NATO ISAF mission, several Chiefs of Defence Staff sitting around the table looked embarrassed, but most said something like "Go Canada!"—with envy. In my sixty-second farewell speech, I thanked my peers for their comradeship and friendship, wished them well and mentioned, once again, my belief that the world needed NATO, no country more so than Canada, and that a revolution in its focus, organization and approach was needed to ensure survival and future relevancy. These were friends, after all, sitting around the table, and Joyce and I had gotten to know particularly well the U.S., U.K., German, Polish, Greek, Norwegian,

Dutch, Danish and Turkish Chiefs, and their wives, over the previous years. We would miss them.

Back in Canada, preparations to select a new CDS were ongoing, with a committee selected at Privy Council Office and chaired by the Minister of National Defence, to interview candidates. Unfortunately, from my perspective, that committee included only bureaucrats and no former CDS or military leaders, so the understanding of operational focus and key characteristics required for the job was slim. Obviously, PCO wanted a selection process that would, if possible, deliver a tame bureaucrat—that much seemed clear to me. My confidants continued to advise me on the transition, including the time and place for the "Connect to Canadians" event that the change of command ceremony would be. I said I wanted the transition to occur in late June or early July, and we looked at locations where many Canadians could participate. Sadly, Parliament Hill was unworkable around the Canada Day celebrations, and early July was clearly becoming the window for the change.

The committee recommending a new CDS completed its work, and Peter MacKay recommended Walt Natynczyk to the Prime Minister as my replacement. We could narrow the time frame for the change immediately, and the Prime Minister was available on July 2. We selected the tarmac at Ottawa Airport, which used to be a part of the old Canadian Forces Base Ottawa, as the site. The July 2 date proved disappointing to some, who could not accuse me of dodging new legislation constraining lobbying, since I was now retiring after the law went into effect on July 1, 2008.

I declined to make a farewell tour of CF units around the country as encouraged, although I did take my command team's advice and decided not to press my luck by squeezing in a last visit to Afghanistan. However, during the course of everyday events in May and June, I had the opportunity to personally thank a significant number of our men and women in the CF. I joined the company of HMCS *Charlottetown* for their last day at sea when the ship returned to Halifax after a seven-month mission in the Persian Gulf. I visited our wounded and recovering soldiers during the International Ice Hockey Federation World Championship games in Halifax, where Shaun Fevens, wounded in an attack that killed six of his comrades on Easter Sunday in 2007, presented the award to the Canadian player of the game. I flew with the Snowbirds in the Carleton Place Airport Airshow on June 30, my birthday. It was non-stop.

I witnessed the fierce pride in our men and women serving in the CF and that of their families who supported them. They walked tall, heads held erect, proud of being a soldier, sailor, airman or airwoman. They believed, again, that to be a "soldier" in Canada, to be part of a profession of arms, is a wonderful thing; everyone I met noted this change. One medic said, "Sir, I have seventeen years' service, and up until now, I couldn't wait to complete twenty and retire. Now, I don't ever want to leave!" The pride was evident in everything they did and brought even greater credit to Canada. The dark and dismal days in the '90s flashed through my mind many times when the word "pride" was mentioned. Now we wore our uniforms proudly, on buses, trains and planes and at sporting events. We let everyone know that we were Canada's armed forces, defending them at home and abroad. The CF's image had seen a sea change.

Lastly, I was of the fervent belief that most of the 33 million Canadians who call this great country home were equally

changed. From coast to coast to coast, Canadians had been educated about who the men and women in uniform are and made
aware of their huge value to our nation. They now see that their
military has made this country secure and has helped make it
the number one place in the world to live. Canadians saw our
soldiers for probably the first time since the Second World War
as Canada's, as *their* armed forces. Canada's moms and dads had
finally recognized that it was Canada's sons and daughters who
were serving in the uniform of the CF, and their response was
overwhelming.

Canadians were proud of the CF, of the work done by those
who served and the legacy of our past heroes, and understood the
risk those modern-day veterans had accepted daily on behalf of all.
Every part of our society seemed to be acknowledging, in some way,
what incredible ambassadors they were for our country around
the world. In every town, city and province, Canadians were holding Rallies in Red, forming support groups, mailing packages of
gifts to deployed troops, buying coffee for people in uniform at
Tim Hortons and showing support for the kind of expenditure
and programs our soldiers need to be successful. During my last
several weeks, as I travelled through Ottawa Airport, I saw a lot
of men and women in desert combat uniform checking in, obviously returning to the mission in Afghanistan. It was a busy time
at the airport, and it seemed, during the fifteen minutes I sat and
watched, that at least two hundred people approached those in
uniform, thanked them, patted them on the back, shook their
hand or offered to buy them a coffee. It wasn't very long ago that
those two hundred would not have known who the uniformed
men and women were, and if they did recognize them, would have

just remained silent, unwilling or uncertain about approaching them, much less thanking them for their work.

What I found most touching were the thousands of Canadians who supported us during the darkest of days, when we brought home the bodies of soldiers killed in action and drove them and their families from Trenton to Toronto along Highway 401, now the Highway of Heroes. Those thousands who lined the fifty overpasses on that route, saluting with hand over their heart, waving a flag or simply standing silently in respect, showed that they too appreciated the sacrifice, what it takes to put your life on the line, what the families were experiencing and that their sacrifice must never be forgotten. The hundreds who lined the fences at CFB Trenton across from where our families stood touched all of us, particularly the one lady who waved her small Canadian flag with the names of each of those who had died on it.

When I established the Military Families Fund in April 2007, the business community lined up to show their support to the families of our troops, and therefore to those troops themselves. Many contributed directly to the fund; others organized their own events to recognize and support their employees who also served. Still others shaped their company policies to support reservists who deployed to serve Canada and the families of both reservists and regular-force men and women who might be working for them.

Most importantly, everyone who wore a uniform had experienced a cultural revolution. We were proud to wear our uniforms, but we also had confidence in who we were—warriors first and foremost, able to do any task—with a first responsibility to finish tough, often violent tasks when Canada needed them done. Our country had not seen this kind of military culture since the Second World War. The immense frustration at the ignorance of so many who labelled us "only" peacekeepers had disappeared. Canadians knew that no matter how easy or tough the mission, whatever it was our country needed doing, we could do it. That was as important for those in uniform to learn as it was for those outside the CF. Amusingly, this actually made life

more difficult in Ottawa. We were at war in Afghanistan, while the mandarins processed paper.

We made our final decisions for the change of command, planning a small reception, inviting the Governor General, the Prime Minister, the Minister of National Defence and other VIPs, as well as a foreign contingent. We decided how we would use this unique event to showcase the talents of men and women in the Canadian Forces. We would also show off their equipment, the C-17 strategic lifter, the main battle tank, our exciting Snowbirds and the daring paratroopers called the SkyHawks. If that couldn't focus Canadians on us even more, nothing would. Most importantly, we wanted the parade to show who we were—air, land, sea, special forces, families, those who had lost their loved ones, our wounded, supporters, heroes and those so unique that they made a difference in an often troubled world.

July 2, my last day in uniform, dawned bright and warm. I was still on a high from the performance with the Snowbirds just thirty-six hours before, when the exhilaration of close-formation aerobatics with the nine best pilots in the world gave me the memory of a lifetime. Family and friends, the same group who had been there when I assumed the appointment, were in town to participate in the change-of-command ceremony, but I left all of them early that morning and went to the National Military Cemetery in Beechwood. My intent was simple: to remember those who had died under my command, to promise them they were not forgotten and to tell them how much I appreciated their courage. It was an emotional experience that left me somewhat ill prepared to respond to media interviews immediately afterwards (I should have remembered my experience at the memorial service in Pembroke in 2003).

My family and the VIPs arrived for the pre-parade reception, and soon enough it was time to start. After the Governor General's arrival and an official salute to her by the troops on parade, we inspected the ranks and visited with the official participants. What I found most emotional and difficult was the few minutes with the wounded, the families and our heroes. It was a time for hugs, tears and laughter as I trailed the GG down that side of the parade. All I wanted to do now was finish. Departing on the tank was a pleasant surprise—this was my background in the army, and also the fastest way off parade and out of Walt Natynczyk's hair! I had been surprised by this kind deed, finding out about it only the previous night, and had immediately phoned the CF Regimental Sergeant Major, Greg Lacroix. I said I appreciated it but did not want anything special. Greg said, "Sort yourself out. A lot of people wanted this to happen for you, so suck it up." Never one to mince words, that man. Climbing upon the tank was a last thrill and, with the departure, an opportunity to both salute all those who had served with me, both in my personal salute and by lowering the tank's gun barrel in a traditional cavalry salute. I was surprised at how unemotional it was. I felt really good until the Leopard tank got near the exit and I spotted one of our junior NCOs, who was saluting me and crying openly. God, I loved being a soldier! Joyce and I then met about a hundred friends from across Canada at a local restaurant and celebrated with them.

We had come far in just three and a half years but again, to quote Churchill, this was not the end of the changes needed, not the beginning of the end of those changes, but it might have been the end of the beginning of what we needed to do. The CF needs more people, immediately. Equipment is fundamental to success, and our troops have to get what they need much more quickly and efficiently than they are now. We need to continue to change how we support families, those who lose loved ones in the service of Canada, and the wounded. Our recognition system still sucks. Where the population goes, politicians go, and if the CF is to have the money and decisions to enable the men and women in uniform to be successful, Canadians will have to continue to show that support. This will be particularly important in times of renewed deficit, when many will desire to do less. Canada, at only half of the NATO spending average and objectives on defence, must continue to increase its investment. For those who will scream to high heaven that we cannot afford to do so, it is my view that this G8 nation cannot afford *not* to do it. Our standing around the world—and on this continent—depends on it.

My intentions are to never retire. I'll continue to support both my successors as CDS and the men and women who serve them. If you want Rick Hillier as your enemy, disrespecting those uniformed treasures and their families will be the surest way to guarantee it. I want to continue to write, as witnessed by this first of two books (the second will be on leadership), and I've formed a leadership company to help companies or countries develop. Lastly, I join to those efforts speaking opportunities about the incredibly inspirational men and women who I served with. That combination, plus my honorary appointment as Chancellor of Memorial University, allows me to support several substantial charitable causes, none more than the Military Families Fund.

Since July 2, 2008, Joyce and I have managed to spend more time with our sons, daughter-in-law, future daughter-in-law, and grandson, and were present soon after the second grandson arrived. No enjoyment is greater than hearing them sing out "Poppy!"

The one thing I feared most in leaving the CF was missing the camaraderie of my "battle buddies." After all, I had grown up in the CF, and those were my lifelong friends. I shouldn't have worried. Every day, perhaps helped by the fact that our son Chris is a soldier, we find ourselves surrounded by uniformed men and women and their families no matter where we go. At speeches, I still introduce them and ask an audience to show their appreciation. Charitable events that I attend invariably become "Support the Troops" rallies, and I became one of the people who shook the hand of those uniformed folks at Ottawa airport. My fears were misplaced.

I had already started to make the adjustment to life after Chief of the Defence Staff, aided, as always, by Joyce. The day after I announced my decision, on April 16, my small security team picked me up at home and we headed downtown just after 6 a.m. Focused on that day's events, I almost missed the surroundings in our neighbourhood and what an important day it was.

Suddenly alert to it, however, and despite the early hour, I phoned Joyce on my cell and she, sleepily, answered. I said, "Joyce, do you know what day it is?" She, being the romantic one in our partnership—and still half asleep—assumed this was profound and said something like, "The first day of the rest of our lives?"

To which I responded, "Yes, but it's also garbage day, and I forgot to put the garbage out. So can you get up and do it?"

That was my life, operating at strategic level but, like every other person in our country, required to take out the garbage every week. We both looked forward to the next stage of our lives.

POSTSCRIPT

Life after uniformed service has been awesome. I had spent thirty-five years, three months, one day and fourteen hours in uniform and would not trade it for anything. Yet, while I enjoyed serving, clearly I missed out on many things that could have been part of my life. I have now been discovering that, in this great country of ours, we can contribute to our society in many ways, have a lot of fun doing it and, yes, make a living at the same time. In very few nations is this possible.

Leaving on July 2, 2008, in hindsight, was exactly the right decision for me, my family and, I believe, the Canadian Forces. I've never doubted that decision, not once in the now more than two years of this new life. One of the questions I get asked a lot by soldiers, sailors, airmen and airwomen that I meet is "Do you miss it?" I always answer that no, I don't, though I always have to qualify my answer, to not have it sound negative, because it's not. Joyce and I learned long ago that you can never go back. From the time of my first command through to being the Chief of the Defence Staff, it was easy to think of myself as the most important person in the world to that unit, until I walked off the parade after handing that command over to someone else and realized that now I was the same as everyone else. After having handed over many commands, that part was clear to Joyce and me; we could not go back—and we are actually pretty comfortable with who we are as individuals and as a family.

I loved being a soldier and will be one until I die, regardless of the fact that I no longer wear a uniform. Being a soldier is not what you do, but who you are: someone who believes that action speaks loudly; someone who lives by a code of values and accepts the need for tough decisions and equally tough actions to safeguard the precious country we have; and someone who realizes the awesome responsibility that we, as Canadians, have to help those around the world who are so much less fortunate than us. That help inevitably requires an acceptance of much risk and a reliance on those with whom you have built a bond of trust —your battle buddies. I'll always be a soldier, and my retirement doesn't change that in the slightest. So I don't miss that part.

Lastly, I don't miss it because I left with no regrets or remorse. Many things changed in the CF in recent years, and the vast majority of the changes were for the better. Being a part of that evolution was probably the most satisfying thing in my life, and I watch and appreciate, with some awe, the enormous respect people from all over the country have for Canada's sons and daughters in the CF. Compared to the days of service in the first 80 to 90 per cent of my career, the current situation is as different as night and day. The CF is probably our most respected Canadian institution these days and that is hugely satisfying. So,

I don't miss my time in uniform, particularly, as mentioned, now that I have the chance to continue in a different way.

I would be remiss, however, if I did not say that there was one part that did cause me fear as my date of departure approached, something that everyone retired from the CF had told me they missed—the camaraderie of those battle buddies with whom you have spent most of your life. After all, my wife and I had truly grown up in the army, and everything we had done in our lives to date had involved the forces in some way. Our friends had all served, our regiment was like family, and I feared that, in leaving, the formal separation from both would be traumatic. But the truth is that I have not left that part behind at all. We are fortunate that our closest friends are also retired and live close to us in Ottawa. I meet uniformed men and women, and their families, no matter where I go. They come up to say hello in airports, shopping malls, on the street, in doctors' offices (my civilian doctor looked after me in the National Defence Medical Centre before I retired) and on golf courses. I meet them at dinners, in pubs, while fishing, during events to honour them and everywhere else I go. So my one fear, that of being separated from those important to me, has not come to pass.

It helps, of course, to be extremely busy, and aside from a few days after leaving my appointment as CDS, I have been. Just before the Change of Command ceremony on July 2, 2008, Joyce asked what I wanted to do. "I want to disappear," I said, "for at least a couple of weeks, and it's really difficult, probably impossible, to do that in Canada."

"Okay," she said. "So where do you want to go?"

"Well, I've visited many battlefields in Europe, but I've never been to the beaches of Normandy," I said. "After so many years of meeting veterans from the D-Day invasion, reading about it and watching movies about it, I want to go there." I felt we could truly be anonymous on and around the beaches of Normandy.

So, a couple of days later, we both flew to Paris, where we joined our friends Georges and Maureen Rousseau; Georges was completing the last weeks of his posting there as Canada's military attaché to France and Spain, and he was within days of retirement himself. We spent one night in Paris with Georges and Maureen, and then drove to Normandy with them the next day, where we rented a small cottage on the farm of the man who heads the Franco-Canadian Juno Beach Committee. He and his wife reminded us of just how much affection and appreciation exists in that part of France for Canada, Canadians and our brave veterans who gave them back their freedom. That afternoon we continued on to Juno Beach. I was first at the door to the beautiful Juno Beach Centre, the memorial to those who came ashore and fought in the Normandy campaign. As I opened the door, waving Joyce, Maureen and Georges in, I noticed a man about twenty feet behind us, and I held the door so he could enter as well. "Ah, General Hillier," he said. "I bet you thought you could disappear over here!"

Later that day we were all invited down to the Queen's Own House. This house, which stood right on Juno Beach during the D-Day invasion on June 6, 1944, and still stands there today, is prominent in the background of the documentaries about the invasion, when the ramps drop in the landing craft delivering Canadian soldiers into that hell of fire and death. The owners of the house hosted us for an hour. I absorbed the history everywhere inside and out, and Joyce made friends with their beautiful little granddaughter.

I was inspired yet again by everything I saw over the next week. The valour of ordinary Canadian men, supported by the millions of men and women across our country, combined with their dedication, training, refusal to accept failure under even the harshest conditions, and *joie de vivre* made me even prouder, if that were possible, to be Canadian—prouder to have served in uniform than I ever imagined—and I am forever thankful for what they have done. Many cultures or religions have a require-ment to do something once in your life—to visit Mecca, for example, if you are Muslim and can make the pilgrimage. Every Canadian, I believe, should visit two places, if at all possible: Vimy Ridge and Juno Beach. At these battlefields, you understand the great history of our country, the sacrifice that makes us a great country today and the need for tough people to do tough things on our behalf. I still get shivers down my spine when I visualize those two monuments to greatness. And they're Canadian!

I returned to Canada all too soon, but we took a vacation to eastern Canada and Newfoundland, where I spoke at a grad-uating class for the Royal Newfoundland Constabulary, among other things. Premier Danny Williams had asked me to become the chancellor of Memorial University in St. John's, and I said yes. Memorial, which is my and Joyce's alma mater, was established in 1925 to be a living memorial to the men from Newfoundland and Labrador, serving primarily in the Royal Newfoundland Regiment, who had died during the First World War. Most of them died during one terrible day at a little place called Beaumont-Hamel in France. There, in the early, sunny morning of July 1, 1916, the regiment, and much of the future leadership of our province, was slaughtered in about thirty-five minutes in the horrible attacks that began the Battle of the Somme. Through the efforts of Newfoundlanders, the battlefield was preserved. Every year Newfoundlanders commemorate the losses of July 1, 1916. In considering the chancellorship of Memorial, I felt that as a Newfoundlander, former CDS and lifelong soldier, no role could be more fitting. This honorary appointment has permitted me to become engaged in this important part of our province, to contribute to where I grew up and studied ("studied" might be an exaggeration) and to get to know more of those who give Newfoundland its unique and endearing charm. One such person is Dr. Nigel Rusted. In July 2009, Nigel attended a dinner I hosted for supporters of the university. He drove to the event from his house, where he lives alone, in his own car, which he had recently purchased. This may sound routine until you realize that Nigel was a student in the very first Memorial class in 1925 and graduated in 1928. He had just turned 102 and, as he told me, he had purchased an extended warranty on that new car. We Newfoundlanders live long, that's for sure.

Many other opportunities have come along; I've established relationships with the TD Bank Financial Group, Gowlings law firm, Telus and Provincial Aerospace Ltd. in St. John's. In one way or another, each opportunity has allowed me to work with outstanding people across Canada and the world, to continue to further the causes of servicemen and servicewomen and to enjoy myself in new surroundings. Unfortunately, the one downside is the constant travel, but I have nobody except myself to blame for that.

Moving into private enterprise coincided with my decision to write *A Soldier First*, to be followed by a second book that focuses specifically on leadership lessons I've learned and observed over my life. HarperCollins guided me through the process on both books with the ready help of my ghostwriter

Chris Wattie. I had known Chris as a reporter and reserve officer and knew that he had spent time in Kandahar with the 2nd
Battalion, Princess Patricia's Canadian Light Infantry. His own
book, *Contact Charlie*, is excellent, so I was very comfortable in
asking for his help. What I had not counted on was the enormous amount of work required to produce the two books.

All of these things were enough to keep me busy, but I also
accepted speaking engagements and donated a lot of my time,
an enormous amount really, to charities, particularly those supporting the causes to which I had a personal commitment: the
Military Families Fund, the Soldier On program, the True Patriot
Love Foundation, Canada Company, Project Hero, Honour
House, McDermott House and others, including the 10th anniversary of the Motorcycle Ride for Dad (for prostate cancer and
the Military Families Fund) with Don Cherry, and the 25th anniversary of the Ottawa Food Bank. It is important to contribute to
causes where you live (and here I steal from Telus, whose motto
is "We Give Where We Live").

There were many highlights in all those good causes but
being at the True Patriot Love Dinner in Toronto on November
10, 2009, where almost 2,000 people attended to show their support and raise money for military families to the tune of about
two million dollars, was special. With the Prime Minister, the
Premier and the Lieutenant Governor of Ontario, Don Cherry
and numerous other well-known Canadians and performers
showing their support, it was indeed a night to remember. Many
of us reflected yet again on how far this country has come in
the last few years in support of its sons and daughters serving in
the CF and, equally, in support of the military families who also
sacrifice for Canada.

However, a couple of irritating situations from my days as CDS continued beyond my departure. I had often railed against the culture in Ottawa that had turned normal, good, common-sense risk assessment into total risk aversion, and, I had warned, as I spoke during the Change of Command ceremony on July 2, 2008, about risk-averse, bureaucratic "field marshal wannabes" and how the command and control of the CF must never be entrusted to them. I absolutely refused, for more than a year before my retirement, to condone any direct role in the command and control of the CF contingent in Afghanistan by any of the bureaucrats. This would have been dangerous to our young men and women, to the mission and to the bureaucrats, who had had no preparation, training or experience in such command and were not qualified for it. The lives of Canadian boys and girls are too precious to be entrusted to those not ready. Additionally, the CDS, and therefore the CF, works for the government of Canada, specifically reporting to the Minister of Defence, advising the PM and enacting direction given by Cabinet or by a specific act of Parliament.

The senior mandarins never rest, however, and a paper produced this last year by (you guessed it) other mandarins spoke about the responsibility that the Clerk of the Privy Council and the Deputy Minister of National Defence have to guide the CF. What crap! The National Defence Act is clear—our sons and daughters need to have direction from the leaders that Canadians have elected, and they need to have that direction passed through their Chief of the Defence Staff without interference from bureaucrats who have no preparation or training for this task, and no responsibility for those same lives. Any governments who permit anything different should have their rear ends booted out of office by the moms and dads of those serving sons and daughters.

The second continuing issue concerned detainees. Specifically, one individual out of hundreds who had been involved in the mission made wide-reaching claims about abuse of detainees and knowledge of that abuse by the government of Canada at senior levels, including within the CF, and stated that essentially nothing had been done about it. I had spent my life in uniform to try to help guarantee the right of individual Canadians to make claims like that, to have that freedom of speech, and so was unperturbed. What was disappointing to me, however, was the response of our parliamentarians on the committee who decided to discuss the issue. Despite the lack of correlation by anyone else (in fact, with differing and contradictory assessments by many), clear evidence of action by the CF when anything did come up and, most importantly, the absence of any evidence, inflammatory indictments of the leadership of Canada, including me, were the order of the day. I, along with the previous commander in Afghanistan, Major-General Dave Fraser, and the retired former commander of international operations, Lieutenant-General (retired) Mike Gauthier, testified in front of the parliamentary committee, articulating how we in the CF had met our Canadian and international obligations, acted when we needed to act, and led men and women whose values are of the highest order. In fact, nobody was even listening to what we had to say. (At one point when I was answering a question by an MP, I actually stopped and said, "Well, you asked the question, and if you want me to answer it, you should at least listen." The MP in question was busy talking to a colleague.) Sadly, our appearance helped make what was happening in Parliament an even greater farce.

My assessment was instant. The committee reflected the lack of ethics in our Parliament. Clearly, the committee members were, for the most part, uninterested in facts and truth, and, equally, they were clearly interested in making what was a non-issue into something to throw at the government. That they were tarring and insulting soldiers, despite their denials of doing just that, while they played partisan politics was obviously unimportant to them. In Ottawa, anyone, including those magnificent men and women who serve our country in uniform, would be run over in a heartbeat if those involved thought it would give them a few more votes. After all, here were MPs, who had voted to abandon hundreds of thousands of innocent Afghans to their fate by withdrawing our troops, now professing to be overwhelmingly concerned about a few people who had been detained. Not detained because they were farmers in the wrong place at the wrong time, but detained because they were killing Canadian boys and girls, trying to kill Canadian boys and girls, found with sophisticated explosive residue on their hands or seized in raids where the plans and materials to kill more people were found. It seemed as if our primary focus in Ottawa was to ensure the rights of Taliban serial killers, Afghan equivalents to Paul Bernardo or Clifford Olson, were guarded at all costs.

Of course, if the committee had had the entire set of documentation, containing all the message traffic even remotely released to these claims, unredacted (that is, with all of the documents readable as opposed to having large amounts of information crossed out), then their deliberations would have been short indeed, because nothing in those documents backed any of the claims in the committee or the media. No wonder Canadians are turned off by what happens in Ottawa.

When we started the CF transformation, I often spoke about how we, serving in the armed forces of our country, had to be worthy of the country's confidence. Now, I believe that those who have turned our Parliament into an embarrassment are unworthy of those in uniform who serve with such valour. It is not surprising that in the last federal election, only some 60 per cent of Canadians bothered to vote. In my travels and discussions with thousands of Canadians, the contempt for parliamentarians, those in the Senate and in the House of Commons, is overwhelming. I said to the International Knightly Order of Saint George that if the words from their vows ("honour, integrity and truth") were more prevalent in Parliament, most Canadians would not be screaming for the Auditor General to have access to the enormous sums of our taxes spent there. The fact that so many want the Auditor General to have that access speaks volumes of Canadian opinions. One weeps.

The issues around detainees and civil service control of the CF, irritating though they are, simply reflect a process at work that most large bureaucracies have. We deal with it and move on. But the issue that was perhaps most disappointing to me personally since my retirement was a very localized backlash to Project Hero.

Project Hero was the brainchild of someone who is both a good friend and a great Canadian, Kevin Reed, who felt that our universities and colleges could do more to show their support to those who serve in the forces. Kevin asked a number of post-secondary institutions if they'd agree to make a small but genuine demonstration of support for children who had lost a parent in service to Canada: education at no cost. His idea was met with an avalanche of support all across the country, as people applauded the decision simply to honour those who served at the direction of our Parliament, on behalf of all Canadians, and fell while serving our country. Amid the enthusiasm was only one cry of indignation. That came from a small group of professors at the University of Regina, who insisted that their "university not be connected with the increasing militarization of Canadian society and politics." (Ironically, the generous contracts of university professors typically guarantee their own children free university education.) To their shame—and to the credit of thousands of Canadians—their views were dismissed by the outpouring of support for the children of heroes, and the university itself noted that the program would continue there. My faith, yet again, in the generous spirit of the millions of Canadians who benefit from the sacrifice of our servicemen and women, to the point that they live in the best country in the world, was validated.

But in my retirement, I take pleasure from the important things in life. (Not surprisingly, I ruled out going into politics.) I turned fifty-five. My golf is still not good. Our oldest son, Chris, completed an eight-month tour in Kandahar and returned home safely. Our youngest, Steven, got engaged to his girlfriend, Amanda, and we will soon therefore have a second daughter-in-law. Our grandsons, Jack and Matthew, are the joy in our lives, and we can never see them enough. And most of all, I continue to be so proud to be Canadian. God bless this great country.

—July 2010

INDEX

A NOTE ON THE TYPE

The text of this book is set in Minion, a typeface designed by Robert Slimbach in 1990 for Adobe Systems. The name comes from the traditional naming system for type sizes, in which *minion* is between *nonpareil* and *brevier*. Inspired by late Renaissance-era type, it is extremely compact and economical and was intended by Slimbach to be a replacement for Times New Roman.

ABOUT THE AUTHOR

General Rick Hillier, born in Newfoundland and Labrador, enlisted in the Canadian Forces in 1973 through the Regular Officer Training Plan program. He graduated from Memorial University in 1975 with a B.Sc. degree. In May 2003 Hillier was appointed Commander of the Army, and in October 2003 he was selected as the Commander of the NATO-led International Security Assistance Force (ISAF) in Kabul, Afghanistan. General Hillier was promoted to Chief of the Defence Staff in February 2005 and stepped down in the summer of 2008.